A SCIENCE OF CONCURRENT PROGRAMS

Turing Award-winner Leslie Lamport shares the key lessons he has learned about concurrent and distributed computing over decades of writing and reasoning about their algorithms.

Algorithms are not programs, and they shouldn't be written in a programming language. Instead, this book explores how to write them and reason about them by using mathematics. It explains the principles underlying abstract programs and understanding those principles helps avoid concurrency errors. Designing an abstract program before writing any code can lead to better, more reliable programs.

The book has very few mathematical prerequisites, with an appendix summarizing the necessary knowledge. Many of the examples are available online, written in the formal language TLA^+, and can be checked with the TLA^+ tools.

This is a fascinating read for any graduate students and researchers in theoretical computer science, concurrency, and distributed systems.

LESLIE LAMPORT was Distinguished Scientist at Microsoft Research until his retirement. Dr. Lamport won the 2013 Turing Award for "fundamental contributions to the theory and practice of distributed and concurrent systems." He is a member of the National Academies of Science and Engineering and the American Association of Arts and Sciences.

A SCIENCE OF CONCURRENT PROGRAMS

LESLIE LAMPORT
Researcher Emeritus, Microsoft

Shaftesbury Road, Cambridge CB2 8EA, United Kingdom

One Liberty Plaza, 20th Floor, New York, NY 10006, USA

477 Williamstown Road, Port Melbourne, VIC 3207, Australia

314-321, 3rd Floor, Plot 3, Splendor Forum, Jasola District Centre, New Delhi - 110025, India

Cambridge University Press is part of Cambridge University Press & Assessment, a department of the University of Cambridge.

We share the University's mission to contribute to society through the pursuit of education, learning and research at the highest international levels of excellence.

www.cambridge.org
Information on this title: www.cambridge.org/9781009719858
DOI: 10.1017/9781009719841

© Leslie Lamport 2026

This publication is in copyright. Subject to statutory exception and to the provisions of relevant collective licensing agreements, no reproduction of any part may take place without the written permission of Cambridge University Press & Assessment.

When citing this work, please include a reference to the DOI 10.1017/9781009719841

First published 2026

Cover image: Filo/DigitalVision Vectors/Getty Images

A catalogue record for this publication is available from the British Library

A Cataloging-in-Publication data record for this book is available from the Library of Congress

ISBN 978-1-009-71985-8 Hardback

Cambridge University Press & Assessment has no responsibility for the persistence or accuracy of URLs for external or third-party internet websites referred to in this publication and does not guarantee that any content on such websites is, or will remain, accurate or appropriate.

For EU product safety concerns, contact us at Calle de José Abascal, 56, 1°, 28003 Madrid, Spain, or email eugpsr@cambridge.org

To Ellen

Contents

About this Book xiii

Acknowledgments xiv

1 Introduction   **1**
- 1.1 Who Am I? 1
- 1.2 Who Are You? 2
- 1.3 The Origin of the Science 2
  - 1.3.1 The Origin of the Theory 2
  - 1.3.2 The Origin of the Practice 3
- 1.4 Correctness 5
- 1.5 A Preview 6
- 1.6 Why Math? 9

2 Ordinary Math   **12**
- 2.1 Arithmetic as a Mathematical Theory 13
- 2.2 The Mathematical Theory of Algebra 14
- 2.3 Mathglish 17
- 2.4 Boolean Arithmetic (Propositional Logic) 18
- 2.5 ZF 21
- 2.6 Meaningless Expressions 23
- 2.7 Quantification and Bound Variables 25
  - 2.7.1 Quantification 25
  - 2.7.2 Bound Variables 26
- 2.8 Defining Mappings and Functions 28
  - 2.8.1 Mappings 28
  - 2.8.2 Functions 30
  - 2.8.3 Sequences and Tuples 31
- 2.9 Some Useful Notation 32
  - 2.9.1 IF/THEN/ELSE 32
  - 2.9.2 Conjunction and Disjunction Lists 32

3 Describing Abstract Programs with Math   34
- 3.1 The Behavior of Physical Systems 34
- 3.2 Behaviors of Digital Systems 37
  - Math I 37
  - 3.2.1 From Continuous to Discrete Time 37
  - 3.2.2 An Example: *Sqrs* 40
  - 3.2.3 A Finer-Grained Example: *FGSqrs* 44
- 3.3 Nondeterminism 46
  - Math II 46
  - 3.3.1 Sources of Nondeterminism 47
  - 3.3.2 An Example: *Increment* 48
- 3.4 Temporal Logic 52
  - Math III 52
  - 3.4.1 The Logic of Actions 53
    - 3.4.1.1 Eliminating State Numbers 53
    - 3.4.1.2 The Semantics of the Logic of Actions . 55
    - 3.4.1.3 The Prime Operator 56
    - 3.4.1.4 Action Composition 58
  - 3.4.2 The Temporal Logic RTLA 59
    - 3.4.2.1 Simple RTLA 60
    - 3.4.2.2 The Complete RTLA 62
    - 3.4.2.3 The $\Box$ Operator 63
    - 3.4.2.4 Eventually ($\Diamond$) 64
    - 3.4.2.5 Eventually Always ($\Diamond\Box$) ... 66
    - 3.4.2.6 Infinitely Often ($\Box\Diamond$) 66
    - 3.4.2.7 The End of the Line 67
    - 3.4.2.8 Leads To ($\leadsto$) 68
    - 3.4.2.9 Warning 69
- 3.5 TLA 70
  - Math IV 70
  - 3.5.1 The Problem 71
  - 3.5.2 The Solution 72
  - 3.5.3 Stuttering Insensitivity 74
  - 3.5.4 The Definition of TLA 76

4 Safety, Liveness, and Fairness   79
- 4.1 Safety and Liveness 79
  - Math V 79
  - 4.1.1 Definitions 81
  - 4.1.2 A Completeness Theorem 82

	4.1.3	The Operator $\mathcal{C}$	84
	4.1.4	What Good is Liveness?	85
4.2	Fairness		86
	4.2.1	Traditional Programs and Enabled	86
	4.2.2	Concurrent Programs	87
		4.2.2.1 Mutual Exclusion	88
		4.2.2.2 Machine Closure	92
	4.2.3	Weak Fairness	93
	4.2.4	Temporal Logic Reasoning	96
	4.2.5	Reasoning With Weak Fairness	97
		4.2.5.1 Liveness for Mutual Exclusion	97
		4.2.5.2 The One-Bit Algorithm	98
		4.2.5.3 Proving Liveness	100
	4.2.6	Strong Fairness	104
		4.2.6.1 Starvation Free Mutual Exclusion	104
		4.2.6.2 The Definition of Strong Fairness	105
		4.2.6.3 Using a Strongly Fair Semaphore	106
	4.2.7	Properties of WF and SF	107
	4.2.8	What is Fairness?	109

5 Interlude — 111
5.1 Possibility and Accuracy — 111
- 5.1.1 Possibility Conditions — 111
- 5.1.2 Expressing Possibility in TLA — 112
- 5.1.3 Checking Accuracy — 114

5.2 Real-Time Programs — 115
Math VI — 116
- 5.2.1 Fischer's Algorithm — 117
- 5.2.2 Correctness of Fischer's Algorithm — 120
- 5.2.3 Fairness and Zeno Behaviors — 121
- 5.2.4 Discrete Time — 123
- 5.2.5 Hybrid Systems — 125

6 Refinement — 126
6.1 A Sequential Algorithm — 128
Math VII — 128
- 6.1.1 A One-Step Program — 129
- 6.1.2 Two Views of Refinement Mappings — 131
- 6.1.3 A Step and Data Refinement — 132

6.2 Invariance Under Refinement — 135

- 6.3 An Example: The Paxos Algorithm 135
  - 6.3.1 The Consensus Problem 136
  - 6.3.2 The Paxos Consensus Algorithm 138
    - 6.3.2.1 The Specification of Consensus 139
    - 6.3.2.2 The Voting Algorithm 139
    - 6.3.2.3 The Paxos Abstract Program 142
  - 6.3.3 Implementing Paxos 144
- 6.4 Proving Refinement 145
  - Math VIII 146
  - 6.4.1 The Refinement Mapping 148
  - 6.4.2 Refinement of Safety 149
  - 6.4.3 Refinement of Fairness 152
  - 6.4.4 A Closer Look at $\mathbb{E}$ 155
    - 6.4.4.1 A Syntactic View 155
    - 6.4.4.2 Computing $\mathbb{E}$ 156
    - 6.4.4.3 The Trouble With $\mathbb{E}$ 158
- 6.5 A Warning 161

7 Auxiliary Variables 163
- 7.1 Variable Hiding 163
  - Math IX 163
  - 7.1.1 Introduction 164
  - 7.1.2 Reasoning About $\exists$ 166
  - 7.1.3 The Definition of $\exists$ 167
- 7.2 History Variables 169
  - 7.2.1 How to Add a History Variable 169
  - 7.2.2 History Variables and Fairness 173
  - 7.2.3 A Completeness Result for History Variables 174
- 7.3 Stuttering Variables 175
  - Math X 175
  - 7.3.1 The Example 176
  - 7.3.2 Adding Stuttering Steps After an Action 178
  - 7.3.3 Adding Stuttering Steps Before an Action 182
  - 7.3.4 Fairness and Stuttering Variables 183
  - 7.3.5 Infinite-Stuttering Variables 186
- 7.4 Prophecy Variables 187
  - Math XI 187
  - 7.4.1 Simple Prophecy Variables 188
  - 7.4.2 Predicting the Impossible and Liveness 192
  - 7.4.3 General Prophecy Variables 193

		7.4.3.1	A Sequence of Prophecies	194
		7.4.3.2	A Set of Prophecies	197
		7.4.3.3	Further Generalizations	200
7.5	The Existence of Refinement Mappings			202
7.6	The FIFO Queue			203

- 7.6.1 *Fifo* – A Linearizable Specification 203
- 7.6.2 *POFifo* – A More General Specification 205
  - 7.6.2.1 The Background 205
  - 7.6.2.2 Program *POFifo* 207
- 7.6.3 Showing *IPOFifo* Implements *Fifo* 211
  - 7.6.3.1 The Prophecy Variable 212
  - 7.6.3.2 The History Variable *qBar* 213
  - 7.6.3.3 Stuttering and the Refinement Mapping . . . 216
- 7.7 Prophecy Constants 217

8 Loose Ends 220

- 8.1 Reduction 220
  - 8.1.1 Introduction 220
    - 8.1.1.1 What Reduction Is 220
    - 8.1.1.2 The TLA Approach 222
  - 8.1.2 An Example 224
    - 8.1.2.1 The Reduced Behaviors 224
    - 8.1.2.2 The Program $S \otimes S^R$ 226
    - 8.1.2.3 The Invariant 230
  - 8.1.3 Reduction In General 232
  - 8.1.4 The Hypothesis $\Box \Diamond \neg \mathcal{L}$ 236
  - 8.1.5 Adding Liveness 236
    - 8.1.5.1 Fairness of Subactions of E^R 237
    - 8.1.5.2 Fairness of Subactions of M^R 240
    - 8.1.5.3 The Reduction Theorem with Fairness . . . 243
  - 8.1.6 An Example: Making Critical Sections Atomic 244
  - 8.1.7 Another Example: Pipelining 247
- 8.2 Decomposing and Composing Programs 251
  - 8.2.1 Decomposing Programs 253
    - 8.2.1.1 Writing a Program as a Conjunction 253
    - 8.2.1.2 Decomposing Proofs 255
  - 8.2.2 Composing Components 261

Appendix 266

A Miscellany 266
- A.1 Ordinary Math Summary 266
  - A.1.1 Arithmetic 266
  - A.1.2 Propositional Logic 266
  - A.1.3 Predicate Logic 267
  - A.1.4 Sets 267
  - A.1.5 The CHOOSE Operator 268
  - A.1.6 Functions 269
  - A.1.7 Sequences 269
  - A.1.8 Notation 270
  - A.1.9 Recursive Definitions 270
- A.2 Structured Proofs 271
- A.3 Why Not All Mappings Are Sets 274
- A.4 How Not to Write x''' 275
- A.5 Hoare Logic 276
- A.6 Another Way to Look at Safety and Liveness 279
  - A.6.1 Metric Spaces 279
  - A.6.2 The Metric Space of Behaviors 282

B Proofs 284
- B.1 Invariance Proof of *Increment* 284
- B.2 Proof of Theorem 4.3 287
- B.3 Proof of Theorem 4.4 289
- B.4 Proof of Theorem 4.5 290
- B.5 Proof of Theorem 4.6 291
- B.6 Proof of Theorem 4.7 291
- B.7 Proof of Theorem 4.8 293
- B.8 Proof Sketch of Theorem 4.9 295
- B.9 Proof of Theorem 7.2 296
- B.10 Proof Sketch of Theorem 7.3 298
- B.11 Proof Sketch of Theorem 7.6 299
- B.12 Proof of Theorem 8.2 302
- B.13 Proof of Theorem 8.3 302

Bibliography 304

Index 310

About this Book

The first chapter, which is a little over ten pages, explains what this book is about. I believe it will tell you whether you should read the book. If you decide to read it, here are some things you should know.

The book's science is embodied in a language called TLA$^+$. Many of its examples have been written in TLA$^+$ and checked with the TLA$^+$ tools. However, TLA$^+$ is not used here because the requirements of handling industrial applications require it to be a little more complicated than is necessary for the book. The TLA$^+$ versions of the examples and an explanation of how to translate from the book's notation to TLA$^+$ will be available at https://www.cambridge.org/9781009719858.

The book has no formal exercises, but the text proposes a number of problems for you to solve that can help you learn the material. To learn how the science can be put into practice, you should try writing your own examples in TLA$^+$, checking what you do with the TLA$^+$ tools.

Acknowledgments

This book presents things that I have learned over decades. During that time, I have discussed them with many wonderful colleagues. I learned many things from them, and I cannot possibly remember who taught me what. Here is a list containing only my coauthors of published papers who I can remember contributing to the content of this book. Omitted are a number of colleagues who taught me a lot that does not appear in the book, and a few who taught me things contained here but with whom I never wrote a published paper.

> Martín Abadi, Krzysztof Apt, Brannon Batson, Manfred Broy, K. Mani Chandy, Ernie Cohen, Edsger Dijkstra, Damien Doligez, Urban Engberg, Georges Gonthier, Jim Gray, Peter Grønning, Markus Kuppe, Robert Kurshan, Peter Ladkin, David Langworthy, Nancy Lynch, Michael Melliar-Smith, Stephan Merz, Susan Owicki, Richard Palais, Fred Schneider, Carel Scholten, Robert Shostak, Mark Tuttle, Friedrich H. Vogt, and Yuan Yu.

The following people not in the list above read preliminary versions of the book and reported errors or sent me comments that led to significant changes.

> Petros Angelatos, Paul Banks, Sergey Bronnikov, Siegfried Bublitz, Hugo Sanz González, Bruno Grenet, Matthias Grundmann, Rob Hagemans, Pedro de las Heras Quirós, Lorin Hochstein, Dave Hughes, Johannes Laire, Tom Moertel, Ron Pressler, Chris Newcombe, Divyanshu Ranjan, Michael Roeleveld, Mark Rogers, Scarlet Schwiderski-Grosche, Peter Sovietov, Alexander Vasilev, and Ugur Y. Yavuz.

Chapter 1

Introduction

1.1 Who Am I?

Dear Reader. I am inviting you to spend many pages with me. Before deciding whether to accept my invitation, you may want to know who I am.

I was educated as a mathematician; my doctoral thesis was on partial differential equations. While a student, I worked part-time and summers as a programmer. At that time, almost all programs were what I will call *traditional* programs—ones with a single thread of control that take input, produce output, and stop.

After obtaining my doctorate, I began working on concurrent algorithms—ones comprising multiple independent threads of control, called *processes*, that are executed concurrently. The first concurrent algorithms were meant to be executed on a single computer, with processes communicating through a shared memory. Later came distributed algorithms—concurrent algorithms designed to be executed on multiple computers in which processes communicate by message passing.

This is not the place for modesty. I was very good at concurrency—both writing concurrent algorithms and developing the theory underlying them. The first concurrent algorithm I wrote, published in 1974, is still taught at universities. In 1978 I published what is probably the first paper on the theory of distributed computing. I have received many awards and honors for this work, including a Turing award (generally considered the Nobel prize of computer science) for "fundamental contributions to the theory and practice of distributed and concurrent systems".

1.2 Who Are You?

You probably belong to one of two classes of people who I will call *scientists* and *engineers*. By scientists, I mean computer scientists who are interested in concurrent computing. If you are a scientist, you should be well-prepared to decide if this book interests you and to read it if it does.

By engineers, I mean people involved in building concurrent programs. If you are an engineer, you might have a job title such as programmer, software engineer, or hardware designer. I need to warn you that this book is about a science, not about its practical application. Practice is discussed only to explain the motivation for the science. If you are interested just in using the science, you should read about the language TLA$^+$ and its tools, which are the practical embodiment of the science [28, 35]. But if you want to understand the underlying science, then this book may be for you.

Like many sciences, the book's science of concurrent programs is based on mathematics. The book assumes only that you know the math one learns before entering a university. The basics of all the ordinary math you will need—"ordinary" meaning not peculiar to this science—is explained in Chapter 2. Some additional ordinary mathematics is introduced later as needed. The appendix contains a brief summary of all this math, most of which is taught at universities in an introductory math course for computer science students, though probably not the way it is presented here. Scientists should be used to reading math. You may find the math hard if you're an engineer. But unless mis-education has burdened you with an insurmountable fear of mathematics, I encourage you to give the book a try. Learning the math will improve your thinking.

1.3 The Origin of the Science

The science that is the subject of this book, which I will call *our* science, is a mathematical theory with a practical goal. That goal is to help build concurrent programs that work correctly. Exactly what "working correctly" means and why it's an important goal are explained in Section 1.4. The origin of our science explains how I came to believe it's a good foundation for trying to achieve that goal.

1.3.1 The Origin of the Theory

The first concurrent algorithm was published in 1965 by Edsger Dijkstra [9]. I started writing concurrent algorithms around 1973, and I quickly learned that they were hard to get right. The many possible orders in which the operations of different processes can be executed leads to an enormous number of possible executions that have to be considered. The only way to ensure that the algorithm worked correctly was to prove that it did.

By the 1970s, a standard approach had been developed for proving correctness of traditional programs. Around 1975, I and a few other computer scientists began extending that approach to concurrent algorithms [4, 24, 29, 45]. Concurrent algorithms were usually written in pseudocode plus some informal explanation of what the pseudocode meant. I came to realize that all these methods for proving correctness could be explained by describing a concurrent algorithm as what I am now calling an *abstract program*; and an abstract program could be described mathematically.

Correctness of an algorithm was expressed by properties required of its executions. I came to realize that correctness can also be expressed by an abstract program—a more abstract, higher-level one than the abstract program describing the algorithm. Proving correctness means showing that the abstract program describing the algorithm implements the abstract program describing its correctness, and I developed a method for doing that.

This work culminated around 1990 with a way to write an abstract program as a single formula [32]. The formula is written in an obscure form of math called temporal logic. The particular temporal logic is called TLA (for the Temporal Logic of Actions). Most of the TLA formula for an abstract program consists of ordinary math that expresses essentially what was described by pseudocode. Temporal logic replaces the informal explanation of the pseudocode. The assertion that one abstract program implements another is expressed as logical implication together with mathematical substitution.

Throughout this period, I was writing correctness proofs of the algorithms I was inventing. This showed me that my way of reasoning with abstract programs worked in practice. However, I discovered that as my algorithms got more and more complicated and the formulas describing them became larger, the method of writing proofs used by mathematicians became unreliable. It could not ensure that all the details were correct. I had to devise a method of hierarchically structuring proofs to keep track of those details.

1.3.2 The Origin of the Practice

I have spent most of my career as a member of industrial research labs. The computer science I have done has been motivated by the problems facing system builders—sometimes before they were aware of those problems. I have devoted the last part of my career to developing tools to help them— both intellectual tools to help them think better and programs to help them detect errors before they are implemented in code. These tools are based on what I learned by writing and reasoning about concurrent algorithms.

Programming is not just coding. It requires thinking before we code. Writing algorithms taught me that there are two things we need to decide before writing and debugging the code: *what* the program should do, and *how* the program should do it. Most programmers think that the code itself adequately describes "how the program should do it", but I learned that we need a higher-level, more abstract description of what the program does. To emphasize that programming is more than just coding, I will use the name *coding language* for what are commonly called programming languages.

An algorithm is an example of a description of how a program should do something. Concurrent algorithms are hard to understand. To invent them, I had to be able to write them in the simplest way possible. Algorithms were usually written in pseudocode to avoid the complexity that real code requires for efficient execution. I developed a way to describe concurrent algorithms in math that was more precise and no harder to understand than pseudocode.

Engineers who build complex systems usually recognize the need for describing what their programs do in a simpler, more abstract way than with code. I decided that abstract programs written in math provided such a way for describing the aspects of a system that involve concurrency. By about 1995, I had designed a complete language called TLA$^+$ that engineers could use to write abstract programs in TLA.

The abstract programs I know of that have been written by engineers to describe what a system should do generally consist of about 200–2000 lines of TLA$^+$. All but a few of those lines are ordinary math, not temporal logic. As with code, those formulas are made easy to understand by decomposing them into smaller pieces. This is done using simple definitions, rather than the more complex constructs of coding languages.

To formalize mathematics and make it easier to write long formulas, I had to add to TLA$^+$ some concepts and syntax not present in the math commonly used by mathematicians—for example, variable declarations, grouping definitions into modules, and notation for substitution. This book uses TLA, but not TLA$^+$, because the examples with which it illustrates our science are short and simple.

The kind of hierarchically structured proofs I devised can also be written in TLA$^+$, and there is a program for checking the correctness of those proofs.

However, with today's proof-checking technology, writing machine-checked proofs takes more time than engineers generally have. By the time I designed TLA⁺, model checking had become a practical tool for checking the correctness of abstract programs and was often used by engineers. A model checker can essentially check correctness of all possible executions of a very small instance of an abstract program. This turns out to be very effective at detecting errors. There are two model checkers for abstract programs written in TLA⁺, using two complementary approaches.

A program's code can, in principle, be described by a (concrete) abstract program and could, in principle, be written as a TLA⁺ formula. For a simple program (or part of a program), the code can be hand-translated to TLA⁺ and checked with the TLA⁺ tools. Usually, the length of the program and the complexity of the coding language makes this impractical.

From the point of view of our science, it makes no difference how long the formula describing an abstract program is. We therefore consider a program written in a coding language to be an abstract program. And since we are considering only abstract programs, we will let *program* mean abstract program. We will call an (abstract) program written in code a *concrete* program.

Although we don't write them as formulas, viewing concrete programs as (abstract) programs provides a new way of thinking about them. One benefit of this way of thinking is that understanding what it means for a concrete program to implement a higher-level abstract program can help avoid coding errors.

1.4 Correctness

Thus far, our science has been described as helping to build concurrent programs that work correctly. Working correctly is a vague concept. Here is precisely what it is taken to mean in this book.

We define a *behavioral property* to be a condition that is or is not satisfied by an individual execution of a program. For example, *termination* is a behavioral property; an execution either terminates or else it doesn't terminate, meaning that it keeps executing forever. We say that a program satisfies a behavioral property if every possible execution of the program satisfies it. A program is considered to *work correctly*, or simply to *be correct*, if it satisfies its desired behavioral properties.

That every possible execution of a program satisfies its behavioral properties may seem like an unreasonably strong requirement. I would be happy if a program that I use does the right thing 99.99% of the times I run it. For many programs, extensive testing can ensure that it does. But it can't for most concurrent programs. What a concurrent program does can depend on the relative order in which operations by different processes are executed. This makes the program nondeterministic, meaning that different executions can do different things, even if the program receives identical inputs. This can result in an enormous number of possible executions, and testing can examine only a tiny fraction of them. Moreover, a concurrent program that has run correctly for years can start producing frequent errors because a small change to the computer hardware, the operating system, or even the other programs running at the same time causes incorrect executions that have never occurred before. The only way to prevent this is to ensure that every possible execution satisfies the behavioral properties.

Model checking is more effective at finding errors in concurrent programs than ordinary testing because it checks all possible executions. However, it does this only on a few small instances of the program—for example, an instance with few processes or one that allows only a small number of messages to be in transit at any time.[1] Engineering judgment is required to decide if correctness of those instances provides enough confidence in the correctness of the program.

There is one way testing could find errors in concrete programs. When building a concurrent system, an abstract program is often used to model how the processes interact with one another, and the correctness of that program is checked. The concrete program is then coded by implementing each process of the more abstract program by a separate process in the code. Since there is no concurrency within an individual process, testing that the concrete program implements the more abstract program has a good chance of finding coding errors. Research on this approach is in progress.

1.5 A Preview

To give you an idea of what our science is like, this section describes informally a simple abstract program for Euclid's algorithm—a traditional algorithm that computes a value and stops. It's a very simple concurrent program in which the number of processes equals 1. Our science applies to single-process programs, although there are simpler sciences that work quite

---

[1]There are techniques for proving the correctness of a program by model checking a simpler program, but they have not been implemented for abstract programs written in TLA⁺.

1.5. A PREVIEW

well for them.

Euclid's algorithm computes the greatest common divisor (GCD) of two positive integers that we will call M and N. For example, the GCD of 12 and 16, written $GCD(12, 16)$, equals 4 because 4 is the largest integer such that 12 and 16 are both multiples of that integer. The algorithm is an abstract program containing two variables that we name x and y. Here is its prose description.

> Start with x equal to M and y equal to N and repeatedly perform the following action until the program stops:
>
>> If the values of variables x and y are equal, then stop; otherwise, subtract from the variable having the larger value the value of the other variable.[2]
>
> When the program has stopped, x and y equal $GCD(M, N)$.

I believe most engineers and many scientists can't explain why an execution of Euclid's algorithm computes $GCD(M, N)$, which means that they don't understand the algorithm. Here is the explanation provided by our science, beginning with how we view executions.

We consider an execution to be a sequence of states. For Euclid's algorithm, a state is an assignment of values to the program variables x and y. We write the state that assigns 7 to x and 42 to y as $[x :: 7,\ y :: 42]$. Here is the sequence of states that is the execution of Euclid's algorithm for $M = 12$ and $N = 16$.

$$\begin{bmatrix} x :: 12 \\ y :: 16 \end{bmatrix} \rightarrow \begin{bmatrix} x :: 12 \\ y :: 4 \end{bmatrix} \rightarrow \begin{bmatrix} x :: 8 \\ y :: 4 \end{bmatrix} \rightarrow \begin{bmatrix} x :: 4 \\ y :: 4 \end{bmatrix}$$

The states in the sequence are separated with arrows because we naturally think of an execution going from one state to the next. But in terms of our science, the algorithm and its execution just *are*; they don't go anywhere.

What an algorithm does in the future depends on its current state, not on what happened in the past. This means that in the final state of the execution, in which x and y are equal, they equal $GCD(M, N)$ because of some property that is true of every state of the execution. To understand Euclid's algorithm, we must know what that property is.

That property is $GCD(x, y) = GCD(M, N)$. (Chapter 3 explains how we show that every state satisfies this property.) Because an execution

---

[2] You may have seen a more efficient modern version of Euclid's algorithm that replaces the larger of x and y by the remainder when it is divided by the smaller. For the purpose of this example, it makes little difference which we use.

stops only when x and y are equal, and $GCD(i,i)$ equals i for any positive integer i, this property implies that x and y equal $GCD(M,N)$ in the final state of the execution.

That the formula $GCD(x,y) = GCD(M,N)$ is true in every state of a program's execution is a behavioral property. A behavioral property that asserts a formula is true in all states of an execution is called an *invariance* property, and the formula is called an *invariant* of the program. Correctness of any concurrent program depends on it satisfying an invariance property. To understand why the program is correct, we have to know the invariant of the program that explains its correctness.

The invariant $GCD(x,y) = GCD(M,N)$ shows that, if Euclid's algorithm terminates, then it produces the correct output. A traditional program must also satisfy the behavioral property of termination. The two behavioral properties

- The program produces correct output if it terminates.

- The program terminates.

are special cases of the following two classes of behavioral properties that can be required of a concurrent program:

Safety What the program is allowed to do.

Liveness What the program must eventually do.

These two classes of properties are defined precisely in Section 4.1. Termination is the only liveness property required of a traditional program. There are many kinds of liveness properties that can be required of concurrent programs.

Euclid's algorithm satisfies its safety requirement (being allowed to terminate only if x and y equal $GCD(M,N)$) because the only thing it is allowed to do is start with $x = M$ and $y = N$ and execute its action. That is, it satisfies its safety requirement because it is assumed to satisfy the safety property of doing only what the description of the algorithm allows it to do.

Euclid's algorithm satisfies its liveness requirement (eventually terminating) because it is assumed to satisfy the liveness property of eventually performing any action that its description allows it to perform. (Section 3.4.2.8 shows how we prove that the algorithm terminates.)

I have found it best to describe and reason about safety and liveness in different ways. In our science, temporal logic plays almost no role in handling safety, but it is central to handling liveness. The TLA formula for an abstract program is the logical conjunction of a safety property and a liveness property.

A single-process algorithm that computes a value and stops doesn't seem to be a good example for a science of concurrent programs. So, let's consider a concurrent version of Euclid's algorithm. It's a two-process version of the algorithm, suitable for execution on a single computer with the processes communicating through shared variables. We call the two processes the x process and the y process. The algorithm uses the same program variables as the one-process version of Euclid's algorithm and it begins in the same starting state, with $x = M$ and $y = N$. If the x process hasn't stopped, it is allowed to execute the following action whenever the *when* condition is true:

When $x \geq y$, stop if $x = y$, else subtract the value of y from x.

Process y is the same as process x, except with x and y interchanged.

Written in pseudocode, this version of Euclid's algorithm looks different from the one-process version. However, if we consider the executions of the two versions, we see that they are the same. That is, they have the same sequence of states, where a state is an assignment of values to x and y. Whether we view Euclid's algorithm as a one- or two-process algorithm may affect how we implement it with a concrete program. An implementation of the two-process algorithm with a two-process concrete program would probably be less efficient than a single-process implementation of the one-process algorithm. But since these two versions of the algorithm have the same executions, from the point of view of correctness they are the same algorithm. Both versions are written as the same TLA formula. More precisely, their formulas are equivalent. There are many equivalent ways to write a mathematical formula. How we choose to write the TLA formula for Euclid's algorithm can depend on whether we view it as a one- or two-process algorithm.

1.6 Why Math?

The science of bridge building has a mathematical basis, but bridge designers don't represent a bridge by a mathematical formula. Why should we describe an abstract program with one? The simple answer is, because we can. A concrete program is not a physical object; it's a concept. Code is just one representation of that concept. While possible in theory, writing a mathematical representation of a concrete program is not practical. However, for simpler abstract programs, it is possible; and I've found it to be a good way to represent them.

Math has been developed over thousands of years to be simple and expressive. An abstract program ignores many implementation details, which often means allowing multiple possible implementations. This is simple to express in math. Code is designed to describe one way of computing something, and it can be hard or even impossible to write code that allows all those possibilities. Even pseudocode, being based on concepts from coding languages, lacks the simplicity and expressiveness of math.

One place we want to allow many possible implementations is in describing what the program's environment can do. A program can't work in an arbitrary environment. An implementation of Euclid's algorithm will not produce the correct answer if the operating system can arbitrarily modify the variables x and y. A concurrent program can interact with its environment in complicated ways, and we have to state explicitly what the program assumes about its environment to know if it's correct. We usually want to assume as little as necessary about the environment, which means the abstract program should allow it to have many different behaviors.

Unanticipated behavior of the environment is a serious source of errors in concurrent programs. Part of the environment of a program is likely to be another program, such as an operating system. Avoiding errors may require finding answers to subtle questions about exactly what that other program does. This is often difficult because the only description of what it does, other than its code, is likely to be imprecise prose. When writing the abstract program to describe what our concrete program does, describing what the environment can do will tell us what questions we have to ask.

The expressiveness of math, embodied in TLA, provides a practical method of writing and checking the correctness of high-level designs of systems. Such checking can catch errors early, when they are easier to correct. TLA+ is used by a number of companies, including Amazon [42], Microsoft, and Oracle. Math also provides a new way of thinking about programs that can lead to better programming. While there is usually no way to quantify the result of better thinking, it was possible in the following instance.

Virtuoso was a real-time operating system. It controlled some instruments on the European Space Agency's Rosetta spacecraft that explored a comet. Its creators decided to build the next version from scratch, and they started by writing a high-level design in TLA+. They described their experience in a book [49]. The head of the project, Eric Verhulst, wrote this in an email to me:

1.6. WHY MATH?

The [TLA⁺] abstraction helped a lot in coming to a much cleaner architecture. One of the results was that the code size is about 10× less than in [Virtuoso].[3]

This result was unusual. It was possible only because the design of the entire system was described with TLA⁺. Usually, TLA⁺ is used to describe only critical aspects of a system that involve concurrency, which represent just a small part of the system's code. But this example dramatically illustrates that describing abstract programs with mathematics can produce better programs.

---

[3]The book states the reduction in code size to be a factor of 5–10. Verhulst explained to me that it was impossible to measure the reduction precisely, so the book gave a conservative estimate; but he believes it was actually a factor of 10.

Chapter 2

Ordinary Math

We will write an abstract program as a mathematical formula. A program can be quite complex, leading to a long formula. A long formula with a lot of esoteric mathematics would be impossible to understand. So, almost all the math used in our formulas is ordinary math, consisting of arithmetic, simple logic, sets, and functions. You should know most of it already if you took an introductory university math course for computer science or engineering students. Ordinary math does not include the temporal logic introduced in Sections 3.4 and 3.5.

This chapter explains the foundation of the ordinary math used in this book and the math needed to begin our study of abstract programs. Later chapters introduce additional math as needed, in special sections named Math I through Math XI. Math introduced in one chapter may be used in later chapters. A brief summary of all the ordinary math used in the book is in Appendix Section A.1. Longer and perhaps easier to understand intuitive explanations of most of the math we will use can be found on the Web.

We can write an abstract program as a TLA formula. While most of that formula consists of ordinary math, TLA is a temporal logic, and temporal logic is not ordinary math. The meaning of TLA formulas will be explained in terms of ordinary math. However, although not hard to understand, temporal logic doesn't satisfy all the properties of ordinary math. Avoiding mistakes when using it requires understanding what its formulas mean. Giving a meaning to the formulas of a logic is called defining a semantics of the logic. This chapter explains how to define a semantics by defining the meaning of formulas of ordinary math. Even if you're familiar with the math presented here, the explanation of its semantics may be new to you. Therefore, you should at least skim this chapter carefully.

In mathematics, the truth of an assertion is established by proof. A mathematician's proof is usually a sequence of paragraphs. This way of writing proofs is adequate for simple proofs. However, it's not reliable for complicated proofs. It's particularly unsuited to handling the many details in a proof of correctness of a program. This book uses a way of structuring proofs that makes them easier to read, and therefore makes it harder to prove things that aren't true. Ordinary paragraph proofs are used only to prove simple results, and for proof sketches that aren't meant to be proofs.

Most of the proofs in this book are in the appendix. Before reading them, you should read Appendix Section A.2, which explains our structured proof style. I hope that, some day, all engineers will be able to write proofs of correctness of their abstract programs. The proofs mathematicians write are too unreliable to provide confidence that a program is correct. Engineers will have to use some way of structuring proofs like the one described in this book. Scientists would also benefit from using it.

Understanding a science of program correctness requires understanding how to prove correctness of a program. Later chapters of the main text therefore contain some proofs, explaining what you need to know about our proof style to understand their proofs.

The description of Euclid's algorithm in Chapter 1 used the program variables x and y. Program variables are different from the variables of ordinary math, such as the ones used in elementary algebra. The values of the program variables x and y in Euclid's algorithm change during execution of the algorithm. The values of the variables x and y of elementary algebra remain the same throughout a calculation. They are like the constants M and N of Euclid's algorithm. For now, we will use the term *variable* to mean a variable of ordinary math, like the ones of elementary algebra.

We begin with what I believe is the hardest math that you will have to know—a branch of math that takes people years to learn. It's much too difficult to explain here, so I will have to assume that you've already learned it. It's called arithmetic.

2.1 Arithmetic as a Mathematical Theory

Arithmetic is about numbers. The first numbers you learned about are the positive integers 1, 2, 3, etc. You then learned about more and more kinds of numbers until eventually you learned about the real numbers, which include integers, rational numbers like 3/4, and lots of other numbers like $-\sqrt{2}$ and π (which equals 3.14159...). Although the numbers we will use are almost always integers, most of our discussion here applies to all real numbers, so we let *number* mean *real number*.

We use the same notation for the operators of arithmetic that you learned in school—for example $+$, $/$ (division), and $\geq$; except that multiplication is written "$*$" because mathematicians use $\times$ to mean something else.

An operator like $*$ is what we call a *mapping*. A mapping M takes some fixed number of arguments. If M takes two arguments, then $M(v, w)$ is a value for some values v and w. For the mapping $*$, if v and w are numbers, then $*(v, w)$ equals the number we usually write $v * w$. For the mapping $=$, if v and w are numbers, then $=(v, w)$ is a value we call TRUE if v equals w, and it's a different value we call FALSE if v doesn't equal w.[1] The values TRUE and FALSE are called *Booleans*. A mapping such as $=$ whose value is a Boolean for all values of its arguments is called a *predicate*.

A mathematical theory contains expressions. An expression in the theory of arithmetic is a syntactically correct sequence of numbers, the operators of arithmetic, and parentheses—for example $2 * (3 + 42)$. It's best to think of $2 * (3 + 42)$ as a way of writing the expression $*(2, +(3, 42))$. Since it's the normal way of writing expressions, we'll write $2 * (3 + 42)$; but we'll think of it as $*(2, +(3, 42))$.

An expression like $2*(3+42)$ whose value is a number is called a *numeric expression*. An expression like $2 + 2 > 22$ whose value is a Boolean is called a *Boolean expression* or, more commonly, a *formula*.

The semantics of a mathematical theory is a mapping that assigns a meaning to each expression. We write the meaning of an expression exp as $[\![exp]\!]$. But you spent years learning the meaning of arithmetic expressions, so there's no need for me to explain it to you. If I define something in terms of arithmetic expressions, then you will understand it.

2.2 The Mathematical Theory of Algebra

By algebra, we mean here elementary algebra, which you probably learned as a teenager. In addition to numbers, algebra has variables that "stand for" numbers. For example, $3 * x - 2 * y$ is a numeric expression of algebra, and $3 * x - 2 * y = 7$ is an algebraic formula, where x and y are variables.

The meaning of an algebraic expression is the value obtained by substituting arbitrary numbers for the variables. To state this precisely, we define

---

[1] Arithmetic has two different operators named $-$. One takes two arguments, and $-(v, w)$ is the number we usually write $v - w$; the other takes a single argument, and $-(v)$ is the number we usually write $-v$.

2.2. THE MATHEMATICAL THEORY OF ALGEBRA

I have been told that many engineers are intimidated by formulas containing Greek letters like Υ. If you're one of them, don't worry. You had no trouble dealing with π as a child; you can handle a few more Greek letters now. They're used sparingly in this book, but sometimes representing a particular kind of object with Greek letters makes the text easier to read. Here are all the Greek letters used in the book, along with their English names. You don't have to remember their names; you just need to distinguish them from one another.

Lowercase

α	alpha	λ	lambda	π	pi	τ	tau
β	beta	μ	mu	ρ	rho	ϕ	phi
δ	delta	ν	nu	σ	sigma	ψ	psi
ϵ	epsilon (also written ε)						

Uppercase

Λ	Lambda	Υ	Upsilon	Π	Pi	Φ	Phi
Δ	Delta						

Figure 2.1: Greek letters used in this book.

---

an *interpretation* to be a mapping from variables to numbers. The meaning of an expression of algebra is then a mapping from interpretations to values, where a value is a number or a Boolean. If *exp* is an expression and[2] Υ is an interpretation, then $[\![exp]\!](\Upsilon)$ equals the value of the arithmetic expression obtained by replacing each variable v that occurs in *exp* with $\Upsilon(v)$. For example, suppose Υ is an interpretation such that $\Upsilon(x)$ equals 1 and $\Upsilon(y)$ equals -2, then $[\![3 * x - 2 * y]\!](\Upsilon)$ equals $3 * 1 - 2 * (-2)$, which equals 7.

Observe that the $*$ and $-$ in $[\![3*x-2*y]\!](\Upsilon)$ are different operators than the $*$ and $-$ in $3 * 1 - 2 * (-2)$. In $[\![\ldots]\!](\Upsilon)$ they are operators of algebra; in $3 * 1 \ldots$ they are operators of arithmetic. The meaning of the operator $*$ of algebra is defined in terms of the operator $*$ of arithmetic by the rule that, for any algebraic expressions exp_1 and exp_2 and any interpretation Υ:

$$[\![exp_1 * exp_2]\!](\Upsilon) \;=\; [\![exp_1]\!](\Upsilon) * [\![exp_2]\!](\Upsilon)$$

There are similar rules for $-$ and the other operators of algebra. There are also two other rules:

- $[\![v]\!](\Upsilon)$ equals $\Upsilon(v)$, for any variable v.

---
[2] If you're not used to reading formulas with Greek letters, go now to Figure 2.1.

- ⟦*exp*⟧(Υ) equals *exp*, if *exp* contains no variables (so it's an expression of arithmetic).

We can apply these rules to compute $⟦3 * x - 2 * y⟧(\Upsilon)$ as follows:

$$
\begin{aligned}
⟦3 * x - 2 * y⟧(\Upsilon) & \\
= ⟦3 * x⟧(\Upsilon) - ⟦2 * y⟧(\Upsilon) \quad & \text{by the rule for } - \\
= ⟦3⟧(\Upsilon) * ⟦x⟧(\Upsilon) - ⟦2⟧(\Upsilon) * ⟦y⟧(\Upsilon) \quad & \text{by the rule for } * \\
= 3 * \Upsilon(x) - 2 * \Upsilon(y) \quad & \text{by the two rules above}
\end{aligned}
$$

An important class of formulas are ones that equal TRUE no matter what values are substituted for their variables. Such a formula is said to be *valid*; and the assertion that F is valid is written $\models F$. For example, we write

(2.1) $\models p * (q + r) = p * q + p * r$

The thing we write as $\models F$ is not a formula of algebra. It's an assertion about the formula F. Formally, $\models F$ is a metamathematical formula or meta-formula. We usually call it something else like an assertion or a condition. When $\models F$ is true for an interesting formula F, mathematicians generally call F a theorem.[3] We might call (2.1) a theorem of algebra. An axiom is a theorem that we take to be an assumption. I will sometimes call $\models F$ a meta-formula to remind you that it's not a formula.

A proof rule tells us how to deduce the validity of one formula from the validity of one or more other formulas. A basic proof rule of algebra is that if a formula is valid, then the formula obtained by substituting numeric expressions for the formula's variables is also valid. For example, we can deduce from (2.1) the following meta-formula, for any numeric expressions exp_1, exp_2, and exp_3,

$$\models exp_1 * (exp_2 + exp_3) = exp_1 * exp_2 + exp_1 * exp_3$$

Implicit in the informal definition of an interpretation given above is that an interpretation assigns values to all possible variables, not just the ones in any particular expression. The value of $⟦F⟧(\Upsilon)$ for a formula F depends only on the values the interpretation Υ assigns to variables that occur in F. But letting an interpretation assign values to all variables simplifies things, because it means we don't have to keep track of which variables an interpretation is assigning values to.

---

[3]Logicians call a formula a theorem only if it can be proved from some collection of axioms and proof rules.

2.3. MATHGLISH

We assume that there are infinitely many variables. We do this for the same reason we assume there are infinitely many integers even though we only ever use relatively few of them: it makes things simpler not to have to worry about running out of them.

2.3 Mathglish

Math is precise, but this book isn't written in math. It's written in English that explains math. Explaining the precise meaning of math in the imprecise language of English is not easy. To help them do this, English-speaking mathematicians speak and write in a dialect of English I call Mathglish. (I expect mathematicians use similar dialects of other languages.) Mathglish differs from English in two ways: It eliminates some of the imprecision of English by giving a precise meaning to some imprecise English words, and it makes the written language more compact by using mathematical formulas to replace English phrases.

This book is written in Mathglish. This chapter explains the Mathglish you need to know to read the book. This section discusses the second feature of Mathglish—the use of formulas to replace prose.

Consider these two sentences that might appear in a math book:

1. Substituting $y+1$ for z in formula (42) yields $x \geq y+1$.

2. Formula (42) shows us that $x \geq y+1$.

Grammatically, we can see that the two uses of "$x \geq y+1$" are different. In sentence 1 it's a noun, while in sentence 2 it's a complete clause. In sentence 1, "$x \geq y+1$" is a formula; in sentence 2 it's an abbreviation for "x is greater than or equal to $y+1$". This grammatical difference tells us that the two sentences have very different meanings. Sentence 2 asserts that the formula $x \geq y+1$ is true. The first doesn't tell us whether it's true or false. For example, sentence 1 could be followed by:

Since (41) implies $x < y+1$, this proves that (42) is false.

It isn't always possible to tell from the grammar which way a formula is being used in a sentence. Sometimes we have to look at the context in which the sentence appears. The formula $x \geq y+1$ can be true only in a context in which some assumptions have been made about the values of x and y—assumptions that are expressed by formulas that are assumed to be true. Without such assumptions, the formula can be used only as a formula, which may be true or false. In this book, I have tried to make it clear by grammar or context what it means when a formula appears in a sentence.

2.4 Boolean Arithmetic (Propositional Logic)

Arithmetic is about numbers. Boolean arithmetic, also called *propositional logic*, is about Boolean values. Since there are only two Boolean values, TRUE and FALSE, Boolean arithmetic is infinitely simpler than ordinary arithmetic. A lot of mathematical reasoning can be described as Boolean arithmetic calculation. We'll first see how it's used in algebra.

We obtained an operator of algebra such as $+$ from the corresponding operator $+$ of arithmetic by defining $[\![exp_1 + exp_2]\!](\Upsilon)$ to equal $[\![exp_1]\!](\Upsilon) + [\![exp_2]\!](\Upsilon)$, for any numeric expressions exp_1 and exp_2 and any interpretation Υ. We can do the same thing with the operators of Boolean arithmetic. For example, the operator $\wedge$ of Boolean arithmetic, which is defined below, can be made an operator of algebra by defining $[\![F \wedge G]\!](\Upsilon)$ to equal $[\![F]\!](\Upsilon) \wedge [\![G]\!](\Upsilon)$ for any formulas (Boolean-valued expressions) F and G and any interpretation Υ.

When you studied algebra, you learned how to solve equations such as

(2.2) $\quad 3*x - 2*y = 7 \text{ and } 7*x + 3*y = 1$

You would have found the solution $x = 1$ and $y = -2$. It is the only solution, because calculating the solution actually proves that equations (2.2) imply $x = 1$ and $y = -2$. The concepts of *and* and *imply* are expressed by the operators $\wedge$ and $\Rightarrow$ of Boolean logic. In solving equations (2.2), you actually proved this theorem:

(2.3) $\quad \models (3*x - 2*y = 7) \wedge (7*x + 3*y = 1) \Rightarrow (x = 1) \wedge (y = -2)$

Mathematical theories generally have formulas, and the operators of Boolean arithmetic are turned into operators on formulas in all those theories in the same way that it's done with elementary algebra.

Since you probably already know them, the operators of Boolean arithmetic are presented only briefly. Here they are, along with their names and how they're read in Mathglish:

$\neg$	negation	not	$\Rightarrow$	implication	implies
$\wedge$	conjunction	and	$\equiv$	equivalence	if and only if
$\vee$	disjunction	or			

Implication is sometimes written $\rightarrow$ or $\supset$, and $\equiv$ is sometimes written $\Leftrightarrow$ or $\leftrightarrow$. Negation and conjunction are defined by

$\neg \text{TRUE} = \text{FALSE} \qquad\qquad \text{TRUE} \wedge \text{TRUE} = \text{TRUE}$
$\neg \text{FALSE} = \text{TRUE} \qquad\qquad \text{TRUE} \wedge \text{FALSE} = \text{FALSE}$
$\qquad\qquad\qquad\qquad\qquad\quad \text{FALSE} \wedge \text{TRUE} = \text{FALSE}$
$\qquad\qquad\qquad\qquad\qquad\quad \text{FALSE} \wedge \text{FALSE} = \text{FALSE}$

2.4. BOOLEAN ARITHMETIC (PROPOSITIONAL LOGIC)

The other operators can be defined in terms of $\neg$ and $\wedge$. In the following definitions, A and B represent Boolean values and $\triangleq$ means *equals by definition*:

$$A \vee B \triangleq \neg(\neg A \wedge \neg B)$$
$$A \Rightarrow B \triangleq (\neg A) \vee B$$
$$A \equiv B \triangleq (A \Rightarrow B) \wedge (B \Rightarrow A)$$

If you're not familiar with Boolean arithmetic, you should write out the complete definitions of $\vee$, $\Rightarrow$, and $\equiv$, the way it's done above for $\neg$ and $\wedge$. Here is a brief explanation of what these operators and their Mathglish counterparts mean—where "is true" means "equals TRUE".

$\neg A$ asserts that A is *not* true, where *not* means the same thing in English and Mathglish.

$A \wedge B$ asserts that A is true *and* B is true, where *and* has the same meaning in both languages.

$A \vee B$ asserts that A is true *or* B is true (or both A and B are true). Unlike *or* in English, *or* in Mathglish allows the possibility that both formulas are true. (Thus, *or* in Mathglish means *and/or* in English.)

$A \Rightarrow B$ asserts that A is true *implies* B is true. This means that B must be true if A is true, but says nothing about B if A is false. Thus, FALSE $\Rightarrow$ TRUE and FALSE $\Rightarrow$ FALSE both equal TRUE. Reading $\Rightarrow$ as *implies* is confusing because A *implies* B in English means that A being true causes B to be true, while *implies* in Mathglish does not. Only in Mathglish would we say that $2+2 = 5$ *implies* $2+2 = 4$. A good way to understand $\Rightarrow$ and the Mathglish *implies* is that we want

$$(x > 20) \underset{\text{implies}}{\Rightarrow} (x > 10)$$

to be true for all numbers x, and substituting different numbers for x shows that we want $A \Rightarrow B$ to equal TRUE except when $A =$ TRUE and $B =$ FALSE. Observe that in (2.3), the formula to the left of the $\Rightarrow$ equals FALSE for an interpretation Υ unless $\Upsilon(x) = 1$ and $\Upsilon(y) = -2$.

$A \equiv B$ asserts that A is true *if and only if* B is true. Thus, $\equiv$ is the equality relation for Boolean values. We read $\equiv$ as *is equivalent to*. Because we often want to express equivalence, written Mathglish has the abbreviation *iff* for *if and only if*. We sometimes write *equals* instead of *is equivalent to* because it's shorter.

Boolean arithmetic is often described as arithmetic with the two numbers 0 and 1, where FALSE is 0 and TRUE is 1. There is the following correspondence between the Boolean operators on FALSE and TRUE and the arithmetic operators on 0 and 1

$$\land \leftrightarrow * \qquad \lor \leftrightarrow + \qquad \Rightarrow \,\leftrightarrow\, \leq \qquad \equiv \,\leftrightarrow\, =$$

except that $1+1$ is taken to equal 1. Under this correspondence, the following laws of ordinary arithmetic become the following laws of Boolean arithmetic, where A, B, and C are any Boolean values:

- $\land$ and $\lor$ are associative and commutative—where an operator $\star$ is associative iff $(A \star B) \star C$ equals $A \star (B \star C)$, and $\star$ is commutative iff $A \star B$ equals $B \star A$.

- $\Rightarrow$ and $\equiv$ are transitive, where $\star$ is transitive iff $A \star B$ and $B \star C$ imply $A \star C$. Transitivity is often used in proofs. For example, transitivity of $\Rightarrow$ allows us to prove $A \Rightarrow Z$ by proving $A \Rightarrow B$ and $B \Rightarrow C$ and ... and $Y \Rightarrow Z$.

- $\land$ distributes over $\lor$, which means that $A \land (B \lor C)$ equals $(A \land B) \lor (A \land C)$.

Boolean arithmetic also has the extra rule that $\lor$ distributes over $\land$.

Negation is related to subtraction by $\neg A \leftrightarrow 1 - A$, which leads to the following rules of Boolean arithmetic:

$$\neg(A \land B) \text{ equals } (\neg A) \lor (\neg B) \qquad \neg(A \lor B) \text{ equals } (\neg A) \land (\neg B)$$

All expressions of Boolean arithmetic are Boolean valued, so they are formulas. When parsing these formulas, $\neg$ has higher precedence (binds more tightly) than $\land$ and $\lor$, which have higher precedence than $\Rightarrow$ and $\equiv$. Thus

$$\neg A \land B \Rightarrow C \lor D \quad \text{equals} \quad ((\neg A) \land B) \Rightarrow (C \lor D)$$

I don't know how the following expressions should be parsed, so don't write them:

$$A \land B \lor C \qquad A \equiv B \Rightarrow C$$

When these operators are incorporated into algebra, they have lower precedence than arithmetic operators like $+$ and $>$. However, it's best to put parentheses around purely algebraic formulas (such as those of (2.2)) when using operators from Boolean arithmetic.

I like the name *Boolean arithmetic* because it makes the subject sound as simple as it really is. However, it's usually called *propositional logic*, so that's what we'll call it from now on. You can find propositional logic calculators on the Web that will check whether a formula like $(A \Rightarrow B) \Rightarrow (\neg B \Rightarrow \neg A)$ is true for all Boolean values A and B. They can help you become facile with propositional logic.

2.5 ZF

Computers do a lot more than numerical computation. To describe what computer systems do mathematically, our math needs more kinds of values than just numbers. The simplest way I know to make the math we need rigorous is to base it on what is called ZF set theory or simply ZF, where Z and F stand for the mathematicians Ernst Zermelo and Abraham Fraenkel. One thing that makes ZF simple is that every value is a set. In ZF, the terms *set* and *value* mean exactly the same thing. Sometimes I will write *set/value* instead of *set* or *value* to remind you that the two words are synonyms.

You've probably learned that a set is a collection of things. In ZF, those things are sets, so a set is a collection of sets. However, we will see below that not all collections are sets—in particular, the collection of all sets isn't a set. The fundamental operator on sets is $\in$, which is read "is an element of" or simply "in". For every value/set S, the formula $e \in S$ equals TRUE iff e is one of the values/sets that S is a collection of. We call the values in a set S the *elements* of S. Two values/sets are equal iff they have the same elements.

Two sets that we will use are the set $\mathbb{R}$ of all real numbers and the set $\mathbb{I}$ of integers. Thus, $\sqrt{2}$ is an element of $\mathbb{R}$ but not an element of $\mathbb{I}$. Since the elements of a set are sets, this means a number must be a set. While logicians have used the operators of ZF set theory to define the set of real numbers, there's no need for us to do that. We just assume the real numbers exist and the arithmetic operators satisfy their usual properties. This means that 42 and $\sqrt{2}$ are sets, but we don't specify what their elements are. We know that $\sqrt{2} \in 42$ equals either TRUE or FALSE, but we don't know which. The Booleans TRUE and FALSE are also values.[4] We generally use the term *value* for a set/value like 42 or TRUE when we don't know what its elements are; and we use the term *set* for a set/value when we do know what its elements are.

---

[4] As usually defined, ZF does not consider TRUE and FALSE to be sets. Making them sets will allow the value of a program variable to be a Boolean.

We define the semantics of ZF the same way we defined the semantics of algebra. The meaning $[\![exp]\!]$ of an expression exp of ZF is a mapping from interpretations to values, where an interpretation is a mapping from variables to values. The operators of propositional logic are incorporated into ZF the same way they were incorporated into algebra. A formula is an expression F such that $[\![F]\!](\Upsilon)$ is a Boolean for every interpretation Υ.

You've probably learned a number of operations on sets, and you will need them if you want to write abstract programs that describe real systems. But the examples in this book are so simple that we'll need only a few of them. We often speak of one set being a subset of another—for example, $\mathbb{I}$ is a subset of $\mathbb{R}$ because every integer is a real number. The assertion that S is a subset of T is written $\subseteq$. It is effectively defined by this axiom:

$$\models S \subseteq T \equiv ((v \in S) \Rightarrow (v \in T))$$

where S, T, and v are variables.

A simple way to describe a set is by enumerating its elements. If $v_1, \ldots, v_n$ are any values, then they are the (only) elements of the set $\{v_1, \ldots, v_n\}$. This set need not have n elements. For example, the set $\{3, \sqrt{2}, 3, 2+1, 42, 3\}$ contains only the three elements $\sqrt{2}$, 3, and 42. It is equal to the set $\{42, 42, 3, \sqrt{2}\}$. (It is as silly to say that a set has two copies of the number 42 as it is to say that a football team has two copies of one of its players.) For $n = 0$, this defines $\{\}$ to be the empty set, which has no elements.

ZF contains the construct that mathematicians call *set comprehension*, but that I prefer to call *subsetting*. The expression $\{v \in S : F\}$ equals the set whose elements are all the elements in the set S for which the formula F is true. For example, we can define the set $\mathbb{N}$ of natural numbers, which consists of all non-negative integers, by:

$$\mathbb{N} \triangleq \{n \in \mathbb{I} : n \geq 0\}$$

In the expression $\{v \in S : F\}$, the symbol v is what is called a *bound variable*. It can be used only in the formula F, but not in S. Bound variables are discussed in Section 2.7.

A kind of set that is often used in describing programs is a finite set of consecutive integers, such as $\{-1, 0, 1, 2\}$. This set is written $-1 \mathinner{..} 2$. In general, we define:

$$m \mathinner{..} n \triangleq \{i \in \mathbb{I} : m \leq i \leq n\}$$

This definition implies that $m \mathinner{..} n$ equals the empty set $\{\}$ if $m > n$.

It's an axiom of ZF that if S is a set, then $\{v \in S : F\}$ is a set for any formula F. This axiom implies that the collection of all sets can't be a set. To show this, we assume the collection $\mathbf{V}$ of all values/sets is a set and obtain a contradiction. If $\mathbf{V}$ is a set, then $\{v \in \mathbf{V} : \neg(v \in v)\}$ is a set; let's call that set S. Since S is a set, the definition of $\mathbf{V}$ implies $S \in \mathbf{V}$ is true. The definition of the subsetting construct then implies $S \in S$ is true iff $\neg(S \in S)$ is true, which is impossible since TRUE doesn't equal FALSE. Therefore, $\mathbf{V}$ can't be a set. This argument is called Russell's paradox, because it was discovered by the mathematician and philosopher Bertrand Russell. Intuitively, the collection of all sets is too big to be a set.

2.6 Meaningless Expressions

The formula $x + y = y + x$ is a valid formula of algebra. However, validity of a formula in ZF means that it is true for every interpretation, where an interpretation is an assignment of a value/set to every variable. For $x + y = y + x$ to be a valid formula of ZF, $\mathbb{N} + \text{TRUE} = \text{TRUE} + \mathbb{N}$ would have to equal TRUE; and there's no reason why it should. What should be a valid formula of ZF is:

$$(x \in \mathbb{R}) \wedge (y \in \mathbb{R}) \Rightarrow (x + y = y + x)$$

But for this formula to be valid, this formula should be true:

(2.4) $(\mathbb{N} \in \mathbb{R}) \wedge (\text{TRUE} \in \mathbb{R}) \Rightarrow (\mathbb{N} + \text{TRUE} = \text{TRUE} + \mathbb{N})$

and (2.4) contains the meaningless expressions $\mathbb{N} + \text{TRUE}$ and $\text{TRUE} + \mathbb{N}$. How can we say whether or not two meaningless expressions are equal? This seems to be a problem.

Most computer scientists would say that the problem is solved by using types. The variables x and y in the formula $x + y = y + x$ should have type *real number*, so validity of that formula means that it's true for interpretations that assign real numbers to x and y. Types would make (2.4) an illegal formula.

I believe types are wonderful in a coding language, and I wouldn't want to write code in an untyped language. However, I have found the kind of types provided by coding languages to be unsuitable for representing abstract programs. For example, type correctness for Euclid's algorithm means that the values of the variables x and y are positive integers. The simple type systems of most coding languages don't allow a type like *positive integer*. Moreover, those type systems are overly restrictive, disallowing some reasonable expressions.

There are type systems that allow the type *positive integer* and are not restrictive. They are needed to formalize the kind of math that mathematicians do, so their proofs can be checked by computer. However, those type systems are so complicated that I never tried to learn them. I didn't have to because I realized that they are not needed for the math used to describe and reason about abstract programs. Instead, type correctness can be treated as a simple invariance property of programs. For example, type correctness of Euclid's algorithm is the invariance of the formula $(x \in \mathbb{N}^+) \wedge (y \in \mathbb{N}^+)$, where $\mathbb{N}^+$ is the set $\{n \in \mathbb{I} : n > 0\}$ of positive integers.

The solution to the problem of the meaningless formula (2.4) is to realize that it's not a problem, and formula (2.4) equals TRUE. The expressions $\mathbb{N} + \text{TRUE}$ and $\text{TRUE} + \mathbb{N}$ are meaningless only in the sense that we have not assigned them a meaning. All we know about them is that they are values/sets. But that's enough to tell us that $\mathbb{N} + \text{TRUE} = \text{TRUE} + \mathbb{N}$ equals either TRUE or FALSE. We don't know whether or not $\mathbb{N}$ and TRUE are numbers. We know that 42 is a set, but we don't know what its elements are. It's possible that 42 is the set $\mathbb{N}$, or that it equals the value/set TRUE. However, it doesn't matter if $\mathbb{N}$ and TRUE are numbers. If either or both of them is not a number, then (2.4) equals FALSE $\Rightarrow$ ($\mathbb{N} + \text{TRUE} = \text{TRUE} + \mathbb{N}$), which equals TRUE since $\mathbb{N} + \text{TRUE} = \text{TRUE} + \mathbb{N}$ is a Boolean. The other possibility is that $\mathbb{N}$ and TRUE are both numbers. In that case, no matter what numbers they are, $\mathbb{N} + \text{TRUE} = \text{TRUE} + \mathbb{N}$ equals TRUE.

Since we haven't given the expression $\mathbb{N} + \text{TRUE}$ a meaning, we will call it meaningless. But there's nothing harmful in writing such a meaningless expression. The expression is just useless because we don't know what it means. If correctness of a program depends on the value of a meaningless expression, then we can't prove that the program is correct. Moreover, a tool for checking correctness should report an error because it has to determine the value of a meaningless expression to decide if the program is correct. In practice, the kind of error in an abstract program that a simple type checker can catch is almost always quickly caught by model checking, and it is easily caught when trying to prove something about a type-incorrect expression.

Though not described in this way, ZF is usually considered to have a type system containing two types: Boolean and non-Boolean. For example, the commutativity of $\wedge$ is expressed as

(2.5) $\models (A \wedge B) \equiv (B \wedge A)$.

2.7. QUANTIFICATION AND BOUND VARIABLES

The assumption that A and B are Booleans isn't needed because it can be inferred that A and B have type Boolean.[5] We can maintain that simplicity without having to introduce types by assuming that rules of predicate logic such as (2.5) are true for all values A and B, not just for Booleans. We do that by assuming a mapping *Bool* such that $Bool(\text{TRUE}) = \text{TRUE}$, $Bool(\text{FALSE}) = \text{FALSE}$, and $Bool(v) \in \{\text{TRUE}, \text{FALSE}\}$ for all values v. We can then define predicate logic operators like $\wedge$ such that $v \wedge w$ equals $Bool(v) \wedge Bool(w)$ for all values v and w. This means that, although we don't know what $2 \wedge \{3\}$ equals, we know that it's a Boolean value and that it equals $\{3\} \wedge 2$.

2.7 Quantification and Bound Variables

2.7.1 Quantification

Math has two Boolean-valued constructs called quantifiers whose symbols, names, and Mathglish pronunciation are:

$\forall$ universal quantification   *for all*
$\exists$ existential quantification   *there exists*

They have the following meanings, where v is a variable and F is any formula of ZF:

$\forall v : F$ is true iff F is true when any value is substituted for v.

$\exists v : F$ is true iff there is some value that, when substituted for v, makes F true.

These are called *unbounded* quantifiers because they make an assertion about all values.[6] As we saw with the formula $x + y = y + x$, we are seldom interested in formulas that are satisfied by all values of a variable. We usually want to assert that a formula is true for all values in some set. It's also of little use to know that there exists a value of x such that $x^2 = 2$ if we don't know that that value is a number, since it's possible that $\text{TRUE}^2 = 2$ even if TRUE isn't a number. We therefore usually use the two *bounded* quantifiers $\forall v \in S$ and $\exists v \in S$, defined by:

$$\forall v \in S : F \triangleq \forall v : (v \in S) \Rightarrow F$$
$$\exists v \in S : F \triangleq \exists v : (v \in S) \wedge F$$

---

[5]The rules of Boolean algebra were described in Mathglish in Section 2.4. They couldn't be expressed there as theorems because we had not yet introduced Boolean-valued variables.

[6]The *bound* in *unbounded* bears no relation to the *bound* in *bound variable*.

For example, the following formula asserts that there exists a (real) number whose square equals y:

$$(2.6) \quad \exists\, x \in \mathbb{R} : y = x^2$$

Since x^2 is a non-negative real number for any real number x, and a real number y has a square root (that's a real number) iff $y \geq 0$, this formula is equivalent to $(y \in \mathbb{R}) \wedge (y \geq 0)$.

The two bounded quantifiers are related by these theorems:

$$(2.7) \quad \models (\forall\, v \in S : F) \equiv (\neg \exists\, v \in S : \neg F)$$
$$\models (\exists\, v \in S : F) \equiv (\neg \forall\, v \in S : \neg F)$$

You should be able to check that they follow from the quantifiers' informal definitions. You should also be able to check that $\forall\, v \in \{\} : F$ equals TRUE and $\exists\, v \in \{\} : F$ equals FALSE for any formula F.

When parsing a formula, the scope of a quantifier extends as far as possible—for example, until it is terminated by the end of the formula or by a right parenthesis whose matching left parenthesis precedes the quantifier. We abbreviate $\forall\, v \in S : \forall\, w \in T : F$ as $\forall\, v \in S, w \in T : F$, and we abbreviate $\forall\, v \in S : \forall\, w \in S : F$ as $\forall\, v, w \in S : F$, with similar abbreviations for $\exists$ and for the unbounded quantifiers.

Quantifiers and the rules for reasoning about them form what is called *predicate logic*. Predicate and propositional logic are the basis for reasoning in ordinary mathematics. A valid formula whose validity is based solely on the laws of predicate and propositional logic, and not on the meanings of any other operators in the formula, is called a tautology. For example, the truth of

$$\models (\exists\, v \in \mathbb{N} : M(v, x) \wedge (v+1 > x)) \Rightarrow (\exists\, v \in \mathbb{N} : M(v, x))$$

doesn't depend on the definitions of $\mathbb{N}$ and the mapping M, or on the meaning of the arithmetic operators $+$ and $>$. Rather, it follows from the rule $\models A \wedge B \Rightarrow A$ of propositional logic and the predicate logic rule that $\models F \Rightarrow G$ implies $\models (\exists\, v \in S : F) \Rightarrow (\exists\, v \in S : G)$. The theorems of predicate and propositional logic themselves are also called tautologies.

2.7.2 Bound Variables

As in the subsetting constructor $\{v \in S : F\}$, the v in the formulas $\forall\, v \in S : F$ and $\exists\, v \in S : F$ is a bound variable that can appear only in F, not in S. More

2.7. QUANTIFICATION AND BOUND VARIABLES

precisely, these expressions declare v to be a variable whose scope is the formula F. Bound variables are somewhat subtle and must be used with care. To understand why, we need to examine variables and scoping.

Like coding languages, formal languages for mathematics usually have explicit variable declarations, and a variable can be used only within the scope of its declaration. In this book and in almost all math books, most of those declarations are implicit. For example, in the discussion of Euclid's algorithm in Section 1.5, the program variables x and y are implicitly declared with scopes that lie entirely within that section. Those program variables are unrelated to the mathematical variables x and y that appear in Section 2.6.

Every expression we write occurs in a context, which specifies the variable declarations within whose scope the expression occurs. For example, the context of the subformula $y = x^2$ of formula (2.6) contains the same variable declarations as the complete formula (2.6), except it includes the declaration of x made by the quantifier $\exists\, x$. A bound variable of a formula F is one that is declared by a quantifier or a subsetting constructer within F. A variable that is not bound in F is called a *free* variable of F. For example, x is a bound variable and y a free variable of formula (2.6).

Things get complicated if formula (2.6) occurs within the scope of another declaration of x. It's best to view the x declared in the context of (2.6) and the x declared by its quantifier as two different variables with the same name. (This means that an interpretation must be a mapping from variables to values, not from variable names to values. That should seem natural if you've done any programming, because a program's code can contain multiple program variables with the same name that may have different values.)

Having two different variables with the same name can produce errors if you're not careful. For example, formula (2.6) is equivalent to $(y \in \mathbb{R}) \wedge (y \geq 0)$. Therefore, substituting an expression *exp* for y in that formula should yield the formula $(exp \in \mathbb{R}) \wedge (exp \geq 0)$. Let's take *exp* to be $x^2 + 1$, where x is the variable whose declaration's scope contains the formula (2.6). Naively substituting $x^2 + 1$ for y in (2.6) produces $\exists\, x \in \mathbb{R} : x^2 + 1 = x^2$, which equals FALSE, rather than $(x^2 + 1 \in \mathbb{R}) \wedge (x^2 + 1 \geq 0)$. The problem is that we should have substituted for y in (2.6) the formula $x^2 + 1$ in which x is the variable declared outside the formula, not the formula's bound variable. Such a substitution would produce a formula that's equivalent to $(x^2+1 \in \mathbb{R}) \wedge (x^2+1 \geq 0)$; but that formula would contain two different variables named x, and our math provides no way to write such a formula.[7] Logicians call the error produced by the naive substitution *variable capture*.

Fortunately, there's an easy way to avoid variable capture. The underlying mathematics doesn't depend on what we name variables. If we change the name of the bound variable in (2.6) to anything other than y, for example writing it as $\exists\, w \in \mathbb{R} : y = w^2$, then we get an equivalent formula. Naively substituting $x^2 + 1$ for y in that formula yields a formula equivalent to $(x^2 + 1 \in \mathbb{R}) \wedge (x^2 + 1 \geq 0)$, as it should.

We can avoid having to rename the bound variable in (2.6) if we use a name different from the name of any variable declared in its context. That is, we can avoid such variable capture by obeying this rule:

> **Safe Scoping Rule** Never declare a bound variable within the scope of a declaration of a variable with the same name.

The rule prevents writing (2.6) in any context in which we could write a formula like $x^2 + 1$ to substitute for y.

The Safe Scoping Rule will help keep you out of trouble, but it isn't enough. There are unlikely situations involving definitions in which this rule alone will not prevent variable capture. Section 2.8.1 below mentions another way variable capture can still occur. So when writing hand proofs, you should always be aware that variable capture is a potential problem, and it may require renaming bound variables to avoid it.

2.8 Defining Mappings and Functions

2.8.1 Mappings

Programs can be quite complex. The way to handle complexity is by hierarchical composition. Mathematics has a very simple and very powerful mechanism for hierarchical composition: the definition. We now examine definitions.

We introduced the symbol $\triangleq$, meaning *is defined to equal*, and defined $\vee$ by writing $A \vee B \triangleq \ldots$. The Boolean operator $\vee$ is a mapping that takes two arguments, and $A \vee B$ is an abbreviation of $\vee(A, B)$. We also defined $\mathbb{N}$ by writing $\mathbb{N} \triangleq \ldots$. We consider $\mathbb{N}$ to be a mapping that takes zero arguments, so we regard every definition as defining a mapping.

---

[7] There are ways to write quantification without using bound variables that allow writing such formulas, but they're inconvenient to use.

2.8. DEFINING MAPPINGS AND FUNCTIONS

The definition

(2.8) $\quad M(a, b) \triangleq a^2 + b^2$

defines the mapping M such that $M(exp_1, exp_2)$ equals $(exp_1)^2 + (exp_2)^2$, for any expressions exp_1 and exp_2. A mapping that has one or more arguments is not a value. The string $M + 42$ is not an expression; it's nonsense, like $3+ = 7$. (Appendix A.3 explains why mappings can't all be values.) The mapping M can appear in an expression only in a subexpression of the form $M(exp_1, exp_2)$. However, (2.8) defines this subexpression to equal $(exp_1)^2 + (exp_2)^2$, for all expressions exp_1 and exp_2 — even if exp_1 equals $\mathbb{R}$ and exp_2 equals FALSE.

The symbols a and b in (2.8) are called the *parameters* of the definition. Definition parameters are bound variables, whose scope is the right-hand side of the definition. However, they pose no problem of variable capture because they are replaced by expressions when the defined symbol appears in a formula. Still, the Safe Scoping Rule should be applied to them because the definition (2.8) would be confusing if it appeared within the scope of the declaration of a variable named a or b.

While definition parameters are bound variables that can't do any "capturing", variable capture is still possible with a definition such as

$$P(a, b) \triangleq (a > b) \wedge \exists x \in \mathbb{R} : b = x^2$$

whose right-hand side declares the bound variable x. The Safe Scoping Rule ensures that this definition does not occur in the scope of a variable named x. However, P may later be used in an expression that *is* in the scope of a variable x. Avoiding variable capture when substituting in that expression may require changing the name of the bound variable in the definition of P.

A fundamental rule of mathematics you may have learned as a teenager is that circular definitions are forbidden. We can't define M in terms of P, and P in terms of Q, and Q in terms of M. The obvious way to enforce this rule is to require that a definition use only previously defined mappings. However, to understand the definitions, it's often best to write them in the opposite order, so higher-level concepts are defined before defining the lower-level concepts on which they are built. So, we will order definitions to make them easier to understand, while avoiding circular definitions.

A special class of circular definitions is allowed in which a mapping is defined in terms of itself. They're called recursive definitions and are introduced in Section 3.5.

2.8.2 Functions

You may have learned about functions, and you undoubtedly did if you studied calculus. If you did learn about them, you may have wondered why I use the term *mapping* rather than *function*. Most mathematicians consider them to be the same. We'll see why they must be different.

For now, we describe functions of only a single argument; functions of multiple arguments are defined in Section 2.8.3 below. We consider a function to be a special kind of mapping that differs from other mappings in two ways:

- A function f has a domain, called DOMAIN(f), and the value of $f(v)$ can be specified only for values v in DOMAIN(f).

- A function is a value; other mappings need not be.

The first difference implies that the mapping M defined by

$$M(S) \triangleq \mathbb{N} \in S$$

defines $M(S)$ to equal the Boolean $\mathbb{N} \in S$ for all values S because its value is specified for every set/value S. We know that $M(S)$ equals $\mathbb{N} \in S$, which is a Boolean, for any value S. But M is not a function, because its domain would have to be the set of all sets/values, and we saw in Section 2.5 that the collection of all sets can't be a set.

If you've studied calculus, you've seen functions like the function f, whose domain is the set $\{x \in \mathbb{R} : x \neq 0\}$ of non-zero real numbers, defined by letting $f(x)$ equal $1/x^2$ for all numbers x in that set. Mathematicians seem to have no convenient notation for writing such a function. We will write it as $v \in \{x \in \mathbb{R} : x \neq 0\} \mapsto 1/v^2$. In general,

$$f \triangleq v \in S \mapsto exp$$

defines f to be the function with DOMAIN(f) equal to S such that $f(v) = exp$ for all $v \in S$. In the expression $v \in S \mapsto exp$, v is a bound variable whose scope is the expression exp. This definition tells us nothing about the value of $f(v)$ if v is not an element of S. However, f is a value. This is important because the value of a program variable must be a value, so we can use functions as ordinary values, just like numbers, when describing abstract programs.

Mathematicians generally define a function to be a set of pairs of values. However, while a function is a set/value, I prefer not to specify what its elements are—in part, because I prefer to define a pair as a function. All

2.8. DEFINING MAPPINGS AND FUNCTIONS

we know about a function is that it is completely determined by its domain and the value it assigns to elements of that domain. Thus, if f and g are two functions with domain S and $f(v) = g(v)$ for all $v \in S$, then the two functions are equal.

2.8.3 Sequences and Tuples

Lists are omnipresent—from shopping lists to lists of transactions on a bank statement. A list is represented mathematically as a sequence, which is a function f whose domain is a consecutive sequence of natural numbers, where $f(i)$ is element number i of the sequence. We will use two kinds of sequences that are numbered in different ways:

Ordinal The items of an ordinal sequence are numbered starting with item 1. The sequence represents a list whose items are naturally named with the ordinal numbers first, second, third, etc. For example, in a list of people waiting to be served, the second person to be served is naturally called person number 2.

Cardinal The items of a cardinal sequence are numbered starting with item 0. It represents a list in which it is natural to name an item by its distance from an item numbered 0. For example, in the list of floors in a building, the ground floor is naturally named floor 0, and floor number 2 is two floors above it.

When I started describing abstract programs with mathematical formulas, I discovered that the formulas were usually simpler if I described finite lists as ordinal sequences. However, the meaning and properties of the formulas are defined in terms of infinite sequences and finite prefixes of those sequences; and the math is simpler if those are cardinal sequences. So, we will use both kinds of sequences.

Mathematicians often use tuples. We represent a tuple as a finite ordinal sequence. Mathematicians enclose tuples in parentheses, but parentheses are used for lots of other things, so we make formulas containing tuples easier to read by using angle brackets $\langle$ and $\rangle$ instead. Thus, the ordinal sequence $\langle John, Mary, John \rangle$ is the function with domain $1..3$ such that $\langle John, Mary, John \rangle(2)$ equals $Mary$. The empty sequence, which is the unique function whose domain is the empty set, is written $\langle \rangle$. It is the one sequence that is both an ordinal and a cardinal sequence. The Cartesian product operator $\times$ is used to describe sets of tuples. For example, $S \times T \times U$ is the set of all triples (3-tuples) $\langle s, t, u \rangle$ such that $s \in S$, $t \in T$, and $u \in U$.

A mapping with n arguments can be considered to be a mapping with a single argument that is an n-tuple. There is no need to do that for arbitrary mappings, but we do it for functions. We define a function of n arguments to be a function whose domain is a set of n-tuples, where $f(v_1, \ldots, v_n)$ is an abbreviation for $f(\langle v_1, \ldots, v_n \rangle)$. As explained in Section Math VI, in ZF any set of n-tuples is a subset of the Cartesian product of n sets.

The lists that we will represent by cardinal sequences consist of things that happen one after the other. They will be written with their items separated by $\rightarrow$ symbols, as in the sequence of four states that is the execution of Euclid's algorithm shown in Section 1.5.

2.9 Some Useful Notation

Here are two pieces of notation that mathematicians don't seem to need, but that I find essential for writing formulas that describe programs.

2.9.1 IF/THEN/ELSE

A programmer who read enough math would notice that mathematicians lack anything corresponding to the **if/then/else** statement of coding languages. Instead, they use either prose or a very awkward typographical convention. We let the expression

IF P THEN exp_1 ELSE exp_2

equal exp_1 if $P =$ TRUE and exp_2 if $P =$ FALSE.

While it's inspired by the **if/then/else** coding language statement, you should not think of an IF/THEN/ELSE expression as instructions for computing something. It's somewhat like the expression written in the C language and its descendants as $P\,?\,exp_1 : exp_2$. However, coding languages usually specify the order in which the expressions P, exp_1, and exp_2 are evaluated. In mathematics there is no concept of evaluation. An expression simply has a value for any particular interpretation.

2.9.2 Conjunction and Disjunction Lists

Abstract mathematical descriptions of real systems can be quite long. Definitions are used to decompose them into shorter formulas that are easier to understand. However, those shorter formulas can still be a few dozen lines long. They are understandable because mathematical formulas have

2.9. SOME USEFUL NOTATION

a natural hierarchical structure. To take full advantage of that structure, we use a simple bit of notation that mathematicians and many computer scientists find heretical, but that engineers appreciate.

There are two simple ideas: (i) a list of formulas bulleted by $\wedge$ or $\vee$ represents the conjunction or disjunction, respectively, of those formulas; (ii) indentation is used to replace parentheses. For example, if $A, B, \ldots, J$ are formulas, then:

$$
\begin{array}{l}
\wedge \vee A \wedge B \\
 \vee C \\
\wedge\, D \Rightarrow E \\
\wedge \vee \exists x : F \\
 \vee \wedge G \equiv H \\
 \wedge J
\end{array}
\qquad \text{equals} \qquad
\begin{array}{l}
(\ (A \wedge B) \\
\ \vee\ C) \\
\wedge\ (D \Rightarrow E) \\
\wedge\ (\ (\exists x : F) \\
\vee\ (\ (G \equiv H) \\
\wedge\ J)\ )
\end{array}
$$

Note how the implicit parentheses in the bulleted lists delimit the scope of the $\Rightarrow$ and $\exists x$ operators in this formula.

Making indentation significant is a feature of the currently popular Python coding language, but it works even better in this notation because the use of $\wedge$ and $\vee$ as "bullets" makes the logical structure easier to see.

Chapter 3

Describing Abstract Programs with Math

In this chapter, we take a leisurely path that begins with a conventional mathematical method of describing computer systems and ends with the definition of almost all of TLA. Along the way, you will learn how to describe the safety part of an abstract program, how to prove it satisfies invariance properties, and the temporal logic that will be used to describe its safety and liveness properties as a single formula.

3.1 The Behavior of Physical Systems

Programs are meant to be executed on physical computers. I have been guided by the principle that any statement I make about a program should be understandable as a statement about its execution on one or more computers. The description of our science of concurrent programs therefore begins by examining the physics of computing devices. We don't care about the actual details of how transistors and digital circuits work. We are just interested in how scientists describe physical systems. As a simple example, we view a planet orbiting a star the way an astronomer might.

We consider the one-planet system's behavior starting at some time t_0, after the star and planet have been formed and the planet has settled into its current orbit. We assume that the planet remains in that orbit forever. Let $\mathbb{R}^{\geq}$ be the set $\{r \in \mathbb{R} : r \geq t_0\}$ of all real numbers r with $r \geq t_0$. The behavior of the one-planet system is described by its state at each instant of time at or after time t_0. We assume the star is much more massive than the planet, so we can assume that it doesn't move. We also assume that there are no other objects massive enough to influence the orbit of the planet, so the state of the system is described by the values of six state variables: three

3.1. THE BEHAVIOR OF PHYSICAL SYSTEMS

describing the three spatial coordinates of the planet's position and three describing the direction and magnitude of its momentum. Let's call those state variables $v_1, \ldots, v_6$; we won't worry about which of the six values each represents. The quantities these variables represent change with time, so the value of each variable v_i is a function, where $v_i(t)$ represents the value at time t. The behavior of the system is described mathematically by the function σ with domain $\mathbb{R}^{\geq}$ such that $\sigma(t)$ is the tuple $\langle v_1(t), \ldots, v_6(t) \rangle$ of numbers, for every $t \in \mathbb{R}^{\geq}$. Physicists call $\sigma(t)$ the *state* of the system at time t.

In this description, the planet is modeled as a point mass. Real planets are more complicated, composed of things like mountains, oceans, and atmospheres. For simplicity, the model ignores those details. This limits the model's usefulness. For example, it's no good for predicting a planet's weather. But models of planets as point masses are sometimes used to plan the trajectories of a real spacecraft. It's also not quite correct to say that the model ignores details like mountains and oceans. The mass of the model's point mass is the total mass of the planet, including its mountains and oceans, and its position is the planet's center of mass. The model abstracts those details, it doesn't ignore them.

The laws that determine the point-mass planet's behavior σ are expressed by six differential equations of this form:

$$(3.1) \quad \frac{dv_i}{dt}(t) = f_i(t)$$

where $t \in \mathbb{R}^{\geq}$ and each f_i is a function with domain $\mathbb{R}^{\geq}$ such that $f_i(t)$ is a formula containing the expressions $v_1(t), \ldots, v_6(t)$. Don't worry if you haven't studied calculus and don't know what equation (3.1) means. All you need to know is that it asserts the following approximate equality for small non-negative values of dt:

$$(3.2) \quad v_i(t + dt) \approx v_i(t) + f_i(t) * dt$$

and the approximation gets better as dt gets smaller. (It reaches equality when $dt = 0$.) The differential equations (3.1) have the property that for any time $t > t_0$ and any time $r > t$, the values of the six numbers $v_i(t)$ and the functions f_i completely determine the six values $v_i(r)$ and hence the value of $\sigma(r)$. That is, the equations imply:

History Independence For any time $t \in \mathbb{R}^{\geq}$, the state $\sigma(r)$ of the system at any time $r > t$ depends only on its state $\sigma(t)$ at time t, not on anything that happened before time t.

The generalization from a planetary system to an arbitrary physical system starting at time t_0 is straightforward. The system is described by state variables $v_1, \ldots, v_n$, and its behavior σ is described mathematically as the function with domain $\mathbb{R}^2$ such that $\sigma(t)$ equals $\langle v_1(t), \ldots, v_n(t) \rangle$. History independence is satisfied by any isolated physical system—that is, by any system that is assumed not to be influenced by anything outside the system.[1]

There is one way our one-planet system differs from most systems. For this system, it is possible to solve the differential equations (3.1) to write the functions v_i as formulas in terms of ordinary mathematical operations. Even for two planets around a star that is not much heavier than them, it is impossible to write such a solution. The functions v_i can be proved to exist and be unique, but the best we can do in general is find very close approximations to those functions for some finite interval of time.

Physics describes systems with math. Remember that in math, there are infinitely many variables. A description of any particular system contains only a finite number of them—the system variables. The description (3.1) of a planet orbiting a star contains only the six system variables describing the planet's state. It doesn't say that there is nothing else in the universe. It just says nothing about any other planets. Instead of thinking of (3.1) and (3.2) as describing a planet orbiting a star, it's more accurate to think of them as describing a universe in which the planet is orbiting the star. They also describe a universe containing both the planet and a spacecraft that orbits the star; they just say nothing about the spacecraft, since the spacecraft is too small to affect the planet's motion. (The spacecraft's motion could be affected by the planet.) Formulas (3.1) and (3.2) just say nothing about the spacecraft.

Physical science is descriptive. The laws of physics describe how a planet moves; they don't instruct the planet. Programs are prescriptive; they tell a computer what to do. This may make it seem strange to use physical science as a guide to a science of programs. But being descriptive or prescriptive is not a property of the math. It's just how we choose to view that math. We can view the equations of planetary motion not only as a description of how a planet moves, but also as commands given to the planet by nature. The math is agnostic. Our science views a program as a description of what behaviors it allows, not as commands for producing those behaviors. This view allows much more freedom in describing programs.

---

[1] In classical physics, the state at time t_0 uniquely determines the system's subsequent behavior. The situation is less clear in quantum physics where multiple subsequent behaviors seem possible, but the set of those behaviors is completely determined by the state.

3.2 Behaviors of Digital Systems

Math I

The Operator % For any integers m and n with $n > 0$, the value of $m \% n$ is defined to be the remainder when m is divided by n. The precise definition is that $m \% n$ equals the unique integer r satisfying

$$(m = d * n + r) \wedge (0 \leq r < n)$$

for some integer d. The operator $\%$ is pronounced *modulo* and is written *mod* by mathematicians.

Mathematical Induction You have probably encountered mathematical induction; if not, you may want to read about it on the Web. Simple mathematical induction proves that a formula is true for all $n \in \mathbb{N}$ by proving that it is true for $n = 0$ and that if it is true for n then it is true for $n+1$. It is stated more precisely by this proof rule, where P is any mapping:

$$\models P(0) \text{ and } \models \forall\, n \in \mathbb{N} : P(n) \Rightarrow P(n+1) \text{ implies } \models \forall\, n \in \mathbb{N} : P(n)$$

This rule is a meta-formula, and the Mathglish terms *and* and *implies* are used to represent the Boolean operators $\wedge$ and $\Rightarrow$ to make it clear that it is a meta-formula and not a formula.

Strong mathematical induction allows proving that the formula is true for $n+1$ by assuming that it is true for all numbers in $0..n$, not just true for n. It is stated as:

$$\models \forall\, n \in \mathbb{N} : (\forall\, m \in 0..(n-1) : P(m)) \Rightarrow P(n)$$
$$\text{implies } \models \forall\, n \in \mathbb{N} : P(n)$$

In this rule, for $n = 0$ the hypothesis implies

$$\models (\forall\, m \in 0..-1 : P(m)) \Rightarrow P(0)$$

which equals $\models P(0)$, since $\forall\, m \in \{\} : P(m)$ equals TRUE.

3.2.1 From Continuous to Discrete Time

Digital systems are physical systems, usually electromagnetic, in which certain stable states represent a collection of one-bit values. For example, at a certain point in a circuit, 0 volts may represent a 0 and 3.3 volts may represent a 1. Classical physics describes the behavior of physical systems as continuous.[2] If the voltage at some point in a circuit changes from 0 volts to 3.3 volts, it must pass through 1 and $\sqrt{2}$ volts.

Computers and other digital systems are designed so that each bit can be thought of as passing instantaneously from one stable state to the next. This means that we can think of there being a sequence of discrete times t_0, t_1, t_2, ... that are the only times at which the value of a bit can change. (We assume there is an event at time t_0 that initializes all the bits of the device.) We pretend that between times t_j and t_{j+1}, the part of the circuit representing each bit is in a stable state. Moreover, whether a bit changes its value at time t_{j+1} depends on the (stable) values of the bits immediately before time t_{j+1}.[3] Thus, the system is history independent.

Although built from one-bit registers, digital systems are designed so that larger components can also be viewed as changing their state instantaneously—for example, a 128-bit register or even all the bits in a chip controlled by a single clock. We can pretend that the entire component changes its value in discrete steps that can occur only at the times t_j. Thus, we can view a digital system as one whose components are represented by state variables that can have more than two values.

When a digital system is executing a program, the state of the program does not correspond directly to the state of the system. The value of a program variable might be represented by different parts of the system at different times. For example, its value may at some times be stored in a memory chip, at some times it may be in a register of a processor chip, and at some times it might be stored on a disk. Later, we'll see what it means mathematically for a digital system to implement a program in this way. For now, consider a concrete program to be just a digital system described by discretely changing variables whose values are not just bits but may be any data structure provided by the language—for example, 128-bit integers. An abstract program is the same, except the value of a variable may be any value—for example a real number such as $\sqrt{2}$, not just a finite-precision approximation like 1.414213562. Modeling a science of programs on the science of physical systems ensures that it can address real problems, and we are not just creating a science of angels dancing on the head of a pin.

---

[2] Here, classical physics includes relativity but not quantum mechanics. I believe that quantum mechanics also describes a continuous universe, but a discussion of that would take us too far afield.

[3] The t_j are pretend times, not exact physical times. Two bits that change at the same pretend time may change at different physical times because the clock pulse that generates the change may reach one of them a fraction of a nanosecond before the other. Chip designers must ensure that we can pretend that they change at the same time.

3.2. BEHAVIORS OF DIGITAL SYSTEMS

(However, the science should be able to describe any discretely behaving angels, wherever they might be dancing.)

We are seldom interested in the actual times t_j at which state variables can change. To simplify things, we consider only the sequence of states through which the system passes, ignoring the times at which it enters and leaves those states. We call the state created at time t_j state number j. Instead of letting a state variable v be a function that assumes the value $v(t)$ at time t, we consider it to be a function that assumes the value $v(j)$ in state number j. In other words, the value of a state variable v is a cardinal sequence of values. A behavior σ of a program is also a sequence, where $\sigma(j)$, its state number j, describes the values of the device's variables in that state.

If a program or a digital device runs forever, then the sequence of times t_j is infinite and therefore so is the sequence σ of its states. But if a program terminates, then those sequences can be finite. Other than parallel programs, in which concurrency is added to a traditional program so it can run faster by using multiple processors, most concurrent programs are not supposed to stop. A concrete concurrent program will not really run forever, but we describe it as running forever for the same reason we assume there are an infinite number of variables even though we use only a finite number of them: it makes things simpler.

Still, some concurrent programs are supposed to stop, so we have to describe them. For simplicity, we describe those programs as well with infinite state sequences. Exceptionally observant readers will have noticed that while the times t_j had to be chosen so we can pretend that the state changes only at those times, we did not require that the state *had* to change at each of those times. There can be times t_j at which none of the program variables' values change. In particular, if the program stops, we can add an infinite number of times t_j after it has stopped. This leads to an infinite sequence of states such that, for some k, the values of the program's variables after state number k are the same. We call a pair $\langle \sigma(j), \sigma(j+1) \rangle$ of successive states in a behavior σ a *step* of σ. A step in which the values of the program's variables do not change is called a *stuttering step* of the program.

We call a behavior ending in infinitely many stuttering steps a *halting* behavior of the program. It describes an execution in which the program stops. There are many reasons a program might stop—for example, an error might cause it to abort. If the program stops because it has completed what it was supposed to do, we say that it *terminates*. The term *halting* covers all cases when the program stops.

Mathematically, a behavior of a digital system or an abstract program

```
variables x = 1, y = 1;
while TRUE do
    a: x := x + y + 2 ;
       y := y + 2
end while
```

Figure 3.1: The simple abstract program *Sqrs*.

is an infinite cardinal sequence of states, where each state is an assignment of values/sets to variables. There is a natural tendency to think of state number j of a behavior as occurring at time j on some clock that ticks at a constant rate. Don't think of it like that. A microsecond might elapse between when the system reaches state number j and when it reaches state number $j+1$, and a day or a femtosecond might then elapse before it reaches state number $j+2$. All we know is that the system can't reach state number $j+1$ before it reaches state number j.

By removing any information about the physical time at which things happen, it may appear that we have eliminated the possibility of describing how much actual time it takes for something to happen. That's not the case, and Section 5.2 explains how to describe the times at which things happen. However, correctness of few programs depends on exactly how long it takes the program to do something, and I know of no commonly used coding language that allows us to write such programs. To my knowledge, nothing in the definition of the Java coding language assures us that executing the statement x = x+1 takes less than a century.

3.2.2 An Example: *Sqrs*

Our first example is a very simple abstract program called *Sqrs* that is described in Figure 3.1 with pseudocode. The **variables** statement describes the program variables and their initial values (their values in state 0). In this example, the program variables are x and y, and their initial values are both 1. The program's code consists of a **while** TRUE loop, which means that the body of the loop is repeatedly executed forever. Program *Sqrs* is an abstract program because it runs forever, producing a behavior with an infinite number of states, unlike a concrete program that would halt with an error when x became too big.

In a science, it would be crazy to let "=" mean anything other than what it has meant in mathematics for several centuries, so we use ":=" to mean assignment. Except for the label *a* that you can ignore for the moment,

3.2. BEHAVIORS OF DIGITAL SYSTEMS

it should be obvious what an execution of the loop body does. What's not obvious in most pseudocode and in virtually all real code is how to represent the execution as a behavior—which means as a sequence of states. In particular, how many different steps in the behavior describe a single execution of the loop body?

We would expect to describe execution of the loop body of *Sqr* with at least one step. But should there be more? For example, should evaluating $x+y$ in the first assignment statement be a separate step? Coding languages seldom answer this question because it makes no difference to the result computed by a traditional program. However, it can make a big difference for concurrent programs.

We will adopt the PlusCal algorithm language's [37] convention of using labels to indicate what the separate steps of a behavior are. The rule is that execution from one label to the next constitutes a single step. This means that a step begins and ends with program execution at a label. For program *Sqrs*, this implies that execution of the entire loop body, starting from label *a* and finishing when the program reaches *a* again, is a single step. With this choice of what constitutes a step in the behavior, the values $x(j)$ and $y(j)$ of the variables in each state j of the behavior are determined by two formulas:

(3.3) $(x(0) = 1) \land (y(0) = 1)$

(3.4) $\forall j \in \mathbb{N} : \land\ x(j+1) = x(j) + y(j) + 2$
$\qquad\qquad\quad \land\ y(j+1) = y(j) + 2$

We call (3.3) the *initial predicate*. It determines the initial state. Formula (3.4) is called the *step predicate*. It's the discrete analog of the differential equations (3.1) that describe the orbiting planet. Instead of describing how the values of the variables change in the continuous behavior when time increases by the infinitesimal amount dt, the step predicate (3.4) describes how they change when the state number of the discrete behavior increases by one.

You can check that (3.3) and (3.4) define a behavior that begins as follows where, for example, $[x :: 16,\ y :: 7]_3$ indicates that state number 3 assigns the values 16 to x and 7 to y, and the arrows are purely decorative.

$$\begin{bmatrix} x :: 1 \\ y :: 1 \end{bmatrix}_0 \rightarrow \begin{bmatrix} x :: 4 \\ y :: 3 \end{bmatrix}_1 \rightarrow \begin{bmatrix} x :: 9 \\ y :: 5 \end{bmatrix}_2 \rightarrow \begin{bmatrix} x :: 16 \\ y :: 7 \end{bmatrix}_3 \rightarrow \begin{bmatrix} x :: 25 \\ y :: 9 \end{bmatrix}_4 \rightarrow \ \cdots$$

These first few states of the behavior suggest that in the complete behavior, x and y equal the following functions:

(3.5) $\quad x = (j \in \mathbb{N} \mapsto (j+1)^2)$
$\quad\quad\quad y = (j \in \mathbb{N} \mapsto 2*j+1)$

To prove that (3.3) and (3.4) imply (3.5), we must prove that they imply:

(3.6) $\quad \forall j \in \mathbb{N} : (x(j) = (j+1)^2) \wedge (y(j) = 2*j+1)$

A proof by (simple) mathematical induction that (3.3) and (3.4) imply (3.6) is a nice exercise in algebraic calculation.

We can think of (3.5) as the solution of (3.3) and (3.4), just as the formulas describing the position and momentum of the planet at each time t are solutions of the differential equations (3.1). It is mathematically impossible to find solutions to the differential equations describing arbitrary multi-planet systems. It is mathematically possible to write explicit descriptions of variables as functions of the state number like (3.5) for the abstract programs written in practice, but those descriptions are almost always much too complicated to be of any use. Instead, we reason about the initial predicate and the step predicate, though in Section 3.4.1 we'll see how to write them in a more convenient way.

The interesting thing about program *Sqrs* is that the sequence of values assumed by x in an execution of the program is the sequence of all positive integers that are perfect squares, and this is accomplished using only addition. This is obvious from (3.5), but for nontrivial examples we won't have such an explicit description of each state of a behavior. Remember that history independence implies that, at any point in a behavior, what the program does in the future depends only on its current state. What is it about the current state that ensures that if x is a perfect square in that state, then it will equal all greater perfect squares in the future? There is a large body of work on reasoning about traditional programs, initiated by Robert Floyd in 1967 [15], that shows how to answer this question. If you're familiar with that work, the answer may seem obvious. If not, it may seem like it was pulled out of a magician's hat. Obvious or magic, the answer is that the following formula is true for every state number j in the behavior of *Sqrs*:

(3.7) $\quad \wedge (x(j) \in \mathbb{N}) \wedge (y(j) \in \mathbb{N})$
$\quad\quad\quad \wedge\; y(j) \,\%\, 2 = 1$
$\quad\quad\quad \wedge\; x(j) = \left(\dfrac{y(j)+1}{2}\right)^2$

3.2. BEHAVIORS OF DIGITAL SYSTEMS

This formula implies that $x(j)$ is a perfect square, since the first two conjuncts imply that $y(j)$ is an odd natural number. Moreover, since $y(j+1) = y(j) + 2$, the last conjunct implies that $x(j+1)$ is the next larger perfect square after $x(j)$. So, the truth of (3.7) for every state number j explains why the algorithm sets x to all perfect squares in increasing order.

A predicate like (3.7) that is true for every state number j of a behavior is called an *invariant* of the behavior. By mathematical induction, we can prove that a predicate is an invariant by proving these two conditions:

I1. The predicate is true for $j = 0$.

I2. For any $k \in \mathbb{N}$, if the predicate is true for $j = k$ then it's true for $j = k + 1$.

For (3.7), I1 follows from the initial predicate (3.3), and I2 follows from the step predicate (3.4). (You should have no trouble writing the proof if you're used to writing proofs; otherwise, it might be challenging.)

A predicate that can be proved to be an invariant by proving I1 from an initial predicate and I2 from a step predicate is called an *inductive invariant*. Model checkers can check whether a state predicate is an invariant of small instances of an abstract program. But the only way to prove it is an invariant is to prove that it either is or is implied by an inductive invariant. For any invariant P, there is an inductive invariant that implies P. However, writing an inductive invariant for which we can prove I1 and I2 is a skill that can be acquired only with practice. Tools to find it for you have been developed [16, 40], but I don't know how well they would work on industrial examples.

The first conjunct of the invariant (3.7) asserts the two invariants $x(j) \in \mathbb{N}$ and $y(j) \in \mathbb{N}$. An invariant of the form $v(j) \in S$ for a variable v is called a *type invariant* for v. An inductive invariant almost always must imply a type invariant for each of its variables. For example, without the hypotheses that $x(j)$ and $y(j)$ are numbers, we can deduce nothing about the values of $x(j+1)$ and $y(j+1)$ from the step predicate (3.4).

Most mathematicians would not bother to write the first conjunct of (3.7), simply assuming it to be obvious. However, mathematicians aren't good at getting things exactly right. They can easily omit some uninteresting corner case—for example, the assumption that a set is nonempty. Those "uninteresting corner cases" are the source of many errors in programs. To avoid such errors, we need to state explicitly all necessary requirements, including type invariants.

variables $x = 1$, $y = 1$, $pc = a$;
while TRUE **do**
  $a\colon x := x + y + 2$;
  $b\colon y := y + 2$
end while

Figure 3.2: The finer-grained abstract program *FGSqrs*.

3.2.3 A Finer-Grained Example: *FGSqrs*

Now consider a modified version of our abstract program *Sqrs* in which the execution of each assignment statement in the body of the **while** loop is represented as a separate step of the behavior. This is specified in the pseudocode by adding a label right before the second assignment statement. The label is *b* and the program is called *FGSqrs*.

The natural way to describe the state of *FGSqrs* is with the variables x and y and an additional variable to specify which assignment statement is the next one to be executed.[4] Such a variable isn't needed in *Sqrs* because that program has just a single label. The variable we add is traditionally called *pc* (for *program counter*). We will let its value equal the label from which the execution described by the next step begins. (That execution ends when it reaches the following label.) We assume that *a* and *b* are two arbitrary distinct values.

The pseudocode for *FGSqrs* is in Figure 3.2. The **variables** declaration contains *pc* and its initial value, even though we know *pc* is needed because there's more than one label, and program execution is normally assumed to start at the beginning of the code. But, a little redundancy doesn't hurt. A little redundancy doesn't hurt.

Here is the mathematical description of the behavior of program *FGSqrs*. As with *Sqrs*, it consists of an initial predicate and a step predicate.

Initial Predicate $(x(0) = 1) \wedge (y(0) = 1) \wedge (pc(0) = a)$

---

[4]In program *FGSqrs*, an additional variable isn't needed because which statement should be executed next can be deduced from the values of the variables x and y, but that's not the case in most programs written in pseudocode.

3.2. BEHAVIORS OF DIGITAL SYSTEMS

Step Predicate $\forall j \in \mathbb{N} :$ IF $pc(j) = a$
$$\begin{array}{ll} \text{THEN} & \wedge\ x(j+1) = x(j) + y(j) + 2 \\ & \wedge\ y(j+1) = y(j) \\ & \wedge\ pc(j+1) = b \\ \text{ELSE} & \wedge\ x(j+1) = x(j) \\ & \wedge\ y(j+1) = y(j) + 2 \\ & \wedge\ pc(j+1) = a \end{array}$$

When they see this step predicate, most programmers and many computer scientists think that the conjuncts $y(j+1) = y(j)$ and $x(j+1) = x(j)$ are unnecessary. They think that not saying what the new value of a variable equals should mean that it equals its previous value. But if that were the case, then what we wrote wouldn't be math. We would be giving up the benefits of centuries of mathematical development—the benefits that are the reason science is based on math. An essential aspect of math is that a formula means exactly what it says—nothing more and nothing less. If the step predicate didn't say what $y(j+1)$ equals when $pc(j) = a$ is true, then there would be no more reason for it to equal $y(j)$ than for it to equal the function $i \in \mathbb{N} \mapsto \sqrt{-42}$.

You may find it discouraging that the mathematical description of *FGSqrs* is more complicated than its pseudocode in Figure (3.2). Please be patient. You will see in Section 3.4.1 how a little notation can simplify it. We can always write an abstract program more compactly in pseudocode than in math, as long as we don't have to explain precisely what the pseudocode means. But science is precise, and a science of abstract programs must explain exactly what they mean. Moreover, tools can't check an imprecise description of a program. Math is the simplest way to explain things precisely.

PlusCal is a precise language for describing abstract programs in what looks like pseudocode. (However, it's infinitely more expressive than ordinary pseudocode because its expressions can be any mathematical expressions—even uncomputable ones.) A PlusCal program is translated to a mathematical description of the program in TLA⁺. I often find it easier to write an abstract program in PlusCal than directly in TLA⁺. However, I reason about the TLA⁺ translation, not the PlusCal code. And for many abstract programs, including most distributed algorithms, it's easier to write the program directly in TLA⁺ than in PlusCal.

The code whose execution is described as a single step of the behavior is called an *atomic operation*. Because a single step in a behavior describing the execution of *Sqrs* is replaced by two steps in the behavior describing the execution of *FGSqrs*, we say that *FGSqrs* has a *finer grain of atomicity* than *Sqrs*. Having a finer grain of atomicity implies that the step predicate is more complicated.

Having a finer grain of atomicity also implies that the inductive invariant that explains why the abstract program works will be more complicated. However, there is a trick for obtaining the invariant for *FGSqrs* from the invariant (3.7) of *Sqrs*. Define $yy(j)$ to equal $y(j)$ if execution of *FGSqrs* is at label a, and to equal the value $y(j)$ will have after executing statement b if execution is at b. The mathematical definition is:

$$yy(j) \triangleq \text{IF } pc(j) = a \text{ THEN } y(j) \text{ ELSE } y(j) + 2$$

Observe that x and yy are changed at the same time by statement a of *FGSqrs* exactly the same way that the loop body of *Sqrs* changes x and y. Statement b of *FGSqrs* leaves x and yy unchanged. This implies that, because (3.7) is an inductive invariant of *Sqrs*, the formula obtained from (3.7) by substituting yy for y satisfies condition I2 for *FGSqrs*. It's easy to check that this formula also satisfies I1, so it is an inductive invariant of *FGSqrs*. This trick of finding an expression (such as $yy(j)$) that is changed by the fine-grained program the way the coarse-grained program changes a variable (such as y) can often be used to obtain an invariant for a finer-grained abstract program from an invariant of a coarser-grained one. It is also at the heart of program refinement, the subject of Chapter 6.

3.3 Nondeterminism

Math II

The # Operator The operator # is defined so that if S is a finite set, then $\#(S)$ equals the number of elements in S. If S is not a finite set (so it must be an infinite set), then $\#(S)$ is a meaningless expression.

More About Functions For any sets D and S, ZF defines $D \to S$ to be the collection, which is assumed to be a set, of all functions f with domain D such that $f(x) \in S$ for all $x \in D$. A value f is a function with domain D iff f equals $v \in D \mapsto f(v)$. Therefore, this is an axiom of ZF:

$$\models f \in (D \to S) \;\equiv\; \land\; f = (v \in D \mapsto f(v)) \\ \land\; \forall v \in D : f(v) \in S$$

An array in coding languages is described mathematically as a function, where the expression $f[x]$ in the language means $f(x)$. For a variable f

3.3. NONDETERMINISM

whose value is an array/function, assigning the value 4.2 to $f[14]$ changes the value of f to a new array/function that we can write as:

$$x \in \text{DOMAIN}(f) \mapsto \text{IF } x = 14 \text{ THEN } 4.2 \text{ ELSE } f(x)$$

Mathematicians have little need to write such a function, but it occurs often when math is used to describe programs, so we need a more compact notation for it. We write it like this:

$$f \text{ EXCEPT } 14 \mapsto 4.2$$

3.3.1 Sources of Nondeterminism

The laws of classical physics, such as the laws of planetary motion, are deterministic. Given the initial values of all the variables, their values at any later time are completely determined. Causes of nondeterminism are either negligible because they have an insignificant effect—for example, meteor showers—or are simply assumed not to happen—for example, cataclysmic collisions with errant asteroids.

A program is nondeterministic if the initial state of a behavior doesn't determine the complete behavior. Even when executed on supposedly deterministic digital systems, nondeterminism is the norm in programs—especially concurrent ones. Here are some sources of nondeterminism in programs:

User Input The user giving a value to the program is usually described as an action of the program that nondeterministically chooses the value provided by the user. The user can also be described as a separate process that nondeterministically chooses the value to provide.

Random Algorithms Some algorithms can achieve better average performance by making random choices. Our science of programs is not meant for describing average properties of possible behaviors, so it can't distinguish this case from one in which random choices are the result of user input.

Generality We may want an abstract program to allow multiple possible implementations. Those possibilities appear as nondeterminism in the abstract program.

Failure Physical devices don't always behave the way they're supposed to. In particular, they can fail in various ways. Programs that tolerate failures describe a failure as an operation that may or may not be executed.

Timing Uncertainty The time taken to perform operations in an individual process can vary from one execution to another for several reasons, including (i) being run on different hardware and (ii) competition for resources with other processes in the same program or in concurrently executed programs. This results in multiple behaviors in which operations in different processes are executed in different orders. Those different orders can lead to very different behaviors.

Timing uncertainty is the most important source of errors due to nondeterminism that affects all concurrent programs (not just fault-tolerant ones). Let's examine a simple example of it.

3.3.2 An Example: *Increment*

The example is a trivial abstract multiprocess program called *Increment*. It has a variable x that initially equals 0, and each process just increments x by 1 and terminates. A process does this in two steps: the first step reads the current value of x, and the second step sets x to one plus the value it read. You should convince yourself that with N processes, an execution can terminate with x having any value from 1 through N. The final value of x will be N if each process executes its two steps with no intervening step by any other process. The final value will be 1 if all processes read x before any process sets the value of x.

This abstract program is described with pseudocode in Figure 3.3, where *Procs* is the set of processes. (*Procs* is really a set of process identifiers, but for convenience we call its elements processes.) The only assumption we make about this set is that it is finite and nonempty. The **process** statement declares that there is a process for every element of *Procs*, and it gives the code for an arbitrary process p in *Procs*. The variables t and pc are local to process p, each process having its own copy of these two variables. Variable x is global, accessed by all the processes. Process p saves the result of reading x in its variable t. The initial value of t doesn't matter, but letting all variables have reasonable initial values makes a type invariant (and sometimes other invariants) simpler, so we let t initially equal 0.

The mathematical description of the abstract program *Increment* is in Figure (3.4), where a, b, and *done* are assumed to be three different values. The process-local variables t and pc are represented by mathematical variables whose values in each state are functions with domain *Procs*, where $t(p)$ and $pc(p)$ are the values of those variables for process p. The initial predicate, describing the values of the variables in state number 0, is simple.

3.3. NONDETERMINISM

>
> **variables** $x = 0$;
> **process** $p \in Procs$
>   **variables** $t = 0, pc = a$;
> $a: t := x$;
> $b: x := t + 1$
> **end process**

Figure 3.3: The *Increment* abstract program for a set *Procs* of processes.

Initial Predicate
$\wedge \ x(0) = 0$
$\wedge \ t(0) = (p \in Procs \mapsto 0)$
$\wedge \ pc(0) = (p \in Procs \mapsto a)$

Step Predicate
$\forall j \in \mathbb{N} : PgmStep(j) \vee Stutter(j)$
  where
  $PgmStep(j) \triangleq \exists p \in Procs : aStep(p, j) \vee bStep(p, j)$
  $aStep(p, j) \triangleq \wedge \ pc(j)(p) = a$
                 $\wedge \ x(j+1) = x(j)$
                 $\wedge \ t(j+1) = (t(j) \text{ EXCEPT } p \mapsto x(j))$
                 $\wedge \ pc(j+1) = (pc(j) \text{ EXCEPT } p \mapsto b)$
  $bStep(p, j) \triangleq \wedge \ pc(j)(p) = b$
                 $\wedge \ x(j+1) = t(j)(p) + 1$
                 $\wedge \ t(j+1) = t(j)$
                 $\wedge \ pc(j+1) = (pc(j) \text{ EXCEPT } p \mapsto done)$
  $Stutter(j) \triangleq \wedge \ \forall p \in Procs : pc(j)(p) = done$
               $\wedge \ \langle x(j+1), t(j+1), pc(j+1) \rangle = \langle x(j), t(j), pc(j) \rangle$

Figure 3.4: The *Increment* abstract program in math.

The possible steps in a behavior are described by a predicate that, for each j, gives the values of $x(j+1)$, $t(j+1)$, and $pc(j+1)$ for any assignment of values to $x(j)$, $t(j)$, and $pc(j)$. It asserts that there are two possibilities, described by formulas $PgmStep(j)$ and $Stutter(j)$, that are explained below.

$PgmStep(j)$ describes the possible result of some process executing one step starting in state j. The predicate equals true iff there exists a process p for which $aStep(p,j)$ or $bStep(p,j)$ is true, where:

$aStep(p,j)$ describes a step in which process p executes its statement labeled a in state number j. Its last three conjuncts describe the values of the three variables x, t, and p in state $j+1$. Many people are tempted to write $t(j+1)(p) = x(j)$ and $pc(j+1)(p) = b$ instead of the third and fourth conjuncts. But that would permit $t(j+1)(q)$ and $pc(j+1)(q)$ to equal any values for $q \neq p$. Instead we must use the EXCEPT operator defined in Math II. The first conjunct is a predicate that is true or false of state j. It is an *enabling condition*, allowing the step described by the following three conjuncts to occur iff that condition is true.

$bStep(p,j)$ describes a step in which process p executes its statement labeled b in state number j. It is similar to $aStep(p,j)$. Its enabling condition is $pc(j)(p) = b$. The step sets $pc(j+1)(p)$ to *done*, which is a value indicating that the process has reached the end of its code and terminated.

$Stutter(j)$ describes a stuttering step starting in state j. It is enabled iff $pc(j)(p)$ equals *done* for all $p \in Procs$, so all processes have terminated. At that point, $PgmStep(j)$ is not enabled, so only an infinite sequence of stuttering steps can occur, as required for a terminated abstract program. The second conjunct in the definition of $Stutter(j)$ uses the fact that two tuples are equal iff their corresponding elements are equal to write the following formula more compactly:

$$(x(j+1) = x(j)) \land (t(j+1) = t(j)) \land (pc(j+1) = pc(j))$$

A property we might like to prove about abstract program *Increment* is that, when it has terminated, the value of x lies between 1 and the number of processes. Let's define N to equal $\#(Procs)$, the number of processes. Since a process has terminated iff its local pc variable equals *done*, the property we want to prove is that this formula is an invariant of *Increment*—that is, true for every $j \in \mathbb{N}$:

(3.8) $(\forall p \in Procs : pc(j)(p) = done) \Rightarrow (x(j) \in 1\mathbin{..} N)$

3.3. NONDETERMINISM

This is not an inductive invariant because condition I2 is not satisfied. For example, suppose the following is true:

- $pc(j)(p) = b$ and $pc(j)(q) = done$ for all $q \neq p$
- $t(j)(p) = N$

Then (3.8) is true in state number j, but false in state number $j + 1$.

To show that (3.8) is an invariant of *Increment*, we must find an inductive invariant that implies it. Stopping now and trying to find that inductive invariant by yourself is a good exercise. But it's not easy if you don't have practice finding inductive invariants and don't have a tool to check if what you think is an inductive invariant actually is one. So, I will write one for you.

An inductive invariant almost always requires a type invariant for each variable. We start by defining *TypeOK* to assert a type invariant for each of the three variables:

$$
\begin{aligned}
TypeOK(j) \triangleq\ & \wedge\ x(j) \in 0\,..\,N \\
& \wedge\ t(j) \in (Procs \rightarrow 0\,..\,N) \\
& \wedge\ pc(j) \in (Procs \rightarrow \{a, b, done\})
\end{aligned}
$$

TypeOK is an invariant, but not an inductive invariant. For example, if $x(j) = 1$, $t(j)(p) = N$, and $pc(j)(p) = b$, then $TypeOK(j)$ is true but a step satisfying $bStep(p, j)$ makes $TypeOK(j+1)$ false. We can make $TypeOK$ an inductive invariant by weakening it, replacing the two occurrences of $0\,..\,N$ with $\mathbb{N}$. However, I prefer a stronger, more informative type invariant.

To write the rest of the inductive invariant, we define $NumberDone(j)$ to be the number of processes that have terminated in state j. The precise definition is:

$$NumberDone(j) \triangleq \#(\{p \in Procs : pc(j)(p) = done\})$$

The complete inductive invariant, which we call *Inv*, is defined by:

(3.9) $\begin{aligned}[t] Inv(j) \triangleq\ & \wedge\ TypeOK(j) \\ & \wedge\ \forall\, p \in Procs : \\ & \qquad (pc(j)(p) = b) \Rightarrow (t(j)(p) \leq NumberDone(j)) \\ & \wedge\ x(j) \leq NumberDone(j) \end{aligned}$

To prove that *Inv* is an inductive invariant of program *Increment*, we must prove I1 and I2. I1 asserts that the initial predicate implies $Inv(0)$, and I2 asserts that the step predicate implies $Inv(j) \Rightarrow Inv(j + 1)$. We will not consider how these conditions are proved until we have a more convenient way of writing them.

3.4 Temporal Logic

Math III

Proof by Contradiction An ordinary proof of $P \Rightarrow Q$ assumes that P is true and proves Q is true. A proof by contradiction proves $P \Rightarrow Q$ by assuming that $P \wedge \neg Q$ is true and proving FALSE. Russell's paradox, explained in Section 2.5, is a proof by contradiction of:

$\{v \in S : F\}$ is a set for any formula F
implies the collection of all sets isn't a set

Proof by contradiction is an application of this theorem of propositional logic:

$$\models (P \Rightarrow Q) \equiv (P \wedge \neg Q \Rightarrow \text{FALSE})$$

Many mathematicians dislike proofs by contradiction because they find them inelegant. If you write a proof to make sure that what you're trying to prove is true, then you should always write a proof by contradiction. It's never harder and can make it easier to write the proof. I like to view proofs by contradiction in terms of this theorem of propositional logic:

$$\models (P \Rightarrow Q) \equiv (P \wedge \neg Q \Rightarrow Q)$$

It asserts that to prove P implies Q, we can assume both P and $\neg Q$ and prove Q. This gives us an additional hypothesis. Moreover, it's a very strong hypothesis. If $P \Rightarrow Q$ is true, then P implies that $\neg Q$ is equivalent to FALSE, which is the strongest possible hypothesis (since FALSE implies anything). If you wind up not using the additional hypothesis, you can just delete it.

Structured Proofs Mathematicians write proofs in prose. This works fine, if the prose satisfies two conditions:

1. It's short. This usually means one paragraph of less than about a dozen lines.

2. It explicitly mentions every assumption and previously proved fact that is needed by the proof.

Proofs that are not short should be structured. The simplest structured proof consists of a sequence of numbered steps, each consisting of an assertion and its prose proof satisfying conditions 1 and 2. The assertion of the

3.4. TEMPORAL LOGIC

last step is Q.E.D., which stands for the goal of the proof—that is, what must be proved to prove the theorem. Each step's proof may assume the assertions of previous steps. General structured proofs, in which a step's proof may also be a structured proof, are introduced in Section 6.4.

3.4.1 The Logic of Actions

3.4.1.1 Eliminating State Numbers

There's an easy way to simplify initial predicates, step predicates, and invariants: remove the explicit state numbers. It's obvious that an initial predicate is about state number 0, so we can eliminate every "(0)" in it. An invariant is true for all states, so we don't have to say which states it's about. For a step predicate, we just have to distinguish between $v(j)$ and $v(j+1)$ for a variable v. A notation for doing this that dates back at least to the early 1980s is to replace $v(j)$ by v and $v(j+1)$ by v'. The initial and step predicates of program *Increment* have been rewritten this way in Figure 3.5, where they've been given the names *Init* and *Next*. The inductive invariant (3.9) is also rewritten without the "(j)" and named *Inv*. (The "(j)" has been implicitly removed from the definition of *NumberDone*.) Make sure that you understand Figure 3.5 by comparing it with Figure 3.4 and definition (3.9).

Mathematically, the big leap from Figure 3.4 to Figure 3.5 is removing the explicit mention of state numbers—for example, writing x instead of $x(j)$. In Figure 3.4, *Procs* and x are both ordinary mathematical variables. The value of *Procs* is a set of processes and the value of x is a function whose domain is $\mathbb{N}$. In Figure 3.5, the value of *Procs* is a set of processes—the same set throughout a behavior of the program. However, the value of x depends on the state of the behavior.

The price of removing explicit state numbers from our formulas is leaving the domain of ordinary math, with a single kind of variable, and entering a new kind of math in which there are two kinds of variables: mathematical variables like *Procs*, whose values are the same in every state of a behavior, and program variables like x that are implicit functions of the state. Program variables like x look weird to mathematicians. In math, the value of a variable x is fixed. We've seen in Chapter 2 that when a mathematician does something else and introduces a variable x, it's really a completely different variable that happens also to be written "x". Of course, you're familiar with program variables because they're the variables of coding languages, whose values change in the course of a computation.

Initial Predicate

$Init \triangleq \land\ x = 0$
$\land\ t = (p \in Procs \mapsto 0)$
$\land\ pc = (p \in Procs \mapsto a)$

Step Predicate

$Next \triangleq PgmStep \lor Stutter$

where

$PgmStep \triangleq \exists\, p \in Procs : aStep(p) \lor bStep(p)$

$aStep(p) \triangleq \land\ pc(p) = a$
$\land\ x' = x$
$\land\ t' = (t \text{ EXCEPT } p \mapsto x)$
$\land\ pc' = (pc \text{ EXCEPT } p \mapsto b)$

$bStep(p) \triangleq \land\ pc(p) = b$
$\land\ x' = t'(p) + 1$
$\land\ t' = t$
$\land\ pc' = (pc \text{ EXCEPT } p \mapsto done)$

$Stutter \triangleq \land\ \forall\, p \in Procs : pc(p) = done$
$\land\ \langle x', t', pc' \rangle = \langle x, t, pc \rangle$

Inductive Invariant

$Inv \triangleq \land\ TypeOK$
$\land\ \forall\, p \in Procs : (pc(p) = b) \Rightarrow (t(p) \le NumberDone)$
$\land\ x \le NumberDone$

where

$TypeOK \triangleq \land\ x \in 0\,..\,N$
$\land\ t \in (Procs \to 0\,..\,N)$
$\land\ pc \in (Procs \to \{a, b, done\})$

$NumberDone \triangleq \#(\{p \in Procs : pc(p) = done\})$

Figure 3.5: Abstract program *Increment* and its invariant *Inv* in simpler math.

3.4. TEMPORAL LOGIC

Since this book is about a science of programs, we will henceforth use the name *variable* for program variables. Mathematical variables like *Procs* will be called *constants*. When describing a program mathematically, variables correspond to what we normally think of as program variables. Constants are parameters of the program, such as a fixed set of processes. Early coding languages had constants as well as variables. In modern coding languages, constants are buried in the code, where they are called static final variables of an object.

In this book, the variables in pseudocode are explicitly declared, and undeclared identifiers like *Procs* are constants. For formulas, the text indicates which identifiers are variables and which are constants.

In addition to having both variables and constants, the formulas in Figure 3.5 have primed variables, like x'. An expression that may contain primed and unprimed variables, constants, and the operators and values of ordinary math (which means everything described in Chapter 2) is called a *step expression*. A Boolean-valued step expression is called an *action*. The math whose formulas are actions is called the Logic of Actions, or LA for short.

3.4.1.2 The Semantics of the Logic of Actions

As we did in defining the semantics of elementary algebra in Section 2.2, we define the meaning $[\![exp]\!]$ of an expression of LA to be a mapping on interpretations. An interpretation assigns values to variables. Since LA has both constants and variables, there are two parts to an interpretation: an assignment of values to constants and an assignment of values to variables.

Since constants are ordinary mathematical values, and we have already discussed the semantics of ordinary math, we will ignore the part of an interpretation for LA that assigns values to them. When discussing a formula of LA, we assume that there is some fixed interpretation Υ that assigns values to the constants. Constants are usually assumed to satisfy some conditions. For example, the constants M and N of Euclid's algorithm in Section 1.5 are assumed to be positive integers, and the constant *Procs* of program *Increment* in Section 3.3 is assumed to be a finite set. We assume that the fixed interpretation Υ satisfies those assumptions. We define $\models F$ for a formula F of LA to mean that $[\![F]\!]$ is true for all interpretations in which the assignment of values to the constants satisfies the assumptions.

In LA, there are effectively two kinds of variables: unprimed and primed. An interpretation of LA assigns values to each of those kinds of variables, where the values assigned to v and v' are independent of one another.

We have defined a state to be an assignment of values to program variables. So, since we're neglecting constants, an interpretation for an LA formula is a pair of states—the first assigning values to the unprimed variables and the second assigning values to the primed variables. We have used the term *step* to mean a pair of successive states in a behavior. We now let it mean any pair of states. We will write the step consisting of the states s and t as $s \to t$ rather than $\langle s, t \rangle$ because that makes it clear that s and t are states.

To define the semantics of LA, we therefore have to define $[\![exp]\!](s \to t)$ for any states s and t. We have not yet defined any operators for LA, so the only operators that can appear in an LA expression are ordinary mathematical operators like $+$ and $\in$. They have the usual semantics in LA. For example

$$[\![exp1 + exp2]\!](s \to t) \triangleq [\![exp1]\!](s \to t) + [\![exp2]\!](s \to t)$$

For an unprimed variable v, we define $[\![v]\!](s \to t)$ to equal $s(v)$, the value assigned to variable v by state s. For a primed variable v', we define $[\![v']\!](s \to t)$ to equal $t(v)$.

We call an LA expression a *step expression* and an LA formula an *action*. For an action A and step $s \to t$, we say that $s \to t$ satisfies A or is an A step iff $[\![A]\!](s \to t)$ equals TRUE.

A *state expression* is an LA expression that contains no primed variables, and a *state formula* is a Boolean-valued state expression. For a state expression exp, the value of $[\![exp]\!](s \to t)$ depends only on s, so we can write it as $[\![exp]\!](s)$.

Because the meaning of an LA expression assigns different values to v and v', we can treat v and v' as two unrelated variables. This means that we can reason about LA formulas as if constants, unprimed variables, and primed variables were all different mathematical variables. Thus, for LA as defined so far, we can regard LA as ordinary math with some mathematical variables having names like v' ending with $'$.

3.4.1.3 The Prime Operator (')

In Figure 3.5, only variables are primed. In the Logic of Actions, we can prime not just a variable but any state expression—that is, any expression containing no primes. For a state expression exp, the value of the step expression exp' on a step $s \to t$ is the value of exp on t. More precisely, the meaning of exp' is defined by $[\![exp']\!](s \to t) = [\![exp]\!](t)$. This means that

3.4. TEMPORAL LOGIC

exp' is equivalent to the step expression obtained by priming all the variables in exp. The priming operator ($'$) can be applied only to state expressions. In LA, priming an expression that contains a prime is a syntax error. That means that it is illegal to prime an expression containing a defined symbol whose definition contains a prime. For example, if e is defined to equal $x' + 1$, then e' is syntactically illegal.

A constant has the same value in both states of a step. Therefore, $\models c' = c$ is true for any constant c. More generally, a *constant expression* is an expression with no (primed or unprimed) variable; and $\models exp' = exp$ is true for any constant expression exp. The bound identifiers of predicate logic are like ordinary mathematical variables, which means they are treated like constants in the Logic of Actions. For example, $(\exists i \in \mathbb{N} : y = x + i)'$ equals $\exists i \in \mathbb{N} : y' = x' + i$. We therefore call bound identifiers *bound constants*. Appendix Section A.4 gives an example of how you can get into trouble by forgetting that bound identifiers are constants.

The semantics of LA imply that the prime operator distributes over the operators and constructs of ordinary math—for example, that $(F \vee G)'$ equals $F' \vee G'$. By expanding all definitions and distributing primes in this way, we obtain a formula in which the prime operator is applied only to variables. We don't have to expand all definitions to obtain such a formula. We need only expand definitions that contain a prime or that appear within a primed expression and contain a variable. Once we have reached an expression in which only variables are primed, we can reason about the resulting expression as if constants, variables, and primed variables were all ordinary mathematical variables. We therefore need no additional rules for reasoning about LA formulas.

Section 3.2.2 defined an inductive invariant *Inv* of a program to be a state predicate satisfying conditions I1 and I2, which we can restate as:

I1. *Inv* is implied by the program's initial state.

I2. If *Inv* is true in a state, then the program's next-state predicate implies that it is true in the next state.

For program *Increment*, whose initial predicate is *Init* and whose next-state action is *Next*, these two conditions can be expressed in LA as:

(3.10) $\models Init \Rightarrow Inv$
$\models Inv \wedge Next \Rightarrow Inv'$

The proof of these conditions for program *Increment* is discussed in Appendix Section B.1.

Thus far, the correctness properties of programs that have concerned us have been invariance properties. All the reasoning we have done to verify that a program satisfies an invariance property is naturally expressed in LA. The safety property usually proved of a traditional program is that it cannot produce a wrong answer—which is expressed as the invariance of the property asserting that the program has not terminated with a wrong answer. The most popular way of proving such a property is Hoare logic [22]. Appendix Section A.5 explains Hoare logic and its relation to the Logic of Actions. (Remember that to understand its structured proof, you should first read Appendix Section A.2.)

3.4.1.4 Action Composition

The Logic of Actions contains another operator that is almost never used in describing abstract programs and will not play a major role for us until Section 8.1. However, it does make brief appearances in Sections 5.1.2 and 6.4.4.3, so it is explained here.

For actions A and B, the action $A \cdot B$ is defined to be true of a step $s \to t$ iff there is a state u such that $s \to u$ is an A step and $u \to t$ is a B step. If actions A and B describe two pseudocode statements S_a and S_b, then $A \cdot B$ describes the statement $S_a; S_b$ executed by executing S_a followed by S_b. For example, the statements labeled a and b in process p of program *Increment* shown in Figure 3.3 are described by actions $aStep(p)$ and $bStep(p)$ of Figure 3.5, and:[5]

$$
\begin{aligned}
aStep(p) \cdot bStep(p) \equiv\ & \land\ pc(p) = a \\
& \land\ x' = t(p) + 1 \\
& \land\ t' = (t \text{ EXCEPT } p \mapsto x) \\
& \land\ pc' = (pc \text{ EXCEPT } p \mapsto done)
\end{aligned}
$$

Replacing the actions $aStep(p)$ and $bStep(p)$ with $aStep(p) \cdot bStep(p)$ in the definition of the next-state action *Next* of program *Increment* produces a program with a coarser grain of atomicity. Choosing the grain of atomicity of an abstract program involves a tradeoff between making the program detailed enough to be useful and simple enough to be usable. Section 8.1 addresses this tradeoff using action composition.

The operator "$\cdot$" is associative, meaning $(A \cdot B) \cdot C = A \cdot (B \cdot C)$ for any actions A, B, and C. We can therefore omit parentheses and simply write

---

[5]If you believe that the second and third conjuncts in this formula are in the wrong order, then you're thinking in terms of coding languages, not math. Remember that $F \land G$ is equivalent to $G \land F$.

3.4. TEMPORAL LOGIC

$A \cdot B \cdot C$.

For any action A, we define the action A^+ to be satisfied by a step $s \to t$ iff state t can be reached from state s by a sequence of one or more A steps. In other words:

$$A^+ \triangleq A \vee (A \cdot A) \vee (A \cdot A \cdot A) \vee (A \cdot A \cdot A \cdot A) \vee \cdots$$

3.4.2 The Temporal Logic RTLA

In 1977, Amir Pnueli [48] had the idea of using an obscure branch of mathematics called temporal logic to express time-dependent properties without explicitly mentioning times or state numbers. He used a temporal logic containing the single temporal operator $\Box$ and operators defined in terms of $\Box$. You can read $\Box$ as *always*, but when you become more familiar with it you'll probably just call it *box*. Intuitively, the formula $\Box F$ asserts that the formula F is true at all times. For example, if P is a state predicate, then $\Box P$ asserts that P is true in all states of a behavior.

From now on, we will be discussing and using temporal logic. We will continue to ignore assignments of values to constants, assuming some fixed interpretation satisfying the assumptions made about those constants.

In the kind of temporal logic Pnueli used, called *linear-time* temporal logic, the meaning of a formula is a predicate on behaviors, where a *behavior* is an infinite cardinal sequence of states. In other words, a behavior σ is a function from $\mathbb{N}$ to states. We think of $\sigma(n)$ as the state at time n, so the first state of σ is $\sigma(0)$. But remember, the only resemblance of the state number n to a time is that state $\sigma(n)$ does not occur later than state $\sigma(n+1)$. (In Section 5.2, we'll see that they could both occur at the same time.) We'll sometimes write σ as $\sigma(0) \to \sigma(1) \to \cdots$.

RTLA is the temporal logic containing the same temporal operators as Pnueli's original logic, all defined in terms of $\Box$, but having the formulas of LA as the basic formulas. The formulas of RTLA can all be written as LA formulas and formulas obtained from them using the operator $\Box$ and the usual Boolean operators and quantifiers of ordinary math. The only expressions of RTLA are formulas. Prime (′) can appear only in the basic LA formulas. It's illegal to prime a formula containing a $\Box$.

The TLA in RTLA stands for *Temporal Logic of Actions*. The R stands for *Raw*, in the sense of *unrefined*. We'll see later that RTLA allows us to write formulas that we shouldn't write. TLA is the logic obtained by restricting RTLA to make it impossible to write those formulas. But that's a complication we don't need to worry about now, so we'll start with the simpler "raw" logic.

In temporal logic formulas, the operator $\Box$ binds more tightly than the operators of propositional logic. For example, $\Box F \vee G$ is parsed as $(\Box F) \vee G$.

3.4.2.1 Simple RTLA

In RTLA, the operator $\Box$ can be applied to any RTLA formula, so we can write formulas like $\Box(A \Rightarrow \Box B)$ where A and B are actions. We will begin by considering simple RTLA, in which the operator $\Box$ is applied only to actions, not to formulas containing $\Box$.

A formula of a temporal logic is called a *temporal formula*. For any assignment of values to constants, the meaning $[\![F]\!]$ of a temporal formula is a *behavior predicate*—that is, a mapping that assigns Boolean values to behaviors. An action A is a formula of RTLA, where it is viewed as a behavior predicate. As a formula of LA, we've viewed A as a step predicate. As a formula of RTLA, we view it as a behavior predicate that is true on a behavior iff, viewed as a step predicate, it is true of the behavior's first step.

To state that precisely, let $[\![A]\!]_{LA}$ be the meaning of A as an LA formula. We define its meaning $[\![A]\!]_{RTLA}$ as an RTLA formula as follows. For any behavior σ, which equals $\sigma(0) \to \sigma(1) \to \sigma(2) \to \cdots$, we define

$$(3.11) \quad [\![A]\!]_{RTLA}(\sigma) \triangleq [\![A]\!]_{LA}(\sigma(0) \to \sigma(1))$$

From now on, $[\![F]\!]$ means $[\![F]\!]_{RTLA}$ for all RTLA formulas, including actions. We will explicitly write $[\![A]\!]_{LA}$ to denote the meaning of A as an LA formula.

For an action A, we define $\Box A$ to be the temporal formula that is true of a behavior iff A is true of all steps of the behavior. In other words, we define the meaning $[\![\Box A]\!]$ of the RTLA formula $\Box A$ by

$$(3.12) \quad [\![\Box A]\!](\sigma) \triangleq \forall n \in \mathbb{N} : [\![A]\!]_{LA}(\sigma(n) \to \sigma(n+1))$$

Like most logics, RTLA contains the propositional logic operators, where they have their standard meanings. For example, $[\![F \wedge G]\!](\sigma)$ equals $[\![F]\!](\sigma) \wedge [\![G]\!](\sigma)$. We will write a quantified formula like $\exists i \in S : F$ with F a temporal formula only when S is a constant expression, in which case $[\![\exists i \in S : F]\!](\sigma)$ equals $\exists i \in [\![S]\!] : [\![F]\!](\sigma)$, where $[\![S]\!]$ is the value of S under the assumed assignment of values to constants. As in LA, bound identifiers are called *bound constants* and they act like constants, having the same value in all states of a behavior.

It's important to remember that a behavior is *any* cardinal sequence of states. It doesn't have to be a behavior of any particular program. Since any step is the first step of lots of behaviors, it's obvious that if A is an LA

3.4. TEMPORAL LOGIC

formula, then $\models A$ is true when A is viewed as an RTLA formula iff it's true when A is viewed as an LA formula.

Now let's return to the description of program *Increment* in Figure 3.5. It tells us that a behavior σ is a behavior of the program iff (i) the initial predicate *Init* is true of its first state $\sigma(0)$ and (ii) the step predicate *Next* is true for every step $\sigma(n) \to \sigma(n+1)$ of σ. Condition (i) is expressed by $[\![\mathit{Init}]\!]$, since (3.11) tells us that $[\![\mathit{Init}]\!](\sigma)$ equals $[\![\mathit{Init}]\!]_{LA}(\sigma(0) \to \sigma(1))$; and since *Init* is a state predicate, it's true of a step iff it's true of the first state of the step. By (3.12), condition (ii) is expressed as $[\![\Box \mathit{Next}]\!]$. Thus (the meaning of) the formula $\mathit{Init} \land \Box \mathit{Next}$ is true of a behavior σ iff σ is a behavior of program *Increment*.

Of course, this is true for an arbitrary program. The behaviors that satisfy a program with initial predicate *Init* and next-state action *Next* are described by the simple RTLA formula $\mathit{Init} \land \Box \mathit{Next}$. Any program is described by an RTLA formula of this form. As promised, we can write any program as a mathematical formula. It's an RTLA formula rather than a TLA formula, and we'll see that it needs to be modified. But for now, it's close enough to the final TLA formula.

By (3.12), the state predicate *Inv* is true in all states of a behavior iff $\Box \mathit{Inv}$ is true of that behavior. That *Inv* is an invariant of *Increment* means that, for any behavior σ, if σ is a behavior of *Increment* then *Inv* is true in all states of σ. Thus, that *Inv* is an invariant of *Increment* is expressed by this condition:

(3.13) $\models \mathit{Init} \land \Box \mathit{Next} \Rightarrow \Box \mathit{Inv}$

Remember that in (3.10) and (3.13), when *Init*, *Next*, and *Inv* are the formulas defined in Figure 3.5, $\models F$ means that F is true for all interpretations satisfying the assumptions we made about the constants of *Increment*—namely, that *Procs* is a nonempty finite set and the values of a, b, and *done* are different from one another.

In general, the conditions I1 and I2 for showing that a state predicate *Inv* is an invariant of a program $\mathit{Init} \land \Box \mathit{Next}$ are expressed in LA by conditions (3.10). It is an RTLA proof rule that these conditions imply (3.13). When we prove a safety property like (3.13), the major part of the reasoning depends on the definitions of the formulas *Init*, *Next*, and *Inv*. That reasoning is reasoning about actions, which is formalized by LA. The temporal logic reasoning, which is done in RTLA, is trivial. Describing the program with a single formula is elegant. But it is really useful only when verifying liveness properties, which requires nontrivial temporal reasoning.

Because it's often forgotten, it is worth repeating that a state is *any* assignment of values to variables, and a behavior is *any* infinite sequence of states. Even when we are discussing program *Increment*, "state" means any state, including states in which x has the value $\langle \sqrt{2}, 1 .. 147 \rangle$. In (3.13), $\models$ means true for *any* behavior, even behaviors in which the initial value of x is $\langle \sqrt{2}, 1 .. 147 \rangle$. It is true for those behaviors because *Init* equals FALSE for them (unless $\langle \sqrt{2}, 1 .. 147 \rangle$ happens to equal 0, which it might).

3.4.2.2 The Complete RTLA

Simple RTLA suffices for reasoning about safety properties, but not for liveness properties. For example, we want to express the liveness property of program *Increment* that a process p eventually terminates. Termination of p means that $pc(p)$ eventually equals *done* and remains equal to *done* forever. In terms of explicit state numbers, where $pc(n)$ is the value of pc in state number n, this property can be written:

(3.14) $\quad \exists j \in \mathbb{N} : \forall k \in \mathbb{N} : pc(j+k)(p) = \textit{done}$

To write it without explicit state numbers, we need full RTLA, in which $\square$ can be applied to any RTLA formula, not just to an action. To define the meaning of all RTLA formulas, we first define σ^{+n}, for any behavior σ and natural number n, to be the behavior obtained by removing the first n states from the sequence σ. That is, σ^{+n} is the behavior

$$\sigma(n) \to \sigma(n+1) \to \sigma(n+2) \to \cdots$$

so σ^{+n} equals $i \in \mathbb{N} \mapsto \sigma(i+n)$.

For any RTLA formula F, the RTLA formula $\square F$ is true of a behavior σ iff it is true of the behaviors σ^{+n} for all $n \in \mathbb{N}$. In other words:

(3.15) $\quad [\![\square F]\!](\sigma) \triangleq \forall n \in \mathbb{N} : [\![F]\!](\sigma^{+n})$

for any behavior σ. When F is an action A, this is the same definition as (3.12) because the first step $\sigma^{+n}(0) \to \sigma^{+n}(1)$ of σ^{+n} is $\sigma(n) \to \sigma(n+1)$.

Although $\square$ has a simple definition, temporal formulas can be hard to understand at first. It helps to think of a temporal formula as an assertion about the present and future. The state $\sigma(n)$ of a behavior σ is the state at time n, and the behavior σ^{+n} is the part of the behavior σ that begins at time n. We can then think of $[\![F]\!](\sigma^{+n})$ as asserting that F is true at time n of behavior σ. Thus, $[\![F]\!](\sigma)$ asserts that F is true at time 0 of σ, and $[\![\square F]\!](\sigma)$ asserts that F is true at all times of σ. The formula $\square F$ therefore

3.4. TEMPORAL LOGIC

asserts that F is true at all times—that is, F is always true. (Remember that time n is just some instant of time; it is *not* n time units after time 0.)

We now drop the $[\![\ ]\!]$ and think about temporal logic the same way we think about ordinary math, conflating a formula with its meaning. So, we'll think of a temporal formula F as a Boolean-value function on behaviors. However, we will still turn to the formal meaning (3.15) of $\Box$ when it is useful.

Since we will now be working with temporal logic formulas, we consider a tautology to be any valid formula whose validity depends only on theorems of temporal logic, which include theorems of ordinary predicate and propositional logic. We will therefore call theorems of temporal logic tautologies. Sections 3.4.2.3–3.4.2.8 below examine $\Box$ and temporal operators defined in terms of $\Box$. They present quite a few temporal logic tautologies. Understanding intuitively why those tautologies are true will make you comfortable reading temporal logic formulas and thinking in terms of them.

3.4.2.3 The $\Box$ Operator

We first consider some temporal logic tautologies—theorems about arbitrary temporal formulas. If they are not obvious, rewrite them in terms of the meanings of the formulas. The first tautology asserts the obvious fact that if F is always true, then it is true now:

(3.16) $\models \Box F \Rightarrow F$

The next tautology asserts that $F \wedge G$ true at all times is equivalent to F true at all times and G true at all times:

(3.17) $\models \Box(F \wedge G) \equiv (\Box F) \wedge (\Box G)$

You should check that (3.17) follows from the definition (3.15) of $\Box$ and the predicate-logic tautology:

$\models (\forall n \in S : P \wedge Q) \equiv (\forall n \in S : P) \wedge (\forall n \in S : Q)$

Observe that $\Box(F \vee G)$ and $(\Box F) \vee (\Box G)$ are not equivalent. For example, $\Box(F \vee G)$ is true of a behavior in which F is true only in the initial state and G is false in the initial state and true in all other states. However, neither $\Box F$ nor $\Box G$ is true of that behavior.

We can generalize (3.17) to any conjunction, including an infinite conjunction—that is, quantification over an infinite set of formulas. If F_i is a temporal formula for all $i \in S$, then:

(3.18) $\models \Box(\forall i \in S : F_i) \equiv (\forall i \in S : \Box F_i)$

The next tautology should also be obvious. It asserts that if F implies G is true at all times, then F is true at all times implies G is true at all times:

(3.19) $\models \Box(F \Rightarrow G) \Rightarrow (\Box F \Rightarrow \Box G)$

Perhaps less obvious is this proof rule, which is sort of a converse of (3.16):

(3.20) $\models F$ implies $\models \Box F$

The assertion $\models F$ means that F is true of all behaviors. The assertion $\models \Box F$ asserts that for any behavior, F is true of the part of that behavior starting at any time. But that part of the behavior is itself a behavior, so $\models F$ implies that F is true of it. If this is not obvious to you, then you may be thinking of a behavior as a behavior of some program. A behavior is any infinite sequence of states, so if you remove the first n states of any behavior, you get a behavior.

From (3.19) and (3.20) we easily derive:

(3.21) $\models F \Rightarrow G$ implies $\models \Box F \Rightarrow \Box G$

This rule lies at the heart of much temporal logic reasoning. Another rule we will need is

(3.22) $\models \Box(F \wedge G \Rightarrow H)$ implies $\models \Box F \Rightarrow \Box(G \Rightarrow H)$

It follows from (3.21) and the equivalence of $F \wedge G \Rightarrow H$ and $F \Rightarrow (G \Rightarrow H)$.

We now examine some additional temporal assertions that can be defined using $\Box$.

3.4.2.4 Eventually ($\Diamond$)

The operator $\Diamond$ is defined by $\Diamond F \triangleq \neg \Box \neg F$. Like $\Box$, the operator $\Diamond$ binds more tightly than the operators of propositional logic, so $\Diamond F \wedge G$ is parsed as $(\Diamond F) \wedge G$. To understand $\Diamond$, we derive the meaning $[\![\Diamond F]\!]$ of a formula $\Diamond F$ from (3.15):

$$
\begin{aligned}
[\![\Diamond F]\!](\sigma) &\equiv [\![\neg \Box \neg F]\!](\sigma) && \text{by definition of } \Diamond \\
&\equiv \neg [\![\Box \neg F]\!](\sigma) && \text{by the meaning of } \neg \\
&\equiv \neg \forall n \in \mathbb{N} : [\![\neg F]\!](\sigma^{+n}) && \text{by (3.15)} \\
&\equiv \neg \forall n \in \mathbb{N} : \neg [\![F]\!](\sigma^{+n}) && \text{by the meaning of } \neg \\
&\equiv \exists n \in \mathbb{N} : [\![F]\!](\sigma^{+n}) && \text{by (2.7) of Section 2.7}
\end{aligned}
$$

3.4. TEMPORAL LOGIC

Hence, $\Diamond F$ asserts that F is true at some time—either now or in the future. We read $\Diamond$ as *eventually*, where by being eventually true we include the possibility of being true only now. Corresponding to the tautologies (3.16) and (3.17) for $\Box$ are these tautologies for $\Diamond$:

$$(3.23) \quad \models F \Rightarrow \Diamond F \qquad \models \Diamond(F \vee G) \equiv (\Diamond F \vee \Diamond G)$$

Make sure you understand why they are true from the meaning of $\Diamond$ as *eventually*. These two tautologies can be derived from (3.16) and (3.17). For example:

$$(3.24) \quad (F \Rightarrow \Diamond F) \equiv (\neg(\neg F) \Rightarrow \neg(\Box \neg F)) \quad \text{By logic and the definition of } \Diamond.$$
$$\equiv (\Box \neg F \Rightarrow \neg F) \quad \text{By propositional logic.}$$

and $\models \Box \neg F \Rightarrow \neg F$ follows from (3.16). You should convince yourself that $\Diamond(F \wedge G)$ and $(\Diamond F) \wedge (\Diamond G)$ need not be equivalent. The equivalence of $\Diamond(F \vee G)$ and $\Diamond F \vee \Diamond G$ generalizes to arbitrary disjunctions:

$$\models \Diamond(\exists i \in S : F_i) \equiv (\exists i \in S : \Diamond F_i)$$

Here are three tautologies relating $\Diamond$ and $\Box$. The first is obtained by negating $\Diamond F$ and its definition; the third by substituting $\neg F$ for F in the first; and the second by negating both sides of the equivalence in the third:

$$(3.25) \quad \models \neg \Diamond F \equiv \Box \neg F \qquad \models \neg \Box F \equiv \Diamond \neg F \qquad \models \Box F \equiv \neg \Diamond \neg F$$

They should be obvious from thinking of $\Box$ as *always* and $\Diamond$ as *eventually*. The first two tell us that moving $\neg$ over a temporal operator $\Box$ or $\Diamond$ changes $\Box$ to $\Diamond$ and $\Diamond$ to $\Box$. Note the similarity between $\Box/\Diamond$ and $\forall/\exists$, a similarity that arises from the meanings of $\Box$ and $\Diamond$. Here is another tautology that follows from the intuitive meanings of $\Box$ and $\Diamond$:

$$(3.26) \quad \models (\Box F \wedge \Diamond G) \Rightarrow \Diamond(\Box F \wedge G)$$

It asserts that if F is true from now on and G is true at some time in the future, then at some time in the future F is true from then on and G is true then.

We can express liveness properties with $\Diamond$. For example, the assertion that some state predicate P is eventually true is a liveness property. The assertion that the program whose formula is F satisfies this property is $\models F \Rightarrow \Diamond P$. Since the assertion that something eventually happens is a liveness property, most of the formulas we write that contain $\Diamond$ express liveness.

To prove that a program described by formula F satisfies the liveness property $\Diamond P$, we must prove $\models F \Rightarrow \Diamond P$. A proof by contradiction proves this by proving $\models F \wedge \neg \Diamond P \Rightarrow \Diamond P$. By the equivalence of $\neg \Diamond P$ and $\Box \neg P$, this is equivalent to proving $\models F \wedge \Box \neg P \Rightarrow \Diamond P$. In particular, if P is a state predicate, this allows us to assume that $\neg P$ is an invariant of F when proving that F implies $\Diamond P$. We can use the invariance $\neg P$ to prove other invariants of F. This form of reasoning is at the heart of most proofs that a program satisfies a liveness property.

3.4.2.5 Eventually Always ($\Diamond\Box$)

Recall that termination of process p of program *Increment* means that $pc(p)$ eventually equals *done* and remains forever equal to *done*, a property expressed with explicit state numbers by (3.14). This is expressed in RTLA as $\Diamond\Box(pc(p) = done)$, because $[\![\Diamond\Box(pc(p) = done)]\!](\sigma)$ equals

$$\exists j \in \mathbb{N} : \forall k \in \mathbb{N} : [\![pc(p) = done]\!]((\sigma^{+j})^{+k})$$

and $(\sigma^{+j})^{+k}$ equals $\sigma^{+(j+k)}$, so $pc(j+k)(p)$ in (3.14) equals $[\![pc(p)]\!]((\sigma^{+j})^{+k})$.

We can think of $\Diamond\Box$ as a temporal operator meaning *eventually always*. Convince yourself that this is a tautology:

$$\models \Diamond\Box(F \wedge G) \equiv (\Diamond\Box F) \wedge (\Diamond\Box G)$$

3.4.2.6 Infinitely Often ($\Box\Diamond$)

It should now seem natural to think of $\Box\Diamond F$ as meaning *always eventually* F is true. If you're not used to thinking about infinite sequences, it may not be obvious that *always eventually* is equivalent to *infinitely often*. So, let's prove it.

Theorem 3.1 *F is infinitely often true iff it is always eventually true.*

Define S_σ to be the set of times at which F is true of a behavior σ.

1. F is infinitely often true of σ iff S_σ is an infinite set.

    PROOF: By definition of *infinitely often*.

2. S_σ is an infinite set iff for every time n, there is a time $m \geq n$ such that $m \in S_\sigma$.

    PROOF: A nonempty set of natural numbers is infinite iff it has no largest element.

3.4. TEMPORAL LOGIC

3. The statement that for every time n there exists a time $m \geq n$ such that $m \in S_\sigma$ is equivalent to the statement that F is always eventually true.

   PROOF: By the definitions of S_σ and *always eventually*.

4. Q.E.D.

   PROOF: By propositional logic, because steps 1–3 are of the form A iff B, B iff C, and C iff D, and the theorem asserts A iff D.

It is usually most helpful to think of $\Box\Diamond$ as meaning *infinitely often* rather than *always eventually*. For example, consider the formula $\Box\Diamond(F \vee G)$. It asserts that $F \vee G$ is true infinitely often, which means that F or G is true infinitely often. But F or G is true infinitely often iff at least one of them is true infinitely often. This yields the following tautology:

$$(3.27) \quad \models \Box\Diamond(F \vee G) \equiv (\Box\Diamond F) \vee (\Box\Diamond G)$$

The rules for moving $\neg$ over $\Box$ and $\Diamond$ that are implied by the first two tautologies of (3.25) yield the following two tautologies. For example, the first comes from $\neg\Box\Diamond F \equiv \Diamond\neg\Diamond F \equiv \Diamond\Box\neg F$.

$$(3.28) \quad \models \neg\Box\Diamond F \equiv \Diamond\Box\neg F \qquad \models \neg\Diamond\Box F \equiv \Box\Diamond\neg F$$

3.4.2.7 The End of the Line

You might expect that we can keep constructing more and more complicated operators like $\Box\Diamond\Diamond\Box\Diamond\Box$ with sequences of $\Box$ and $\Diamond$. We can't. Any such sequence is equivalent to $\Box$, $\Diamond$, $\Box\Diamond$, or $\Diamond\Box$. To see this, first observe that *always always* is the same as *always*. That is, $\Box\Box F$ is equivalent to $\Box F$. That's because $\forall i, j \in \mathbb{N} : P(i+j)$ is equivalent to $\forall k \in \mathbb{N} : P(k)$, for any P.

Similarly, *eventually eventually* is the same as *eventually*, so $\Diamond\Diamond F$ is equivalent to $\Diamond F$. The equivalence of $\Diamond\Diamond$ and $\Diamond$ also follows from the definition of $\Diamond$ and the equivalence of $\Box\Box$ and $\Box$ by:

$$\Diamond\Diamond F \equiv \neg\Box\neg\neg\Box\neg F \equiv \neg\Box\Box\neg F \equiv \neg\Box\neg F \equiv \Diamond F$$

So, we can only get a new operator by alternating $\Box$ and $\Diamond$. However, $\Box\Diamond$ and $\Diamond\Box$ is as far as we can go because of the following tautologies:

$$(3.29) \quad \models \Diamond\Box\Diamond F \equiv \Box\Diamond F \qquad \models \Box\Diamond\Box F \equiv \Diamond\Box F$$

The first one is obvious if we read $\Diamond\Box\Diamond$ as *eventually infinitely often*, because F is true at infinitely many times iff it is true at infinitely many times after some time has passed. You can convince yourself that the second is true by realizing that infinitely often F always true is equivalent to F being always true starting at some time. Alternatively, you can show that the first tautology implies the second by figuring out why each of the following equivalences is true:

$$\Box\Diamond\Box F \equiv \neg\Diamond\neg\neg\Box\neg\neg\Diamond\neg F \equiv \neg\Diamond\Box\Diamond\neg F \equiv \neg\Box\Diamond\neg F$$
$$\equiv \neg\neg\Diamond\neg\neg\Box\neg\neg F \equiv \Diamond\Box F$$

3.4.2.8 Leads To ($\leadsto$)

Although there are no more operators to be defined by directly stacking $\Box$ and $\Diamond$, there is another useful temporal operator defined in terms of them: the operator $\leadsto$, read *leads to*, defined by:

(3.30) $\quad F \leadsto G \triangleq \Box(F \Rightarrow \Diamond G)$

The operator $\leadsto$ is parsed like $\Rightarrow$, meaning it has lower precedence (binds less tightly) than $\neg$, $\land$, and $\lor$, and it has the same precedence as $\equiv$.

Formula $F \leadsto G$ asserts of a behavior that, whenever F is true, G is true then or later. You should convince yourself that $\leadsto$ is transitive, meaning:

$$\models (F \leadsto G) \land (G \leadsto H) \Rightarrow (F \leadsto H)$$

Here are two additional tautologies that should be obvious:

(3.31) $\quad \models ((F \lor G) \leadsto H) \equiv (F \leadsto H) \land (G \leadsto H)$
$\qquad \models (F \leadsto G) \land \Box(G \Rightarrow H) \Rightarrow (F \leadsto H)$

The first of these tautologies generalizes to:

(3.32) $\quad \models ((\exists\, i \in S : F_i) \leadsto H) \equiv (\forall\, i \in S : (F_i \leadsto H))$

Here are three more tautologies involving $\leadsto$; try to understand why they're true.

(3.33) (a) $\models \Box F \land (F \leadsto G) \Rightarrow \Box\Diamond G$
$\qquad$ (b) $\models (F \leadsto G) \equiv (F \land \Box\neg G \leadsto G)$
$\qquad$ (c) $\models (F \land \Box G \leadsto H) \equiv (F \land \Box G \leadsto H \land \Box G)$

Here's how I understand them:

(a) $F \leadsto G$ implies that whenever F is true, G is true then or later; and $\Box F$ implies that F is always true. Therefore, $\Box F \land (F \leadsto G)$ implies G is true infinitely often.

3.4. TEMPORAL LOGIC

(b) $F \leadsto G$ $\equiv$ $\Box(F \Rightarrow \Diamond G)$ Definition of $\leadsto$.
           $\equiv$ $\Box(F \wedge \neg \Diamond G \Rightarrow \Diamond G)$ Propositional logic.
           $\equiv$ $\Box(F \wedge \Box \neg G \Rightarrow \Diamond G)$ By (3.25).
           $\equiv$ $F \wedge \Box \neg G \leadsto G$ Definition of $\leadsto$.

(c) $F \wedge \Box G \leadsto H$ asserts that, for all t, if $F \wedge \Box G$ is true at time t, then H is true at some time $u \geq t$; and $\Box G$ true at time t implies it is still true at time u, so $H \wedge \Box G$ is true at time u.

Observe that tautology (b) justifies a proof by contradiction: to prove that F true implies G is eventually true, we can assume that G is never true.

Proving $\leadsto$ properties is at the heart of liveness proofs. For example, here's how we prove termination of Euclid's algorithm, discussed in Section 1.5. The algorithm terminates because while $x \neq y$ is true, the sum of x and y keeps decreasing, which can't continue forever because the algorithm satisfies the invariant that x and y are positive integers. Therefore, eventually $x = y$ and the algorithm terminates. This argument is formalized in RTLA as follows.

To prove termination, we must prove that every behavior of the algorithm satisfies $\Diamond(x = y)$. The proof uses this tautology, which follows from the meanings of the operators $\Box$, $\leadsto$, and $'$:

$$(3.34) \quad \models \Box(P \Rightarrow Q') \Rightarrow (P \leadsto Q)$$

The tautology $\models \Diamond P \vee \Box \neg P$ allows us to prove $\Diamond(x = y)$ by assuming that a behavior of the algorithm satisfies $\Box(x \neq y)$ and obtaining a contradiction. Let R_i be the state predicate $x + y \leq i$. We prove that $\Box(x \neq y)$ and the invariant that x and y are positive integers imply that, for all $i > 0$, the program satisfies $\Box(R_i \Rightarrow (R_{i-1})')$. By (3.34), this implies $R_i \leadsto R_{i-1}$. By the transitivity of $\leadsto$ and mathematical induction, this implies $R_{M+N} \leadsto R_0$. Since the program implies that R_{M+N} is true in the initial state, this implies that $\Diamond R_0$ is true, contradicting the invariant that x and y are always positive.

3.4.2.9 Warning

Although elegant and useful, temporal logic is weird. It's not ordinary math. In ordinary math, any operator Op we can define satisfies the condition, sometimes called *substitutivity*, that the value of an expression $Op(e_1, \ldots, e_n)$

is unchanged if we replace any e_i by an expression equal to e_i. If Op takes a single argument, substitutivity means that

$$(3.35) \quad \models (exp_1 = exp_2) \Rightarrow (Op(exp_1) = Op(exp_2))$$

is true for any expressions exp_1 and exp_2. For example, (3.35) is true for the operator $\neg$. However, the temporal operator $\Box$ is not substitutive. For example let exp_1 and exp_2 be the state predicates $x = 0$ and $y = 0$, respectively; and let σ be a behavior such that for each $j \in \mathbb{N}$, the state $\sigma(j)$ assigns the value 0 to x and the value j to y. Then exp_1 and exp_2 both equal TRUE for σ because they are both true for $\sigma(0)$. Formula $\Box exp_1$ is true for σ because $x = 0$ is true in all its states, but $\Box exp_2$ is false for σ because $y = 0$ is true only in the first state $\sigma(0)$. Hence, the value of the formula $(exp_1 = exp_2) \Rightarrow (\Box exp_1 = \Box exp_2)$ for this behavior is (TRUE = TRUE) $\Rightarrow$ (TRUE = FALSE), which equals FALSE. The operator $'$ (prime) is similarly not substitutive, so it too is weird. This weirdness affects all temporal logics and makes temporal logic reasoning tricky.

3.5 TLA

Math IV

Simple Recursive Definitions A recursive definition of a mapping M is one in which M appears in its definition. (Mathematicians call them inductive definitions.) A simple recursive definition defines a function f with domain $\mathbb{N}$ by defining the value of $f(0)$ to equal some expression not containing f and, for every $n > 0$, defining $f(n)$ in terms of $f(n-1)$. The classic recursive definition is that of $n!$ (pronounced n *factorial*), which equals the product of the numbers from 1 through n, with $0!$ defined to equal 1. If we consider $n!$ to be an abbreviation of $!(n)$ for the function $!$, we can define $!$ by

$$! \;\triangleq\; n \in \mathbb{N} \mapsto \text{IF } n = 0 \text{ THEN } 1 \text{ ELSE } n * !(n-1)$$

An arbitrary definition $f \triangleq n \in \mathbb{N} \mapsto exp$ where f appears in the expression exp does not necessarily define f to equal $n \in \mathbb{N} \mapsto exp$. For example, if I had written $!(n+1)$ instead of $!(n-1)$ in the definition of $!$, then it's not obvious what that definition would mean. (Its meaning is defined in Appendix Section A.1.9.) But all you need to know is that it would define $!(n)$ to be a meaningless expression for any value n.[6]

---

[6] This particular definition would define $!$ to be a function with domain $\mathbb{N}$, but with $!(n)$ a meaningless expression for any n. However, it's usually not the case that such a

3.5. TLA

The actual definition given above does define ! to be a function that equals the right-hand side of its definition. The intuitive reason is that the definition allows us to compute $!(n)$ in a finite number of steps for any natural number n. For example, we can compute $!(42)$ by computing $!(41)$, which we can compute by computing $!(40)$, which we can compute by ..., which we can compute by computing $!(0)$, which equals 1.

3.5.1 The Problem

There is something terribly wrong with our RTLA descriptions of abstract programs, because there is something terribly wrong with the descriptions like the one in Figure 3.4 that we wrote using explicit step numbers. To see why, let's return to the discussion in Section 3.1 of how astronomers describe a planet orbiting a star. As explained there, the mathematical description of the orbiting planet is best thought of as describing a universe containing the planet, saying nothing about what else is or is not in the universe. In particular, that description applies just as well to a universe in which there is a spacecraft close to the star that orbits it very fast—perhaps going around the star 60 times every time the planet goes around it once. Since the spacecraft is too small to affect the motion of the planet, we would obtain a description of the system composed of the planet and the spacecraft by adding (conjoining) a description of the spacecraft's motion to the description of the planet's motion. The description of the planet's motion remains an accurate description of that planet in the presence of the spacecraft. It would be crazy if we had to write different formulas to describe the planet because of the spacecraft that has no effect on it.

Now consider the descriptions of abstract programs we've been writing. In particular, consider an RTLA formula HM describing how the values of the hour and minute displays of a 24-hour clock change. Using the variables hr and min to describe the current hour and minute being displayed, we might define HM to equal $Init \wedge \Box Next$, where:

(3.36) $Init \triangleq (hr = 0) \wedge (min = 0)$
$Next \triangleq \wedge\ min' = (min + 1) \% 60$
$\wedge\ hr' =$ IF $min = 59$ THEN $(hr + 1) \% 24$ ELSE hr

But suppose that the clock also displays seconds. The RTLA formula HMS that also describes the second display might use a variable sec to describe that display. A behavior σ allowed by HMS would not be allowed by HM

---
non-terminating recursion can be proved to define a function.

because *HM* requires every step to change the value of *min*, while σ must change the value of *sec* in every step and the value of *min* in only every 60th step.

It is just as crazy for an abstract program describing an hour-minute clock not to describe a clock that also displays seconds as it is for a description of a planet's motion no longer to describe that motion because of a spacecraft that doesn't affect the planet. It means that anything we've said about the hour and minute display might be invalid if there's also a second display. And it doesn't matter if the minute display is on a digital clock on my desk and the second display is on a phone in my pocket. More generally, it means if we've proved things about completely separate digital devices and we look at those two devices at the same time, nothing we've proved about them remains true unless those devices are somehow synchronized to run in lock step. The more you think about it, the crazier it seems.

3.5.2 The Solution

To figure out how to fix this problem, let's first see where we went wrong. It happened in Section 3.2.1, when we went from a sequence t_0, t_1, t_2, ... of times to a sequence 0, 1, 2, ... of state numbers. We were writing a description of a particular system. But math and science don't describe a system; they describe a universe containing that system. And that universe can contain many systems. A different system might lead to a different sequence u_0, u_1, u_2, ... of times, with only t_0 and u_0 equal. Our error was converting two possibly different times t_i and u_i into the same state number. The result was that when we thought we were writing a description of a particular system, we were actually writing a description of a universe in which the values of all variables, including ones describing other systems, could change only when the variables of that particular system changed.

You might think that because the error occurred when we were throwing away times, we need to represent the time at which a state holds, not just a state number. Fortunately, there is a simpler solution. It's the one we used to eliminate finite behaviors and consider only infinite behaviors. We observed that we could do that by adding *stuttering steps* at the end of a finite sequence of states—steps that just repeat the previous state of the program. Eliminating finite behaviors was not simply a matter of convenience. The real reason to do it was to eliminate one source of craziness. Since a behavior is not just a behavior of a particular program but a behavior of the entire universe, a finite behavior is one in which everything in the universe stops changing. The description of a halting program execution as

3.5. TLA

a finite behavior therefore asserts that the entire universe halts when the program does. Those infinitely many stuttering steps, in which the value of no variable of the program changes, allow other programs' variables to keep changing.

We can add those stuttering steps because of the observation that the conversion from times to state numbers requires that a program variable be allowed to change only at time t_i for some i. It does not require that any variable does change at that time. The mistake was writing descriptions that, until the program halts, require some variable to change value at each time t_i. Instead, we should have added to the sequence of times t_i times at which no program variable changes. Adding such a time adds a step in which other variables describing other programs can change while the program's variables remain unchanged. Thus, if the description allows a behavior σ, then it should allow the behavior obtained by inserting stuttering steps of the program in σ. This is easy to do. For the description of the hour/minute display, we just change the definition of HM to

$$HM \triangleq Init \wedge \Box(Next \vee ((hr' = hr) \wedge (min' = min)))$$

We can write this formula more compactly as

$$(3.37) \quad HM \triangleq Init \wedge \Box(Next \vee (\langle hr, min \rangle' = \langle hr, min \rangle))$$

because $\langle hr, min \rangle'$ equals $\langle hr', min' \rangle$, and two tuples are equal iff their corresponding components are equal.

We can similarly fix every other example we've seen so far by changing the next-state action $Next$ in its RTLA description to $Next \vee (v' = v)$, where v is the tuple of all variables that appear in the RTLA formula. Since this will have to be done all the time, we abbreviate $A \vee (v' = v)$ as $[A]_v$ for any action A and state expression v.

We can add stuttering steps to a pseudocode description of an algorithm by adding a separate process that just takes stuttering steps. However, we won't bother to do this. We will just consider all pseudocode to allow stuttering steps.

When HM is defined by (3.37), if HMS is true of a behavior then HM is also true of the behavior. This remains true when HMS is modified to allow stuttering steps. Thus, HMS implements HM, and $\models HMS \Rightarrow HM$ is true. Implementation is implication. How elegant!

There is an apparent problem with formula HM of (3.37). It allows behaviors in which the program takes a finite number of steps (possibly zero steps) and then takes nothing but stuttering steps. In other words, it allows behaviors in which the clock stops. Most computer scientists will say that we should never allow behaviors in which an abstract program stops when it is possible for it to continue executing. This is because they are used to thinking about traditional programs. In many cases, we don't want to require a concurrent abstract program to do something just because it can.

Never stopping is a liveness property. Taking only steps satisfying $[Next]_v$ is a safety property. My experience has taught me that we should describe safety properties separately from liveness properties, because we reason about them differently and we should think about them differently. Formula *HM* describes the safety property that the hour-minute clock should satisfy. We will see in Section 4.2 how we conjoin a liveness property to *HM* if we want to require the clock to run forever. It is a feature not a problem that this definition of *HM* asserts only what the clock *may* do and not what it *must* do.

In general, the safety property of an abstract program is written in the form $Init \land \Box[Next]_v$, where *Init* is the initial predicate and $[Next]_v$ is the next-state action. The formula $\Box[Next]_v$ always allows stuttering steps because $[Next]_v$ has the form $\ldots \lor (v' = v)$, and $v' = v$ allows stuttering steps. However, $v' = v$ allows lots of non-stuttering steps. In particular, it allows steps in which any variable that does not appear in v can have any values in the two states of the step. To describe an abstract program, the state expression v in $\Box[Next]_v$ must ensure that $v' = v$ allows only steps that do not change any of the program's variables. Therefore, unless stated otherwise, in a formula of the form $\Box[Next]_v$ where *Next* is the next-state action of a program, the subscript v is assumed to be the tuple of all program variables. (However, that subscript need not be called v.)

3.5.3 Stuttering Insensitivity

We have seen that the safety property of an abstract program should have the form $Init \land \Box[Next]_v$, so it allows stuttering steps. But what can we say in general about formulas for describing systems or abstract programs?

Stuttering steps are created by adding extra times t_i at which we report the values of a program's variables. A stuttering step does not represent the program doing anything. It's just a mathematical way to allow the descriptions of the universe with which we describe different abstract programs to be made consistent with one another. Therefore, any assertion we make about a behavior of an abstract program should not depend on whether we add or remove steps that leave the program's variables unchanged. Since the

3.5. TLA

assertion depends only on the values a behavior assigns to the program's variables, this condition is satisfied iff the assertion does not depend on whether we add or remove steps that leave *all* variables unchanged. We've used the term *stuttering step* to mean a step that leaves a program's variables unchanged. We will now call such a step a stuttering step *of the program*. We define a stuttering step to be a step that leaves *all* variables unchanged.

A sensible predicate F on behaviors should satisfy the condition that the value of $[\![F]\!](\sigma)$ is not changed by adding stuttering steps to, or removing them from, a behavior σ. This means that the value of $[\![F]\!](\sigma)$ is not changed even if an infinite number of stuttering steps are added and an infinite number removed. (However, the behavior must still be infinite, so if σ ends in an infinite number of stuttering steps, those steps can't be removed.) A predicate on behaviors satisfying this condition for all behaviors σ is called *stuttering insensitive*, or SI for short. When describing abstract programs or the properties they satisfy, we should use only SI predicates on behaviors.

To define SI precisely, we first define $\natural(\sigma)$ to be the behavior obtained by removing from the behavior σ all stuttering steps except those belonging to an infinite sequence of stuttering steps at the end. We do this by defining $\natural(\sigma)(n)$ to equal $\sigma(f_\sigma(n))$ where the function f_σ is defined recursively by $f_\sigma(0) = 0$ and $f_\sigma(n)$ for $n > 0$ equals either the smallest value i greater than $f_\sigma(n-1)$ such that $\sigma(i)$ is unequal to $\sigma(f_\sigma(n-1))$, or else equals $f_\sigma(n-1) + 1$ if σ stutters forever after state number $f_\sigma(n-1)$.

To write the definition of f_σ, we first let $Min(S)$ be the smallest element of S for any set S of natural numbers. Such a smallest element exists for any nonempty subset S of $\mathbb{N}$, even if S is infinite. We next let $n^>$ be the set $\{i \in \mathbb{N} : i > n\}$ of all natural numbers greater than n. The recursive definition of f_σ is then:

$$f_\sigma \triangleq n \in \mathbb{N} \mapsto$$
$$\text{IF } n = 0$$
$$\text{THEN } 0$$
$$\text{ELSE } \text{IF } \forall i \in f_\sigma(n-1)^> : \sigma(i) = \sigma(f_\sigma(n-1))$$
$$\text{THEN } f_\sigma(n-1) + 1$$
$$\text{ELSE } Min(\{i \in f_\sigma(n-1)^> : \sigma(i) \neq \sigma(f_\sigma(n-1))\})$$

We define $\natural(\sigma)$ to equal $n \in \mathbb{N} \mapsto \sigma(f_\sigma(n))$.

A predicate on behaviors is defined to be SI iff, for any behavior σ, the predicate is true of σ iff it is true of $\natural(\sigma)$. SI is a semantic condition—that is, a condition on the meanings of formulas. Since we are conflating formulas and their meanings, saying that a formula F is SI means that $[\![F]\!]$ is SI.

We have been using the term *property* informally to mean some condition on the behaviors of a system or abstract program. We now define it to mean an SI predicate on behaviors. *Behavior predicate* still means any predicate on behaviors, not just SI ones.

3.5.4 The Definition of TLA

We now define TLA to be a language that is a sublanguage of RTLA in which every formula is a property—that is, an SI formula. Defining a language means giving syntactic rules for a formula to belong to the language.

We begin by defining a state predicate to be a TLA formula. Recall that we defined a state predicate to be the RTLA formula that is true of a behavior iff it's true of the behavior's first state. A state predicate is SI because the first state of a behavior isn't changed by adding or removing stuttering steps.

The operators of propositional logic applied to SI formulas produce SI formulas. For example, if adding or removing stuttering steps doesn't change whether formulas F and G satisfy a behavior, then they don't change whether $F \vee G$ satisfies the behavior. So, we let TLA include all formulas obtained by applying propositional logic operators to TLA formulas. Similarly, we can let TLA include all formulas obtained by applying the ordinary operators of predicate logic. For example, $\exists x \in S : F$ is a TLA formula if F is one and S is a constant expression.[7]

For any formula F, a behavior σ satisfies $\Box F$ iff every suffix σ^{+n} of σ satisfies F. It follows from this that $\Box F$ is SI iff F is. Therefore, for every TLA formula F, we let $\Box F$ be a TLA formula. Every RTLA formula is built from actions, $\Box$, and operators of ordinary logic; and every state predicate is a TLA formula. Therefore any RTLA formula in which the only actions are state predicates—which means any RTLA formula containing no primes—is a TLA formula.

It's easy to find actions A that, when viewed as a temporal formula, are not SI. For example, $x' \neq x$ is not SI because if σ is a behavior that satisfies $x' \neq x$, then the behavior obtained by adding a stuttering step to the beginning of σ doesn't satisfy it. However, the formula $\Box[A]_v$ is SI for any action A and state expression v, because it's true of a behavior iff every step of the behavior that changes v is an A step, and adding or removing stuttering steps doesn't change the steps that change v. So, we let TLA contain all such formulas.

---

[7] We could let S be a state expression, but there is no need to.

3.5. TLA

The formula $\Box[A]_v$ asserts that action $[A]_v$ is true of all steps of a behavior. For reasoning about liveness, we will need to assert that an action is true in some step of a behavior. The formula $\Diamond A$ is not SI for an arbitrary action A because if A is true on some stuttering step, then $\Diamond A$ might be false on a behavior σ and true on a behavior obtained by adding such a stuttering step to σ. However, if A does not allow stuttering steps, then adding or removing stuttering steps doesn't alter whether a behavior satisfies $\Diamond A$, so $\Diamond A$ is SI. Since $A \wedge (v' \neq v)$ does not allow stuttering steps, the formula $\Diamond(A \wedge (v' \neq v))$ is SI for any state expression v. We define $\langle A \rangle_v$ to equal $A \wedge (v' \neq v)$; and we let TLA contain all formulas $\Diamond \langle A \rangle_v$, for any action A and state expression v.

We can also see that $\Diamond \langle A \rangle_v$ is SI because of the tautology:

(3.38) $\quad \models \Diamond \langle A \rangle_v \equiv \neg \Box [\neg A]_v$

This tautology follows the definition of $\Diamond$ and

$$\models \langle A \rangle_v \equiv \neg [\neg A]_v$$

which follows from the definitions of $[\ ]_v$ and $\langle\ \rangle_v$ and propositional logic. From (3.38) we see that $\neg \Diamond \langle A \rangle_v$ is equivalent to $\Box [\neg A]_v$. This means that an $\langle A \rangle_v$ step never occurs in a behavior iff every step of the behavior is a $[\neg A]_v$ step. This fact is used in proofs by contradiction of formulas of the form $\Diamond \langle A \rangle_v$.

The only temporal operator we have defined besides $\Box$ and $\Diamond$ is $\rightsquigarrow$. We define $F \rightsquigarrow \langle A \rangle_v$ to be a TLA formula if F is one, A is an action, and v is a state expression. This formula is SI, since by definition of $\rightsquigarrow$ it equals $\Box(F \Rightarrow \Diamond \langle A \rangle_v)$.

Combining all this, we see that a TLA formula is one of the following:

- A state predicate.

- Obtained by applying propositional logic operators and the operators $\Box$, $\Diamond$, or $\rightsquigarrow$ to TLA formulas.

- $\forall\exists\, c : F$ or $\forall\exists\, c \in S : F$ where $\forall\exists$ is $\forall$ or $\exists$, for a bound constant c, a TLA formula F, and a constant expression S.

- $\Box[A]_v$, $\Diamond \langle A \rangle_v$, or $F \rightsquigarrow \langle A \rangle_v$, for an action A, a state expression v, and a TLA formula F.

Abstract programs and the properties they satisfy should be TLA formulas. However, we can use RTLA proof rules and even RTLA formulas when reasoning about TLA formulas. For example, we can prove that Inv is an invariant of $Init \wedge \Box[Next]_v$ by substituting $[Next]_v$ for $Next$ in the RTLA proof rule that (3.10) implies (3.13). This yields the following rule:

$$\models (Init \Rightarrow Inv) \wedge (Inv \wedge [Next]_v \Rightarrow Inv')$$
$$\text{implies} \quad \models Init \wedge \Box[Next]_v \Rightarrow \Box Inv$$

In this rule, the first $\models$ means validity in LA while the second $\models$ means validity in TLA. A feature of TLA is that as much reasoning as possible is done in LA, which becomes ordinary mathematical reasoning when the necessary definitions are expanded and primes are distributed across operators, so only variables are primed.

Chapter 4

Safety, Liveness, and Fairness

We have seen how to write the safety property of an abstract program in TLA. We now see how to write its liveness property. This chapter precisely defines safety and liveness properties, and shows why and how the liveness property of an abstract program is written as a particular kind of liveness property called a fairness property. In principle, any property that can be described mathematically can be expressed in TLA by such an abstract program. The chapter also shows how to use TLA to prove that a program satisfies a liveness property.

4.1 Safety and Liveness

Math V

ASSUME/PROVE **Proof Steps** We usually prove a formula of the form $F \Rightarrow G$ by assuming F is true and proving G is true. In our structured proof style, we write such a proof with the following proof step:

> ASSUME: F
> PROVE: G
>   PROOF: ...

This step asserts the truth of $F \Rightarrow G$. However, the proof of a step that asserts the formula $F \Rightarrow G$ has as its goal to prove $F \Rightarrow G$. (It might do that by proving $F \Rightarrow H$ and $H \Rightarrow G$ for some H.) The proof of this ASSUME/PROVE step has as its goal to prove G, using the assumption that F is true. The statement of a theorem is sometimes written as such an ASSUME/PROVE. It has the same meaning as for a proof step, asserting $F \Rightarrow G$ and that the proof assumes F and proves G.

Instead of being a single formula, the ASSUME clause can be a list of assertions—sometimes a numbered list. That's equivalent to assuming the conjunction of those assertions. A paragraph proof should state what previous steps and assumptions it uses, identifying them by step and assumption numbers.

Countable Sets A countable set is one whose elements can be counted. That is, a set S is countable iff we can assign a different natural number to each of its elements. More precisely, a set S is countable iff there exists a function $f \in \mathbb{N} \to S$ such that $\forall s \in S : \exists n \in \mathbb{N} : f(n) = s$. All finite sets are countable. Here is a function f that shows that the set $\mathbb{I}$ of all integers is countable.

$$
\begin{array}{cccccccccc}
n: & 0 & 1 & 2 & 3 & 4 & 5 & 6 & 7 & 8 & \ldots \\
& \downarrow & \downarrow & \downarrow & \downarrow & \downarrow & \downarrow & \downarrow & \downarrow & \downarrow & \\
f(n): & 0 & 1 & -1 & 2 & -2 & 3 & -3 & 4 & -4 & \ldots
\end{array}
$$

This function f equals:

$$n \in \mathbb{N} \;\mapsto\; \text{IF } n \% 2 = 0 \text{ THEN } -n/2 \text{ ELSE } (n+1)/2$$

We will need this theorem:

Theorem 4.1 If S is a countable set, then there is a function f in $\mathbb{N} \to S$ such that for every $s \in S$, there are infinitely many $n \in \mathbb{N}$ with $f(n) = s$.

PROOF: Since S is countable, we can number its elements s_0, s_1, s_2, ... If S is finite, we can let f equal $n \in \mathbb{N} \mapsto s_{(n \% \#(S))}$. Therefore, we can assume S is infinite. Here is a picture that shows how such a function f can be defined:

$$
\begin{array}{ccccccccccc}
n: & 0 & 1 & 2 & 3 & 4 & 5 & 6 & 7 & 8 & 9 & \ldots \\
& \downarrow & \downarrow & \downarrow & \downarrow & \downarrow & \downarrow & \downarrow & \downarrow & \downarrow & \downarrow & \\
f(n): & s_0 & s_0 & s_1 & s_0 & s_1 & s_2 & s_0 & s_1 & s_2 & s_3 & \ldots
\end{array}
$$

However, I don't see an easy way to define that function mathematically. Here's an easy way to define a function f that works. Let g be the function in $\mathbb{N} \to \mathbb{N}$ such that $g(n)$ is the largest integer satisfying $g(n)^2 \leq n$, so $g(n^2) = n$ and $g(n)^2 \leq n < (g(n)+1)^2$ for all $n \in \mathbb{N}$. Define $f(n) \triangleq s_{n-g(n)^2}$ for all $n \in \mathbb{N}$. This function has the desired property because for any $n \in \mathbb{N}$, for any $m \geq n$ there exists $i \in m^2\,..\,((m+1)^2 - 1)$ such that $f(i) = s_n$. END PROOF

4.1.1 Definitions

Safety and liveness properties have been described intuitively as specifying what the program is allowed to do and what it must do. To define them precisely, we begin by observing that they have these characteristics:

Safety If a behavior doesn't satisfy a safety property, then we can point to the place in the behavior where it violates the property. For example, if a behavior doesn't satisfy an invariance property, it violates the property in the first state in which the invariant is false.

Liveness We have to look at an entire infinite behavior to see that it doesn't satisfy a liveness property. For example, we can't see that the property *x eventually equals 42* is violated by looking at a finite part of the behavior.[1]

This characterization was turned into precise definitions of safety and liveness for arbitrary behavior predicates by Alpern and Schneider [3]. Since we're interested only in properties (which are SI), we will use a somewhat simpler definition of safety. But first, we need a few preliminary definitions.

We call a finite, nonempty cardinal sequence of states a *finite behavior*. (A *behavior*, without the adjective *finite*, still means an infinite cardinal sequence of states.) We'll write a finite behavior ρ as $\rho(0) \to \cdots \to \rho(n)$. A nonempty finite prefix of a behavior is a finite behavior. We define the *completion* $\rho^\uparrow$ of a finite behavior to be the behavior obtained by repeating the last state of ρ infinitely many times—that is, adding infinitely many stuttering steps. A finite behavior ρ is defined to satisfy a behavior predicate iff its completion $\rho^\uparrow$ satisfies it. We can now precisely define safety and liveness.

Safety A property F is a safety property iff it satisfies the following condition: A behavior satisfies F iff every nonempty finite prefix of the behavior satisfies F.

Liveness A property F is a liveness property iff every finite behavior is the prefix of a behavior that satisfies F.

A state predicate is a safety property because it is satisfied by a behavior iff the state predicate is true on the initial state, and a behavior and all its

---
[1] Remember that a behavior means any infinite sequence of states, not just one that satisfies some program. If we know that a behavior satisfies the program, we can often tell that $\Diamond(x = 42)$ is false by looking at the behavior predicate that describes the program, without looking at the behavior at all.

nonempty prefixes have the same initial state. The formula $\Box[A]_v$ is a safety property for any action A and state expression v; here is the proof that every nonempty finite prefix of a behavior σ satisfies $\Box[A]_v$ iff σ satisfies $\Box[A]_v$.

1. ASSUME: Every nonempty finite prefix of σ satisfies $\Box[A]_v$.
   PROVE: σ satisfies $\Box[A]_v$

   PROOF: σ satisfies $\Box[A]_v$ iff every step of σ satisfies $[A]_v$, and every step of σ is a step of some finite prefix of σ, so σ satisfies $\Box[A]_v$ by the assumption.

2. ASSUME: σ satisfies $\Box[A]_v$
   PROVE: Every nonempty finite prefix of σ satisfies $\Box[A]_v$.

   PROOF: Every step of a nonempty finite prefix of σ is either a step of σ, so it satisfies $[A]_v$ by the assumption, or it is a stuttering step, which satisfies $[A]_v$ by definition of $[\ ]_v$.

3. Q.E.D.
   PROOF: Obvious, by steps 1 and 2.

It also follows easily from the definition of safety that the conjunction of safety properties is a safety property. Therefore, as expected, the formula $Init \land \Box[Next]_v$ that we have been calling the safety property of a program is indeed a safety property.

The property that asserts that a program halts is a liveness property. That property is true of a behavior σ iff σ ends with infinitely many steps that leave the program's variables unchanged. It's a liveness property because every finite behavior ρ is a prefix of its completion $\rho^\uparrow$, which satisfies the property.

Safety and liveness are conditions on properties, which are SI behavior predicates. When we say that a TLA formula $\Box[A]_v$ is a safety property, we are conflating the formula with its meaning. It's actually $[\![\Box[A]_v]\!]$ that is the safety property.

4.1.2 A Completeness Theorem

TLA is quite simple, adding only the two operators $'$ (prime) and $\Box$ to ordinary math. In theory, this simplicity makes it quite inexpressive. For example, here is a property F_{12} that neither TLA nor RTLA can express: the value of x must equal 1 before it can equal 2. It's expressed in terms of explicit states as:

(4.1) $F_{12} \triangleq \forall j \in \mathbb{N} : (x(j) = 2) \Rightarrow \exists k \in \mathbb{N} : (k < j) \land (x(k) = 1)$

4.1. SAFETY AND LIVENESS

This behavior predicate is a property because it's SI; adding or removing stuttering steps doesn't affect whether a behavior satisfies it. Property F_{12} is a safety property because it's not satisfied by a behavior σ iff there's a point in σ at which it's violated—namely, a state $\sigma(j)$ in which $x = 2$ and $x \neq 1$ in all the states $\sigma(0), \ldots, \sigma(j-1)$.

If TLA is inexpressive, how can we describe programs with it? The answer is, by using variables. We can express F_{12} as an abstract program described by a TLA formula S_{12} if we add a Boolean-valued variable, let's call it y, whose value is TRUE iff x equals 1 or has previously equaled 1. We let the initial predicate $Init$ of S_{12} assert that $x \neq 2$ and that $y =$ TRUE iff $x = 1$. The next-state relation $Next$ allows x' to equal 2 only if $y =$ TRUE, and it sets y to TRUE if $x = 1$. Here are the definitions:

(4.2)
$$S_{12} \triangleq Init \wedge \Box[Next]_{\langle x, y \rangle}$$
$$Init \triangleq (x \neq 2) \wedge (y = (x = 1))$$
$$Next \triangleq \wedge (x' = 2) \Rightarrow y$$
$$\wedge y' = (y \vee (x = 1))$$

It's not obvious in what sense formula S_{12} expresses property F_{12}, since S_{12} contains the variables x and y while F_{12} describes only the values of x. Intuitively, S_{12} makes the same assertion as F_{12} if we ignore the value of y. Section 7.1 describes a TLA operator $\exists$ such that $\exists y : S_{12}$ means S_{12} *if we ignore the value of y*. We'll then see that $[\![\exists y : S_{12}]\!]$ equals F_{12}. However, there's no need to introduce $\exists$ here. The relevant condition that S_{12} satisfies is that if G is any TLA formula that does not contain the variable y, then

$$\models F_{12} \Rightarrow [\![G]\!] \quad \text{iff} \quad \models S_{12} \Rightarrow G$$

The idea of adding a variable to express a property works in general. We state it now only for safety properties. We can't express *every* safety property as a TLA formula. A formula is a finite string of finitely many symbols, and there are only a countable number of such strings; but there are uncountably many safety properties. (For example, there are uncountably many real numbers, so there are uncountably many properties asserting that the initial value of x is a particular real number.) What we can show is that any safety property (which is a predicate on behaviors) that can be described by a mathematical formula—that is, by a formula of ZF—can be expressed as a TLA formula. We do that by showing that if the mapping F from behaviors to Boolean values is a safety property, then we can use F to write a TLA formula that describes it the way S_{12} describes F_{12} in our example. One condition satisfied by a mathematical formula is that it contains only a finite number of variables, and its value depends only on the values of those variables. Remember that we are assuming that the language LA for writing actions contains all the operators of ZF.

The theorem is expressed with the convention of letting a boldface identifier like **x** be the list $x_1, \ldots, x_n$ of subscripted non-bold versions of the identifier, for some n. Thus, $\langle \mathbf{x} \rangle$ is the tuple of those identifiers. The theorem is a special case of Theorem 4.9 in Section 4.2.7 below, so the proof is omitted.

Theorem 4.2 Let **x** be the list $x_1, \ldots, x_n$ of variables and let F be a safety property such that $F(\sigma)$ depends only on the values of the variables **x** in a behavior σ. There exists a formula S equal to $\mathit{Init} \wedge \square[\mathit{Next}]_{\langle \mathbf{x},y \rangle}$, where Init and Next are defined in terms of F, y is a variable not among the variables **x**, and the variables of S are **x** and y, such that $\models F \Rightarrow [\![G]\!]$ iff $\models S \Rightarrow G$, for any property G.

This theorem is a completeness result, showing that TLA can express as an abstract program any safety property that can be expressed semantically. While this shows that there is no fundamental lack of expressiveness in TLA, it is of little practical significance. The proof assumes a description of the property F and uses it to write F as an abstract program. If there were a better way to describe properties mathematically than with abstract programs, we should use it. There are other temporal logics that can express the simple property F_{12} with a formula that's easier to understand than S_{12}. However, S_{12} is not hard to understand, and abstract programs are the only practical way I know to express all the properties of concrete concurrent programs that we need to describe.[2]

4.1.3 The Operator $\mathcal{C}$

We now define the operator $\mathcal{C}$ so that $\mathcal{C}(F)$ is the strongest safety property implied by F, for any property F. Remember that property G stronger than property H means every behavior satisfying G satisfies H—that is, $\models G \Rightarrow H$. The operator $\mathcal{C}$ is not part of the TLA language; we do not use it to write abstract programs. What we do is show that, under certain conditions, some G equals $\mathcal{C}(F)$ for some other program F. It would be more precise to write that $[\![G]\!]$ equals $\mathcal{C}([\![F]\!])$, but we won't bother because we regularly conflate a formula and its meaning.

---

[2] Remember that *property* means predicate on behaviors. There are many conditions we want programs to satisfy besides properties.

4.1. SAFETY AND LIVENESS

If we want $\mathcal{C}(F)$ to be the strongest safety property implied by F, it should be satisfied by the behaviors satisfying F plus the fewest additional behaviors needed to make it a safety property. The appropriate definition is: A behavior σ satisfies $\mathcal{C}(F)$ iff every finite prefix of σ is a prefix of a behavior that satisfies F. For example, suppose F is the property satisfied only by behaviors in which x initially equals 0, x keeps being incremented by 1, and eventually the behavior halts. For this property F, the property $\mathcal{C}(F)$ is satisfied by a behavior that either satisfies F or in which x initially equals 0 and keeps being incremented by 1 forever. The following theorem shows that this is the correct definition of $\mathcal{C}$. Its proof is in the Appendix.

Theorem 4.3 If F is a property, then $\mathcal{C}(F)$ is a safety property such that $\models F \Rightarrow \mathcal{C}(F)$ and, for any safety property G, if $\models F \Rightarrow G$ then $\models \mathcal{C}(F) \Rightarrow G$.

Alpern and Schneider proved that every property is the conjunction of a safety property and a liveness property.[3] They actually proved this stronger result, whose proof is in the Appendix:

Theorem 4.4 Every property F is equivalent to $\mathcal{C}(F) \wedge L$ for a liveness property L.

We have been describing abstract programs by formulas of the form $Init \wedge \Box[Next]_v$, which are safety properties. As we've observed, like any safety property, this formula allows behaviors that halt at any point in the behavior. We usually don't want to allow such behaviors, so we must conjoin a liveness property to this formula to describe most abstract programs. For example, we can rule out behaviors of program *Increment* that don't halt prematurely with the liveness property

$$\forall p \in Procs : \Diamond(pc[p] = done)$$

However, we'll see later why that's not a good liveness property to use.

There's another method of describing safety and liveness that helps me understand them intuitively. It's based on topology. The method and the necessary topology are explained in Appendix Section A.6.

4.1.4 What Good is Liveness?

Safety properties constrain the finite behavior of a system. They describe what must be true of finite prefixes of a behavior. Liveness properties say

---
[3]Their result was stated for arbitrary behavior predicates, not properties.

nothing about finite prefixes; they describe what must be true if the system runs forever. Since we don't live forever, why should we care about liveness properties?

In theory, liveness is useless; but in practice it's useful. Consider the liveness property required of a traditional program: it eventually terminates. In theory, that's useless because it might not terminate in a billion years. In practice, proving that a program will terminate within a given amount of time isn't easy. Proving that it eventually terminates is easier, and it is useful because the program is certainly not going to terminate soon enough if it never does. But proving liveness provides more than that. Understanding why a program eventually terminates requires understanding what it must do in order to finish. That understanding helps you decide if it will terminate soon enough. This applies to other liveness properties as well.

Using a model checker doesn't give you the understanding that you get from writing a proof. However, using a model checker to check liveness properties is a good way to detect errors—both in the program you intended to write and in what you actually wrote. A program that does nothing satisfies most safety properties, and an error in translating your intention into mathematics might disallow behaviors in which the program fails to satisfy a safety property. Checking that the program satisfies liveness properties that it should can catch such errors, as well as errors in the program you wanted to write. Section 5.1 discusses checking liveness to check if the program you wrote is the one you wanted to write.

4.2 Fairness

Expressing mathematically the way computer scientists and engineers described their algorithms and programs led us to describe the safety property satisfied by an abstract program with the formula $Init \land \Box[Next]_v$, where v is the tuple of all the program's variables. We must conjoin to that formula another formula to describe the program's liveness property. To see how this should be done, we first examine how scientists and engineers have expressed liveness.

4.2.1 Traditional Programs and the Enabled Operator $\mathbb{E}$

We start with traditional programs. It was assumed, usually without needing to be stated explicitly, that a traditional program kept executing statements until it terminated. If termination is expressed by $pc = done$, then

4.2. FAIRNESS

this assumption can be stated as the requirement that when $pc \neq done$, a *Next* step must eventually occur. This is expressed by the TLA formula

(4.3) $(pc \neq done) \rightsquigarrow \langle Next \rangle_v$

The $\langle \ldots \rangle_v$ is a bit of a nuisance, but it's required by TLA to prevent a liveness property from being satisfied by a stuttering step, which would make no sense. Usually, the next-state action *Next* does not permit stuttering steps, so (4.3) is equivalent to the RTLA formula $(pc \neq done) \rightsquigarrow Next$.

We can't expect a program to take steps if it has halted for any reason, not just if it has terminated. We should therefore replace (4.3) by $E \rightsquigarrow \langle Next \rangle_v$, where E is a state predicate that is true in a state iff it's possible to take a $\langle Next \rangle_v$ step in that state. We write that state predicate E as $\mathbb{E}\langle Next \rangle_v$, where $\mathbb{E}$ is read *enabled*.

In general, for any action A, we define $\mathbb{E}(A)$ to be the state predicate that is true in a state s iff there exists a state t such that $s \to t$ is an A step. In other words, $\mathbb{E}$ is an LA operator, where for any action A the state predicate $\mathbb{E}(A)$ is defined by letting $[\![\mathbb{E}(A)]\!](s)$ equal TRUE for a state s iff there exists a state t such that $[\![A]\!](s \to t)$ equals TRUE. In the common case when A has the form $\langle B \rangle_v$, we omit the parentheses and write simply $\mathbb{E}\langle B \rangle_v$. The liveness property assumed of a traditional program whose safety property is described by the formula $Init \wedge \Box[Next]_v$ is $\mathbb{E}\langle Next \rangle_v \rightsquigarrow \langle Next \rangle_v$.

4.2.2 Concurrent Programs

In traditional programs, when the program hasn't terminated there is just one program statement that can be executed. In multiprocess programs, it is usually possible for there to be multiple statements that can be executed, each in a different process. Moreover, a process can stop not just because it has terminated, but because it is waiting for another process to do something. The liveness property $\mathbb{E}\langle Next \rangle_v \rightsquigarrow \langle Next \rangle_v$ ensures that the program keeps executing statements as long as some process hasn't halted. It is satisfied if one process keeps executing statements. It allows other processes to halt, even if they could keep executing statements. Those other processes are said to be *starved*.

It was generally accepted that processes should be treated "fairly". Multiprocess programs were usually executed on computers having fewer processors than there were processes—for many years, usually just a single processor. It was sometimes proposed that fairness should guarantee the stronger condition that each process gets a fair share of processor time. However, it came to be generally accepted that fairness should not specify how long (in terms of program steps) a process that can execute a statement might wait before executing it. Therefore, fairness came to mean simply that no process should be starved.

In a program with a set *Procs* of processes, the next-state action is defined by

$$Next \triangleq \exists p \in Procs : PNext(p)$$

where $PNext(p)$ is the next-state action of process p. The obvious generalization of the liveness requirement for a traditional program suggests that fairness for all the processes in a multiprocess program should mean:

(4.4) $\forall p \in Procs : \mathbb{E}\langle PNext(p)\rangle_v \rightsquigarrow \langle PNext(p)\rangle_v$

However, this is *not* the way fairness should be expressed, and it is not an appropriate liveness property for multiprocess programs. To see why, we consider mutual exclusion algorithms.

4.2.2.1 Mutual Exclusion

The concept of fairness in a concurrent program appeared implicitly in Edsger Dijkstra's seminal 1965 paper that launched the study of concurrent algorithms [9]. That paper defined mutual exclusion and presented the first algorithm that implemented it.

In mutual exclusion, we assume a set of processes that each alternately executes two sections of code called the *noncritical* and *critical* sections. A mutual exclusion algorithm must ensure that no two processes can be executing their critical sections at the same time. For example, the processes may occasionally print output on the same printer, and two processes printing at the same time would produce an unreadable mixture of the two outputs. To prevent that, the processes execute a mutual exclusion algorithm, and a process prints only when in its critical section.

The outline of a mutual exclusion algorithm is shown in Figure 4.1, where *Procs* is the set of processes. We don't care what the processes do in their noncritical and critical sections, so we represent them by atomic **skip** statements labeled *ncs* and *cs* that do nothing when executed except change the value of pc. The nontrivial part of the algorithm consists of the two sections of code, the *waiting* and *exiting* sections, that begin with the labels *wait* and *exit*. Each of those sections can contain multiple labeled statements, using variables declared in the two **variables** statements.

4.2. FAIRNESS

```
variables ... ;         global variables
process p ∈ Procs
    variables pc = ncs, ... ;    process-local variables
    while TRUE do
        ncs:  skip ;    noncritical section
        wait:  ⋮         waiting section

        cs:   skip ;    critical section
        exit:  ⋮        exiting section
    end while
end process
```

Figure 4.1: The outline of a mutual exclusion algorithm.

The safety property that a mutual exclusion algorithm must satisfy is that no two processes are executing their critical sections at the same time—meaning that $pc(p)$ and $pc(q)$ cannot both equal cs for two different processes p and q. This is an invariance property. A cute way of expressing it compactly is:

(4.5) $\Box\,(\forall\,p, q \in \textit{Procs} : (p \neq q) \Rightarrow (\{pc(p), pc(q)\} \neq \{cs\})\,)$

We will not yet state a precise liveness condition a mutual exclusion algorithm should satisfy. All we need to know for now is that if some processes enter the waiting section, they can't all wait forever without any process entering the critical section.

Most people viewing the outline in Figure 4.1 will think this is an unrealistic description of a mutual exclusion algorithm because, by describing the execution of the critical section with a single **skip** step, we are assuming that the entire critical section is executed as a single step. Of course, we realize that this isn't the case. It no more says that the critical section is executed as a single step than our description of an hour-minute clock says that nothing else happens between the step that changes the clock's display to 7:29 and the step that changes it to 7:30. Just as 59 changes to a seconds display can occur between those two steps, process p can print the entire Bhagavad Gita while $pc(p)$ equals cs. A mutual exclusion algorithm simply describes all that printing as stuttering steps of the algorithm.

Figure 4.2 describes a program named UM, which is an abbreviation of *Unacceptable Mutual exclusion algorithm*. Technically, it's a mutual exclusion algorithm because it satisfies property (4.5) with *Procs* equal to the

> **variables** $x = (p \in \{0, 1\} \mapsto \text{FALSE})$;
> **process** $p \in \{0, 1\}$
>   **variables** $pc = ncs$;
>   **while** TRUE **do**
> ncs: **skip** ;
> $wait$: $x[p] := \text{TRUE}$;
> $w2$: **await** $\neg x[1 - p]$;
> cs: **skip** ;
> $exit$: $x[p] := \text{FALSE}$
>   **end while**
> **end process**

Figure 4.2: The unacceptable mutual exclusion algorithm *UM*.

set $\{0, 1\}$ of processes. But for reasons that will be discussed later, it isn't considered to be an acceptable algorithm.

This pseudocode program is the first one we've seen with an **await** statement. For a state predicate P, the statement **await** P can be executed only when control is at the statement and P equals TRUE. We could write the statement $a:$ **await** P as:

a: **if** $\neg P$ **then goto** a **end if**

Executing this statement in a state with P equal to TRUE just moves control to the next statement. Executing it in a state with P equal to FALSE does not change the value of any program variable, so it's a stuttering step of the program. Since a stuttering step is always allowed, executing the statement **await** P when P equals FALSE is the same as not executing it. So, while we can think of the statement **await** P continually evaluating the expression P and moving to the next statement iff it finds P equal to TRUE, mathematically that's equivalent to describing it as an action A such that $\mathbb{E}(A)$ equals $(pc = a) \wedge P$.

This is also the first pseudocode we've seen with explicit array variables. An array variable x is an array-valued variable, where an array is a function and $x[p]$ just means $x(p)$. We've already seen implicit array variables— namely, the local variables t and pc of program *Increment* are represented by function-valued variables in Figure 3.5. I have decided to write $x[p]$ instead of $x(p)$ in pseudocode to make the pseudocode look more like real code. However, the value of an array variable can be any function, not just (as in some coding languages such as C) a finite ordinal sequence; and we write $x(p)$ instead of $x[p]$ when discussing the program mathematically. As

4.2. FAIRNESS

we've seen in Figure 3.5, an assignment statement $x[p] := \ldots$ is described mathematically as $x' = (x \text{ EXCEPT } p \mapsto \ldots)$.

Algorithm *UM* is quite simple. The processes communicate through the variable x, with process p modifying $x(p)$. The initial value of $x(p)$ for each process p is FALSE. To enter the critical section, process p sets $x(p)$ to TRUE and then enters its critical section when $x(1-p)$ (the array element written by the other process) equals FALSE.

It's easy to see that the two processes cannot be in their critical sections at the same time. If they were, the last process p to enter its critical section would have read $x(1-p)$ equal to TRUE when executing statement $w2$, so it couldn't have entered its critical section. Since mutual exclusion is an invariance property, it can be proved mathematically by finding an inductive invariant that implies mutual exclusion. You can check that the following formula is such an inductive invariant of *UM*:

$$
\begin{aligned}
(4.6) \quad & \wedge \; TypeOK \\
& \wedge \; \forall p \in \{0,1\} : \wedge \; (pc(p) \in \{w2, cs\}) \Rightarrow x(p) \\
& \phantom{\wedge \; \forall p \in \{0,1\} :} \wedge \; (pc(p) = cs) \Rightarrow (pc(1-p) \neq cs)
\end{aligned}
$$

where *TypeOK* is the type-correctness invariant:

$$
\begin{aligned}
TypeOK \; \triangleq \; & \wedge \; x \in (\{0,1\} \to \{\text{TRUE}, \text{FALSE}\}) \\
& \wedge \; pc \in (\{0,1\} \to \{ncs, wait, w2, cs, exit\})
\end{aligned}
$$

Let *UMSafe* be the safety property described by the pseudocode. We want to conjoin a property *UMLive* to *UMSafe* to state a fairness requirement of the program's behaviors. Let's make the obvious choice of defining *UMLive* to be formula (4.4) with *Procs* equal to $\{0,1\}$ and v equal to $\langle x, pc \rangle$. This implies that both processes keep taking steps forever, executing their critical sections infinitely often, which makes it seem like a good choice. Actually, that makes it a bad choice.

Algorithm *UM* is unacceptable because formula *UMSafe*, which describes the pseudocode, permits deadlock. If both processes execute statement *wait* before either executes *w2*, then the algorithm reaches the deadlocked state in which neither **await** statement is enabled. Conjoining *UMLive* to *UMSafe* produces a formula asserting that such a deadlocked state cannot occur. It ensures the liveness property we want, that processes keep executing their critical sections. However, it does this not by requiring only that processes keep taking steps, but also by preventing them from taking some steps—namely, ones that produce a deadlocked state. A fairness property shouldn't do that.

Before going further, let's see why *UMSafe* ∧ *UMLive* doesn't allow such a deadlocked state to be reached. The reason is that the formula satisfies this invariant:

(4.7) $\quad \neg(pc(0) = pc(1) = w2)$

This is an invariant of *UMSafe* ∧ *UMLive* because it is true initially and it can be made false only by a step in which a process p executes its *wait* statement in a state s with $pc(1-p) = w2$; and we now show that such a step cannot occur.

It's an invariant of *UMSafe*, and hence of *UMSafe* ∧ *UMLive*, that $pc(p) = wait$ implies $x(p) = $ FALSE. Hence, $pc(1-p) = w2$ and $x(p) = $ FALSE in state s, which implies $\mathbb{E}\langle PNext(1-p)\rangle_v$ is true. Therefore, *UMLive* implies that $\Diamond\langle PNext(1-p)\rangle_v$ must be true at state s of the behavior. This implies that the process p step can't occur, because it would lead to deadlock which would make such a $\langle PNext(1-p)\rangle_v$ step impossible. Therefore, no step of the program can make (4.7) false. Since it is true in an initial state, (4.7) is an invariant of *UMSafe* ∧ *UMLive*.

Thus, *UMLive* should not be the fairness property for algorithm *UM*, because it disallows a program step allowed by *UMSafe*. Before determining what the fairness property should be, let's characterize exactly what's wrong with property *UMLive*.

4.2.2.2 Machine Closure

The general principle illustrated by program *UM* is that fairness for a program should require only that something eventually happens, so it should rule out only infinite behaviors in which that thing never happens. It should not rule out finite behaviors.

A liveness property by itself does not rule out any finite behaviors. A liveness property L by definition allows any finite behavior to be completed to a behavior that satisfies L. Property *UMLive* is a liveness property, so the finite behavior in which the program reaches a deadlocked state can be completed to a behavior satisfying *UMLive*. For example, we can concatenate to that finite behavior a complete behavior satisfying *UMSafe* ∧ *UMLive*. (There are many behaviors of *UMSafe* that don't deadlock.) Since that concatenation contains infinitely many steps of each process, it satisfies *UMLive*. However, it doesn't satisfy *UMSafe* because the step between the last state of the deadlocked finite behavior (which is a deadlocked state) and the first state of a complete behavior does not satisfy the program's next-state action.

4.2. FAIRNESS

It is impossible to complete that deadlocked behavior to a behavior satisfying both *UMLive* and *UMSafe* because the next-state action of *UMSafe* does not allow any non-stuttering step from a deadlocked state.

For a liveness property L to be a fairness property for *UMSafe*, it should not just require that any finite behavior can be completed to a behavior satisfying L; it should require that any finite behavior that satisfies *UMSafe* can be completed to a behavior that satisfies $UMSafe \wedge L$.

In general, a pair $\langle S, L \rangle$, where S is a safety property and L a liveness property, is defined to be *machine closed* iff every finite behavior satisfying S can be completed to a behavior satisfying $S \wedge L$. We require that a fairness property for a program having the safety property S be a liveness property L such that $\langle S, L \rangle$ is machine closed. The following theorem, proved in the Appendix, provides a nice mathematical characterization of machine closure.

Theorem 4.5 If S is a safety property and L a liveness property, then $\langle S, L \rangle$ is machine closed iff $\models \mathcal{C}(S \wedge L) \equiv S$.

4.2.3 Weak Fairness

Let's now see how to describe fairness with a machine-closed liveness property. Using the requirement that

(4.8) $\quad \mathbb{E}\langle PNext(p)\rangle_v \rightsquigarrow \langle PNext(p)\rangle_v$

is true for all p in *Procs* worked fine for program *Increment*. It failed for program *UM*. The reason it worked for program *Increment* is that when $PNext(p)$ is enabled, it remains enabled until a $PNext(p)$ step occurs. In program *UM*, process p can reach a state in which $pc(p)$ equals $w2$ and $PNext(p)$ is enabled, but process $1 - p$ can then take a step that disables action $PNext(p)$.

To obtain a machine-closed condition, we have to weaken (4.8) so it rules out fewer behaviors. The obvious way to do that is by requiring a $PNext(p)$ step to occur not if $PNext(p)$ just becomes enabled, but only if it remains enabled until a $PNext(p)$ step occurs. Let $F \, \mathcal{U} \, G$ be the temporal formula asserting that F is true until G is true. (We'll discuss later exactly what $\mathcal{U}$ means.) As our choice of fairness property, we will replace property (4.8) by:

(4.9) $\quad (\, \mathbb{E}\langle PNext(p)\rangle_v \, \mathcal{U} \, \langle PNext(p)\rangle_v \,) \rightsquigarrow \langle PNext(p)\rangle_v$

However, rather surprisingly, (4.9) is equivalent to:

(4.10) $\quad \Box \mathbb{E}\langle PNext(p)\rangle_v \rightsquigarrow \langle PNext(p)\rangle_v$

To prove this, we first have to examine the definition of $\mathcal{U}$. When we say that E is true until P is true, we usually mean that P is eventually true and E is true until P becomes true. But if $E\,\mathcal{U}\,P$ implies that $\Diamond P$ is true, then (4.9) would be trivially true and thus useless, since it would assert that $\langle PNext(p)\rangle_v$ conjoined with some other condition leads to $\langle PNext(p)\rangle_v$. So we have to interpret $E\,\mathcal{U}\,P$ to mean that either P is eventually true and E is true until it is, or P is not eventually true and E is true forever. Thus, whatever the precise meaning of $\mathcal{U}$ is, we have:

$$(4.11) \quad \models (E\,\mathcal{U}\,P) \equiv (\Diamond P \wedge E\,\mathcal{U}\,P) \vee (\neg \Diamond P \wedge \Box E)$$

The equivalence of (4.9) and (4.10) follows from this RTLA theorem, which is proved in the Appendix.

Theorem 4.6 (4.11) implies $\models ((E\,\mathcal{U}\,P) \rightsquigarrow P) \equiv (\Box E \rightsquigarrow P)$ for any formulas E and P.

A liveness property commonly assumed of multiprocess algorithms, called *weak fairness*, is that (4.10) is true for every process p. We generalize this concept to define weak fairness of an arbitrary action A to be the formula $\mathrm{WF}_v(A)$ defined by:

$$(4.12) \quad \mathrm{WF}_v(A) \triangleq \Box \mathbb{E}\langle A\rangle_v \rightsquigarrow \langle A\rangle_v$$

Another form of fairness called strong fairness that is sometimes assumed is discussed later. We will see how weak and strong fairness are used to write machine-closed descriptions of abstract programs. A special case of the general result is that if S is the formula $Init \wedge \Box[Next]_v$ and $Next$ equals $\exists p \in Procs : PNext(p)$, then $\langle S, \forall p \in Procs : \mathrm{WF}_v(PNext(p))\rangle$ is machine closed. But before we get to all that, let's examine weak fairness.

The first thing we observe is that for a multiprocess program described with pseudocode, weak fairness of a process's next-state action is equivalent to the conjunction of weak fairness of all the actions described by the process's statements. That is, if $PNext(p)$ equals $\exists i \in I : A_i(p)$ for a set I, where action $A_i(p)$ describes the statement with label i, and v is the tuple of program variables, then:

$$(4.13) \quad \models \mathrm{WF}_v(PNext(p)) \equiv \forall i \in I : \mathrm{WF}_v(A_i(p))$$

This is because $\langle PNext(p)\rangle_v$ is enabled iff $\langle A_{pc(p)}(p)\rangle_v$ is enabled, in which case $pc(p)$ can be changed only by an $\langle A_{pc(p)}(p)\rangle_v$ step. Thus, in any state of a behavior with $pc(p) = i$, the formula $\mathbb{E}\langle PNext(p)\rangle_v \Rightarrow \Diamond \langle PNext(p)\rangle_v$

4.2. FAIRNESS

is equivalent to $\mathbb{E}\langle A_i(p)\rangle_v \Rightarrow \Diamond\langle A_i(p)\rangle_v$. A rigorous justification of (4.13) is that it is a special case of Theorem 4.8 in Section 4.2.7 below.

The following tautology is useful for deducing properties from weak fairness assumptions:

$$(4.14) \quad \models \mathrm{WF}_v(A) \equiv (\Diamond\Box\mathbb{E}\langle A\rangle_v \Rightarrow \Box\Diamond\langle A\rangle_v)$$

It makes weak fairness look stronger than the definition because $\Box\Diamond\langle A\rangle_v$ is a stronger property than $\Diamond\langle A\rangle_v$. Here's an informal proof of (4.14). The definition of $\mathrm{WF}_v(A)$ implies the right-hand side of the equivalence because $\Diamond\Box\mathbb{E}\langle A\rangle_v$ implies that eventually $\langle A\rangle_v$ is always enabled, whereupon $\mathrm{WF}_v(A)$ keeps forever implying that an $\langle A\rangle_v$ step occurs, so there must be infinitely many $\langle A\rangle_v$ steps, making $\Box\Diamond\langle A\rangle_v$ true. The opposite implication is true because $\Box\mathbb{E}\langle A\rangle_v$ implies $\Diamond\Box\mathbb{E}\langle A\rangle_v$, so the right-hand side of the equivalence implies that $\Box\Diamond\langle A\rangle_v$ is true and hence $\Diamond\langle A\rangle_v$ is true. A rigorous proof of (4.14) is by the following RTLA[4] reasoning, substituting $\mathbb{E}\langle A\rangle_v$ for F and $\langle A\rangle_v$ for G:

$$\begin{aligned}
\Box F \leadsto G &\equiv \Box(\Box F \Rightarrow \Diamond G) && \text{by definition (3.30) of } \leadsto \\
&\equiv \Box(\neg\Box F \vee \Diamond G) && \text{by propositional logic} \\
&\equiv \Box(\Diamond\neg F \vee \Diamond G) && \text{by } \neg\Box F = \Diamond\neg F \text{ (3.25)} \\
&\equiv \Box\Diamond(\neg F \vee G) && \text{by (3.23)} \\
&\equiv \Box\Diamond\neg F \vee \Box\Diamond G && \text{by (3.27)} \\
&\equiv \neg\Box\Diamond\neg F \Rightarrow \Box\Diamond G && \text{by propositional logic} \\
&\equiv \Diamond\Box F \Rightarrow \Box\Diamond G && \neg\Box\Diamond\neg F \equiv \Diamond\neg\Diamond\neg F \equiv \Diamond\Box\neg\neg F \text{ by (3.25)}
\end{aligned}$$

The following tautology is useful for proving a weak-fairness formula, because it has an additional hypothesis in the implication:

$$(4.15) \quad \models \mathrm{WF}_v(A) \equiv (\Box\mathbb{E}\langle A\rangle_v \wedge \Box[\neg A]_v \leadsto \langle A\rangle_v)$$

It is proved by expanding the definition of $\leadsto$ and applying the propositional logic tautology $\models (F \Rightarrow G) \equiv (F \wedge \neg G \Rightarrow G)$ and the TLA tautology $\models \neg\Diamond\langle A\rangle_v \equiv \Box[\neg A]_v$. Using (4.15) to prove $\mathrm{WF}_v(A)$ is essentially a proof by contradiction.

Proving these kinds of temporal logic tautologies is a good exercise. However, there are temporal logic theorem provers that can do it for you.

---

[4]With these definitions of F and G, the formula $\Box\Diamond(\neg F \vee G)$ is not a TLA formula.

4.2.4 Temporal Logic Reasoning

Thus far, the only properties we've verified that programs satisfy have been invariance properties. Proving invariance requires no temporal logic reasoning. To prove $\models Init \wedge \Box[Next]_v \Rightarrow \Box Inv$, we prove the LA formulas $\models Init \Rightarrow Inv$ and $\models Inv \wedge [Next]_v \Rightarrow Inv'$ and then apply a single temporal logic proof rule.

Nontrivial temporal logic reasoning is required for proving that programs satisfy liveness properties. We often prove liveness properties of the form $P \leadsto Q$. This property asserts that something is true at all "times" in a behavior—namely, that whenever P is true, Q is eventually true. The description $Init \wedge \Box[Next]_v$ of a program cannot be used directly to prove $P \leadsto Q$ because it asserts only that something is true initially. For that reason, the first thing we do when proving $P \leadsto Q$ is to prove that some formula Inv is an invariant of the program, so the program implies $\Box Inv \wedge \Box[Next]_v$. We then use $\Box Inv \wedge \Box[Next]_v$ to prove $P \leadsto Q$.

A formula F that asserts something is true at all times is called a $\Box$ formula. The formula $\Box Inv \wedge \Box[Next]_v$ is a $\Box$ formula because it's equivalent to the RTLA formula $\Box(Inv \wedge [Next]_v)$. A formula F is a $\Box$ formula iff $\models F \equiv \Box F$ is true, because $\models F \equiv \Box G$ implies $\models \Box F \equiv \Box\Box G$ by (3.21), and $\Box\Box G$ is equivalent to $\Box G$. By (3.17), the conjunction of $\Box$ formulas is a $\Box$ formula. In general, (3.18) implies $\forall i \in S : F_i$ is a $\Box$ formula if each F_i is a $\Box$ formula.

In a proof, we almost always want every temporal logic formula asserted by a statement to be a $\Box$ formula. A theorem with statement F asserts $\models F$. The proof rule (3.16) tells us that $\models F$ implies $\models \Box F$. This means that whenever we prove F, we have proved $\Box F$. However, that does not mean that when we have proved a step in a proof that asserts F, we have proved $\Box F$. When we prove a step

    4.2.7. $G \leadsto H$

we have not proved $\models G \leadsto H$. We have proved $\models Asp \Rightarrow (G \leadsto H)$, where Asp is the conjunction of all the assumptions in effect at statement 4.2.7. By the proof rule (3.21), $\models Asp \Rightarrow (G \leadsto H)$ implies $\models \Box Asp \Rightarrow \Box(G \leadsto H)$. If Asp is a $\Box$ formula, so it's equivalent to $\Box Asp$, then proving 4.2.7 proves $\models Asp \Rightarrow \Box(G \leadsto H)$. Therefore proving 4.2.7 is equivalent to proving

    4.2.7. $\Box(G \leadsto H)$

if Asp is a $\Box$ formula. Since the conjunction of $\Box$ formulas is a $\Box$ formula, Asp is a $\Box$ formula if all the assumptions in effect at statement 4.2.7 are $\Box$ formulas.

4.2. FAIRNESS

We assure that every statement that asserts a temporal formula F asserts $\Box F$ by making every temporal formula in an ASSUME clause be a $\Box$ formula. Any temporal formula F asserted by a statement can then be considered to assert $\Box F$. The following are $\Box$ formulas for all temporal formulas F and G, state expressions v, and actions A: $\Box\Diamond F$ (obviously), $\Diamond\Box F$ by (3.29), $F \leadsto G$ by the definition (3.30) of $\leadsto$, and $\mathrm{WF}_v(A)$ by the definition (4.12) of WF.

4.2.5 Reasoning With Weak Fairness

We now see how to show that an abstract program with weak fairness conditions satisfies a liveness property. We will do this with a modification of algorithm *UM* called the *One-Bit* algorithm that is an acceptable mutual exclusion algorithm. But first, we examine what liveness condition the algorithm should satisfy.

4.2.5.1 Liveness for Mutual Exclusion

The liveness condition Dijkstra required of the mutual exclusion algorithm outlined in Figure 4.1 was that if some process is at statement *wait*, then eventually some process enters its critical section—expressed by:

(4.16) $(\exists p \in \mathit{Procs} : pc(p) = \mathit{wait}) \leadsto (\exists p \in \mathit{Procs} : pc(p) = \mathit{cs})$

This condition is usually called *deadlock freedom*. That's a misuse of the term, because deadlock freedom is actually the safety property asserting that the program never reaches a deadlocked state—one in which no process can take a step. Property (4.16) also rules out what is called *livelock*, in which no process enters its critical section although some processes keep executing statements in their waiting sections. However, when discussing mutual exclusion, we will use deadlock freedom to mean property (4.16). This condition allows one or more processes to be starved—that is, to remain forever in their waiting section—while other processes enter and leave the critical section.

Dijkstra also required that processes be allowed to remain forever in their noncritical sections. Just because a process might send output to the printer, we don't want to insist that it does. This requirement rules out simple algorithms in which processes take turns entering the critical section. A process that does not want to enter its critical section cannot be required to do anything to allow other processes to enter their critical sections.

```
variables x = (p ∈ {0, 1} ↦ FALSE) ;
process p ∈ {0, 1}
  variables pc = ncs ;
  while TRUE do
    ncs: skip ;
    wait: x[p] := TRUE ;
    w2:  if p = 0 then await ¬x[1]
                 else if x[0] then w3: x[1] := FALSE ;
                                  w4: await ¬x[0] ;
                                      goto wait
                      end if
         end if ;
    cs:   skip ;
    exit: x[p] := FALSE
  end while
end process
```

Figure 4.3: Algorithm OB.

4.2.5.2 The One-Bit Algorithm

The basic idea of the One-Bit algorithm is to modify algorithm UM to prevent deadlock by having process 1 wait when both processes are concurrently trying to enter the critical section. This is done by modifying process 1 so that if it sees that $x[0]$ equals TRUE in statement $w2$, then it sets $x[1]$ to FALSE and waits until $x[0]$ equals FALSE (so process 0 has exited its critical section) before going back to statement $wait$ and trying again. The pseudocode for the algorithm, which we call OB, is in Figure 4.3.[5]

Algorithm OB satisfies mutual exclusion because the processes use the same protocol as in algorithm UM to enter the critical section: Each process p sets $x[p]$ to TRUE and can then enter the critical section only if $x[1-p]$ equals FALSE. In fact, that OB satisfies mutual exclusion can be proved with the same inductive invariant (4.6) as UM except that the type invariant $TypeOK$ must be modified because $pc(1)$ can now also equal $w3$ or $w4$. For

---

[5] Algorithm OB is the two-process case of an N-process algorithm that was discovered independently by James E. Burns and me in the 1970s, but not published until later [7, 30].

4.2. FAIRNESS

algorithm OB, we define:[6]

(4.17) $TypeOK \triangleq$ $\land\ x \in (\{0,1\} \to \{\text{TRUE, FALSE}\})$
$\land\ pc \in (\{0,1\} \to \{ncs, wait, w2, w3, w4, cs, exit\})$
$\land\ pc(0) \notin \{w3, w4\}$

However, the resulting inductive invariant isn't strong enough for proving liveness. We now consider liveness.

Let $OBSafe$, the safety property of OB described by the pseudocode, be the formula $Init \land \Box[Next]_v$, where v equals $\langle x, pc \rangle$ and

$$Next \triangleq \exists\, p \in \{0,1\} : PNext(p)$$

The fairness condition we want OB to satisfy is weak fairness of each process's next-state action, except when the process is in its noncritical section. A process p remaining forever in its noncritical section is represented in our abstract program by no $PNext(p)$ step occurring when $pc(p)$ equals ncs. The fairness condition we assume of program OB is therefore:

$$OBFair \triangleq \forall\, p \in \{0,1\} : \text{WF}_v((pc(p) \neq ncs) \land PNext(p))$$

The formula $OBSafe \land OBFair$, which we call OB, satisfies the liveness property that if process 0 is in its waiting section, then it will eventually enter its critical section. That is, OB implies:

(4.18) $(pc(0) \in \{wait, w2\}) \rightsquigarrow (pc(0) = cs)$

This implies deadlock freedom, because if process 0 stops entering and leaving its critical section, then it eventually stays forever in its noncritical section. If process 1 is then in its waiting section, it will read $x[0]$ equal to FALSE and enter its critical section.

The inductive invariant obtained from the inductive invariant of UM isn't strong enough because it doesn't assert that $x[p] =$ FALSE when process p is in its noncritical section, which is at the heart of why OB is deadlock free. For that we need this stronger invariant, where $TypeOK$ is defined by (4.17):

(4.19) $\land\ TypeOK$
$\land\ x[0] \equiv (pc[0] \in \{w2, cs, exit\})$
$\land\ x[1] \equiv (pc[1] \in \{w2, w3, cs, exit\})$
$\land\ \forall\, p \in \{0,1\} : (pc[p] = cs) \Rightarrow (pc[1-p] \neq cs)$

---
[6]For any infix predicate symbol like $=$ or $\in$, putting a slash through the symbol negates it, so $e \notin S$ means $\neg(e \in S)$.

$\Box Inv \wedge \Box[Next]_v \wedge OBFair$

```
┌─────────────────────────────────────────────────────────────────┐
│  pc(0) ∈ {wait, w2}  ──1──▶  pc(0) = w2  ──3──▶  pc(0) = cs    │
│              ╲1            ╱2                                   │
│               pc(0) = wait                                      │
└─────────────────────────────────────────────────────────────────┘
```

Figure 4.4: Leads-to lattice for the proof of (4.18).

4.2.5.3 Proving Liveness

We will now see how to reason more rigorously about liveness. Even if you never write rigorous correctness proofs, learning how to reason about liveness will help you better understand liveness properties.

There are two kinds of liveness properties that we prove: that a program implies leads-to properties such as (4.16), and that a program implies the fairness properties of a more abstract program. Here we consider leads-to properties. Proving fairness properties is discussed in Section 6.4.

The proof of a leads-to formula is usually decomposed into proving simpler leads-to formulas. Figure 4.4 shows how we decompose the proof of formula (4.18) using what is called a *leads-to lattice* [46].

First, let's pretend that the box and the formula labeling it aren't there. We then have just a directed graph whose nodes are formulas. A formula F and its outgoing edges represent the assertion that F leads to the disjunction of the formulas those edges point to. (The edges are numbered so we can refer to them.) Thus, the two edges numbered 1 assert the formula:

$$(pc(0) \in \{wait, w2\}) \rightsquigarrow ((pc(0) = wait) \vee (pc(0) = w2))$$

By the meaning of *leads to*, the property asserted by each formula F in the graph means that if the program is ever in a state for which F is true, then it will eventually be in a state satisfying a formula pointed to by one of the outgoing edges from F. The graph has a single sink node (one having no outgoing edge). Every path in the graph, if continued far enough, leads to the sink node. By transitivity of the $\rightsquigarrow$ relation, this means that if all the properties asserted by the diagram are true of a behavior, then the behavior satisfies the property $F \rightsquigarrow H$, where H is the sink-node formula and F is any formula in the lattice. In particular, the properties asserted by the diagram imply formula (4.18). By (3.32), that every formula in the graph leads to the sink-node formula means that the disjunction of all the formulas in the graph leads to the sink-node formula.

4.2. FAIRNESS

Now to explain the box. Let Λ equal $\Box Inv \wedge \Box[Next]_v \wedge OBFair$, the formula that labels the box. Formula Λ is implicitly conjoined to each of the formulas in the graph. It is a $\Box$ formula, since the conjunction of $\Box$ formulas is a $\Box$ formula, and $OBFair$ is the conjunction of WF formulas, which are $\Box$ formulas.

Since Λ is conjoined to every formula in it, the leads-to lattice makes assertions of the form

$$\Lambda \wedge G \leadsto (\Lambda \wedge H_1) \vee \ldots \vee (\Lambda \wedge H_j)$$

Since Λ equals $\Box\Lambda$, and once $\Box\Lambda$ is true it is true forever, this formula is equivalent to $\Lambda \wedge G \leadsto H_1 \vee \ldots \vee H_j$. (This follows from (3.33c) and propositional logic.)

If H is the unique sink node of the lattice, then proving the assertions made by the lattice proves $\models \Lambda \wedge G \leadsto H$ for every node G of the lattice. By definition of $\leadsto$ and (3.22), $\models \Lambda \wedge G \leadsto H$ implies $\models \Box \Lambda \Rightarrow (G \leadsto H)$. Thus, if Λ is a $\Box$ formula, then proving $\models \Lambda \wedge G \leadsto H$ proves $\models \Lambda \Rightarrow (G \leadsto H)$. In general, we label a box in a leads-to lattice only with a $\Box$ formula.

Remember what the proof lattice of Figure 4.4 is for. We want to prove that OB implies (4.18). By proving the assertions made by the proof lattice, we show that the formula Λ labeling the box implies (4.18). By definition of OB and because OB implies $\Box Inv$, formula Λ is implied by OB. Therefore, by proving the leads-to properties asserted by the proof lattice, we prove that OB implies (4.18). Note how we had to use the $\Box$ formula $\Box Inv \wedge \Box[Next]_v$ instead of $OBSafe$, which is true only initially.

To complete the proof that OB implies (4.18), we now prove the leads-to properties asserted by Figure 4.4. The leads-to property asserted by the edges numbered 1 is:

$$\Lambda \wedge (pc(0) \in \{wait, w2\}) \leadsto ((pc(0) = wait) \vee (pc(0) = w2))$$

It is trivially true, since $pc(0) \in \{wait, w2\}$ implies that $pc(0)$ equals $wait$ or $w2$, and $\models F \Rightarrow G$ implies $F \leadsto G$.

The formula $\Lambda \wedge (pc(0) = wait) \leadsto (pc(0) = w2)$ asserted by edge number 2 is true because Λ implies $\Box Inv \wedge \Box[Next]_v$, which implies that if $pc(0) = wait$ is true then it must remain true until a $PNext(0)$ step makes $pc(0) = w2$ true, and such a step must occur by the weak fairness assumption of process 0, which Λ also implies.

The formula

(4.20) $\quad \Lambda \wedge (pc(0) = w2) \leadsto (pc(0) = cs)$

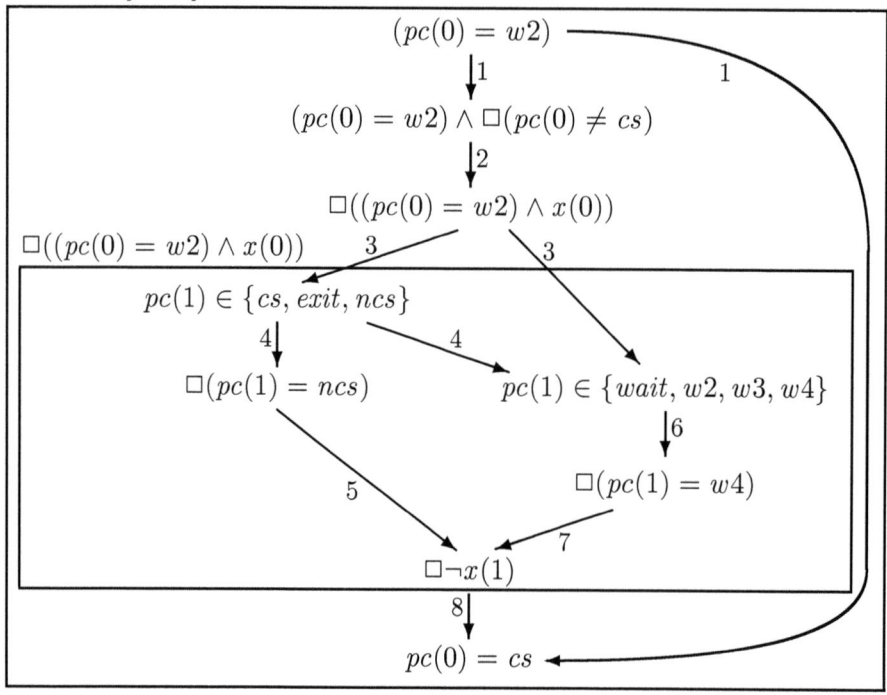

Figure 4.5: Leads-to lattice for the proof of (4.20).

asserted by edge number 3 is the interesting one. Its proof is decomposed with the proof lattice of Figure 4.5.

The property asserted by the edges numbered 1 in this leads-to lattice has the form $\Lambda \wedge F \leadsto (G \vee (F \wedge \Box \neg G))$. This formula is a tautology. Intuitively, it's true because if F is true now, then either G is true eventually or F is true now and $\neg G$ is true from now on. It's proved by:

$$
\begin{aligned}
\Lambda \wedge F &\Rightarrow F \wedge (\Diamond G \vee \Box \neg G) & &\Diamond G \vee \Box \neg G \text{ equals TRUE} \\
&\Rightarrow \Diamond G \vee (F \wedge \Box \neg G) & &\text{by propositional logic} \\
&\Rightarrow \Diamond G \vee \Diamond(F \wedge \Box \neg G) & &\text{by (3.23)} \\
&\equiv \Diamond(G \vee (F \wedge \Box \neg G)) & &\text{by (3.23)}
\end{aligned}
$$

which shows $\models (\Lambda \wedge F \Rightarrow \Diamond(G \vee (F \wedge \Box \neg G)))$, from which we can deduce $\models \Lambda \wedge F \leadsto (G \vee (F \wedge \Box \neg G))$ by (3.20) and the definition of $\leadsto$.

The leads-to formula asserted by edge 2 is an implication. It's true because $\Box Inv \wedge \Box[Next]_v$ implies that, if $pc(0) = w2$ and $\Box(pc(0) \neq cs)$ are ever true, then $pc(0) = w2$ must remain true forever, which by $\Box Inv$ implies $x(0)$

4.2. FAIRNESS

must equal TRUE forever. It is proved by proving that $(pc(0) = w2) \wedge x(0)$ is an invariant of an abstract program. The initial predicate of this program is $Inv \wedge (pc(0) = w2)$. Its next-state relation is:

$$Next2 \triangleq Inv \wedge Next \wedge (pc(0) \neq cs)'$$

The formula $\Box[Next2]_v$ is implied by $\Box Inv$ and $\Box[Next]_v$ and the conjunct $\Box(pc(0) \neq cs)$ of the formula at the tail of the edge 2 arrow. (Note that the prime in this formula is valid because $pc(0) \neq cs$ always true implies that it's always true in the next state.) We are using an invariance property of one program to prove a liveness property of another program. This would seem strange if we were thinking in terms of code. But we're thinking mathematically, and a mathematical proof contains lots of formulas. It's not surprising if one of those formulas looks like the formula that describes a program.

The edges numbered 3 enter a box whose label is the same formula from which those edges come. In general, an edge can enter a box with a label $\Box F$ if it comes from a formula that implies $\Box F$. This is because a box labeled $\Box F$ is equivalent to conjoining $\Box F$ to all the formulas in the box, and $\Box F \leadsto (G_1 \vee \ldots \vee G_n)$ implies $\Box F \leadsto ((\Box F \wedge G_1) \vee \ldots \vee (\Box F \wedge G_n))$. An arrow can always leave a box, since removing the formula it points to from the box just weakens that formula.

Proofs of the assertions represented by the rest of the lattice's edges are sketched below.

edges 3 The formula represented by these edges is true because the disjunction of the formulas they point to asserts that $pc(1)$ is in the set $\{ncs, wait, w2, w3, w4, cs, exit\}$, which is implied by $\Box Inv$.

edges 4 If $pc(1)$ equals cs or $exit$, then $\Box Inv \wedge \Box[Next]_v$ and the fairness condition for process 1 imply that it will eventually be at ncs. Either $pc(1)$ equals ncs forever or eventually it will not equal ncs. In the latter case, $\Box[Next]_v$ implies that the step that makes $pc(1) = ncs$ false must make $pc(1) = wait$ true.

edge 5 This is an implication since $\Box Inv$ implies that if process 1 is forever at ncs, then $x(1)$ is forever false.

edge 6 If process 1 is at $wait$, $w2$, or $w3$, then its weak fairness condition implies it is eventually at $w4$. When process 1 is at $w4$, formulas $\Box[Next]_v$ and $\Box x(0)$ (from the label of the inner box) imply that it must remain forever at $w4$.

edge 7 This is an implication, because Inv and $pc(1) = w4$ imply $\neg x(1)$.

edge 8 $\Box \neg x(1)$, $\Box(pc(0) = w2)$ (implied by the inner box's label), and $OBFair$ imply that a process 0 step that makes $pc(0)$ equal to cs must eventually occur. (Equivalently, these three formulas are contradictory, so they imply FALSE which implies anything.)

The proof sketches of the properties asserted by edges 4 and edge 6 skim over more details than the proofs of the other properties asserted by the lattice. A more detailed proof would be described by a lattice in which each of the formulas pointed to by the edges numbered 3 were split into multiple formulas—for example, the formula $pc(1) \in \{cs, exit, ncs\}$ would be split into the formulas $pc(1) = cs$, $pc(1) = exit$, and $pc(1) = ncs$. A good check of your understanding is to draw the more detailed lattice and write proof sketches for its new edges.

4.2.6 Strong Fairness

4.2.6.1 Starvation Free Mutual Exclusion

Mutual exclusion was not motivated by sharing a printer. It's needed when multiple processes perform operations on the same data. As we saw from the *Increment* example of Section 3.3, even sharing a simple counter without synchronization can result in increment operations being lost. An easy way to synchronize data sharing is to put every operation to the shared data in a critical section.

The One-Bit Algorithm *OB* implements mutual exclusion with processes that communicate using only simple reads and writes of shared variables. Synchronizing processes in this way is inefficient. Dijkstra proposed the communication mechanism called a *binary semaphore* or *lock*. A lock is a variable that can have two values, traditionally taken to be 0 and 1. Let's call that variable *sem*. Initially *sem* equals 1. A process can execute two atomic lock operations, $P(sem)$ and $V(sem)$. These operations are described in pseudocode as:

$P(sem)$	$V(sem)$
await $sem = 1$;	$sem := 1$
$sem := 0$	

Locks were originally implemented with operating system calls. Modern multiprocessor computers provide machine instructions to implement them.

4.2. FAIRNESS

variables $sem = 1$;
process $p \in Procs$
  while TRUE **do**
    ncs: **skip** ;
    $wait$: $P(sem)$;
    cs: **skip** ;
    $exit$: $V(sem)$
  end while
end process

Figure 4.6: Program LM: mutual exclusion with a semaphore.

Using a lock, mutual exclusion for any set *Procs* of processes can be implemented with the trivial algorithm LM of Figure 4.6.

Let $PNext(p)$ now be the next-state action of process p of program LM. With weak fairness of $(pc(p) \neq ncs) \wedge PNext(p)$ for each process p as its fairness property, algorithm LM satisfies the deadlock freedom condition (4.16). However, deadlock freedom allows individual processes to be starved, remaining forever in the waiting section.

Let $Wait(p)$, $Cs(p)$, and $Exit(p)$ be the actions described by the statements in process p with the corresponding labels *wait*, *cs*, and *exit*. Weak fairness of $(pc(p) \neq ncs) \wedge PNext(p)$ is equivalent to the conjunction of weak fairness of the actions $Wait(p)$, $Cs(p)$, and $Exit(p)$. Program LM allows starvation of individual processes because weak fairness of the $Wait(p)$ actions ensures only that if multiple processes are waiting to execute that action, then some process will eventually execute it. But if processes continually reach the *wait* statement, some individual processes p may never get to execute $Wait(p)$.

It's reasonable to require the stronger condition of *starvation freedom*, which asserts that no process starves. This is the property

(4.21) $\forall p \in Procs : (pc(p) = wait) \leadsto (pc(p) = cs)$

which asserts that any process reaching *wait* must eventually enter its critical section. For LM to satisfy this property, it needs a stronger fairness property than weak fairness of the $Wait(p)$ actions.

4.2.6.2   The Definition of Strong Fairness

By the usual meaning of *fair*, the fairest lock would be one in which processes execute their $Wait(p)$ actions in the order in which they set $pc(p)$ to *wait*.

Some implementations of locks ensure this property. However, we don't consider it to be a fairness property because it produces a description of program LM that is not machine closed. It rules out finite behaviors in which processes execute their $Wait(p)$ actions in the wrong order—executions in which a process p reaches the $wait$ statement after process q, but p enters the critical section before q does. Machine closure means that the liveness condition does not forbid any finite behaviors allowed by the program's safety property described by the pseudocode.

There is a standard way to strengthen weak fairness that produces machine-closed program descriptions. Weak fairness of an action A asserts that if ever A is always enabled, then an A action must eventually occur. To strengthen this condition, we replace the requirement that A be always enabled by the weaker requirement that it be infinitely often enabled. We therefore define *strong fairness*, of A, written $\text{SF}_v(A)$, by:

$$(4.22) \quad \text{SF}_v(A) \triangleq \Box\Diamond \mathbb{E}\langle A\rangle_v \rightsquigarrow \langle A\rangle_v$$

Analogous to formulas (4.14) and (4.15) for weak fairness are:

$$(4.23) \quad \models \text{SF}_v(A) \equiv (\Box\Diamond \mathbb{E}\langle A\rangle_v \Rightarrow \Box\Diamond\langle A\rangle_v)$$

$$(4.24) \quad \models \text{SF}_v(A) \equiv (\Box\Diamond \mathbb{E}\langle A\rangle_v \wedge \Box[\neg A]_v \rightsquigarrow \langle A\rangle_v)$$

The informal justification and the proof of (4.23) are similar to the ones for (4.14). The proof of (4.24) is essentially the same as that of (4.15).

4.2.6.3 Using a Strongly Fair Semaphore

To make program LM starvation free, meaning that it satisfies (4.21), we conjoin to the safety property $LMSafe$ defined by the pseudocode the fairness property $LMFair$ equal to $\forall p \in Procs : LMPFair(p)$, where $LMPFair(p)$ is the fairness requirement for process p. If we let $LMPFair(p)$ be the conjunction of strong fairness of $Wait(p)$ and weak fairness of $Cs(p)$ and $Exit(p)$, then the following argument shows $LMSafe \wedge LMFair$ implies starvation freedom. Starvation means that a process p waits forever with $pc(p) = wait$. That is possible only if other processes keep entering and leaving their critical sections. But whenever a process executes the $Exit$ action, it sets sem to 1, which makes $\mathbb{E}\langle Wait(p)\rangle_v$ true. Thus $\mathbb{E}\langle Wait(p)\rangle_v$ must be true infinitely often, which by strong fairness of $Wait(p)$ implies that $Wait(p)$ is eventually executed, so p must enter its critical section.

There are several ways of writing formula $LMPFair(p)$. First, we observe that weak and strong fairness are equivalent for the actions $Cs(p)$ and

4.2. FAIRNESS

$Exit(p)$. This is because the action is enabled iff $pc(p)$ has the appropriate value, so it remains enabled until a step of that action occurs to change $pc(p)$. Thus, when the action is enabled, it is continuously enabled until it is executed. We can therefore write *LMFair* as the conjunction of strong fairness of the three actions $Wait(p)$, $Cs(p)$, and $Exit(p)$.

The same sort of reasoning that led to (4.13) of Section 4.2.3, as well as Theorem 4.8 of Section 4.2.7, imply that the conjunction of strong fairness of these three actions is equivalent to strong fairness of their disjunction. Therefore, we can write *LMFair* as strong fairness of their disjunction, which equals $(pc(p) \neq ncs) \wedge PNext(p)$.

While $\mathrm{SF}_v((pc(p) \neq ncs) \wedge PNext(p))$ is compact, I prefer not to define *LMPFair(p)* this way because it suggests to a reader of the formula that strong fairness of $Cs(p)$ and $Exit(p)$ is required, although only weak fairness is. Usually, the process's next-state action will be the disjunction of many actions, and strong fairness is required of only a few of them. I would define *LMFair* to equal

$$\mathrm{WF}_v((pc(p) \neq ncs) \wedge PNext(p)) \;\wedge\; \mathrm{SF}_v(Wait(p))$$

This is redundant because the first conjunct implies weak fairness of $Wait(p)$ and the second conjunct asserts strong fairness of it. But a little redundancy doesn't hurt, and its redundancy should be obvious because strong fairness implies weak fairness.

4.2.7 Properties of WF and SF

This section presents three theorems that justify assertions made earlier. First, Section 4.2.3 asserts that if *Next* is the disjunction of actions $PNext(p)$, and L is the conjunction of weak fairness of those actions, then $\langle Init \wedge \Box[Next]_v, L \rangle$ is machine closed. In general, this is true if L is the conjunction of any countable set of weak and/or strong fairness conditions on subactions of *Next*, where an action A is defined to be a *subaction* of an action *Next* iff $\models A \Rightarrow Next$ is true. The subactions of *Next* for which fairness is asserted are usually disjuncts in the definition of *Next*—for example, $Wait(p)$ is a subaction of the next-state action *Next* of algorithm *OB*. Often, we assert fairness of an action $P \wedge A$ where A is a disjunct of *Next* and P is a state predicate—for example, the action $(pc(p) \neq ncs) \wedge PNext(p)$ of *OB*. Here is the precise theorem, whose proof is in the Appendix.[7]

---

[7] The two theorems stated here are true if we allow a subaction A to be one satisfying $\models Inv \wedge A \Rightarrow Next$, where *Inv* is an invariant of the program. However, this generalization does not seem to be needed in practice.

Theorem 4.7 Let *Init* be a state predicate, *Next* an action, and v a tuple of all variables occurring in *Init* and *Next*. If A_i is a subaction of *Next* for all i in a countable set I, then the pair

$$\langle\, \mathit{Init} \wedge \Box[\mathit{Next}]_v \,,\ \forall\, i \in I\, :\, \mathrm{XF}^i_v(A_i)\,\rangle$$

is machine closed, where each XF^i_v may be either WF_v or SF_v.

The theorem allows I to be an infinite set. Writing an infinite conjunction of fairness properties may not seem to be something we would do in practice. However, the next-state action of an abstract program sometimes does contain an infinite disjunction—that is, existential quantification over an infinite set of subactions—and we might want a fairness condition for each of those subactions. For example, a program that dynamically creates processes may be described as having an infinite number of processes, only a finite number of which have their next-state action enabled at any time. We might want a fairness condition for each of those processes.

Let Q equal $(pc(p) \neq ncs) \wedge \mathit{PNext}(p)$. Section 4.2.3 also asserts that for program LM, weak fairness of Q is equivalent to weak fairness of its three subactions $\mathit{Wait}(p)$, $\mathit{Cs}(p)$, and $\mathit{Exit}(p)$; and Section 4.2.6.3 asserts this for strong fairness. Those assertions are true because when any one of these subactions is enabled, a step of that subaction must occur before a step of either of the other two subactions can occur. Let's call these three subactions A_1, A_2, and A_3. This condition can then be asserted as:

(4.25) $\quad \forall\, i \in 1..3\, :\, \mathbb{E}\langle A_i\rangle_v\ \Rightarrow\ (\mathbb{E}\langle Q\rangle_v \Rightarrow \mathbb{E}\langle A_i\rangle)\,\mathcal{U}\,\langle A_i\rangle_v$

where $\mathcal{U}$ is the *until* operator with which we first defined weak fairness of $\mathit{PNext}(p)$ as (4.9). Similarly to what we did for weak fairness, we can remove the $\mathcal{U}$ by observing that $F\,\mathcal{U}\,G$ implies that if G is never true, then F must remain true forever. That $\langle A_i\rangle_v$ is never true is asserted by $\neg\Diamond\langle A_i\rangle_v$, which is equivalent to $\Box[\neg A_i]_v$. Therefore (4.25) implies

(4.26) $\quad \forall\, i \in 1..3\, :\, \mathbb{E}\langle A_i\rangle_v \wedge \Box[\neg A_i]_v\ \Rightarrow\ \Box(\mathbb{E}\langle Q\rangle_v \Rightarrow \mathbb{E}\langle A_i\rangle)$

While (4.25) implies (4.26), the formulas are not equivalent. Formula (4.26) is strictly weaker than (4.25). However, it's strong enough to imply that strong or weak fairness of all the A_i is equivalent to strong or weak fairness of Q—assuming that Q is the disjunction of the A_i. Here is the precise theorem. Its proof is in the Appendix.

4.2. FAIRNESS

Theorem 4.8 Let A_i be an action for each $i \in I$, let $Q \triangleq \exists i \in I : A_i$, and let XF be either WF or SF. Then

$$\models (\forall i \in I : \Box(\mathbb{E}\langle A_i\rangle_v \land \Box[\neg A_i]_v \Rightarrow$$
$$\Box[\neg Q]_v \land \Box(\mathbb{E}\langle Q\rangle_v \Rightarrow \mathbb{E}\langle A_i\rangle_v))$$
$$\Rightarrow (\text{XF}_v(Q) \equiv \forall i \in I : \text{XF}_v(A_i))$$

It is perhaps interesting, but of no practical significance, that the theorem is valid even if the set of actions A_i is uncountably infinite.

Section 4.1.2 asserts that the completeness result for safety properties in Theorem 4.2 can be extended to arbitrary properties. Here is that extension, whose proof is sketched in the Appendix.

Theorem 4.9 Let $\mathbf{x}$ be the list x_1, ..., x_n of variables and let F be a property such that $F(\sigma)$ depends only on the values of the variables $\mathbf{x}$ in σ, for any behavior σ. There exists a formula S equal to $\textit{Init} \land \Box[\textit{Next}]_{\langle \mathbf{x},y\rangle} \land \text{WF}_{\langle \mathbf{x},y\rangle}(\textit{Next})$, where $\textit{Init}$ and $\textit{Next}$ are defined in terms of F, y is a variable not among the variables $\mathbf{x}$, and the variables of S are $\mathbf{x}$ and y, such that $\models F \Rightarrow [\![G]\!]$ iff $\models S \Rightarrow G$, for any property G. If F is a safety property, then the conjunct $\text{WF}_{\langle \mathbf{x},y\rangle}(\textit{Next})$ is not needed.

Like Theorem 4.2, this result is of theoretical interest only.

4.2.8 What is Fairness?

Before TLA, concurrent abstract programs were generally written in something like a coding language. Fairness meant that each process had to execute its next atomic statement when it could. Viewed in terms of TLA, each atomic statement was described by an action, and fairness meant fairness of those actions. Usually that meant weak fairness of the action, but when the statement was a synchronization primitive, it sometimes meant strong fairness. For rigorous reasoning, those fairness requirements were expressed as requirements on when control in the process had to move from one control point to another [46].

With TLA, fairness was generalized to weak and strong fairness of arbitrary actions. We have considered a fairness property for a safety property S to be a formula L that is the conjunction of weak and strong fairness conditions on actions such that $\langle S, L\rangle$ is machine closed. However, weak and strong fairness of an action are defined in terms of how the action is written, not in terms of its semantics. While we have given semantic definitions of safety, liveness, and machine closure; we have not done it for fairness.

I only recently learned that a semantic definition of fairness was published in 2012 by Völzer and Varacca [50]. Their definition of what it means for a property L to be a fairness property for a safety property S can be stated in terms of the following infinite two-player game. Starting with *seq* equal to the empty sequence, the two players forever alternately take steps that append a finite number of states to *seq*. The only requirement on the steps is that after each one, *seq* must satisfy S. The second player wins the game if she makes *seq* an infinite sequence that satisfies L. (Since S is a safety property, *seq* must satisfy S.) They defined L to be a fairness property for S iff the second player can always win, regardless of what the first player does (as long as he follows the rules).

It is mathematically meaningless to say that a definition is correct. However, this seems to be the only reasonable definition that includes weak and strong fairness such that fairness implies machine closure and the conjunction of countably many fairness properties is a fairness property. This definition also encompasses other fairness properties that have been proposed, including one called hyperfairness [34].

I believe that weak and strong fairness of actions are the only fairness properties that are relevant to abstract programs. However, this general definition is interesting because it provides another way to think about fairness. More importantly, it's interesting because concepts we are led to by mathematics often turn out to be useful.

Chapter 5

Interlude

We have seen how to use TLA to write abstract programs and show that they satisfy simple safety and liveness properties. In this chapter, we pause in our development to consider two problems. The first is determining if an abstract program written in TLA expresses what we want it to. We consider an approach to this problem that is different from what we have been doing—determining what the program *might* do, rather than what it must or must not do. The second problem is describing and reasoning about the real-time behavior of systems. I hope that seeing how this problem is addressed with TLA helps you appreciate the power of thinking of an abstract program as a predicate on behaviors rather than a generator of behaviors.

5.1 Possibility and Accuracy

5.1.1 Possibility Conditions

Informally, a safety property states what an abstract program is allowed to do and a liveness property states what it must do. If a behavior violates a safety property, then it does so at a particular step in the behavior. Therefore, we can also view a safety property as stating what a program must not do—that is, it must not take a step that violates the property. So, liveness says what must happen and safety says what must not happen. That a program eventually sets x to 0 is a liveness property, that it never sets x to 0 is a safety property.

Possibility says what *might* happen. That a program might set x to 0 is a possibility condition. It is not a property, because it is not a predicate on behaviors. It is satisfied by an abstract program iff there is some behavior of the program in which x is set to 0. We can tell that the program satisfies it if we see such a behavior. But seeing one behavior that doesn't satisfy it doesn't tell us whether or not some other behavior might satisfy it. However, we will see that possibility conditions can be expressed as properties that explicitly mention the program's actions.

Knowing that something might be true of a system, but knowing nothing about the probability of its being true, is of almost[1] no practical use. The only way I know of calculating such probabilities is to view the abstract program as a state-transition system, attach probabilities to the various transitions, and mathematically analyze that system—for example, using Markov analysis [51]. Usually, the state-transition system would be a more abstract program implemented by the program of interest.

While possibility conditions of systems are of little interest, we don't reason about systems; we reason about abstract programs that describe systems. Verifying that a program satisfies a possibility condition can be a way of checking what we will call here the *accuracy* of an abstract program—that it accurately describes the system it is supposed to describe. For example, if the system doesn't control when users send it input, a program that accurately describes the system and its users should satisfy the condition that it's always possible for users to enter input.

5.1.2 Expressing Possibility in TLA

There exist logics for expressing possibility properties and tools for checking them. Such tools could be built to check those properties for abstract TLA programs, and it might be worthwhile to do so. But we will see how that can be avoided.

Even though a possibility condition is not a property, that an abstract program satisfies a possibility condition can be expressed by a TLA formula that depends on the program and the possibility condition. For example, suppose S is a TLA description of an abstract program and the action *Input* is a subaction of its next-state action that describes users entering input. That it is always possible for users to enter input could be considered to mean that the *Input* action is enabled in every reachable state of the program, which is asserted by

$$\models S \;\Rightarrow\; \Box\, \mathbb{E}(\textit{Input})$$

However, "always possible" might instead mean that from any reachable state, there is a sequence of possible steps that reach a state with $\mathbb{E}(\textit{Input})$

---

[1] Section 8.1 explains one way in which a possibility condition can be used to verify a property of a system and could therefore be of practical use.

5.1. POSSIBILITY AND ACCURACY

true—a condition we will call "always eventually possible". To express this and other possibility conditions in TLA, we can use the action composition operator defined in Section 3.4.1.4. Recall that for any action A, the action A^+ is true of a step $s \to t$ iff t is reachable from s by a sequence of one or more A steps.

Now consider an abstract program $Init \wedge \Box[Next]_v$ where $Init$ is a state predicate, $Next$ is an action, and v is the tuple of all variables that appear in $Init$ or $Next$. Let's abbreviate $([Next]_v)^+$ as $[Next]_v^+$. If s is a reachable state of the program, then $s \to t$ is a $[Next]_v^+$ step iff it is possible for an execution of the program to go from state s to state t. (Since $[Next]_v$ allows stuttering steps, t can equal s. In fact, $[Next]_v^+$ is equivalent to $[Next^+]_v$.) A state t is a reachable state of the program iff there is a state s satisfying $Init$ such that $s \to t$ is a $[Next]_v^+$ step. In other words, t is a reachable state of the program iff there is a state s such that $s \to t$ is an $Init \wedge [Next]_v^+$ step.

We can now express the condition that it is always eventually possible for the user to enter input, meaning that from any reachable state it is possible to reach a state in which $\mathbb{E}(Input)$ is true. We generalize this condition by replacing $\mathbb{E}(Input)$ with an arbitrary state predicate P. For the abstract program $Init \wedge \Box[Next]_v$, that P is always eventually possible is expressed as:

(5.1) $\models Init \wedge \Box[Next]_v \Rightarrow \Box \, \mathbb{E}([Next]_v^+ \wedge P')$

This example indicates that it should be possible to express possibility conditions in TLA using $Next^+$ and the $\mathbb{E}$ operator. However, like (5.1), the resulting TLA formulas are quite different from the ones that arise in checking that an abstract program satisfies a property. Different tools would be needed to verify that a program satisfies a possibility condition expressed in this way. It would be nice to be able to verify possibility conditions by verifying the same kind of properties that arise in verifying that an abstract program satisfies a liveness property. Here is how it can be done for the condition that it is always eventually possible to reach a state satisfying P.

This condition obviously holds if the program satisfies the property that in any reachable state, a state satisfying P *must* eventually occur—that is, if the program satisfies the property $\Box \Diamond P$. Let S equal $Init \wedge \Box[Next]_v$. The safety property S will not imply the liveness property $\Box \Diamond P$ unless P is true in all reachable states of F—that is, unless S implies $\Box P$. However, if F is a fairness property for S, so $\langle S, F \rangle$ is machine closed, then $S \wedge F$ has the same set of reachable states as S. So, any state satisfying P can be reached from a reachable state of S iff it can be reached from a state satisfying $S \wedge F$. Therefore, it suffices to verify that a state satisfying P can be reached from every reachable state of $S \wedge F$, which is true if $S \wedge F$ implies $\Box \Diamond P$. Therefore, we can verify that P is always possible by verifying

$$\models \textit{Init} \wedge \Box[\textit{Next}]_v \wedge F \Rightarrow \Box \Diamond P$$

for a fairness property F of $\textit{Init} \wedge \Box[\textit{Next}]_v$. By Theorem 4.7, we can ensure that F is a fairness property for S by writing it as the conjunction of strong fairness properties. (Since strong fairness implies weak fairness, there is no need to use weak fairness properties.) There is a completeness result that essentially says that such a fairness property always exists for any state predicate P if S has the standard form $\textit{Init} \wedge \Box[\textit{Next}]_v$ [33].

I suspect that TLA can in a similar way express possibility for a more general class of possibility conditions than the two possible interpretations of "always possible". However, the only other possibility condition I have found to be useful for checking the accuracy of an abstract program is a very simple one, discussed in the following section.

5.1.3 Checking Accuracy

Using TLA to check that a state predicate P is always eventually possible may not be easy, since it requires finding a fairness condition that implies P is true infinitely often. There's a simpler condition that is easier to check: it's possible for P to be true (at least once). It would be more useful to check the stronger condition of always eventually possible. However, I have found that most people, including me, don't spend enough time checking the accuracy of their abstract programs. The weaker check is likely to be more helpful in practice because it's more likely to be done than one that requires more effort.

It's possible for P to be true means that it is true in some reachable state. This is equivalent to the assertion that $\neg P$ is not true in all reachable states—in other words, that $\neg P$ is not an invariant of the program. We can check this by asking a tool for checking invariance to check if $\neg P$ is an invariant. If the tool reports that it isn't, then it's possible for P to be true. For example, if a model checker reports that your mutual exclusion algorithm satisfies mutual exclusion, you should check that it's possible for a process to enter its critical section. This is especially true if you did not have to make many corrections to reach that point. Remember that a program that takes no non-stuttering steps satisfies most safety properties.

Tools can provide other ways of checking the accuracy of a program. For example, if $\textit{Input}$ is a subaction of the program's next-state action, a TLA$^+$

5.2. REAL-TIME PROGRAMS

model checker called TLC reports how many different steps satisfying *Input* occur in behaviors of the program. If it finds no such steps, then it is not always possible for an *Input* step to occur with either definition of "always possible". Finding too few such steps can also be an indication that the program is not accurate.

Accuracy of an abstract program cannot be formally defined. It means that a program really is correct if it implements the abstract program. In other words, an abstract program is accurate iff it means what we want it to mean, and our desires can't be formally defined. That accuracy can't be formally defined does not mean it's unimportant. There are quite a few important aspects of programs that lie outside the scope of our science of correctness.

5.2 Real-Time Programs

Real-time abstract programs are ones in which timing constraints ensure that safety properties hold. Real time is most often used in concrete programs to ensure not safety but liveness. It appears in timeouts that guarantee something eventually happens. For example, to guarantee that a message is eventually delivered despite possible message loss, a timeout occurs if an acknowledgement of the message is not received soon enough after it is sent, and the message is then resent. A program that uses timeouts only in this way is not a real-time program. The actual time at which a timeout occurs affects only performance, not correctness. Therefore, timeout can be modeled in an abstract program as an event that must eventually occur but can occur at any time. The program can use liveness to abstract away time. We need to write a real-time abstract program only if timing constraints are used to ensure safety properties.

Scientists have been dealing mathematically with real-time systems for centuries by simply representing time as the value of a variable. It has been known for decades that this works for real-time programs too [6]. I will illustrate how it is done with a mutual exclusion algorithm of Michael Fischer.[2]

I believe that most work on the correctness of real-time programs has considered only safety properties. Instead of requiring that something eventually happens, it requires the stronger property that it happens within some fixed amount of time, which is a safety property. Fischer's Algorithm

---

[2]Fischer sent this algorithm in an email to me [13]. I believe Martín Abadi and I were the first to describe it in print [1].

is more general because in addition to using real-time to ensure mutual exclusion, a safety property, it uses fairness to ensure deadlock freedom, a liveness property.

In the past 40 years, I have had essentially no contact with engineers who build real-time systems. I know of only one case in which TLA was used to check that a commercial system satisfied a real-time property [5].[3] From the point of view of our science, there is nothing special about real-time programs. However, how well tools work can depend on the application domain. The TLA$^+$ tools were not developed with real-time programs in mind, and it's unclear how useful they are in that domain.

Math VI

Definitions Within an Expression The scope of an ordinary definition includes everything that comes logically after it in the current context, which in this book might end at the end of the current section. It's sometimes convenient to make a definition whose scope is limited to a single expression *exp*. This is often done for "common subexpression elimination", where *exp* contains multiple occurrences of the same subexpression *subexp*, and we want to give that subexpression a name *nm* and rewrite *exp* as the expression *nmexp* in which each occurrence of *subexp* has been replaced by *nm*. We do that by rewriting *exp* as:

$\quad$ LET $nm \triangleq subexp$ IN $nmexp$

Note that if *exp* occurs in the scope of bound variables and we wanted to do this with an ordinary definition, we would have to define *nm* as an operator with one argument for each of those bound variables. The general form of the LET/IN construct is

$\quad$ LET *defs* IN *exp*

where *exp* is an expression and *defs* consists of one or more definitions. The scope of those definitions is the expression *exp*, and the definitions can include definitions of mappings that take arguments.

The Mapping Set Constructor ZF contains a set constructor that I call the *mapping* constructor. Its general form is $\{exp : v \in S\}$, where v is a bound variable whose scope is the expression *exp*. It equals the set of all

---

[3]The TLA$^+$ design of the real-time operating system mentioned in Section 1.6 was not used to check its real-time properties.

5.2. REAL-TIME PROGRAMS

values obtained by substituting an element of the set S for v in exp. For example, $\{2 * n : n \in \mathbb{N}\}$ is the set of all even natural numbers. As another example, if S is a set of n-tuples, then it is a subset of $S_1 \times \ldots \times S_n$, where S_i is the set $\{v(i) : v \in S\}$.

Don't confuse the mapping constructor with the subsetting constructor, whose form is $\{v \in S : exp\}$. The set of all even natural numbers can be written with the subsetting constructor as $\{n \in \mathbb{N} : n \% 2 = 0\}$.[4]

5.2.1 Fischer's Algorithm

The algorithm without its timing constraints is described by the pseudocode in Figure 5.1. The constant *Procs* is the (finite) set of processes, and *none* is some constant that is not in *Procs*. The global variable x is read and written by all the processes and, as usual, the value of $pc(p)$ is the label of the next statement to be executed by process p. As explained in Section 4.2.2.1, the statement **await** P is a synchronization primitive that allows the process to continue only when the state predicate P is true. Thus, the *wait* statement of process p is described by the action:

$\land\ pc(p) = wait$
$\land\ x = none$
$\land\ pc' = (pc\ \text{EXCEPT}\ p \mapsto w1)$
$\land\ x' = x$

With no time constraints, mutual exclusion is easily violated. Two processes can execute the *wait* statement when x equals *none*, then statements $w1$ and $w2$ can both be executed by the first process and then by the second one, putting both processes in the critical section. Mutual exclusion is ensured by timing constraints.

We assume that each step is executed instantaneously at a certain time, and that each process executes $w1$ at most δ seconds after it executes *wait* and executes $w2$ at least ϵ seconds after it executes $w1$, for constants δ and ϵ with $\delta < \epsilon$. (The algorithm doesn't specify what the time units are; we will call them seconds for convenience.) It's a nice exercise to show that this ensures mutual exclusion by assuming that two processes are in their critical sections and showing that the necessary reads and writes of x that allowed them both to enter the critical section must have occurred in an order that violates the timing constraints if $\delta < \epsilon$. While it may be good enough for

---

[4]The expression $\{v \in S : v \in T\}$ is ambiguous; it could be either a subsetting or a mapping constructor. We will never write such an expression, so we won't worry about which it is.

variables $x = none$;
process $p \in Procs$
  variables $pc = ncs$;
  while TRUE **do**
    ncs: **skip** ;   noncritical section
    $wait$: **await** $x = none$;
    $w1$: $x := p$;
    $w2$:   **if** $x \neq p$ **then goto** $wait$ **end if** ;
    cs: **skip** ;   critical section
    $exit$: $x := none$
  end while
end process

Figure 5.1: Fischer's Algorithm.

such a simple algorithm, this kind of behavioral reasoning is unreliable for more complicated programs.

To verify mutual exclusion more rigorously, we describe Fischer's Algorithm with its timing constraints as an abstract program. This requires adding a variable whose value represents the current time. Scientists usually call that variable t, but I like to call it now. We also add a variable rt, where the value of $rt(p)$ records the time at which certain actions of process p were executed. The program also contains an additional process called $Time$ that advances time.

The algorithm is written in pseudocode in Figure 5.2. The initial value of now can be any number in the set $\mathbb{R}$ of real numbers, and the initial value of rt can be any function from the set of processes to $\mathbb{R}$. Let's now examine the code of process p. Two assignments to $rt(p)$ have been added. Each sets $rt(p)$ to the time at which the action in which it appears is executed, the actions being the ones performed when the program is at control points $wait$ and $w1$. Also added is an **await** statement at $w2$ that allows the action to be performed only when $now - rt(p) \geq \epsilon$. This **await** enforces the requirement that the $w2$ action must not be executed until at least ϵ seconds after execution of the $w1$ action.

Let's now examine the $Time$ process. It repeatedly performs a single atomic action, so it has just one control point that needs no label. That action increases the value of now. The $:\in$ operation is like the assignment operation $:=$ except with $=$ replaced by $\in$. That is, a step of the $Time$ process's action assigns to now an arbitrary element of the set on the right-

5.2. REAL-TIME PROGRAMS

variables $x = \mathit{none}$, $\mathit{now} \in \mathbb{R}$, $rt \in (\mathit{Procs} \to \mathbb{R})$;
process $p \in \mathit{Procs}$
  variables $pc = \mathit{ncs}$;
  while TRUE **do**
    ncs: **skip** ;   noncritical section
    wait: **await** $x = \mathit{none}$;
         $rt(p) := \mathit{now}$;
    $w1$: $x := p$;
         $rt(p) := \mathit{now}$;
    $w2$:   **await** $\mathit{now} - rt(p) \geq \epsilon$;
         if $x \neq p$ **then goto** wait **end if** ;
    cs: **skip** ;   critical section
    exit: $x := \mathit{none}$
  end while
end process

process Time
  while TRUE **do**
    $\mathit{now} :\in \{t \in \mathbb{R} :$
             $\wedge\; t > \mathit{now}$
             $\wedge\; \forall p \in \mathit{Procs} : (pc(p) = w1) \Rightarrow (t \leq rt(p) + \delta)\}$
  end while
end process

Figure 5.2: Fischer's Algorithm with explicit time.

hand side of the $:\in$. The action can assign to *now* any value t greater than its current value, subject to the condition that $t \leq rt(p)+\delta$ for every process p at control point $w1$. It is this condition that enforces the requirement that a process must execute statement $w1$ within δ seconds of when it executes the *wait* statement.

Fischer's Algorithm illustrates the basic method of representing real-time constraints in an abstract program. Lower bounds on how long it must take to do something are described by enabling conditions on the algorithm's actions. Upper bounds are described by enabling conditions on the action that advances time. There are a number of ways of enforcing these bounds. The use of the variable rt in Fischer's algorithm shows one way. Another is to use variables whose values are the number of seconds remaining before an action must be executed (lower bounds) or can be executed (upper bounds)—variables whose values are decremented by the time-advancing action.

The idea of an abstract program constraining the advance of time is mind-boggling to most people, since they view a program as a set of instructions. They see it as the program stopping time. You should by now realize that an abstract program is a description, not a set of instructions. It describes a universe in which the algorithm is behaving correctly. That description may constrain the algorithm's environment, which is the part of the universe that the algorithm doesn't control—for example, its users. Time is an important part of that environment if the amount of time it takes to perform the algorithm's actions is relevant to its correctness.

5.2.2 Correctness of Fischer's Algorithm

Having written Fischer's algorithm as an abstract program, we know how to verify its correctness. Mutual exclusion is an invariance property, and to understand why the algorithm satisfies it we need to find the inductive invariant that explains why the algorithm satisfies that property. As usual, the inductive invariant asserts type-correctness of all the variables. The interesting part of the invariant makes the following assertions about each process p:

- If control is at $w1$, then the current time is at most δ seconds after the time at which p just executed the *wait* statement.

- If control is at cs or $exit$, then $x = p$ and in no process is control at $w1$. (This condition implies mutual exclusion.)

- If p is at $w2$ and $x = p$, then any process with control at $w1$ must execute statement $w1$ before p can execute statement $w2$.

These assertions about every process p are expressed mathematically as:

$$\forall p \in \text{Procs} :$$
$$\land \ (pc(p) = w1) \Rightarrow (rt(p) \leq now \leq (rt(p) + \delta))$$
$$\land \ (pc(p) \in \{cs, exit\}) \Rightarrow (x = p) \land (\forall q \in \text{Procs} : pc(q) \neq w1)$$
$$\land \ (pc(p) = w2) \land (x = p) \Rightarrow$$
$$\quad \forall q \in \text{Procs} : (pc(q) = w1) \Rightarrow ((rt(q) + \delta) < (rt(p) + \epsilon))$$

You should understand why the three conjuncts in this formula are the three assertions expressed informally above. Adding the type-correctness part and proving that it is an inductive invariant is a good exercise if you want to learn how to write proofs.

5.2. REAL-TIME PROGRAMS

Under suitable fairness assumptions, Fischer's Algorithm is deadlock free. Recall that deadlock freedom for a mutual exclusion algorithm means it's always true that if some process is trying to enter the critical section, then some process (not necessarily the same process) will eventually do so. Deadlock freedom of Fischer's Algorithm follows from the algorithm having this additional invariant:

(5.2) $(x \neq none) \Rightarrow (pc(x) \in \{w2, cs, exit\})$

Here's a sketch of a proof by contradiction that the algorithm is deadlock free. Suppose some process is at *wait* and no process is ever in its critical section. Eventually, some set of processes will be forever in their noncritical sections, and one or more processes will forever have control at *wait*, *w1*, or *w2*. Eventually the latter processes will all wind up waiting at the *wait* statement with $x \neq none$. But that contradicts the invariant (5.2), which implies that process x cannot be at *wait*.

5.2.3 Fairness and Zeno Behaviors

What fairness requirements of the abstract program of Figure 5.2 are assumed in the informal argument that the program is deadlock free? If $procStep(p)$ is the next-state action of a process p in *Procs*, then we naturally assume weak fairness of the action $procStep(p) \land (pc \neq ncs)$. What about fairness of the *Time* process? Let's call that process's action $timeStep$. The obvious choice is to let it be strong fairness of $timeStep$. However, that allows the following behavior: While all other processes in *Procs* remain in their noncritical sections, a process p executes the *wait* statement and then, at time t, executes statement $w1$ that sets $rt(p)$ to t. Repeated executions of action $timeStep$ then set now to $t + \epsilon/2$, then $t + 2*\epsilon/3$, then $t + 3*\epsilon/4$, and so on. Process p must wait forever at $w2$ because now is always less than $t + \epsilon$ and the $w2$ action is enabled only when $now \geq t + \epsilon$. Such a behavior, in which time remains bounded, is called a Zeno behavior.

The most natural way to avoid the problem of Zeno behaviors is to make the abstract program describing Fischer's Algorithm disallow them. The obvious way to do that is to conjoin this liveness property:

(5.3) $\forall t \in \mathbb{R} : \Diamond(now > t)$

which asserts that the value of time is unbounded. However, this isn't necessarily a fairness property. It's easy to write an abstract program that allows only Zeno behaviors, so conjoining the liveness property (5.3) produces a program that allows no behaviors. For example, we can add timing constraints to the program of Figure 5.1 that require a process both to execute statement $w1$ within δ seconds after executing statement $wait$ and to wait at least ϵ seconds after executing $wait$ before executing $w1$, with $\delta < \epsilon$. If a process executes $wait$ at time t, then $now \le t + \delta$ must remain true forever. If we added fairness properties that required processes eventually to reach the $wait$ statement and execute it if it's enabled, then the program would allow only Zeno behaviors.

We can ensure that Fischer's Algorithm satisfies (5.3) by having it require an appropriate fairness condition on the advancing of time. The condition we need is strong fairness of the action $timeStep \wedge (now' = exp)$, where exp is the largest value of now' permitted by the values of $rt(p)$ for processes p with control at $w1$, or $now + 1$ if there is no such process. More precisely:

$$exp \triangleq \text{LET } T \triangleq \{rt(p) + \delta \,:\, p \in \{q \in Procs \,:\, pc(q) = w1\}\}$$
$$\text{IN} \quad \text{IF } T = \{\} \text{ THEN } now + 1 \text{ ELSE } Min(T)$$

where $Min(T)$ is the minimum of the nonempty finite set T of real numbers. With this fairness condition on advancing time and the conjunction of the fairness conditions for the processes in $Procs$, Fischer's Algorithm satisfies (5.3) and the proof sketch that the algorithm is deadlock free can be made rigorous.

If we are interested only in safety properties, there is no need for an abstract program to rule out Zeno behaviors. A program satisfies a safety property iff all finite behaviors allowed by the program satisfy it, and a Zeno behavior is an infinite behavior. In many real-time programs, liveness properties are of no interest. Correctness means not that something eventually happens but that it happens within a certain length of time, which is a safety property. Zeno behaviors then make no difference, and there is no reason to disallow them.

Even if Zeno behaviors don't matter, the absence of non-Zeno behaviors can be a problem. Since real time really does increase without a bound, an abstract program in which it is not always possible for time to become arbitrarily large is unlikely to be accurate. Therefore, we almost always want to ensure that a real-time program satisfies the condition that for any $t \in \mathbb{R}$, it is always possible for $now > t$ to be true. This is true iff, for any $t \in \mathbb{R}$, from any reachable state of the program it is always possible for $now > t$ to be true. This is the kind of possibility condition considered in Section 5.1. We saw there that if the program $Safe$ is a safety property that satisfies this condition, then we can verify that it does so by finding a

5.2. REAL-TIME PROGRAMS

conjunction F of fairness properties for *Safe* and verifying:

(5.4) $\models$ *Safe* $\wedge\ F \Rightarrow \Box\Diamond(now > t)$

for all $t \in \mathbb{R}$. (Since a real-time program never allows *now* to decrease, it suffices to verify that *Safe* $\wedge\ F$ implies (5.3).)

5.2.4 Discrete Time

Verifying properties of real-time programs is easier if we assume time is discrete and *now* always equals a multiple of some time unit. It may seem obvious that, since concrete programs run on real computers reading the current time from a clock that advances in discrete steps, we can always assume discrete time. However, different processes can be executed on different computers whose clocks can run at slightly different rates. Still, it seems likely that an abstract program will be sufficiently accurate if it assumes time changes only in one yoctosecond (10^{-24} second) increments. So, in practice we should be able to assume that the values of *now* and any time constants are integers, leaving unspecified how long one time unit is.

When writing proofs, there doesn't seem to be much reason to use discrete time. The main advantage of discrete time is that tools for automatically verifying properties of ordinary abstract programs can, in principle, handle discrete real-time programs. For example, I didn't prove that what I claimed in Section 5.2.2 to be an inductive invariant of Fischer's Algorithm actually is one. Instead, I used a model checker to check that it is, which gave me enough confidence to make the claim.

Many model checkers are based on enumerating reachable states, usually on a small instance of the program—for example, with a small number of processes. This is impossible with continuous time, in which a single state can have possible next states with uncountably many values of *now*. There are still infinitely many reachable states with discrete time because the values of *now* are unbounded, but counterexamples to incorrect safety properties and to (5.3) for a particular time t can be found by examining all reachable states with *now* less than some value.

The number of reachable states that must be examined can be reduced for real-time programs that satisfy a condition called *symmetry under time translation*.

This condition asserts that for every $d \in \mathbb{R}$ there is a *time-translation* mapping T_d from states to states such that: For every state s, the value of *now* in state $T_d(s)$ equals d plus its value in s, and any step $s \to t$ satisfies the program's next-state action iff $T_d(s) \to T_d(t)$ does. For example,

Fischer's Algorithm is symmetric under the time translations T_d defined by letting the values of *now* and $rt(p)$ in $T_d(s)$ equal d plus their values in s, and letting the values of x and pc be the same in s and $T_d(s)$.

Suppose S is a program symmetric under the time-translation functions T_d, and for simplicity assume that the program's initial predicate asserts $now = 0$. Let's call states s and t *translation equivalent* iff $t = T_d(s)$ for some d. If P is a safety property containing only variables whose values are left unchanged by the functions T_d, then to verify that P is satisfied by S we can verify that it is satisfied by the program $\widehat{S}$ obtained from S by considering two translation equivalent states to be the same state. Often, there will be some time λ such that every reachable state of S is translation equivalent to a state in which $now \leq \lambda$, in which case $now \leq \lambda$ in every state of $\widehat{S}$. This implies we can verify that S satisfies (5.3) by checking that it satisfies $\Diamond(now \geq \lambda + 1)$, which requires examining only reachable states with $now \leq \lambda + 1$. The details can be found elsewhere [36].

Being able to reduce verification of a discrete-time program to examining reachable states with *now* less than some value would still leave an enormous number of states to consider if *now* advanced in yoctosecond steps. Henzinger, Manna, and Pnueli proved that for a class of programs called timed transition systems, certain properties can be verified with discrete time in which *now* advances only in reasonably sized steps [18]. Timed transition systems are essentially programs in which, like Fischer's Algorithm, time is used only to require minimum and maximum delays between when a program action becomes enabled and when it either must be executed (maximum delay) or may be executed (minimum delay). If those delays are constants that are all multiples of some time unit Δ, then a certain class of properties can be verified by letting time always be a multiple of Δ. That class of properties are ones in which replacing each state in a behavior by time-translating it by d with $-\Delta < d \leq 0$ does not change whether the behavior satisfies the property. It includes properties that depend only on variables whose values are unchanged by time translation. It also includes the property (5.3).

One reason that has been given for preferring continuous time is that it is necessary for composing programs. It would be difficult to compose a program in which a clock tick represents a nanosecond with one in which a clock tick represents a millisecond. However, we can easily describe a program in terms of a clock that ticks at an unspecified rate and an unspecified constant that equals the number of clock ticks in a second.

Program composition is discussed in Section 8.2, where it is shown how the composition of two abstract programs can be represented as the con-

5.2. REAL-TIME PROGRAMS

junction of the TLA formulas that describe them. Moreover, a real-time abstract program can be written as the conjunction of two formulas, one describing an ordinary, untimed program, the other specifying the required timing constraints [1]. However, this kind of abstract program composition is not yet usable in practice.

5.2.5 Hybrid Systems

A hybrid computer system is one that controls physical processes—for example, one that flies an airplane or runs a chemical plant. An abstract program that describes such a system is a real-time program that describes not only the passage of time but also other physical quantities like altitude or pressure. There is no fundamental difference between programs that describe hybrid systems and other real-time programs. The current altitude or pressure is represented by a variable like any other variable. Abstract programs describing hybrid systems differ from other real-time abstract programs only in the math used to describe them. If the variable prs describes the current pressure, then the time-advancing subaction of the next-state action might contain a subformula like:

$$(5.5) \quad prs' = prs + \int_{now}^{now'} exp \, dt$$

for some expression exp containing the bound variable t and other variables [31].

It may seem that a representation of the behavior of a continuous process by a sequence of discrete states would not be sufficiently accurate. For example, if it is required that the pressure not be too high, violation of that requirement would not be found if it occurred during the time between two successive states of the behavior. This is not a problem because correctness means that a property is true of all possible behaviors, and the possibility of the pressure being too high at some time is revealed by a behavior containing a state in which now equals that time.

Other than the differences implied by the use of continuous math, such as calculus in (5.5), rather than discrete math, proving properties of hybrid programs is the same as proving properties of other real-time abstract programs. Automatic tools like model checkers for ordinary abstract programs seem to be unsuitable for checking abstract programs in which variables represent continuously varying quantities. Methods have been developed for checking such programs [11].

Chapter 6

Refinement

We have discussed one abstract program implementing another. We now consider more carefully what that means. We write abstract programs with TLA formulas, and it is rather weird to talk about one formula implementing another. Computer scientists who view programs mathematically generally use the term *refinement* rather than *implementation*. Henceforth, we will use the two terms interchangeably. There are two aspects to refinement:

Step Refinement The refining program has a finer grain of atomicity. This means that a non-stuttering step of the high-level program can correspond to multiple steps of the refining program, all but one of them implementing stuttering steps of the high-level program. In the example of Section 3.5.1, the hour-minute-second clock *HMS* refines the hour-minute clock *HM*. Every non-stuttering step of *HM*, which advances the minute, corresponds to 60 steps of *HMS*, each changing the second and one of them changing the minute.

Data Refinement A program refining another program can also refine the representation of data used by the higher-level program. This will be illustrated by refining a higher-level program that uses numbers with a program that implements a number by a sequence of digits.

Refinement usually involves both step and data refinement, with step refinement manifest as operations on the lower-level data requiring more non-stuttering steps than the corresponding operations on the higher-level program's data. As we saw with the example of the hour-minute and hour-minute-second clocks in Section 3.5.2, without data refinement, a program S is refined by a program T means that T implies S. We will see that with data refinement, T refines S means that T implies the formula obtained from S by substituting expressions containing the variables of T for the variables of S. To describe this precisely, we need some notation for substitution.

Mathematicians have no standard way of describing substitution, and the notation I've seen used by computer scientists is impractical for the formulas that arise in describing programs. The notation used in this book, illustrated with substitution for three variables, is that

$$E \text{ WITH } v_1 \leftarrow exp_1,\ v_2 \leftarrow exp_2,\ v_3 \leftarrow exp_3$$

is the expression obtained from the expression E by simultaneously substituting exp_1 for v_1, exp_2 for v_2, and exp_3 for v_3; where v_1, v_2, and v_3 are distinct variables and exp_1, exp_2, and exp_3 are expressions. For example:

$$(p*(q+r)) \text{ WITH } q \leftarrow r,\ r \leftarrow q+s\ =\ p*(r+(q+s))$$

As in this example, the WITH expression is usually enclosed in parentheses when it appears as a subexpression in a larger expression, otherwise parsing would be difficult.

When a program S is refined by a program T, the variables in formula T are usually different from the variables in formula S, and the two sets of variables have non-overlapping scopes. Showing that T refines S involves reasoning in the scope of T about formulas containing the variables of S. To do this, we import an expression E containing variables of S into the scope of the variables of T as the expression

$$E \text{ WITH } v_1 \leftarrow exp_1, \ldots, v_m \leftarrow exp_m$$

where the v_i are the variables of S and the exp_i are expressions containing the variables of T. The same thing applies to the constants of T and S, so the v_i are both the variables and constants of S. If v_i is a constant, then exp_i is usually a constant expression. We adopt the convention that if the expression exp_i (which may be a constant or variable) of T has the same name as the constant or variable v_i of S, then we omit the substitution $v_i \leftarrow v_i$. (This is a common case, because the programs S and T are usually abstract views of the same system, where an expression of T and a variable or constant of S have the same name only if they describe the same part of the system's state.)

6.1 A Sequential Algorithm

In step refinement, the additional steps taken by the lower-level program correspond to stuttering steps in the higher-level one. We consider an extreme example of this: a program that terminates after taking a single non-stuttering step that is refined by a traditional sequential program that computes a value and stops.

This example is used because it's simple and nicely illustrates data refinement. Its use does not imply that this way of looking at refinement is the best one to use for traditional programs. There are other methods for reasoning about refinement of traditional programs that are probably better than our science of more general programs [21]. We consider only safety in this example; liveness is straightforward.

The high-level abstract program *Add* begins with variables x and y equal to arbitrary natural numbers, sets the variable z to their sum, and terminates. Termination is indicated by changing the value of a Boolean-valued variable *end* to TRUE. Here is the definition:

$$InitA \triangleq (end = \text{FALSE}) \land (x \in \mathbb{N}) \land (y \in \mathbb{N})$$
$$NextA \triangleq \neg end \land (z' = x + y) \land (end' = \text{TRUE})$$
$$vA \triangleq \langle x, y, z, end \rangle$$
$$Add \triangleq InitA \land \Box[NextA]_{vA}$$

The initial-state predicate *InitA* does not specify the value of z; its initial value doesn't matter. The next-state action *NextA* does not specify the values of x' or y'. As we know, this doesn't mean that they have the same values as x and y; it means that their new values are unspecified. We are assuming that the final values of x and y don't matter; we care only about the final value of z.

Math VII

Sequence Operators We now define some operators for sequences. They are defined for both ordinal and cardinal sequences. For any sequences σ and τ such that σ is finite, we define $\sigma \circ \tau$ to be the sequence obtained by concatenating σ and τ. For example, $\langle 4, 5 \rangle \circ \langle 1, 2 \rangle$ equals $\langle 4, 5, 1, 2 \rangle$, and $(4 \to 5) \circ (1 \to 2 \to 3 \to \cdots)$ equals $4 \to 5 \to 1 \to 2 \to 3 \to \cdots$.

For any (finite or infinite) nonempty sequence σ, we define $Head(\sigma)$ to be the first item of σ and $Tail(\sigma)$ to be the sequence obtained by removing the first element of σ. For example, $Head(\langle 1, 2, 3 \rangle)$ and $Head(1 \to 2 \to 3 \to \cdots)$ both equal 1; $Tail(\langle 1, 2, 3 \rangle)$ equals $\langle 2, 3 \rangle$; and $Tail(1 \to 2 \to 3 \to \cdots)$

6.1. A SEQUENTIAL ALGORITHM

equals $2 \to 3 \to \cdots$. If σ is a nonempty ordinal sequence, then it equals $\langle Head(\sigma) \rangle \circ Tail(\sigma)$.

For any finite sequence σ, we define $Len(\sigma)$ to be the number of items in σ. Thus, DOMAIN(σ) equals $1 \mathinner{..} Len(\sigma)$ if σ is a finite ordinal sequence; and it equals $0 \mathinner{..} (Len(\sigma) - 1)$ if σ is a finite cardinal sequence.

We need the following two operators only for ordinal sequences, so we don't define them for cardinal sequences. For any ordinal sequence σ and value v, we define $Append(\sigma, v)$ to equal $\sigma \circ \langle v \rangle$, the sequence obtained by appending the item v to the end of σ. We define $Seq(S)$ to be the set of all finite ordinal sequences whose items are in S. Thus, if $\sigma \in Seq(S)$ then $\sigma \in (1 \mathinner{..} Len(\sigma) \to S)$.

Set Difference The set difference operator $\setminus$ is defined by
$$S \setminus T \triangleq \{v \in S : \neg(v \in T)\}$$
In other words, $S \setminus T$ is the set of elements of S that are not elements of T.

6.1.1 A One-Step Program

We refine *Add* by a program *AddS* in which a natural number is represented by a finite ordinal sequence of decimal digits—that is, by an element of the set $Seq(0 \mathinner{..} 9)$. For convenience, we number the digits from right to left, so the sequence $\langle 1, 2, 3 \rangle$ represents the number 321. Thus a sequence *seq* of digits represents the number $Val(seq)$ defined as follows, where the empty sequence is defined to represent 0.

$$Val(seq) \triangleq \text{IF } seq = \langle \rangle \text{ THEN } 0$$
$$ \text{ELSE } Head(seq) + 10 * Val(Tail(seq))$$

Let $\oplus$ be addition of numbers represented in this way as sequences of digits. In other words, $\oplus$ satisfies
$$Val(s \oplus t) = Val(s) + Val(t)$$
for all sequences s and t of digits. We would expect *Add* to be refined by the program *AddS* obtained by replacing $+$ by $\oplus$ and $\mathbf{N}$ by $Seq(0 \mathinner{..} 9)$ in the definition of *Add*. To avoid confusing the variables of the two programs, we'll also replace x, y, z, and *end* by u, v, w, and *fin*, so *AddS* is defined by:

$$\begin{aligned}
InitS &\triangleq (\textit{fin} = \text{FALSE}) \wedge (u \in Seq(0 \mathinner{..} 9)) \wedge (v \in Seq(0 \mathinner{..} 9)) \\
NextS &\triangleq \neg\textit{fin} \wedge (w' = u \oplus v) \wedge (\textit{fin}' = \text{TRUE}) \\
vS &\triangleq \langle u, v, w, \textit{fin} \rangle \\
AddS &\triangleq InitS \wedge \Box[NextS]_{vS}
\end{aligned}$$

Exactly what does it mean for *AddS* to refine *Add*? I believe the natural definition is: If we look at any behavior of *AddS* and interpret the numbers represented by the sequences u, v, and w of digits to be the values of x, y, and z, and we interpret the value of *fin* to be the value of *end*, then we get a behavior of *Add*. More precisely, let "←" mean "is represented by". That *AddS* refines *Add* means that a behavior satisfying *AddS* represents a behavior satisfying *Add* with this representation of the variables of *Add* in terms of the variables of *AddS*:

(6.1) $\quad x \leftarrow Val(u) \quad y \leftarrow Val(v) \quad z \leftarrow Val(w) \quad end \leftarrow fin$

Here's an example to illustrate this, where the first two-state sequence is a finite behavior satisfying *AddS* and the second two-state sequence is the finite behavior it represents. Remember that *AddS* leaves unspecified the value of w in an initial state and the values of u and v in a halting state. A "?" in the second behavior means the value is unspecified because, as explained in Section 2.6, *Val(seq)* is a meaningless expression if *seq* isn't a sequence of numbers.

$$\begin{bmatrix} u &::& \langle 1,2,3 \rangle \\ v &::& \langle 3,2 \rangle \\ w &::& \sqrt{2} \\ fin &::& \text{FALSE} \end{bmatrix}_0 \rightarrow \begin{bmatrix} u &::& \langle 5 \rangle \\ v &::& -27 \\ w &::& \langle 4,4,3 \rangle \\ fin &::& \text{TRUE} \end{bmatrix}_1$$

$$\begin{bmatrix} x &::& 321 \\ y &::& 23 \\ z &::& ? \\ end &::& \text{FALSE} \end{bmatrix}_0 \rightarrow \begin{bmatrix} x &::& 5 \\ y &::& ? \\ z &::& 344 \\ end &::& \text{TRUE} \end{bmatrix}_1$$

As you can see, the second finite behavior satisfies *Add*, since $321+23$ equals 344 and *end* has the values the abstract program *Add* says it should.

Let's look closely at this example. What it shows is that when we perform the substitutions (6.1) for the variables of *Add* in a behavior satisfying formula *AddS*, we get a behavior that satisfies formula *Add*. In other words, in any behavior: if the behavior satisfies *AddS*, then it satisfies the formula *Add* when we perform the substitutions (6.1). This means that the following formula is true:

(6.2) $\quad \models AddS \Rightarrow$
$\quad\quad (Add \text{ WITH } x \leftarrow Val(u), y \leftarrow Val(v), z \leftarrow Val(w), end \leftarrow fin)$

This is what it means for *AddS* to refine *Add* under the representation defined by (6.1). That representation is called a *refinement mapping*. Formula (6.2) asserts that *AddS* implements *Add* under this refinement mapping.

6.1. A SEQUENTIAL ALGORITHM

I find (6.2) beautiful. We've already seen that, viewed in terms of TLA, step refinement is implication. Now we see that data refinement is substitution—the ordinary mathematical operation of substituting expressions for variables in a formula. How beautifully simple! In science, beauty is not an end in itself. It's a sign that we're doing something right.

6.1.2 Two Views of Refinement Mappings

There are two ways to view the refinement mapping (6.1) that appears in (6.2). To understand them, let's simplify things by ignoring irrelevant variables and letting *state* mean program state—an assignment of values to the program's variables. Let an *S*-state be a state of *AddS*, which is an assignment of values to the variables u, v, w, and *fin* of *AddS*; and let an *A*-state be an assignment of values to the variables x, y, z, and *end* of *Add*. Let an *S*-behavior or *A*-behavior be a sequence of *S*-states or *A*-states, respectively.

The first way to view the refinement mapping is as a mapping f that maps *S*-states to *A*-states. For any *S*-state s, the values of the variables x, y, z, and *end* that define the state $f(s)$ are related to the vales of the variables u, v, w, and *fin* that define the state s by (6.1). We can define the mapping $\widehat{f}$ from *S*-behaviors to *A*-behaviors in terms of f by $\widehat{f}(\sigma)(i) \triangleq f(\sigma(i))$ for any *S*-behavior σ. That *AddS* implements *Add* under the refinement mapping f means $[\![AddS]\!](\sigma) \Rightarrow [\![Add]\!](\widehat{f}(\sigma))$ for every *S*-behavior σ.

The second way to view refinement is expressed in (6.2), which states that *AddS* implements *Add* under the refinement mapping means $[\![AddS]\!](\sigma) \Rightarrow [\![Add \text{ WITH } \ldots]\!](\sigma)$ for every *S*-behavior σ.

In the first view, the refinement mapping maps low-level behaviors to high-level behaviors—that is, behaviors of *AddS* to behaviors of *Add*. In the second view, it maps the high-level formula *Add* to the low-level formula *Add* WITH .... It may not be obvious, but these two views are equivalent. They're equivalent because

(6.3) $[\![Add \text{ WITH } \ldots]\!](\sigma) \equiv [\![Add]\!](\widehat{f}(\sigma))$

is true for every *S*-behavior σ. And this equivalence is true if *Add* is replaced by any RTLA formula containing only the variables of *Add*. It's true because the values of the variables of *Add* in the state s and the values of the variables of *AddS* in the state $f(s)$ are related by (6.1).

6.1.3 A Step and Data Refinement

Section 3.5.1 illustrated step refinement by showing that an hour-minute-second clock refines an hour-minute clock. We have just illustrated data refinement by showing that *AddS* implements *Add* under a refinement mapping. We now show an example that involves both step and data refinement.

The example involves an algorithm *AddSeq* that adds numbers the way you probably learned to add them as a child. However, we represent those numbers as sequences of digits in the reverse order, as they are in program *AddS*, with the low-order digit being the first one in the sequence. It sets *sum* equal to $u \oplus v$, where u and v are numbers represented by strings of digits. The algorithm computes *sum* digit by digit, keeping it equal to the right-most digits of the sum computed so far. Each step removes the first (right-most) digit from u and v and appends the next (left-most) digit to *sum*, setting *carry* equal to the value 0 or 1 "carried over" from that sum.

A pseudocode description of the algorithm is in Figure 6.1, but it uses some notation that requires explanation. Recall that $Append(seq, val)$ is defined in Section 2.8.3 to equal $seq \circ \langle val \rangle$, the sequence obtained by appending the value *val* to the end of the ordinal sequence *seq* of values. The code assumes that *DigitSeq* is the set $Seq(0..9) \setminus \{\langle \rangle\}$ of nonempty finite sequences of the digits 0 through 9. If u and v are of unequal length, then the number of steps taken by the algorithm you learned in school is usually equal to or one greater than the length of the longer number. For simplicity, the number of steps taken by *AddSeq* always equals one plus the length of the longer number. To simplify the description of what happens when the algorithm runs out of digits in one of the numbers, it uses the operator *Fix* defined as follows to replace the empty sequence by $\langle 0 \rangle$:

$$Fix(seq) \triangleq \text{IF } seq = \langle \rangle \text{ THEN } \langle 0 \rangle \text{ ELSE } seq$$

The algorithm's **define** statement defines *digit* to equal the indicated expression within that statement. The value of $\lfloor n/10 \rfloor$ is the greatest integer less than or equal to $n/10$. To simplify the invariant, *AddSeq* specifies the initial value of *carry* to equal 0 and ensures that it equals 0 at the end. Since the low-order digit of a two-digit number n is $n \% 10$ and its high-order digit is $\lfloor n/10 \rfloor$, it should be clear that *AddSeq* describes an algorithm for adding two decimal numbers. (If it's not, execute it by hand on an example.)

The usual way to express correctness of a program that computes a value *sum* and stops is with an invariant asserting that if the program has stopped then *sum* has the correct value. We can't do that with *AddSeq* because the correct value of *sum* is the initial value of $u \oplus v$, and those initial values

6.1. A SEQUENTIAL ALGORITHM

variables $u \in DigitSeq$, $v \in DigitSeq$, $sum = \langle \rangle$, $carry = 0$, $pc = a$;
while a: $(u \neq \langle \rangle) \lor (v \neq \langle \rangle) \lor (carry \neq 0)$ **do**
   define $digit \triangleq Fix(u)(1) + Fix(v)(1) + carry$;
      $sum \ := Append(sum, digit \% 10)$;
      $carry := \lfloor digit \,/\, 10 \rfloor$
   end define ;
   $u := Tail(Fix(u))$;
   $v := Tail(Fix(v))$
end while ;
$carry := 0$

Figure 6.1: Algorithm *AddSeq*.

have disappeared by the time the program stops. To express correctness, we can add a constant *ans* that equals the initial value of $u \oplus v$. Since stopping means *pc* equals *done* for our pseudocode, correctness means:

(6.4) $\quad \models AddSeq \Rightarrow \Box((pc = done) \Rightarrow (ans = sum))$

The key part of an inductive invariant to prove (6.4) is the assertion that *ans* equals the final value of *sum*. A first approximation to the final value of *sum* is:

$$sum \circ (\langle carry \rangle \oplus (u \oplus v))$$

We haven't said what $s \oplus t$ means if s or t is the empty sequence, but it's clear that we should define the empty sequence to represent 0. However, a close examination of the algorithm indicates that if u and v both equal $\langle \rangle$ and $carry = 0$, then this expression equals a sequence with an extra 0 at the end. The correct assertion that is the key to the inductive invariant is

(6.5) $\quad ans =$ IF $(u \circ v = \langle \rangle) \land (carry = 0)$
               THEN sum ELSE $sum \circ (\langle carry \rangle \oplus (u \oplus v))$

The remainder of the inductive invariant asserts type correctness and that $pc = done$ implies that u, v, and *carry* have their correct final values.

However, the point of this example is not that *AddSeq* implements a particular procedure for adding sequences of digits; it's that it refines the abstract program *Add* that adds two integers in a single step. This is a dramatic example of step refinement, in which a program that can take arbitrarily many non-stuttering steps to finish refines one that always finishes in one non-stuttering step. And we don't have to add the constant *ans* to do it.

Under the refinement mapping, one step in an execution of *AddSeq* must refine a *NextA* step of *Add*; all the other steps must refine stuttering steps of *Add*. The initial values of the variables x and y of *Add* should equal the initial values of $Val(u)$ and $Val(v)$. The initial values of u and v are no longer deducible from the state after *AddSeq* takes its first step. This tells us that the *NextA* step of *Add* must be refined by the first non-stuttering step of *AddSeq*.

An *Add* step changes the value of its variable *done* from FALSE to TRUE. So, the refinement mapping must assign to *done* an expression whose value is changed from FALSE to TRUE by the first non-stuttering step of *AddSeq*. Since further steps of *AddSeq* refine stuttering steps of *Add*, the expression assigned to *done* must remain true for the rest of the execution of *Add*. A suitable expression is $sum \neq \langle\rangle$, so we let the refinement mapping include $done \leftarrow sum \neq \langle\rangle$.

In the initial state of *AddSeq*, the refinement mapping should assign to x and y the values of u and v. Since *Add* allows x and y to have any values in its final state, it doesn't matter what values the refinement mapping assigns to x and y after the first step of *AddSeq*. However, since later steps must refine stuttering steps of *Add*, the values of x and y must not change. Zero seems like a nice value to let x and y equal when their value no longer matters, so we let the refinement mapping include:

$$x \leftarrow \text{IF } sum \neq \langle\rangle \text{ THEN } 0 \text{ ELSE } Val(u),$$
$$y \leftarrow \text{IF } sum \neq \langle\rangle \text{ THEN } 0 \text{ ELSE } Val(v)$$

Finally, we must decide what value the refinement mapping assigns to z. If we add to *AddSeq* the constant *ans* that always equals the result the algorithm finally computes, then we can substitute $Val(ans)$ for z. But we don't have to add it because the invariant (6.5) tells us what expression containing only the variables of *AddSeq* always equals *ans*. We could therefore substitute for z the expression obtained by applying *Val* to the right-hand side of equation (6.5). However, there's a simpler expression that we can use. Convince yourself that the following substitution works:

$$z \leftarrow Val(sum) + 10^{Len(sum)} * (carry + Val(u) + Val(v))$$

This completes the refinement mapping. That *AddSeq* implements *Add*

6.2. INVARIANCE UNDER REFINEMENT

under the refinement mapping means that this theorem is true:

$\models AddSeq \Rightarrow (Add$ WITH
$\quad done \leftarrow sum \neq \langle\rangle\,,$
$\quad x \leftarrow$ IF $sum \neq \langle\rangle$ THEN 0 ELSE $Val(u)\,,$
$\quad y \leftarrow$ IF $sum \neq \langle\rangle$ THEN 0 ELSE $Val(v)\,,$
$\quad z \leftarrow Val(sum) + 10^{Len(sum)} * (carry + Val(u) + Val(v)))$

6.2 Invariance Under Refinement

If an abstract program T implements an abstract program S under a refinement mapping, and Inv is an invariant of S, then the refinement mapping maps Inv to an invariant of T. The precise statement of this is the following theorem, where "..." is any refinement mapping.

Theorem 6.1 $\models T \Rightarrow (S$ WITH $\ldots)$ and $\models S \Rightarrow \Box Inv$ imply
$\models T \Rightarrow \Box(Inv$ WITH $\ldots)$.

The proof is simple:

1. $\models S \Rightarrow \Box Inv$ implies $\models (S \Rightarrow \Box Inv)$ WITH $\ldots$.

    PROOF: Substitution in a true formula produces a true formula.

2. $\models (S \Rightarrow \Box Inv)$ WITH $\ldots$ equals $\models (S$ WITH $\ldots) \Rightarrow \Box(Inv$ WITH $\ldots)$.

    PROOF: By definition of what substitution means.

3. Q.E.D.

    PROOF: The theorem follows from steps 1 and 2 by propositional logic.

Recall the trick used in Section 3.2.3 to obtain an invariant of $FGSqrs$ from an invariant of the coarser-grained algorithm $Sqrs$. We replaced the variable y by the expression yy in the invariant of $Sqrs$. That trick was an application of the theorem, because $FGSqrs$ implements $Sqrs$ under the refinement mapping $x \leftarrow x, y \leftarrow yy$.

6.3 An Example: The Paxos Algorithm

We've seen step and data refinement for a sequential abstract program. Concurrency adds nothing new. Refinement works exactly the same for concurrent programs. This is illustrated with the Paxos consensus algorithm, an example chosen for the following reasons:

- It's a distributed algorithm. Quite a few researchers used to believe that different techniques are needed to reason about correctness of distributed programs; perhaps some still do. Paxos illustrates that there is no mathematical difference between distributed and non-distributed concurrent programs. In fact, Paxos is obtained as a refinement of a non-distributed algorithm.

- It's a widely used algorithm. If you perform any commercial transaction on the Web, there is a good chance that Paxos or an algorithm inspired by it is being executed by a program running on the computers that perform the transaction.

- It illustrates the importance of abstraction. Thinking scientifically means thinking abstractly. The abstract programs in this example are more abstract than ones most computer scientists and engineers would think of. Learning to think more abstractly is the key to building better complex computer systems.

- The complete TLA$^+$ specifications of the abstract programs, as well as videos of a pair of lectures that explain them, are available on the Web [27]. Therefore, the abstract programs are only sketched here.

The Paxos algorithm was invented (at least) twice, first by Barbara Liskov and Brian Oki [43] and then by me. Its consensus algorithm had been invented by Cynthia Dwork, Nancy Lynch, and Larry Stockmeyer [12].

6.3.1 The Consensus Problem

One reason for building distributed systems is fault tolerance. Systems implemented by multiple computers are often required to operate normally even if one or more of the computers fail. What a system should do can be described as a single-process abstract program that executes a sequence of commands it receives as inputs. Correct execution of the system by multiple computers requires that all the computers agree on what that sequence of inputs is. This is achieved by having all the computers agree on what the ith input is for every i. Ensuring that all the computers agree on a single input is called *consensus*. A fault-tolerant system repeatedly executes a consensus algorithm to choose a sequence of inputs.

I was inspired to invent the Paxos algorithm because colleagues were building a distributed fault-tolerant system. I realized that the system had to implement consensus, so it should implement a consensus algorithm. However, my colleagues were writing code; they didn't have an algorithm. I

6.3. AN EXAMPLE: THE PAXOS ALGORITHM

never found out how their program implemented consensus. But based on the state of the art of programming at the time, here is what their program might have done.

A process called the *leader*, running on a single computer, receives all input requests and decides what input should be chosen next. A new leader will have to be selected if the initial leader fails, but we'll worry about that later. (Failure of a process usually means failure of the computer executing the process.) For the system to keep running despite the failure of individual computers, a set of processes called *acceptors*, each running on a different computer, have to know what value was chosen. Moreover, only a subset of the acceptors should have to be working (that is, not failed) for an input to be chosen. If an input v is chosen by a leader and a set of acceptors, and the leader and those acceptors fail, then a different leader and a different set of acceptors must not choose an input different from v. The obvious way to ensure that is to require a majority of the acceptors to agree upon the input v in order for that input to be chosen. Any two majorities have at least one acceptor in common, and that acceptor will know that it agreed to the choice of v.

This reasoning leads to the following algorithm: The leader decides what input v should be chosen. It sends a message to the acceptors saying that they should agree to the choice of v. Any working acceptor that receives the message replies to the leader with a message saying "v is OK". When the leader receives such an OK message from a majority of acceptors, it sends a message to all the acceptors telling them that v has been chosen.

This algorithm works fine, and the system keeps choosing a sequence of inputs, until the leader fails. At that point, a new leader is selected. The new leader sends a message to all the acceptors asking them what they've done. In particular, the new leader finds out from the acceptors if inputs were chosen that it was unaware of. It also finds out if the previous leader had begun trying to choose an input but failed before the input was chosen. If it had, then the new leader completes the choice of that input. When the new leader has received this information from a majority of acceptors, it can complete any uncompleted choices of an input and begin choosing new inputs. Let's call this algorithm the naive consensus algorithm.

There's one problem with the naive algorithm: How is the new leader chosen? Choosing a single leader is just as hard as choosing a single input. The naive consensus algorithm thus assumes the existence of a consensus algorithm. However, because leader failures should be rare, choosing a leader does not have to be done efficiently. So, programmers would probably have approached the problem of choosing a leader the way they approached most programming problems. They would have found a plausible solution and then debugged it. Debugging usually means thinking of all the things that could go wrong and adding code to handle them.

Let's pause and look at the science of consensus. Before Paxos, there were consensus algorithms that worked no matter what a failed process could do [47]. However, they were *synchronous* algorithms, meaning that they assumed known bounds on the time required for messages sent by one process to be received and acted upon by another process. They were not practical for the loosely coupled computers that had become the norm by the 1980s. Although asynchronous algorithms were required, they had to solve a simpler problem because sufficiently reliable systems could be based on the assumption that a process failed by stopping and could not perform incorrect actions. However, the FLP theorem, named after Michael Fischer, Nancy Lynch, and Michael Paterson who discovered and proved it, states that no asynchronous algorithm can implement consensus if even a single process can fail in this benign way [14]. More precisely, any algorithm that ensures the safety property that two processes never choose different values must allow behaviors that violate the liveness property that requires a value eventually to be chosen if enough processes are working and can communicate with one another. Asynchronous algorithms that ensure liveness must allow behaviors in which processes disagree about what input is chosen.

The leader-selection code programmers would have written therefore had to allow either behaviors in which two processes thought they were the leader, probably with serious consequences, or else behaviors in which no leader is selected, causing the system to stop choosing values. With a properly designed algorithm, the probability of never choosing the leader is zero, and a leader will be chosen fairly quickly if enough of the system is working properly. The system my colleagues built ran for several years with about 60 single-user computers, and I don't think their consensus code caused any system error or noticeable stalling. There is no way to know if it had errors that would have appeared in today's systems with thousands of computers and many thousands of users.

6.3.2 The Paxos Consensus Algorithm

We develop the Paxos consensus algorithm as a series of three abstract programs: a trivial specification of the problem the algorithm solves, which is refined by a non-distributed multiprocess algorithm, which is refined by the Paxos algorithm. I believe that this description—in particular, its view of Paxos as a refinement of the non-distributed algorithm—mirrors how I

6.3. AN EXAMPLE: THE PAXOS ALGORITHM

actually found the algorithm.

Only the safety properties of these abstract programs are described. In most applications, violation of safety in a consensus algorithm can be quite serious—for example, causing money deposited to a client's bank account to disappear. We will see later how the algorithm can be implemented to almost always achieve liveness while never violating safety. As mentioned above, the abstract programs are just sketched; complete descriptions are available on the Web [27].

6.3.2.1 The Specification of Consensus

Instead of talking about inputs, we define consensus as choosing an element of some set *Value* of values. Most correctness proofs of consensus algorithms prove only that they satisfy the invariance property that two processes never choose different values. A consensus algorithm must also not allow a value to be unchosen and a different value then chosen. Proving the invariance property is usually sufficient because it's obvious that the algorithm doesn't allow a value to be unchosen. But to illustrate refinement, we write a high-level abstract program that rules out such a possibility.

There are a number of reasonable ways to describe consensus as an abstract program, and it makes little difference which one is used. Perhaps the most obvious way is with a multiprocess abstract program in which each process independently learns what value is chosen. The next-state action would allow a process p that has not learned a value to learn one, with the constraint that if any process has learned that the value v was chosen, then p must also learn that v was chosen.

We take a different approach and let the abstract program describe only the choosing of a value, without mentioning processes that learn the chosen value. This abstract program has a single variable *chosen* that represents the set of values that have been chosen. (In any behavior allowed by the program, that set always contains at most one element.) The initial predicate is *chosen* = {}, and the next-state action is:

$$(\textit{chosen} = \{\}) \land (\exists\, v \in \textit{Value} : \textit{chosen}' = \{v\})$$

As explained above, there is no fairness condition.

6.3.2.2 The Voting Algorithm

In the naive algorithm, leader and acceptor processes communicate by sending messages. It's natural to think about a consensus algorithm in terms of messages being sent. However, remember that we reason about an abstract program in terms of its state, so we should be thinking about states, not about sending messages. And the important part of the state is the state of the acceptors. So, we refine the Consensus program with an abstract program called the Voting algorithm whose state is just the state of the acceptors. This is not just a nice way to describe the Paxos algorithm. Viewing Paxos as a refinement of the non-distributed voting algorithm is what enabled me to discover Paxos.

In good programming, we begin by abstracting away lower-level details and getting the high-level design right. There's a kind of bad programming that sounds similar: We begin writing something that handles the normal behavior, and we then modify it to handle non-normal situations. That's the way the naive consensus algorithm was described, and it's a recipe for creating incorrect programs—both abstract and concrete ones. We should start thinking about the general case, not the normal case.

The general state of acceptors in the naive algorithm is one that is reached after a number of leaders have begun trying to get a value chosen, and some of them may have succeeded. When a leader tries to get a particular value chosen, we say that the leader has begun a *ballot*. When an acceptor has sent an OK message for a value v in that ballot, we say that the acceptor has *voted* for v in that ballot. The algorithm will assign a unique natural number to each ballot.[1] The state of the Voting algorithm records all the votes that each acceptor has cast. This is described by a variable *votes* whose value is a function that assigns to each acceptor a a set $votes(a)$ of pairs $\langle b, v \rangle$, where $b \in \mathbb{N}$ and $v \in Value$. The pair $\langle b, v \rangle$ in $votes(a)$ means that a has voted for v in ballot number b.

Choosing a leader is the weak point in the naive algorithm. The Voting algorithm abstracts away the leaders. A leader serves two functions. The first is to ensure that in any ballot, acceptors can cast votes only for the value proposed by the leader. The Voting algorithm's next-state action takes care of that by not letting an acceptor cast a vote for a value v in ballot b if a vote has already been cast in ballot b for a different value. The second function of the leader is to learn that a value has been chosen, which it does when it has received enough OK messages. The Voting algorithm does away with that function by declaring that the value has been chosen when the requisite number of OK messages have been sent—that is, when

---

[1]Don't confuse different ballots with the different instances of the consensus algorithm being executed. Execution of an instance of the consensus algorithm can consist of multiple ballots.

6.3. AN EXAMPLE: THE PAXOS ALGORITHM

there are enough votes cast for the value in the ballot. More precisely, we define $ChosenAt(b, v)$ to be true iff a majority of acceptors has voted for v in ballot b. The Voting algorithm implements the Consensus abstract program under the refinement mapping

(6.6) $\quad chosen \leftarrow \{v \in Value : \exists\, b \in \mathbb{N} : Chosen(b, v)\}$

In addition to $votes$, the algorithm has one other variable $maxBal$ whose value is a function that assigns to each acceptor a a number $maxBal(a)$. The significance of this number is that a will never in the future cast a vote in any ballot numbered less than $maxBal(a)$. The value of $maxBal(a)$ is initially 0 and is never decreased. The algorithm can increase $maxBal(a)$ at any time.

It may seem strange that the state does not contain any information about what processes have failed. We are assuming that a failed process does nothing. Since we are describing only safety, a process is never required to do anything, so there is no need to tell it to do nothing. A failed process that has been repaired can differ from a process that hasn't failed because it may have forgotten its prior state when it resumes running. A useful property of a consensus algorithm is that, even if all processes fail, the algorithm can resume its normal operation when enough processes are repaired. To achieve this, we require that a process maintains its state in stable storage, so it is restored when a failed process restarts. A process failing and restarting is then no different from a process simply pausing.

The heart of the Voting algorithm is a state expression $SafeAt(b, v)$ that is true iff $ChosenAt(c, w)$ is false and will remain false forever for any $c < b$ and $w \neq v$. That it will remain false forever can be deduced from the current state, because the next-state action implies both that a process a will not cast a vote in ballot c when $c < maxBal(a)$ and that $maxBal(a)$ can never decrease. The key invariant maintained by the algorithm is

(6.7) $\quad \forall\, a \in Acceptor, b \in \mathbb{N}, v \in Value :$
$\qquad (\langle b, v \rangle \in votes(a)) \;\Rightarrow\; SafeAt(b, v)$

where $Acceptor$ is the set of acceptors. The next-state action allows a process a to perform either of two actions:

- Increase $maxBal(a)$. This action is always enabled.

- Vote for a value v in a ballot numbered b. As already explained, this action is enabled only if no process has voted for a value other than v in ballot b and $b \geq maxBal(a)$. An additional enabling condition is required to maintain the invariance of (6.7).

I have given you all the information you need to figure out the definition of $SafeAt(b, v)$ and the enabling condition on acceptors needed to maintain the invariance of (6.7). Can you do it? Few people can. I was able to only because I had simplified the problem to finding an abstract program whose only processes are the acceptors and whose state consists only of the set of votes cast and the value of $maxBal$. I had abstracted away leaders, messages, and failures.

The Voting algorithm requires an acceptor to know the current state of other acceptors to decide what vote it can cast. How can this lead to a distributed consensus algorithm? I abstracted away leaders and messages; I didn't ignore them. I knew that an acceptor didn't have to directly observe the state of other acceptors to know that they hadn't voted for some value other than v in a ballot. The acceptor could know that because of a message it received from a leader. I also knew that it could deduce that the other enabling conditions were satisfied from messages it received. Abstracting away leaders and messages enabled me to concentrate on the core problem of achieving consensus. The solution to that problem told me what the leaders should do and what messages needed to be sent.

6.3.2.3 The Paxos Abstract Program

The Voting algorithm told me what messages needed to be sent. But I had to decide how to represent message passing in an abstract program. Languages expressly designed for describing distributed algorithms usually don't require us to make that decision because they provide built-in message-passing primitives. However, different distributed algorithms and distributed systems have different requirements for message passing. They may or may not tolerate lost messages; they may or may not require messages to be delivered in the order they are sent; they may or may not require that the same message not be received twice; and so on. Our abstract programs require that we choose how to represent message passing, but they make it easy to represent any form of message passing we want.

I have found that most computer scientists and engineers are constrained by thinking in terms of how messages are transmitted in actual systems. They think of messages being sent on communication channels between processes. Few of them would come up with the simple representation of message passing I used in the Paxos abstract program—a representation that is obvious if one thinks mathematically.

Paxos doesn't require that messages be delivered in the order in which they are sent, so there is no need for message channels. The receiver of

6.3. AN EXAMPLE: THE PAXOS ALGORITHM

a message can be inferred from the message, so we can just have a set of messages. Paxos tolerates the same message being received multiple times by a process, so there is no need to remove a message when it is received. This means that if the same message is sent to multiple recipients, there is no need for multiple copies of the message. There is also no need for a separate action of receiving a message. An action that should be taken upon receipt of a message simply has the existence of that message in the set of sent messages as an enabling condition. Paxos tolerates message loss. But since we are describing safety, there's no difference between a lost message and a message that is sent but never received. So, there is no need ever to remove messages that have been sent.

We can therefore represent message passing with a variable *msgs* whose value is the set of all messages that have been sent. A message is sent by adding it to the set *msgs*. The presence of a message in *msgs* enables an action that should be triggered by the receipt of the message. The algorithm has a variable *maxBal* that implements the variable of the same name in the Voting algorithm. It also has two other variables *maxVBal* and *maxVal* whose values are functions with domain the set of acceptors. They are explained below.

The Paxos consensus algorithm can be viewed as a multiprocess algorithm containing two sets of processes: the acceptors that implement the acceptors of the Voting algorithm, and an infinite set of processes, one for each natural number, where process number b is the leader of ballot number b. More precisely, the ballot b leader orchestrates the voting by the acceptors in ballot b of the Voting algorithm.

The next-state action of the algorithm could be (but isn't literally) written in the form $\exists\, b \in \mathbb{N} : BA(b)$ where $BA(b)$ describes how ballot b is performed. The ballot consists of two phases. In phase 1, the ballot b leader sends a message to the acceptors containing only the ballot number b. An acceptor a ignores the message unless $b > maxBal(a)$, in which case it sets $maxBal(a)$ to b and replies with a message containing a, b, $maxVBal(a)$, and $maxVal(a)$. When the ballot b leader receives those messages from a majority of the acceptors, it can pick a value v to be chosen, where v is either a value picked by the leader of a lower-numbered ballot or an arbitrary value. The complete algorithm describes how it picks v. Phase 2 begins with the leader sending a message to the acceptors asking them to vote for v in ballot b. An acceptor a ignores the message unless $b \geq maxBal(a)$, in which case a sets $maxBal(a)$ to b and replies with a message saying that it has voted for v in ballot b.

The Paxos algorithm implements the Voting algorithm under a refinement mapping in which the variable *votes* of Voting is implemented by the expression defined in the obvious way from the set of votes reported by acceptors' phase 2 messages in *msgs*, and in which the variable *maxBal* of Voting is implemented by the variable of the same name in the Paxos abstract program.

The values of *maxVBal* and *maxVal* can be described as functions of the value of *votes*. For any acceptor a, the pair $\langle maxVBal(a), maxVal(a)\rangle$ equals the pair $\langle b, v\rangle$ in the set *votes*(a) with the largest value of b. (Initially, when *votes*(a) is the empty set, it equals $\langle -1, None\rangle$ for some special value *None*.) Making *maxVBal* and *maxVal* variables rather than state expressions makes it clear that they are the only information about what messages have been sent that needs to be part of the acceptors' states.

6.3.3 Implementing Paxos

An implementation of the Paxos consensus algorithm would add a third phase to each ballot in which the leader sends a message announcing that a value v had been chosen after it receives phase 2 messages telling it that a majority of acceptors had voted for v in the ballot. With that addition, a ballot of the Paxos algorithm looks like what the naive algorithm does when a new leader has been selected. Phase 1 of a Paxos ballot corresponds to the new leader finding out if it needs to complete the choosing of a value proposed by the failed leader. Phase 2 corresponds to the leader completing the choosing of a previously proposed value or choosing a new value.

In Paxos, a leader performs phase 1 in every instance of the consensus algorithm, while in the naive algorithm it performs the corresponding actions only once when it is selected. This makes Paxos seem much less efficient, since leaders are infrequently replaced. However, the value to be chosen isn't selected until phase 2. This means that phase 1 can be executed simultaneously for a ballot numbered b in all instances of the consensus algorithm the first time ballot b is executed for any instance. A single message can serve as the leader's phase 1 message for all instances. A single message can also contain the phase 1 responses of a particular acceptor for all the instances, since there is only information to be transmitted for consensus instances that have begun but not yet chosen a value. Thus Paxos uses the same number of messages to choose a value as the naive algorithm.

The Paxos consensus algorithm is an efficient algorithm that has been proved to satisfy the safety requirement of consensus. We still have to see how to get it to satisfy the liveness requirement of actually choosing a value. To solve a problem, we need to understand it, and it's easy to understand

6.4. PROVING REFINEMENT

what prevents Paxos from choosing a value. An acceptor a participating in ballot number b sets $maxBal(a)$ to b, preventing it from responding to any message from the leader of any ballot numbered less than b. Even in the absence of failures or message loss, no value will ever be chosen if higher and higher numbered ballots are begun before any ballot chooses a value.

Conversely, if ballot number b is started and no higher-numbered ballot is begun, and if the ballot b leader and a majority of acceptors are working, then liveness assumptions that require working processes eventually to perform enabled actions (which implicitly assume that messages sent are eventually delivered) imply that a value is eventually chosen. This observation can be stated mathematically as a temporal logic formula and proved. However, it is so obviously true that, to my knowledge, no one has ever bothered doing it.

How do we assure that a ballot numbered b is started and no higher-numbered ballots are? Paxos uses an infinite number of leader processes—one for each ballot number. Those infinitely many processes are executed by a finite number of computers, with each ballot number pre-assigned to a single computer that executes the leader of the corresponding ballot. A single computer, called the coordinator, is selected to be the only one that executes leader processes, and it is easy to add messages that allow it to find a ballot number higher than the values of $mbal(a)$ for a majority of acceptors a.

Like the naive algorithm, Paxos depends on selecting a single coordinator. However, the naive algorithm can fail to maintain its safety requirement if two different computers believe they are the coordinator. If that happens with Paxos, safety is preserved; the algorithm just fails to make progress. An algorithm for choosing a coordinator in Paxos needs to work only most of the time, a much easier problem to solve. One solution uses a synchronous algorithm that implements consensus assuming known bounds on the times needed to transmit and process messages. That algorithm chooses the coordinator assuming values for those bounds that will be satisfied most of the time.

6.4 Proving Refinement

This section sketches how to prove that one abstract program refines another. We use as an example the proof that the One-Bit mutual exclusion algorithm OB of Figure 4.3 in Section 4.2.5.2 refines program LM of Figure 4.6 in Section 4.2.6.1, assuming a weakly fair semaphore.

The proof uses identifiers from the definition of OB and ones from the definition of LM. To avoid confusion, we indicate to which program an identifier belongs with a subscript. We defined OB to equal:

$Init \land \Box[Next]_v \land Fair$
where $Next \triangleq \exists p \in \{0,1\} : PNext(p)$
$Fair \triangleq \forall p \in \{0,1\} : \text{WF}_v(PNext(p))$

We now add subscripts to that definition, so OB equals:

$Init_{OB} \land \Box[Next_{OB}]_{v_{OB}} \land Fair_{OB}$

We assume LM has the same definition, except with the subscripts LM. We sometimes use subscripts even when they aren't necessary—for example writing x_{OB} even though LM has no variable named x.

We define *OBSafe* and *OBFair* as in Section 4.2.5.2, so OB equals *OBSafe* $\land$ *OBFair*. We define *LMSafe* and *LMFair* similarly. As expected, safety and liveness are proved separately. We first show that *OBSafe* refines *LMSafe*. (By machine closure of ⟨*OBSafe*, *OBFair*⟩ and Theorems 4.3 and 4.5, *OBFair* isn't needed to prove that OB refines *LMSafe*.) We then show that OB implies *LMFair*. However, first we must define the refinement mapping under which OB implements LM.

Math VIII

Hierarchical Proofs Thus far, our structured proofs have consisted of a single list of steps. That doesn't work for the long proofs needed to prove complex results, such as correctness of the abstract programs that engineers write. The method of handling complexity that's obvious to an engineer is hierarchical structuring. With structured proofs, a proof consists of either a paragraph proof or a sequence of steps, each step having a proof. The last step in a proof that consists of a sequence of steps is a Q.E.D. step.

The steps of a top-level proof are numbered 1, 2, etc. The steps of a proof of step number 2 are numbered 2.1, 2.2, ... The steps of a proof of step number 3.4 are 3.4.1, 3.4.2, ... and so on. The lowest-level proofs are paragraph proofs. A step can be used only in the proof of later steps of the same proof. For example, the assertion proved as step 3.4.2 can be used in the proofs of steps 3.4.4 and 3.4.5.1, but not in the proof of step 3.5. This ensures that a step is used only where the assumptions under which the step was proved still hold.

This numbering scheme works for three or four levels. For deeper proofs, we can abbreviate step number 2.7.4 as ⟨3⟩4 because it's step number 4 of

6.4. PROVING REFINEMENT

a depth-3 proof. Although many step numbers can have the same abbreviation, at most one of those steps can be used at any point in the proof [38].

For reliable proofs, the paragraph proofs should be short enough so they're easy to understand and obviously correct. If a paragraph proof isn't obviously correct, it should be decomposed into a sequence of steps. Some steps need deeper proofs than others. The proofs of Q.E.D. steps should usually be paragraphs. My rule of thumb is to decompose a proof until I'm sure that every paragraph proof is correct, then decompose the paragraph proofs one level further. The proofs in this book haven't been carried down to that level. This was to keep the book from being too long, and because no program will crash if there's a small mistake in one of the book's theorems.

For machine-checked proofs, paragraph proofs are replaced by instructions to the prover. The proof must be decomposed into steps that are simple enough for the prover to check, which may sometimes be infuriatingly simple. This should eventually change as machine learning is applied to proof checking. Some proof checkers don't support hierarchical structuring. They require you to do the structuring by hand. If you don't structure the proof, you will wind up with an unmanageable unstructured mass of lemmas when trying to prove the correctness of a complex abstract program.

SUFFICES **Proof Steps** A mathematical proof of a formula G often begins by showing that, to prove G, it suffices to prove F. That step in a proof is represented in our structured proof style by a SUFFICES step.

At any step in a proof, there is a current goal. The current goal at the first step is the assertion to be proved. The statement SUFFICES: F changes the current goal to F. If G is the current goal at this SUFFICES statement, then the statement's proof must prove ASSUME: F PROVE: G. That is, the proof must prove G assuming that F is true.

The SUFFICES statement can be used with an ASSUME/PROVE to assert that to prove the current goal, it suffices to assume E is true and prove F is true. The statement

SUFFICES: ASSUME: E
PROVE: F

changes the current goal to F, and it adds E to the set of formulas that can be assumed true by the following steps of the current proof. The proof of this statement is the same as the proof of SUFFICES: $E \Rightarrow F$.

6.4.1 The Refinement Mapping

To define the refinement mapping under which OB implements LM, it's helpful to think of a single behavior in which the variables x_{OB} and pc_{OB} describe a behavior of program OB and the variables sem_{LM} and pc_{LM} describe the corresponding behavior of LM that is implemented by OB under the refinement mapping. To determine what the refinement mapping should be, for each possible step in such a behavior that changes the values of the variables of LM, we decide how that step should change the values of OB.

For example, if a step of the behavior describes the execution of statement cs by a process p of LM, then it should describe the execution of cs by process p of OB. Thus, when the value of $pc_{LM}(p)$ changes from cs to $exit$, the value of $pc_{OB}(p)$ should also change from cs to $exit$. Reasoning in this way, we see that the values of $pc_{LM}(p)$ and $pc_{OB}(p)$ should be equal, except that when $pc_{LM}(p)$ equals $wait$, the value of $pc_{OB}(p)$ can be $wait$, $w2$, $w3$, or $w4$. This tells us that the refinement mapping must substitute for pc_{LM} the value $pcBar_{OB}$ defined by:

$$pcBar_{OB} \triangleq p \in \{0,1\} \mapsto \text{IF } pc_{OB}(p) \in \{w2, w3, w4\} \text{ THEN } wait \\ \text{ELSE } pc_{OB}(p)$$

In a behavior satisfying LM, the value of sem_{LM} can be deduced from the value of pc_{LM}. In particular, sem_{LM} equals 0 iff $pc_{LM}(p)$ equals cs or $exit$ for one of the processes p. From the definition of $pcBar_{OB}$, this means that the refinement mapping must substitute for sem_{LM} the value $semBar_{OB}$ defined by:

$$semBar_{OB} \triangleq \text{IF } (\exists p \in \{0,1\} : pc_{OB}(p) \in \{cs, exit\}) \text{ THEN } 0 \text{ ELSE } 1$$

That OB refines LM under this refinement mapping means:

(6.8) $\models OB \Rightarrow (LM \text{ WITH } pc_{LM} \leftarrow pcBar_{OB}, sem_{LM} \leftarrow semBar_{OB})$

We'll be using a lot of formulas that are obtained from formulas F_{LM} by making the substitutions defined by the refinement mapping for the variables of LM. To keep from having lots of WITHs, we use this abbreviation, for any formula F_{LM}:

$$\overline{F_{LM}} \triangleq (F_{LM} \text{ WITH } pc_{LM} \leftarrow pcBar_{OB}, sem_{LM} \leftarrow semBar_{OB})$$

Thus, (6.8) can be written $\models OB \Rightarrow \overline{LM}$. Also, $\overline{pc_{LM}}$ equals $pcBar_{OB}$ and $\overline{sem_{LM}}$ equals $semBar_{OB}$ (which explains the suffix Bar in the names $pcBar$ and $semBar$).

6.4. PROVING REFINEMENT

6.4.2 Refinement of Safety

We now sketch the proof that $OBSafe$ refines $LMSafe$, which means the proof of

(6.9) $\models OBSafe \Rightarrow \overline{LMSafe}$

By the definitions of these formulas, this requires proving:

(6.10) (a) $\models Init_{OB} \Rightarrow \overline{Init_{LM}}$
(b) $\models Init_{OB} \wedge \Box[Next_{OB}]_{v_{OB}} \Rightarrow \Box\overline{[Next_{LM}]_{v_{LM}}}$

The proof of (a) is simple. To prove (b), we use the invariant Inv_{OB} of OB, which is defined by (4.19), where $TypeOK$ is defined by (4.17). That is, we assume:

(6.11) $\models OBSafe \Rightarrow \Box Inv_{OB}$

To prove (6.10b), it suffices to prove

(6.12) $\models Inv_{OB} \wedge [Next_{OB}]_{v_{OB}} \Rightarrow \overline{[Next_{LM}]_{v_{LM}}}$

By definition of $[\ldots]_v$, we can prove (6.12) by proving:

(6.13) (a) $\models Inv_{OB} \wedge Next_{OB} \Rightarrow \overline{Next_{LM}} \vee (\overline{v_{LM}}' = \overline{v_{LM}})$
(b) $\models (v_{OB}' = v_{OB}) \Rightarrow (\overline{v_{LM}}' = \overline{v_{LM}})$

Part (b) is trivial, since $\overline{v_{LM}}$ is defined in terms of the variables of v_{OB}. For part (a), propositional logic tells us that we prove $F \wedge (G_1 \vee \ldots \vee G_n) \Rightarrow H$ by proving $F \wedge G_i \Rightarrow H$ for each i. So, we decompose the proof of part (a) by writing $Next_{OB}$ as the disjunction of subactions.

We use the notation introduced in Section 4.2.6.1 of naming the action described by a labeled statement with the capitalized label. For example, $Cs_{OB}(p)$ is the action described by statement cs of process p of program OB. We decompose the proof of (6.13a) into proving:

(6.14) $\models Inv_{OB} \wedge Lbl_{OB}(p) \Rightarrow \overline{Next_{LM}} \vee (\overline{v_{LM}}' = \overline{v_{LM}})$

for each label lbl in Figure 4.3 and p in $\{0, 1\}$.

Condition (6.14) asserts that a step of OB described by the statement labeled lbl implements a step of LM under the refinement mapping. We defined the refinement mapping to make that true, so we should be able to prove this assertion. We prove it by showing that each action $Lbl_{OB}(p)$ implements some particular subaction of $Next_{LM}$. In particular, we prove the following seven assertions R1–R7. Three of them assert that actions of OB

imply actions of the form $\overline{\langle A_{LM}\rangle_{v_{LM}}}$. For proving that OB implies $\overline{LMSafe}$, we need only the weaker assertions obtained by replacing such an action by $\overline{A_{LM}}$. However, we will need the stronger assertions later for proving that OB implies $\overline{LMLive}$.

R1. $\models Inv_{OB} \land Ncs_{OB}(p) \Rightarrow \overline{Ncs_{LM}(p)}$

R2. $\models Inv_{OB} \land Wait_{OB}(p) \Rightarrow \overline{(v_{LM}' = v_{LM})}$

R3. $\models Inv_{OB} \land W2_{OB}(p) \Rightarrow$
$\qquad$ IF $p = 0$ THEN $\overline{\langle Wait_{LM}(0)\rangle_{v_{LM}}}$
$\qquad\qquad$ ELSE IF $x_{OB}(0)$ THEN $\overline{v_{LM}' = v_{LM}}$
$\qquad\qquad\qquad$ ELSE $\overline{\langle Wait_{LM}(1)\rangle_{v_{LM}}}$

R4. $\models Inv_{OB} \land W3_{OB}(p) \Rightarrow \overline{(v_{LM}' = v_{LM})}$

R5. $\models Inv_{OB} \land W4_{OB}(p) \Rightarrow \overline{(v_{LM}' = v_{LM})}$

R6. $\models Inv_{OB} \land Cs_{OB}(p) \Rightarrow \overline{\langle Cs_{LM}(p)\rangle_{v_{LM}}}$

R7. $\models Inv_{OB} \land Exit_{OB}(p) \Rightarrow \overline{\langle Exit_{LM}(p)\rangle_{v_{LM}}}$

Assertion R3 is equivalent to these three assertions:

R3a. $\models Inv_{OB} \land W2_{OB}(0) \Rightarrow \overline{\langle Wait_{LM}(0)\rangle_{v_{LM}}}$

R3b. $\models Inv_{OB} \land W2_{OB}(1) \land x_{OB}(0) \Rightarrow \overline{(v_{LM}' = v_{LM})}$

R3c. $\models Inv_{OB} \land W2_{OB}(1) \land \neg x_{OB}(0) \Rightarrow \overline{\langle Wait_{LM}(1)\rangle_{v_{LM}}}$

All these assertions are proved by expanding the definitions of the actions and of the refinement mapping. To see how this works, we consider R3a. We haven't written the definitions of the actions corresponding to the pseudocode statements of algorithms OB and LM. The definitions of $W2_{OB}(0)$ and $Wait_{LM}(0)$ as well as the other relevant definitions are in Figure 6.2. Here is the proof of R3a.

1. SUFFICES: ASSUME: $Inv_{OB} \land W2_{OB}(0)$
$\qquad\qquad$ PROVE: $\overline{\langle Wait_{LM}(0)\rangle_{v_{LM}}}$

   PROOF: Obvious.

2. $(\overline{pc_{LM}}(0) = wait) \land (\overline{pc_{LM}}' = (\overline{pc_{LM}} \text{ EXCEPT } 0 \mapsto cs))$

   PROOF: By the step 1 assumption and the definitions of $W2_{OB}(0)$ and $pcBar_{OB}(0)$, since $\overline{pc_{LM}}$ equals $pcBar_{OB}$.

3. $(\overline{sem_{LM}} = 1) \land (\overline{sem_{LM}}' = 0)$

   PROOF: $W2_{OB}(0)$ implies $(pc_{OB}(0) = w2) \land \neg x_{OB}(1)$, and Inv_{OB} and $\neg x_{OB}(1)$ imply $pc_{OB}(1) \notin \{cs, exit\}$. Hence, $semBar_{OB} = 1$, so $\overline{sem_{LM}} = 1$. The

6.4. PROVING REFINEMENT

$$W2_{OB}(0) \equiv$$
$$\land \; pc_{OB}(0) = w2$$
$$\land \; \neg x_{OB}(1)$$
$$\land \; pc_{OB}' = (pc_{OB} \text{ EXCEPT } 0 \mapsto cs)$$
$$\land \; x_{OB}' = x_{OB}$$

$$Wait_{LM}(0) \equiv$$
$$\land \; pc_{LM}(0) = wait$$
$$\land \; sem_{LM} = 1$$
$$\land \; pc_{LM}' = (pc_{LM} \text{ EXCEPT } 0 \mapsto cs)$$
$$\land \; sem_{LM}' = 0$$

$$Inv_{OB} \triangleq \land \; TypeOK_{OB}$$
$$\land \; \forall p \in \{0,1\} : \land \; (pc_{OB}(p) \in \{w2, cs\}) \Rightarrow x_{OB}(p)$$
$$\land \; (pc_{OB}(p) = cs) \Rightarrow (pc_{OB}(1-p) \neq cs)$$

$$TypeOK_{OB} \triangleq \land \; x_{OB} \in (\{0,1\} \to \{\text{TRUE}, \text{FALSE}\})$$
$$\land \; pc_{OB} \in (\{0,1\} \to \{ncs, wait, w2, w3, w4, cs, exit\})$$
$$\land \; pc_{OB}(0) \notin \{w3, w4\}$$

$$pcBar_{OB} \triangleq p \in \{0,1\} \mapsto \text{IF } pc_{OB}(p) \in \{w2, w3, w4\} \text{ THEN } wait$$
$$\text{ELSE } pc_{OB}(p)$$

$$semBar_{OB} \triangleq \text{IF } \exists p \in \{0,1\} : pc_{OB}(p) \in \{cs, exit\} \text{ THEN } 0 \text{ ELSE } 1$$

$$\overline{pc_{LM}} = pcBar_{OB} \qquad \overline{sem_{LM}} = semBar_{OB}$$

Figure 6.2: Definitions used in the proofs.

definition of $W2_{OB}(0)$ and Inv_{OB} (which implies pc_{OB} is a function with domain $\{0,1\}$) imply $pc_{OB}'(0) = cs$. Hence $semBar_{OB}' = 0$, so $\overline{sem_{LM}}' = 0$.

4. Q.E.D.
   PROOF: Steps 2 and 3 and the definition of $Wait_{LM}(0)$ imply $\overline{Wait_{LM}}(0)$. Step 3 implies $\overline{sem_{LM}}' \neq \overline{sem_{LM}}$ which implies $\overline{v}_{LM}' \neq \overline{v}_{LM}$, proving the goal $\langle \overline{Wait_{LM}}(0) \rangle_{\overline{v}_{LM}}$ introduced by step 1.

How we decomposed the proof that $OBSafe$ implies $\overline{LMSafe}$ into proving R1–R7 was determined by the structure of $Next_{OB}$ as a disjunction of seven subactions and knowing which disjuncts of $\overline{Next_{LM}}$ each of those subactions implements, which followed directly from the definition of the refinement mapping. The decomposition of R3 into R3a–R3c followed from the structure of R3. As illustrated by the proof of R3a, the proof of each of the resulting nine formulas is reduced to ordinary mathematical reasoning by expanding the appropriate definitions. The only place where not understanding the algorithms could result in an error is in the definition of the invariant Inv_{OB} or of the refinement mapping. Catching such an error requires only careful reasoning about simple set theory and a tiny bit of arithmetic, using elementary logic. Someday, computers should be very good at such reasoning.

6.4.3 Refinement of Fairness

This section shows how to prove that a program refines the fairness property of another program by sketching the proof of one example: OB implies $\overline{LMFair}$. Define

$$OBB \triangleq \Box(Inv_{OB} \wedge \overline{Inv_{LM}}) \wedge \Box[Next_{OB}]_{v_{OB}} \wedge OBFair$$

where Inv_{OB} is the invariant satisfied by OB defined by (4.19) and (4.17), and Inv_{LM} is an invariant of LM. For our example, we just require that Inv_{LM} implies type correctness of LM. Formula OBB is a $\Box$ formula that is implied by OB. (We have proved that OB implies $\overline{LMSafe}$, which implies that $\overline{Inv_{LM}}$ is an invariant of OB.) We now prove $\models OBB \Rightarrow \overline{LMFair}$.

We use Theorem 4.8 to write $LMFair$ as the conjunction of weak fairness of $Wait_{LM}(p)$, $CS_{LM}(p)$, and $Exit_{LM}(p)$, for $p \in \{0,1\}$. So, we have to prove $\models OBB \Rightarrow \overline{WF_{v_{LM}}(A_{LM})}$ for A_{LM} equal to each of those six actions. By (4.12), we can do this by proving:

$$(6.15) \quad \models OBB \Rightarrow (\Box\overline{\mathbb{E}\langle A_{LM}\rangle_{v_{LM}}} \rightsquigarrow \overline{\langle A_{LM}\rangle_{v_{LM}}})$$

We prove (6.15) by finding an action B_{OB} and state predicates P_{OB} and Q_{OB} satisfying the following conditions:

A1. 1. $\models Inv_{OB} \wedge \overline{Inv_{LM}} \wedge \overline{\mathbb{E}\langle A_{LM}\rangle_{v_{LM}}} \Rightarrow Q_{OB}$
    2. $\models OBB \Rightarrow (\Box Q_{OB} \rightsquigarrow \Box P_{OB})$

A2. 1. $\models Inv_{OB} \wedge \overline{Inv_{LM}} \wedge P_{OB} \Rightarrow \mathbb{E}\langle B_{OB}\rangle_{v_{OB}}$
    2. $\models OBB \Rightarrow WF_{v_{OB}}(B_{OB})$

A3. $\models Inv_{OB} \wedge \overline{Inv_{LM}} \wedge P_{OB} \wedge \langle B_{OB}\rangle_{v_{OB}} \Rightarrow \overline{\langle A_{LM}\rangle_{v_{LM}}}$

To show that these conditions imply (6.15), we have to show that they imply that in any behavior σ satisfying OBB, if $\Box\overline{\mathbb{E}\langle A_{LM}\rangle_{v_{LM}}}$ is true of σ^{+m}, then $\sigma(n) \to \sigma(n+1)$ is an $\overline{\langle A_{LM}\rangle_{v_{LM}}}$ step for some $n \geq m$. Condition A1.1 implies $\Box Q_{OB}$ is true of σ^{+m}, which by A1.2 implies $\Box P_{OB}$ is true of σ^{+q} for some $q \geq m$. By the definition of WF, conditions A2 imply $\sigma(n) \to \sigma(n+1)$ is a $\langle B_{OB}\rangle_{v_{OB}}$ step for some $n \geq q$, and A3 implies that a $\langle B_{OB}\rangle_{v_{OB}}$ step is an $\overline{\langle A_{LM}\rangle_{v_{LM}}}$ step.

6.4. PROVING REFINEMENT

A_{LM}	Q_{OB}	B_{OB}	P_{OB}
$Wait_{LM}(0)$	$\wedge\ pc_{OB}(0) \in \{wait, w2\}$ $\wedge\ pc_{OB}(1) \notin \{cs, exit\}$	$W2_{OB}(0)$	$\wedge\ pc_{OB}(0) = w2$ $\wedge\ \neg x(1)$
$Wait_{LM}(1)$	$\wedge\ pc_{OB}(1) \in$ $\{wait, w2, w3, w4\}$ $\wedge\ pc_{OB}(0) \notin \{cs, exit\}$	$W2_{OB}(1)$	$\wedge\ pc_{OB}(1) = w2$ $\wedge\ \neg x(0)$
$CS_{LM}(p)$	$pc_{OB}(p) = cs$	$CS_{OB}(p)$	$pc_{OB}(p) = cs$
$Exit_{LM}(p)$	$pc_{OB}(p) = exit$	$Exit_{OB}(p)$	$pc_{OB}(p) = exit$

Figure 6.3: Formulas B_{OB}, P_{OB}, and Q_{OB} for the actions A_{LM}, with $p \in \{0, 1\}$.

The formulas B_{OB}, P_{OB}, and Q_{OB} used for the six actions A_{LM} are shown in Figure 6.3. Condition A2.1 for the actions A_{LM} follows easily from the definitions of B_{OB} and P_{OB}. To show that A2.2 is satisfied, we apply Theorem 4.8 to write $OBFair$ as the conjunction of weak fairness of the actions described by each process's statements other than its ncs statement. That A3 is satisfied for the four actions A_{LM} in Figure 6.3 follows from conditions R3a, R3c, R6, and R7 of Section 6.4.2.

This leaves condition A1 for the actions. A1.1 is proved by using the type correctness invariant implied by Inv_{LM} to show that $\mathbb{E}\langle A_{LM}\rangle v_{LM}$ equals $\mathbb{E}(A_{LM})$, and then substituting $pcBar_{OB}$ for pc_{LM} and $semBar_{OB}$ for sem_{LM} in $\mathbb{E}(A_{LM})$. For our example, this actually shows that $\overline{Inv_{LM}}$ implies $\overline{\mathbb{E}\langle A_{LM}\rangle v_{LM}} \equiv Q_{OB}$ for all the actions A_{LM}. A1.2 is trivially satisfied for $CS_{LM}(p)$ and $Exit_{LM}(p)$, since Q_{OB} and P_{OB} are equal. The interesting conditions are A1.2 for $Wait_{LM}(0)$ and $Wait_{LM}(1)$. They are the kind of leads-to property we saw how to prove in Section 4.2.5. In fact, we now obtain a proof of A1.2 for $Wait_{LM}(0)$ by a simple modification of the proof in Section 4.2.5.3 that OB implies:

$$(6.16) \quad (pc(0) \in \{wait, w2\}) \leadsto (pc(0) = cs)$$

Let's drop the subscript OB, so the variables in any formula whose name has no subscript are the variables of OB. The proof of (6.16) is described by the proof lattice of Figures 4.4 and 4.5. A $\square$ formula in a label on a box in a proof lattice means that the formula is conjoined to each formula inside the box. Since $F \leadsto G$ implies $(\square H \wedge F) \leadsto (\square H \wedge G)$ for any F, G, and H, we obtain a valid proof lattice (one whose leads-to assertions are all true) by conjoining $\square \overline{Inv_{LM}} \wedge OBFair \wedge \square Q$ to the labels of the outer boxes in the lattices of Figures 4.4 and 4.5. This makes those labels equal to $OBB \wedge \Box Q$. Since Q implies $pc(0) \in \{wait, w2\}$, we obtain a valid proof lattice by replacing the source node of the lattice in Figure 4.4 by $\Box Q$. Moreover, since the new label's conjunct $\Box Q$ implies $\Box(pc(0) \neq cs)$, so it's impossible for $pc(0)$ ever to equal cs, we can remove the sink node $pc(0) = cs$ and the edges to and from it from the lattice of Figure 4.5.[2] Since the label on the inner box containing $\Box \neg x(1)$, which is the new sink node, implies $\Box(pc(0) = w2)$, we now have a valid proof lattice that shows:

$$\models OBB \Rightarrow (\Box Q \leadsto \Box((pc(0) = w2) \wedge \neg x(1)))$$

This proves A1.2 for the action $Wait_{LM}(0)$.

To prove A1.2 for action $Wait_{LM}(1)$, it suffices to assume OBB and prove $\Box Q \leadsto \Box P$ for the formulas P and Q given in Figure 6.3 for the action. Here is the proof sketch, which uses without mention some simple temporal logic, including transitivity of $\leadsto$.

1. $\Box Q \Rightarrow \Box \neg x(0)$

    1.1. $\Box Q \Rightarrow \Box(pc(0) \notin \{wait, w2\})$

    PROOF: We proved in Section 4.2.5.3 that $pc(0) \in \{wait, w2\}$ leads to $pc(0) = cs$, and $\Box Q$ implies $\Box(pc(0) \neq cs)$.

    1.2. $\Box Q \wedge \Box(pc(0) \notin \{wait, w2\}) \Rightarrow \Box(pc(0) = ncs)$

    PROOF: Q implies $pc(0) \notin \{cs, exit\}$, which by Inv and $pc(0) \notin \{wait, w2\}$ implies $pc(0) = ncs$.

    1.3. Q.E.D.

    PROOF: By steps 1.1 and 1.2, since $Inv \wedge Q$ imply $pc(0) = ncs$, and Inv and $pc(0) = ncs$ imply $\neg x(0)$.

2. $\Box Q \wedge \Box \neg x(0) \leadsto \Box P$

    2.1. $\Box Q \wedge \Box \neg x(0) \leadsto (pc(1) = w2)$

    PROOF: Q implies $pc(1) \in \{wait, w2, w3, w4\}$, and a straightforward proof using fairness of $PNext(1)$ and $\Box \neg x(0)$ shows

    $$(pc(1) \in \{wait, w2, w3, w4\}) \leadsto (pc(1) = w2)$$

    2.2. $\Box Q \wedge \Box \neg x(0) \wedge (pc(1) = w2) \Rightarrow \Box(pc(1) = w2)$

    PROOF: $\Box Q$ implies $\Box(pc(1) \neq cs)$, and $(pc(1) = w2) \wedge \Box[Next]_v \wedge \Box(pc(1) \neq cs)$ implies $\Box(pc(1) = w2)$.

---

[2]Equivalently, we can remove edge 8 and add an edge from $pc(0) = cs$ to FALSE and an edge from FALSE to $\Box \neg x(1)$, since FALSE implies anything.

6.4. PROVING REFINEMENT

2.3. Q.E.D.

PROOF: Steps 2.1 and 2.2 imply $\Box Q \wedge \Box \neg x(0) \rightsquigarrow \Box(pc(1) = w2)$, and $\Box P$ equals $\Box(pc(1) = w2) \wedge \Box \neg x(0)$.

3. Q.E.D.

PROOF: By steps 1 and 2.

6.4.4 A Closer Look at $\mathbb{E}$

6.4.4.1 A Syntactic View

Section 4.2.1 explained $\mathbb{E}$ semantically, defining $\mathbb{E}(A)$ to be true of a state s iff there exists a state t such that action A is true of the step $s \to t$. We now translate this semantic definition into a syntactic definition of $\mathbb{E}(A)$. A state is an assignment of values to variables, so we can restate that definition as:

E1. $\mathbb{E}(A)$ is true for an assignment of values to the unprimed variables iff there exists an assignment of values to the primed variables that makes A true.

A state predicate is true of a state iff it is true when its variables have the values assigned to them by the state. We can therefore restate E1 as:

E2. $\mathbb{E}(A)$ is true (of a state) iff there exist values of the primed variables for which A is true.

We now translate E2 into a precise syntactic definition of $\mathbb{E}$.

To do this, for any variable x, we regard x and x' as two unrelated symbols. For an expression exp, we take exp' to be the expression obtained by priming all the variables in exp. If exp contains a defined symbol whose definition contains variables, then all the variables in that definition are primed in exp'.

We now define AWITH to be substitution like WITH, except regarding x' as being a different variable from x. For example, if x, y, and z are variables, then:

$(x' = x + 1)$ WITH $x \leftarrow y - z$ equals $(y - z)' = (y - z) + 1$
$(x' = x + 1)$ AWITH $x \leftarrow y - z$ equals $x' = (y - z) + 1$
$(x' = x + 1)$ AWITH $x' \leftarrow y - z$ equals $(y - z) = x + 1$

If sym is a defined symbol, then

$(x' = x + sym)$ AWITH $x' \leftarrow y - z$

equals
$$(y - z) = x + (sym \text{ AWITH } x' \leftarrow y - z)$$
If $sym \triangleq \sqrt{2 * x'}$, then this equals
$$(y - z) = x + \sqrt{2 * (y - z)}$$

Now let A be an action and let $x_1, \ldots, x_n$ be all the variables that appear in A. We can then write E2 as:

(6.17) $\mathbb{E}(A) \triangleq \exists c_1, \ldots, c_n : (A \text{ AWITH } x'_1 \leftarrow c_1, \ldots, x'_n \leftarrow c_n)$

Thus, we obtain $\mathbb{E}(A)$ from A by replacing the primed variables by bound constants that are existentially quantified. We informally describe this definition by saying that $\mathbb{E}(A)$ is obtained from A by existentially quantifying its primed variables.

6.4.4.2 Computing $\mathbb{E}$

The syntactic definition (6.17) of $\mathbb{E}$ immediately provides rules for writing $\mathbb{E}(A)$ in terms of formulas $\mathbb{E}(B_i)$, for B_i subactions of A. From the rule

$$\models (\exists c : A \vee B) \equiv (\exists c : A) \vee (\exists c : B)$$

we have

E1. $\models \mathbb{E}(A \vee B) \equiv \mathbb{E}(A) \vee \mathbb{E}(B)$

For example, in program LM defined in Section 4.2.6.1, the next-state action $PNext(p)$ is the disjunction of actions $Ncs(p)$, $Wait(p)$, $Cs(p)$, and $Exit(p)$. Therefore, rule E1 implies

$$\mathbb{E}(PNext(p)) \equiv \mathbb{E}(Ncs(p)) \vee \mathbb{E}(Wait(p)) \vee \mathbb{E}(Cs(p)) \vee \mathbb{E}(Exit(p))$$

The generalization of E1 is:

E2. $\models \mathbb{E}(\exists i \in S : A_i) \equiv \exists i \in S : \mathbb{E}(A_i)$

where S is a constant or state expression.

Another rule of existential quantification is that if the constant c does not occur in A, then $\exists c : (A \wedge B)$ is equivalent to $A \wedge (\exists c : B)$. From this we deduce:

E3. If no variable appears primed in both A and B, then $\models \mathbb{E}(A \wedge B) \equiv \mathbb{E}(A) \wedge \mathbb{E}(B)$.

6.4. PROVING REFINEMENT

For example, in program LM we have:

$$Wait(p) \triangleq \begin{aligned} &\land (sem = 1) \land (pc(p) = wait) \\ &\land sem' = 0 \\ &\land pc' = (pc \text{ EXCEPT } p \mapsto cs) \end{aligned}$$

Therefore, rule E3 implies

$$(6.18) \quad \mathbb{E}(Wait(p)) \equiv \begin{aligned} &\land \mathbb{E}((sem = 1) \land (pc(p) = wait)) \\ &\land \mathbb{E}(sem' = 0) \\ &\land \mathbb{E}(pc' = (pc \text{ EXCEPT } p \mapsto cs)) \end{aligned}$$

The following two rules also follow easily from (6.17) and properties of existential quantification:

E4. If P is a state predicate, then $\models \mathbb{E}(P) \equiv P$.

E5. If x is a variable and exp is a state expression, then $\models \mathbb{E}(x' = exp) \equiv$ TRUE.

From (6.18), E4, and E5, we deduce that $\mathbb{E}(Wait(p))$ equals $(sem = 1) \land (pc(p) = wait)$. Here is another obvious rule, which can be considered a generalization of E5, since $c = exp$ is equivalent to $c \in \{exp\}$:

E6 If x is a variable and exp is a state expression, then $\models \mathbb{E}(x' \in exp) \equiv (exp \neq \{\})$.

Rules E1–E6 are sufficient for computing $\mathbb{E}(A)$ for almost all subactions A that, like $PNext(p)$, appear in the definition of a program's next-state action. However, the definition of fairness does not contain such formulas $\mathbb{E}(A)$. Instead, it contains formulas of the form $\mathbb{E}\langle A\rangle_v$, which equals $\mathbb{E}(A \land (v' \neq v))$. None of those rules apply to such a formula. In particular, E3 does not apply because v is the tuple of all the program's variables.

Most of the time, a subaction A in the definition of a program's next-state action does not allow stuttering steps. Therefore, $\langle A\rangle_v$ equals A, so $\mathbb{E}\langle A\rangle_v$ equals $\mathbb{E}(A)$ and we can apply the rules. For example, $\mathbb{E}\langle PNext(p)\rangle_v$ equals $\mathbb{E}(PNext(p))$ because a $PNext(p)$ step changes the value of $pc(p)$, so it can't be a stuttering step. We are using the substitutivity rule (3.35) of ordinary math to deduce

$$\models (A \equiv B) \Rightarrow (\mathbb{E}(A) \equiv \mathbb{E}(B))$$

(Even though substitutivity is not valid for TLA or the Logic of Actions, we can apply it to the syntactic definition (6.17) of $\mathbb{E}$, which treats x and x' as two different variables of ordinary math—that is, two different constants.)

However, we can't deduce $PNext(p) \equiv \langle PNext(p) \rangle_v$ from the definition of $PNext(p)$. For example, if $pc(p) = cs$, then the definition of $PNext(p)$ asserts

$$pc' = (pc \text{ EXCEPT } p \mapsto exit)$$

If p is not in the domain of pc, then $pc'(p) = pc(p)$. If pc is not a function, then we have no idea what $pc'(p)$ equals, so it could equal $pc(p)$. Fortunately, we care what $\mathbb{E}\langle PNext(p) \rangle_v$ equals only in reachable states of LM. So, we just have to prove that Inv implies $\mathbb{E}\langle PNext(p) \rangle_v \equiv \mathbb{E}(PNext(p))$ for an invariant Inv of LM that asserts type correctness. To do this, we observe that for any action A and state predicate P, rules E3 and E4 imply $P \wedge \mathbb{E}(A) \equiv \mathbb{E}(P \wedge A)$. So, to prove that Inv implies $\mathbb{E}\langle PNext(p) \rangle_v \equiv \mathbb{E}(PNext(p))$, it suffices to prove

$$\models Inv \Rightarrow (\langle PNext(p) \rangle_v \equiv PNext(p))$$

which is straightforward. In general, we reason about liveness under the assumption that the program's safety property is satisfied, so we can assume $\Box Inv$ is true for an invariant Inv of the program.

Since the formula $\Box[Next]_v$ always allows stuttering steps, there is no need for a next-state action $Next$ to allow them. Usually, it doesn't. However, there is no reason for $Next$ not to allow stuttering steps, and sometimes it's more convenient to write a subaction A that allows them. In that case, we have to use the definition (6.17) to compute $\mathbb{E}\langle A \rangle_v$. However, we apply the definition to $\mathbb{E}(Inv \wedge \langle A \rangle_v)$, which equals $\mathbb{E}\langle Inv \wedge A \rangle_v$, for a program invariant Inv.

6.4.4.3 The Trouble With $\mathbb{E}$

Refinement is based on substitution. Program OB refines LM means:

(6.19) $\models OB \Rightarrow (LM \text{ WITH } pc \leftarrow pcBar, sem \leftarrow semBar)$

We no longer need the subscripts that were added to help us understand which program an identifier refers to. We continue using the abbreviation that, for any formula F:

$$\overline{F} \triangleq (F \text{ WITH } pc \leftarrow pcBar, sem \leftarrow semBar)$$

Almost without thinking, we replaced $\overline{Init \wedge \Box[Next]_v}$ with the equivalent property $\overline{Init} \wedge \Box\overline{[Next]_{\overline{v}}}$. We were actually using these three rules:

- $\overline{F \wedge G} \equiv \overline{F} \wedge \overline{G}$ for any formulas F and G.

6.4. PROVING REFINEMENT

- $\overline{\Box F} \equiv \Box \overline{F}$ for any formula F.

- $\overline{[A]_v} \equiv [\overline{A}]_{\overline{v}}$ for any action A and state expression v.

The first asserts that substitution *distributes over* $\vee$; the second asserts that substitution distributes over $\Box$; and the third asserts that substitution distributes over the construct $[\ldots]_{\ldots}$.

We expect substitution to distribute in this way over all mathematical operators, so we would expect $\overline{\mathbb{E}(A)}$ and $\mathbb{E}(\overline{A})$ to be equal for any action A. In fact, they are equal for most actions encountered in practice. But here's an action A for which they aren't for the refinement mapping of (6.19):

$$A \triangleq \wedge pc' = (p \in \{0, 1\} \mapsto wait)$$
$$ \wedge sem' = 0$$

Rules $\mathbb{E}3$ and $\mathbb{E}5$ imply that $\mathbb{E}(A)$ equals TRUE, so $\overline{\mathbb{E}(A)}$ equals TRUE. By definition of the refinement mapping:

$$\overline{A} \triangleq \wedge pcBar' = (p \in \{0, 1\} \mapsto wait)$$
$$\phantom{\overline{A} \triangleq } \wedge semBar' = 0$$

$\overline{A}$ implies $pcBar'(p) = wait$ for $p \in \{0, 1\}$. By definition of $pcBar$, this implies:

(1) $pc'(p) \in \{w2, w3, w4, wait\}$ for p equal to 0 or 1.

But $\overline{A}$ also implies $semBar' = 0$, which by the definition of $semBar$ implies:

(2) $pc'(p) \in \{cs, exit\}$ for p equal to 0 or 1.

Both (1) and (2) can't be true, so $\overline{A}$ must equal FALSE and thus $\mathbb{E}(\overline{A})$ equals FALSE. Therefore, $\overline{\mathbb{E}(A)}$ does not equal $\mathbb{E}(\overline{A})$, so substitution does not always distribute over $\mathbb{E}$.

The reason substitution doesn't distribute over $\mathbb{E}$ is that $\mathbb{E}(\overline{A})$ performs the substitutions $pc \leftarrow pcBar$ and $sem \leftarrow semBar$ for the primed variables pc' and sem'. However, as we see from (6.17), those primed variables do not occur in $\mathbb{E}(A)$; they are replaced by bound constants. The substitutions should be performed only on the unprimed variables. Therefore:

$$\mathbb{E}(A) \text{ WITH } pc \leftarrow \ldots, sem \leftarrow \ldots$$

does not equal

$$\mathbb{E}(A \text{ WITH } pc \leftarrow \ldots, sem \leftarrow \ldots)$$

Instead, it equals

$$\mathbb{E}(A \text{ AWITH } pc \leftarrow \ldots, sem \leftarrow \ldots)$$

which substitutes only for unprimed variables.

Since WF and SF are defined in terms of $\mathbb{E}$, substitution does not distribute over them either. We proved that OB refines LM by proving that OB implies $\overline{\text{WF}_v(A)}$ for six actions A. To evaluate $\overline{\text{WF}_v(A)}$, we expanded the definition of WF. Since substitution distributes over all the operators other than $\mathbb{E}$ in the definition of $\text{WF}_v(PN)$, including in the definition $PN(p)$, we could perform the substitutions everywhere in the resulting formula except in $\overline{\mathbb{E}\langle A\rangle_v}$. We could then have used (6.17) to expand the definition of $\mathbb{E}$ and perform the substitution on the resulting formula, which contains no primed variables. (This is equivalent to performing the substitution in $\mathbb{E}\langle A\rangle_v$, except using AWITH instead of WITH.)

While expanding the definition of $\mathbb{E}$ in this way would have allowed $\overline{\mathbb{E}\langle A\rangle_v}$ to be evaluated, it would have required applying $\mathbb{E}$ to an action that was more complicated than $\langle A\rangle_v$. That's not what we did in the proof sketch in Section 6.4.3. Instead we showed that $\langle A\rangle_v$ equals A and performed the substitution on $\mathbb{E}(A)$. Showing $\langle A\rangle_v \equiv A$ required an invariant Inv of LM, but because OB refines $LMSafe$, the formula $\overline{Inv}$ is an invariant of OB, allowing us to deduce that $\overline{\mathbb{E}\langle A\rangle_v}$ equals $\overline{A}$.

Substitution not distributing over $\mathbb{E}$ makes $\mathbb{E}$ mathematically weird. You should be suspicious of such weird things. The operators □ and ′ (prime) that TLA adds to ordinary math are weird because they are not substitutive. But substitution does distribute over them. Moreover, temporal logic is a well-studied field of math. I find $\mathbb{E}$ weirder than the temporal logic operators.

However, fairness is an important concept in concurrent programs. The WF and SF operators are the mathematical expressions of what fairness has meant since Dijkstra introduced the assumption of weak fairness in 1965 [9]. There seems to be no good way to express it mathematically without the operator $\mathbb{E}$.

A similarly weird operator has been at the heart of traditional programs since the earliest coding languages—namely, the action composition operator "·" introduced in Section 3.4.1.4. If $x_1, \ldots, x_n$ are all the variables that appear in actions A and B, then $A \cdot B$ can be defined syntactically by:

$$A \cdot B \triangleq \exists c_1, \ldots, c_n : \wedge (A \text{ AWITH } x'_1 \leftarrow c_1, \ldots, x'_n \leftarrow c_n)$$
$$\wedge (B \text{ AWITH } x_1 \leftarrow c_1, \ldots, x_n \leftarrow c_n)$$

The primed variables of A and the unprimed variables of B are replaced by bound constants, and substitution does not distribute over "$\cdot$" for the same reason it doesn't distribute over $\mathbb{E}$.

The common methods for reasoning about traditional programs written in an imperative language can be viewed as a form of Hoare logic. As explained in Appendix Section A.5, such a logic can be viewed mathematically as defining the meaning of a statement S to be an action A_S. If the meanings of statements S and T are the actions A_S and A_T, then the meaning of $S;T$ is the action $A_S \cdot A_T$.

With this way of reasoning, the semicolon of imperative coding languages therefore has the same weirdness as the $\mathbb{E}$ operator. I suspect this was never discovered because people thought of programs in terms of conventional code, and it makes no sense to implement a variable x by an expression when x can appear in an assignment statement $x := \ldots$.

6.5 A Warning

We have defined correctness of a program S to mean $\models S \Rightarrow P$ for some property P. We have to be careful to make sure that we have chosen P so that this implies what we really want correctness of the program to mean. As discussed in Section 5.1, we have to be concerned with the accuracy of P.

When correctness asserts that S refines a program T, the property P is T WITH ... for a refinement mapping "...". That refinement mapping is as important a part of the property as the program T, and it must be examined just as carefully to be sure that proving refinement means what you want it to. As an extreme example, OB also implements LM under this refinement mapping:

$$pc_{LM} \leftarrow (p \in \{0,1\} \mapsto ncs),\ sem_{LM} \leftarrow 1$$

Implementation under this refinement mapping tells us nothing about OB, because under it, every behavior of OB implements a behavior in which all processes remain forever in their noncritical sections. The program obtained by replacing the next-state action of OB by FALSE also implements LM under this refinement mapping.

Such an egregiously useless refinement mapping can often be detected because, under a refinement mapping that implements behaviors of a program T by behaviors of program S that do nothing, S won't implement the fairness properties of T. However, programs often don't require that actions representing the initiation of an operation by the environment ever occur. In such a case, it's a good idea to make sure that S refines T when fairness requirements are added to those actions in both programs. This is an application of the general idea of adding fairness to verify possibility that was introduced in Section 5.1.2.

Chapter 7

Auxiliary Variables

An auxiliary variable is a variable that is added to an abstract program without altering the values assumed by the program's regular variables. It's sometimes necessary to add auxiliary variables to a program in order to prove that it refines another program. Sections 7.2, 7.3, and 7.4 define the three kinds of auxiliary variables that may be needed, illustrating them with silly little examples. Section 7.6 describes a realistic example that makes use of all three kinds of auxiliary variables. We begin with a section that explains variable hiding, which is the basis for auxiliary variables and is also used in Chapter 8.

7.1 Variable Hiding

Math IX

Reasoning About $\exists$ Variable hiding in abstract programs is performed with an existential quantifier of temporal logic. That quantifier obeys the same rules as the unbounded quantifier $\exists$ of ordinary math, so we now examine those rules. We are concerned with two rules: the $\exists$ *Introduction* rule used for proving a formula $\exists\, v : F$, and the $\exists$ *Elimination* rule used for proving that $\exists\, v : F$ implies a formula G. Rules for reasoning about the bounded quantifier $\exists\, v \in S$ can be obtained from these rules by replacing F with $(v \in S) \wedge F$ and then replacing $\exists\, v : (v \in S) \wedge F$ with $\exists\, v \in S : F$.

$\exists$ ***Introduction*** To prove $\exists\, v : F$, we have to show that there is a value of v that makes F true. We do this by explicitly describing that value. This is asserted by the following rule, where *exp* is an arbitrary expression:

$$\models (F \text{ WITH } v \leftarrow exp) \Rightarrow (\exists\, v : F)$$

∃ Elimination Suppose $\exists\, v : F$ is true and $F \Rightarrow G$ is true when v has any value. This implies that G is true for the particular value of v that makes F true, so $\exists\, v : G$ is true. Stated precisely, this rule is:

$$\models F \Rightarrow G \quad \text{implies} \quad \models (\exists\, v : F) \Rightarrow (\exists\, v : G)$$

This doesn't look like an ∃ elimination rule because we use $\exists\, v : F$ to prove another existentially quantified formula $\exists\, v : G$, so we haven't eliminated the ∃. It becomes an elimination rule if v is not a free variable of G, because then $\exists\, v : G$ is equivalent to G. The rule is usually stated with $\exists\, v : G$ replaced by G and the side condition that v is not a free variable of G. This syntactic side condition can be replaced by the more general mathematical condition that substituting 0 (or any other fixed value) for v leaves G unchanged. (This condition is satisfied by the formula $v = v$, in which v occurs.) In practice, the syntactic condition is good enough. But the mathematical condition makes it clear that v not occurring free in G means that v does not occur in G after the definitions of all defined symbols that appear in G have been expanded. With this understanding of what it means, the rule used to eliminate the quantifier from $\exists\, x : G$ is:

(7.1) $\quad \models (\exists\, v : G) \equiv G \quad$ if v does not occur free in G

Of course, the same rule holds for the quantifier ∀ as well.

7.1.1 Introduction

Recall the behavior predicate F_{12}, discussed in Section 4.1.2, that is true of a behavior iff the value of x can equal 2 in a state only if x equaled 1 in a previous state. We gave a semantic definition of F_{12}; it can't be expressed in RTLA or TLA as those languages have been defined so far. We observed that F_{12} can be expressed as the abstract program S_{12}, defined in (4.2), by introducing an additional variable y.

The variable x that we're interested in is called an *interface* variable. The variable y that's used only to describe how the values of x can change is called an *internal* variable. There's a problem with using the internal variable y to describe F_{12}. Consider the abstract program S_x that starts with $x = 0$ and can keep incrementing x by one:

$$S_x \triangleq (x = 0) \wedge \Box[x' = x + 1]_x$$

7.1. VARIABLE HIDING

Since S_x allows x to equal 2 only after it has equaled 1, it satisfies property F_{12}. However, S_x doesn't imply S_{12} because S_{12} describes how the values of x and y change, while S_x allows behaviors in which y can have any values.

We want to express F_{12} by a formula that asserts of a behavior σ that there is some way to assign values to y that makes S_{12} true, but says nothing about the actual values of y. As mentioned in Section 4.1.2, that formula is written $\exists\, y : S_{12}$. The operator $\exists$ is explained here.

In ordinary math, the formula $\exists\, y : x * y^2 = 36$ asserts that there is some value y for which $x * y^2$ equals 36, but says nothing about the actual value of y. The variables of ordinary math correspond to the constants of temporal logic. The y in $\exists\, y : S_{12}$ is a constant, so that formula asserts that there is a constant value y that satisfies S_{12}; and that value equals TRUE if the initial value of x is 1, otherwise it equals FALSE. Formula $\exists\, y : S_{12}$ asserts that x can never equal 2 unless the initial value of x is 1, which is not what F_{12} asserts.

The formula $\exists\, y : S_{12}$ is true of a behavior iff the values of x in that behavior are the same as its values in a behavior satisfying S_{12}, where y is a variable rather than a constant; but it says nothing about the actual values assumed by y. Thus, y is a bound variable, not a free variable, of $\exists\, y : S_{12}$. The precise definition of $\exists$ is subtle and is given below. For now, we just need to know that $[\![\exists\, y : S_{12}]\!]$ equals F_{12}. I like to say that $\exists\, y : S_{12}$ is formula S_{12} with y hidden, because $\exists$ does what hiding is supposed to do in coding languages.

We now generalize abstract programs to allow quantification over variables. As with the operator $\exists$, we let $\exists\, y_1, \ldots, y_n : F$ be an abbreviation for $\exists\, y_1 : \ldots \exists\, y_n : F$. The general form of an abstract program with hidden variables is:

(7.2) $\exists\, y_1, \ldots, y_k : Init \wedge \Box[Next]_v \wedge L$

with internal (bound) variables $y_1, \ldots, y_k$. (The interface variables are the free variables of the formula.) Theorem 4.9 shows that any property that can be described mathematically can be written in this form, with a single bound variable. However, $\exists$ is of little use in practice. The only role it plays is telling us that, when implementing the program, it doesn't matter how the internal variables are refined. That can be stated just as well in a comment; we don't need to introduce a new operator just for that. In fact, although $\exists$ is an operator of TLA$^+$ and is recognized by the parser, none of the current tools handle it. Model checking formulas containing $\exists$ seems to be computationally infeasible. I don't know of any engineer wanting to use it.

The reason to understand the temporal existential quantification operator $\exists$ is that it is the logical underpinning of important concepts such as the auxiliary variables discussed in this chapter.

7.1.2 Reasoning About $\exists$

Allowing an abstract program to be described with a formula of the form (7.2) raises the question of how to reason about such formulas. The answer is that the operator $\exists$ obeys the same introduction and elimination rules as the quantifier $\exists$ of ordinary math, except with program variables (now called variables) replacing the mathematical variables (now called constants). In principle, $\exists$ has the same problem of variable capture as $\exists$, but in practice, $\exists$ is used in such a restricted way that variable capture is not an issue.

We want to reason about a formula of the form $\exists\, y_1, \ldots, y_k : F$. Applying the $\exists$ introduction rule k times to $\exists$, we get the following rule, where the exp_i may be any expressions:

$$\models G \Rightarrow (F \text{ WITH } y_1 \leftarrow exp_1, \ldots, y_k \leftarrow exp_k)$$
$$\text{implies } \models G \Rightarrow \exists\, y_1, \ldots, y_k : F$$

Applying the $\exists$ elimination rule k times to $\exists$, we get the rule:

$$\models F \Rightarrow G \text{ implies } \models (\exists\, y_1, \ldots, y_k : F) \Rightarrow G$$
if no variable y_i occurs free in G.

Of course, we can always ensure that no y_i occurs free in G by renaming the internal variables y_i of F.

Combining these two rules, we see that we can prove that one program of the form (7.2) implements another program of that form by proving an assertion of the form

(7.3) $\quad T \Rightarrow (S \text{ WITH } y_1 \leftarrow exp_1, \ldots, y_k \leftarrow exp_k)$

where S and T have the standard form $Init \wedge \Box[Next]_v \wedge L$ of an abstract program, and none of the internal variables of T are interface variables of S. For every interface variable x of S, which in practice must also be an interface variable of T, the WITH clause includes an implicit substitution $x \leftarrow x$ that substitutes the variable x of T for the variable x of S. Thus, the WITH clause describes a refinement mapping under which T refines S.

This raises a question: If $\models T \Rightarrow \exists\, y_1, \ldots, y_k : S$ is true, do there always exist expressions exp_i for which (7.3) is true? The answer is no, if we can use only the variables that appear in T to define the refinement

7.1. VARIABLE HIDING

mapping. If S has the form $\mathit{Init} \wedge \Box[\mathit{Next}]_v \wedge L$, then the answer is yes if we're allowed to add auxiliary variables to T. Adding an auxiliary variable a (which does not occur in T) to T means writing a formula T^a such that $\exists\, a : T^a$ is equivalent to T. By this equivalence, we can verify $\models T \Rightarrow S$ by verifying $\models (\exists\, a : T^a) \Rightarrow S$. By the $\exists$ Elimination rule, we do this by verifying $\models T^a \Rightarrow S$. And to verify this, we can use a as well as the variables of T to define the refinement mapping. Auxiliary variables are the main topic of this chapter and are discussed after the definition of $\exists$.

7.1.3 The Definition of $\exists$

The standard way temporal existential quantification is defined in most temporal logics is not suitable for TLA because it does not preserve stuttering insensitivity (SI), defined in Section 3.5.3. It's the natural way to define it for RTLA, so we will call the operator defined in that way $\exists_{\mathrm{RTLA}}$.

To define $\exists_{\mathrm{RTLA}}$, we first define $s =_y t$ to be true for states s and t iff the values of all variables except y are the same in states s and t. Remembering that $\sigma(i)$ is state number i of a behavior σ, we define the relation $\simeq_y$ on behaviors by:

$$\sigma \simeq_y \tau \;\triangleq\; \forall\, i \in \mathbb{N} : \sigma(i) =_y \tau(i)$$

Therefore, $\sigma \simeq_y \tau$ asserts that behaviors σ and τ are the same except for the values assigned to y by their states. We then define $\exists_{\mathrm{RTLA}}\, y : F$ to be satisfied by a behavior σ iff it is satisfied by some behavior τ with $\sigma \simeq_y \tau$.

The operator $\exists_{\mathrm{RTLA}}$ is not a suitable hiding operator for properties, and hence not suitable for TLA, because the formula $\exists_{\mathrm{RTLA}}\, y : F$ need not be SI, and thus not a property, even if F is. For example, let F be the following formula, where $\lfloor r \rfloor$ is the largest integer less than or equal to r:

(7.4) $\;(x = y = 0) \wedge \Box[(y' = y + 1) \wedge (x' = \lfloor y'/2 \rfloor)]_{\langle x, y \rangle}$

Ignoring the values of other variables, the property F is satisfied by this non-halting behavior with no stuttering steps:

$$\begin{bmatrix} x :: 0 \\ y :: 0 \end{bmatrix}_0 \to \begin{bmatrix} x :: 0 \\ y :: 1 \end{bmatrix}_1 \to \begin{bmatrix} x :: 1 \\ y :: 2 \end{bmatrix}_2 \to \begin{bmatrix} x :: 1 \\ y :: 3 \end{bmatrix}_3 \to \begin{bmatrix} x :: 2 \\ y :: 4 \end{bmatrix}_4 \to \cdots$$

The non-halting behaviors of $\exists_{\mathrm{RTLA}}\, y : F$ consist of this behavior:

(7.5) $\;\begin{bmatrix} x :: 0 \end{bmatrix}_0 \to \begin{bmatrix} x :: 0 \end{bmatrix}_1 \to \begin{bmatrix} x :: 1 \end{bmatrix}_2 \to \begin{bmatrix} x :: 1 \end{bmatrix}_3 \to \begin{bmatrix} x :: 2 \end{bmatrix}_4 \to \cdots$

and behaviors obtained from it by adding stuttering steps. An SI formula containing the one free variable x that allows behavior (7.5) should also allow this behavior:

(7.6) $\quad [x :: 0]_0 \rightarrow [x :: 1]_1 \rightarrow [x :: 2]_2 \rightarrow [x :: 3]_3 \rightarrow [x :: 4]_4 \rightarrow \cdots$

Since $\exists_{\mathrm{RTLA}}\, y : F$ does not allow this behavior, it is not SI, so it is not a property.

To obtain the proper quantifier $\exists$ for TLA, we modify the definition of $\exists_{\mathrm{RTLA}}$ so $\exists\, y : F$ is satisfied by (7.6). The definition of $\exists$ is the same as that of $\exists_{\mathrm{RTLA}}$ except with the relation $\simeq_y$ on behaviors replaced by a relation $\sim_y$. This relation is defined so $\sigma \sim_y \tau$ means approximately that σ can be obtained from τ by adding and removing stuttering steps and then changing the values of y. The precise definition of $\sim_y$ is subtle. (In fact, its definition in [35] is wrong.)

To define $\sim_y$, we first define the operator $\natural_y$ on behaviors. This operator is the same as the operator $\natural$ defined in Section 3.5.3, except it removes "almost stuttering" steps instead of just stuttering steps, where a step $s \rightarrow t$ is almost stuttering if $s =_y t$. The precise definition is that $\natural_y(\sigma)(n)$ equals $\sigma(f_{y,\sigma})(n)$, where the definition of $f_{y,\sigma}$ is obtained from the definition of f_σ in Section 3.5.3 by replacing $=$ and $\neq$ by $=_y$ and $\neq_y$ in "$\sigma(i) =$" and "$\sigma(i) \neq$".

We now define $\sigma \sim_y \tau$ to equal $\natural_y(\sigma) \simeq_y \natural_y(\tau)$ and define $\exists\, y : F$ to be satisfied by a behavior σ iff there is a behavior τ satisfying F such that $\sigma \sim_y \tau$. Observe that $\sigma \simeq_y \tau$ implies $\sigma \sim_y \tau$, so $\exists_{\mathrm{RTLA}}\, y : F$ implies $\exists\, y : F$ for any behavior predicate F.

One reason not to use $\exists$ is that if S is a safety property, then $\exists\, y : S$ need not be a safety property. Temporal quantification destroys the nice separation of safety and liveness provided by our way of describing abstract programs. For example, let F be this safety property for an abstract program:

(7.7) $\quad \wedge\, (x = 0) \wedge (y \in \mathbb{N})$
$\qquad \wedge\, \Box[(y > 0) \wedge (x' = x + 1) \wedge (y' = y - 1)]_{\langle x,y \rangle}$

In a behavior satisfying this formula, x cannot be incremented forever because eventually y would equal 0, making any further non-stuttering steps impossible. Therefore, formula $\exists\, y : F$ is equivalent to

(7.8) $\quad (x = 0) \wedge \Box[x' = x + 1]_x \wedge \Diamond\Box[x' = x]_x$

To see that this is not a safety property, remember that a behavior σ satisfies a safety property iff every finite prefix of σ satisfies that property. Consider

7.2. HISTORY VARIABLES

a behavior σ in which x does keep being incremented forever. Every finite prefix of σ satisfies (7.8), since completing the prefix with stuttering steps makes the behavior satisfy the liveness property $\Diamond\Box[x' = x]_x$. However, σ doesn't satisfy (7.8) because it doesn't satisfy this liveness property. Therefore, even though formula F, defined to equal (7.7), is a safety property, formula $\exists\, y : F$, which is equivalent to (7.8), is not a safety property.

7.2 History Variables

The simplest kind of auxiliary variable is a history variable. As the name implies, a history variable is used to remember things that happened in the past and can't be deduced from the current state. We may need to add a history variable to T to prove $\models T \Rightarrow S$ when the internal state of S records information about past events that isn't needed to describe the behavior of its interface variables.

7.2.1 How to Add a History Variable

Except in one unusual case described in Section 7.3.5, we add an auxiliary variable to an abstract program by adding it to the safety part of the program. Thus, if T equals $\mathit{Init} \wedge \Box[\mathit{Next}]_v \wedge L$ for a liveness property L, then the formula T^h obtained by adding a history variable h will equal

$$\mathit{Init}^h \wedge \Box[\mathit{Next}^h]_{vh} \wedge L$$

where Init^h and Next^h are obtained by augmenting Init and Next to describe, respectively, the initial value of h and how h can change; and vh is the tuple $v \circ \langle h \rangle$ of the variables of v and the variable h. Since h does not appear in L, the formula $\exists\, h : T^h$ equals

$$(\exists\, h : \mathit{Init}^h \wedge \Box[\mathit{Next}^h]_{vh}) \wedge L$$

We can therefore ignore L for now, so we assume T equals $\mathit{Init} \wedge \Box[\mathit{Next}]_v$ and show how to define Init^h and Next^h.

We use a tiny example to illustrate history variables. There is an abstract program in which a user inputs a sequence of real numbers and the system displays the average of the numbers entered thus far. The interface variables are *inp* and *avg*. Initially, *inp* equals a value *rdy* that is not a number and *avg* = 0. The user's input action sets *inp* to a real number and leaves *avg* unchanged. The system's output action sets *avg* to the new average of the inputs and resets *inp* to *rdy*.

$$InitS \triangleq (inp = rdy) \wedge (avg = 0) \wedge seq = \langle\,\rangle$$

$$User \triangleq\; \wedge\; inp = rdy$$
$$\wedge\; inp' \in \mathbb{R}$$
$$\wedge\; (avg' = avg) \wedge (seq' = seq)$$

$$Syst \triangleq\; \wedge\; inp \in \mathbb{R}$$
$$\wedge\; seq' = Append(seq, inp)$$
$$\wedge\; avg' = SeqSum(seq') / Len(seq')$$
$$\wedge\; inp' = rdy$$

$$NextS \triangleq User \vee Syst$$

$$IS \triangleq InitS \wedge \Box[NextS]_{\langle inp, avg, seq \rangle}$$

$$S \triangleq \exists\, seq : IS$$

Figure 7.1: The abstract averaging program S.

This abstract program is described by formula S of Figure 7.1. It uses an internal variable seq whose value is the ordinal sequence of numbers input so far. Recall that $\mathbb{R}$ is the set of real numbers, and Section Math VII defines these operators on sequences seq: $Append(seq, inp)$ is the sequence obtained by appending inp to the end of seq; $Len(seq)$ is the length of seq; and $Tail(seq)$ is the sequence obtained by removing the first element of seq if seq is nonempty. The operator $SeqSum$ is defined as follows so that $SeqSum(sq)$ is the sum of the elements of a finite sequence sq of numbers:

$$SeqSum(sq) \triangleq \text{IF } sq = \langle\,\rangle \text{ THEN } 0 \text{ ELSE } sq(1) + SeqSum(Tail(sq))$$

Using the internal variable seq to write the behavior predicate S is arguably the clearest way to describe the values assumed by the interface variables inp and avg. It's a natural way to explain that the value of avg is the average of the values that have been input. However, it's not a good way to describe how to implement the system. There's no need for an implementation to remember the entire sequence of past inputs; it can just remember the number of inputs and their sum. In fact, it doesn't even need an internal variable to remember the sum. We can implement it with an abstract program T that implements S using only a single internal variable num whose value is the number of inputs that the user has entered.

We first describe T in pseudocode and construct T^h by adding a history variable h to the code. The TLA translations of the pseudocode show how to add a history variable to an abstract program described in TLA.

7.2. HISTORY VARIABLES

variables $inp = rdy$, $avg = 0$, $num = 0$;
while TRUE **do**
   usr: $inp :\in \mathbb{R}$;
   sys: $avg := (avg * num + inp)/(num + 1)$;
      $num := num + 1$;
      $inp := rdy$
end while

Figure 7.2: Abstract program T in pseudocode.

variables $inp = rdy$, $avg = 0$, $num = 0$, $h = \langle \rangle$;
while TRUE do
   usr: $inp :\in \mathbb{R}$;
   sys: $avg := (avg * num + inp)/(num + 1)$;
      $num := num + 1$;
      $h := Append(h, inp)$;
      $inp := rdy$
end while

Figure 7.3: Abstract program T^h in pseudocode.

It's natural to think of the user and the system in this example as two separate processes. However, the abstract programs S and T are predicates on behaviors, which are mathematical objects. *Process* is not a mathematical concept; it's a way in which we interpret predicates on behaviors. For simplicity, we write T as a single-process program.

The pseudocode for program T is in Figure 7.2. It uses the operator $:\in$ introduced in Figure 5.2, so statement usr sets inp to an arbitrary element of $\mathbb{R}$. Since we're not concerned with implementing T, there's no reason to hide its internal variable num.

Because the sum of n numbers whose average is a is $n * a$, it should be clear that program T implements program S. But showing that T implements S requires defining a refinement mapping under which T implements IS (program S without variable seq hidden). And that requires adding an auxiliary variable that records the sequence of input values. Adding the required auxiliary variable h is simple and obvious. We just add the two pieces of code shown in black in Figure 7.3.

It is a straightforward exercise to prove

$$\models T^h \Rightarrow (IS \text{ WITH } inp \leftarrow inp, avg \leftarrow avg, seq \leftarrow h)$$

using the fact that

$$avg \equiv \text{IF } h = \langle\rangle \text{ THEN } 0 \text{ ELSE } SeqSum(h) / Len(h)$$

is an invariant of T^h. To show that this proves $\models T \Rightarrow S$, we have to show that T^h actually is obtained by adding the auxiliary variable h to T—that is, we have to show that T is equivalent to $\exists\, h : T^h$. This requires showing (i) $\models (\exists\, h : T^h) \Rightarrow T$ and (ii) $\models T \Rightarrow (\exists\, h : T^h)$.

To show (i) we have to show $\models T^h \Rightarrow T$, which is obvious because it's easy to see that the initial predicate and next-state action of T^h imply the initial predicate and next-state action of T. To show (ii), we have to show that for any behavior σ satisfying T, there is a behavior τ satisfying T^h with $\tau \sim_h \sigma$. From the code for T^h, it's easy to obtain a recursive definition of the value of h in each state $\tau(i)$ of τ. The declaration of h provides the value of h in state $\tau(0)$, and the rest of the code defines the value of h in state $\tau(i+1)$ as a function of its value and the value of pc in state $\tau(i)$.

It's pretty obvious how to generalize from this example to adding a history variable h to any abstract program T described by pseudocode. We let the initial value of h be any expression that can contain the variables of T. We modify the pseudocode by adding at most one statement assigning a value to h to any action of the code. The right-hand side of the assignment can contain h as well as the variables of T. Making this precise would require making pseudocode precise, which we don't want to do. When we want to be precise, we use math.

So, let's now see how we add a history variable when the abstract program T is written in TLA. The translation of the code in Figure 7.2 to TLA defines

$$T \triangleq Init \wedge \Box[Next]_{\langle inp, avg, num\rangle} \quad \textbf{where} \quad Next \triangleq Usr \vee Sys$$

Actions Usr and Sys are the actions executed from control points usr and sys, respectively. The TLA translation of the code in Figure 7.3 is

(7.9) $\quad T^h \triangleq Init^h \wedge \Box[Next^h]_{\langle inp, avg, num, h\rangle}$
$\qquad\qquad \textbf{where} \quad Init^h \triangleq Init \wedge (h = \langle\rangle)$
$\qquad\qquad\qquad\qquad\; Next^h \triangleq Usr^h \vee Sys^h$
$\qquad\qquad\qquad\qquad\; Usr^h \triangleq Usr \wedge (h' = h)$
$\qquad\qquad\qquad\qquad\; Sys^h \triangleq Sys \wedge (h' = Append(h, inp))$

Here is the general result that describes how to add a history variable to a program. Its proof is a simple generalization of the proof for our example.

7.2. HISTORY VARIABLES

Theorem 7.1 (History Variable) Let T equal $Init \wedge \Box[Next]_v$, where $Next$ equals $\exists\, i \in I : A_i$ and v is the tuple of variables in T, and assume h is not one of those variables. If T^h equals $Init^h \wedge \Box[Next^h]_{vh}$, where

- $Init^h \triangleq Init \wedge (h = exp)$
- $Next^h \triangleq \exists\, i \in I : A_i \wedge (h' = exp_i)$
- $vh \triangleq v \circ \langle h \rangle$
- exp is a state expression that does not contain the variable h, and the exp_i are step expressions that do not contain h',

then $\models T \equiv \exists\, h : T^h$.

7.2.2 History Variables and Fairness

We add a history variable h to a safety property T of the form $Init \wedge \Box[Next]_v$ to obtain a formula T^h such that $\exists\, h : T^h$ is equivalent to T. If a program also contains a liveness condition L, this gives us the program $T^h \wedge L$. Since the variable h does not occur in L, the formula $\exists\, h : T^h \wedge L$ is equivalent to $(\exists\, h : T^h) \wedge L$ which equals $T \wedge L$. Therefore the history variable h is an auxiliary variable for $T^h \wedge L$.

As explained in Section 4.2.7, the standard form for the liveness condition of a program is the conjunction of weak and/or strong fairness conditions of subactions of its next-state action. Even if $T \wedge L$ has this form, $T^h \wedge L$ will not because a subaction of $Next$ will not be a subaction of $Next^h$. (An action that does not mention h cannot imply $Next^h$.) This means that we can't apply Theorem 4.7 to show that $\langle T^h, L \rangle$ is machine closed. However, we can show as follows that if $\langle T, L \rangle$ is machine closed, then $\langle T^h, L \rangle$ is also machine closed. By definition of machine closure, this means showing that any finite behavior ρ satisfying T^h can be extended to an infinite behavior satisfying $T^h \wedge L$. Since T^h implies T, machine closure of $\langle T, L \rangle$ implies ρ can be extended to a behavior $\rho \circ \sigma$ satisfying $T \wedge L$. By definition of T^h, we can modify the values of h in the states of σ to obtain a behavior τ such that $\rho \circ \tau$ satisfies T^h. Since the truth of L does not depend on the values of h, the behavior $\rho \circ \tau$ also satisfies L, as required.

When using TLA, the fact that L will contain fairness conditions on actions that are not subactions of $Next^h$ makes no difference. However, not everyone uses TLA. In some approaches, abstract programs are described in something like a coding language, and they define fairness only in terms of weak and strong fairness of subactions of the next-state action. So, it is interesting to know if we can replace a fairness condition on a subaction B_i of T with the same fairness condition on a corresponding subaction B_i^h of T^h. We can, under the following condition, which is likely to be satisfied by programs written in those other languages: The next-state action of T must be the disjunction of actions A_i, and each B_i must be a subaction of A_i such that a B_i step is not an A_j step for $j \neq i$. The precise result is the following, whose proof is in the Appendix. In this theorem, letting B_i equal FALSE is equivalent to omitting that fairness condition because weak and strong fairness of FALSE are trivially true. (The action FALSE is never enabled, so (4.23) implies $\text{SF}_v(\text{FALSE})$ equals $\Box\Diamond\text{FALSE} \Rightarrow \Box\Diamond\text{FALSE}$, which equals TRUE.)

Theorem 7.2 With the assumptions of Theorem 7.1, for all $i \in I$ let B_i be a subaction of A_i such that $T \wedge (i \neq j) \Rightarrow \Box[\neg(B_i \wedge A_j)]_v$ for all j in I; and let $B_i^h \triangleq \langle B_i \rangle_v \wedge (h' = exp_i)$. Then

$$T \wedge (\forall i \in I : \text{XF}_v^i(B_i)) \equiv \exists h : T^h \wedge (\forall i \in I : \text{XF}_{vh}^i(B_i^h))$$

where each XF^i is either WF or SF.

7.2.3 A Completeness Result for History Variables

A popular approach to proving safety properties of concurrent programs, derived from work by Owicki and Gries [44], can prove only invariance properties. We can, in theory, reduce proving safety properties to proving invariance. We do this by adding a history variable h to a program T to obtain a program T^h. For any safety property F, we can then define a state predicate I_F that is an invariant of T^h iff (every behavior of) T satisfies F. The idea is simple: We define the value of h to be the sequence of program states in the current behavior up to and including the current state. We then define I_F to be true iff the value of h satisfies F. The result is stated in the following theorem, whose proof is sketched in the Appendix.

Theorem 7.3 Let T equal $\textit{Init} \wedge \Box[\textit{Next}]_{\langle \mathbf{x} \rangle}$ where $\mathbf{x}$ is the list of all variables of S; let F be a safety property such that $F(\sigma)$ depends only on the values of the variables $\mathbf{x}$ in σ, for any behavior σ; and let h be a variable not one of the variables $\mathbf{x}$. We can add h as a history variable to T to obtain T^h and define a state predicate I_F in terms of F such that $\models \llbracket T \rrbracket \Rightarrow F$ is true iff I_F is an invariant of T^h.

A simple example of the theorem is when F is the safety property F_{12} defined semantically by (4.1) of Section 4.1.2. That property asserts x must equal 1

7.3. STUTTERING VARIABLES

before it can equal 2. A program $Init \wedge \Box[Next]_v$ satisfies F_{12} iff the formula $(x = 2) \Rightarrow h$ is an invariant of the program obtained by adding the history variable h to that program as follows:

$$(Init \wedge (h = \text{FALSE})) \wedge \Box[Next \wedge (h' = h \vee (x = 1))]_{vo\langle h \rangle}$$

Theorem 7.3 assumes only that F is a safety property. This might suggest we can show that one program satisfies the safety part of another program by verifying an invariance property. However, I have never seen this done, and in practice it seems unlikely to be possible to describe any but the simplest abstract programs with an invariant.

7.3 Stuttering Variables

Typically, when a lower-level abstract program T implements a higher-level abstract program S, program T takes more steps than S does to perform an operation. Under the refinement mapping, the extra steps of T implement stuttering steps of S. It's also possible for S to take more steps than T. In that case, defining a refinement mapping requires adding steps to behaviors of T that implement those extra steps of S. This is done by adding a *stuttering variable* s to T. The extra steps are ones that change only s, so when s is hidden, those steps become stuttering steps of T.

There are two kinds of stuttering variables used in practice: ones that add stuttering steps immediately after steps of an action, and ones that add stuttering steps immediately before steps of an action. They are described in Sections 7.3.2 and 7.3.3. Multiple such variables can be combined into a single stuttering variable. Section 7.3.5 explains another kind of stuttering variable that is never needed in practice but could, in theory, be required.

This section talks about adding stuttering steps, which literally makes no sense because it's impossible to require or forbid stuttering steps in a TLA formula. Here, adding stuttering steps to an abstract program T means writing a formula T^s containing s and the variables of T by adding steps that change s and leave the variables of T unchanged, so that $\exists\, s : T^s$ is equivalent to T. In this section, a stuttering step usually means one of those additional steps that leave the variables of T unchanged and change s.

Math X

CASE **Proof Steps** A common proof method is case splitting—for example, splitting the proof of a formula containing a number x into proving it first if $x \geq 0$ and then if $x < 0$. This is done with CASE statements, where if G is the current goal, then CASE: F is an abbreviation of $F \Rightarrow G$. A proof by case splitting usually ends with a sequence of CASE steps followed by a Q.E.D. step showing that those steps cover all possible cases.

Well-Founded Relations A relation $\succ$ is said to be *well-founded* on a set S iff there is no infinite sequence $s_1 \succ s_2 \succ \ldots$ with $s_i \in S$ for all i. If we think of $s \succ t$ meaning that t is smaller than s, then well-founded on S means that if you keep taking smaller and smaller elements of S, then you'll eventually reach a minimal element. (There may be many minimal elements.) The prototypical example of a well-founded relation on a set is the relation $>$ on the set $\mathbb{N}$ of natural numbers.

7.3.1 The Example

Stuttering variables are explained with the silly example of a tiny censoring system. An artist paints pictures and submits them to a censor, who decides either to display or reject each picture. This system is described by the abstract program *Cen1* defined as follows.

There are two interface variables *inp* and *disp*. The artist submits a picture w, which is an element of the set *Art* of all possible pictures, by setting the value of the variable *inp* to w. The censor then either displays w by setting the value of the variable *disp* to $\langle w, i \rangle$, where i is set alternately to 0 and 1, or else rejects w. (The second component of *disp* is needed so displaying the same picture twice isn't a stuttering step, which would needlessly complicate the example.) The censor then acknowledges receipt of the picture by setting the value of *inp* to a special value *NotArt* that is not an element of *Art*.

There is also an internal variable *aw* that is hidden. The value of *aw* is initially the empty sequence $\langle \rangle$. It is set to $\langle w \rangle$ when the artist submits a picture w, and it is reset to $\langle \rangle$ when w is either displayed or rejected. The value of *aw* records whether or not the display/reject decision has been made. That information is encoded in *aw* this way so the example is more easily modified to obtain an example in Section 7.4. The complete description of the abstract program is formula *Cen1* in Figure 7.4, where *ICen1* is the program without *aw* hidden. (Initially, any painting may be displayed.)

There is another way to describe the artist/censor system as an abstract program. In *ICen1*, submission of a picture w by the artist is described by an input action that sets *inp* to w and *aw* to $\langle w \rangle$. A separate action *DispOrNot* either displays or rejects w. We define *Cen2* to equal

7.3. STUTTERING VARIABLES

$$Cen1 \triangleq \exists\, aw : ICen1$$

$$ICen1 \triangleq Init \land \Box[Next1]_v$$

$$v \triangleq \langle inp,\ disp,\ aw \rangle$$

$$Init \triangleq\ \land\ inp = NotArt$$
$$\land\ aw = \langle\rangle$$
$$\land\ disp \in Art \times \{0,1\}$$

$$Next1 \triangleq Input \lor DispOrNot \lor Ack$$

$$Input \triangleq\ \land\ (inp = NotArt) \land (aw = \langle\rangle)$$
$$\land\ inp' \in Art$$
$$\land\ aw' = \langle inp' \rangle$$
$$\land\ disp' = disp$$

$$DispOrNot \triangleq\ \land\ aw \neq \langle\rangle$$
$$\land\ \lor\ disp' = \langle aw(1),\ 1 - disp(2) \rangle$$
$$\lor\ disp' = disp$$
$$\land\ aw' = \langle\rangle$$
$$\land\ inp' = inp$$

$$Ack \triangleq\ \land\ (inp \in Art) \land (aw = \langle\rangle)$$
$$\land\ inp' = NotArt$$
$$\land\ (aw' = aw) \land (disp' = disp)$$

Figure 7.4: The program $Cen1$.

$\exists\, aw : ICen2$ where $ICen2$ describes a program in which it is the input action that decides whether to display or reject w, setting aw to $\langle w \rangle$ iff it decides to display w. The displaying action always displays w if aw equals $\langle w \rangle$. The program $Cen2$ is defined in Figure 7.5, where v, $Init$, and Ack are the same as in $Cen1$ and are defined in Figure 7.4.

If we ignore the values of aw, the only difference between behaviors of $ICen1$ and $ICen2$ is that, when a picture is rejected, the behavior of $ICen1$ takes one more step than the corresponding behavior of $ICen2$—a step that leaves inp and $disp$ unchanged. Since inp and $disp$ are the only free variables in the two definitions of Cen, stuttering insensitivity implies that the formulas $Cen1$ and $Cen2$ are equivalent, so they describe the same abstract program.

To show that the two definitions are equivalent, we have to show that $ICen1$ and $ICen2$ each implement the other under a suitable refinement map-

$$Cen2 \triangleq \exists\, aw : ICen2$$
$$ICen2 \triangleq Init \land \Box[Next2]_v$$
$$Next2 \triangleq InpOrNot \lor Display \lor Ack$$
$$\begin{aligned}InpOrNot \triangleq\ & \land (inp = NotArt) \land (aw = \langle\,\rangle)\\ & \land inp' \in Art\\ & \land \lor aw' = \langle inp'\rangle\\ & \ \lor aw' = aw\\ & \land disp' = disp\end{aligned}$$

$$\begin{aligned}Display \triangleq\ & \land aw \neq \langle\,\rangle\\ & \land disp' = \langle aw(1),\ 1 - disp(2)\rangle\\ & \land aw' = \langle\,\rangle\\ & \land inp' = inp\end{aligned}$$

Figure 7.5: The program $Cen2$.

ping. We will see here how to define the refinement mapping under which $ICen2$ implements $ICen1$. Section 7.4 shows how to define the refinement mapping under which $ICen1$ implements $ICen2$.

7.3.2 Adding Stuttering Steps After an Action

To define the refinement mapping that shows $ICen2$ implements $ICen1$, we have to add a stuttering step to an execution of $ICen2$ for each operation of receiving an input and rejecting it. We do that by adding a stuttering variable that adds a stuttering step after each $InpOrNot$ step of the execution that rejects the input—that is, after $InpOrNot$ steps that set aw to $\langle\,\rangle$.

The simplest stuttering variable s is one whose value is a natural number that equals 0 except when it is adding stuttering steps (steps that change only s), in which case s equals the number of such steps it has yet to take. Here's how we add such a variable that adds stuttering steps after a subaction A of the next-state action.

Let T equal $Init \land \Box[Next]_v$, where $Next$ equals $A \lor (\exists\, j \in J : B_j)$ for actions A and B_j. We define T^s to equal $Init^s \land \Box[Next^s]_{vs}$, where $Next^s$ equals $A^s \lor (\exists\, j \in J : B_j^s)$ and $Init^s$, A^s, B_j^s, and vs are defined as follows:

S1. vs is the tuple of variables obtained by appending s to the tuple v of variables.

S2. $Init^s \triangleq Init \land (s = 0)$.

7.3. STUTTERING VARIABLES

S3. $A^s \triangleq \lor (s = 0) \land A \land (s' = exp)$
$ \lor (s > 0) \land (v' = v) \land (s' = s - 1)$

where exp is an expression whose value is a natural number; it can contain the original variables primed or unprimed.

S4. $B_j^s \triangleq (s = 0) \land B_j \land (s' = 0)$, for $j \in J$.

Ignoring the value of s, the behaviors satisfying T^s are the same as behaviors satisfying T, except each A step in a behavior of T is followed in T^s by a finite number (possibly 0) of steps that leave the variables of T unchanged. Therefore, by stuttering insensitivity, T and $\exists s : T^s$ are satisfied by the same sets of behaviors, so they are equivalent.

To show that $ICen2$ implements $ICen1$, we define $ICen2^s$ in this way, where A equals $InpOrNot$ and the B_i are Ack and $Display$. In the definition of $InpOrNot^s$, we let:

$$exp \triangleq \text{IF } aw' = \langle\rangle \text{ THEN } 1 \text{ ELSE } 0$$

This adds a stuttering step to a behavior of $ICen2^s$ after an $InpOrNot$ step that rejects the input.

Programs $ICen1$ and $ICen2^s$ take the same number of steps to process an input. A stuttering step of $ICen2^s$ corresponds to a $DispOrNot$ step of $ICen1$ that rejects the input. If we compare behaviors of these two programs, we find that corresponding states have the same values of the variables inp, $disp$, and aw except when $ICen2^s$ is about to take a stuttering step. In that state, $s = 1$ in $ICen2^s$, and the value of aw for an input w is $\langle\rangle$ in $ICen2^s$ and $\langle w \rangle$ in $ICen1$. This means that the value of aw in a behavior of $ICen1$ always equals the value of the following state function in the corresponding behavior of $ICen2^s$:

(7.10) $awBar \triangleq \text{IF } s = 0 \text{ THEN } aw \text{ ELSE } \langle inp \rangle$

Therefore, $ICen2^s$ implements $ICen1$ under the refinement mapping that substitutes $awBar$ for aw. In other words:

(7.11) $\models ICen2^s \Rightarrow (ICen1 \text{ WITH } aw \leftarrow awBar)$

The proof of (7.11) is similar to, but simpler than, the refinement proof sketched in Section 6.4.2. Here, we give only the briefest outline of a proof to present results that will be used below when discussing liveness.

Let's abbreviate $(F \text{ WITH } aw \leftarrow awBar)$ by $\overline{F}$ for any formula F, so we must prove $\models ICen2^s \Rightarrow \overline{ICen1}$. The proof of $\models Init^s \Rightarrow \overline{Init}$ is trivial, since

$s = 0$ implies $\overline{v} = v$ by definition of $awBar$, so $Init^s$ implies $\overline{Init} = Init$. The main part of the proof is proving:

(7.12) $\models ICen2^s \Rightarrow \Box\overline{[Next1]_v}$

This is proved by proving assertions C1–C4 below, which are the analogs of assertions R1–R7 of the proof in Section 6.4.2. Again, assertions containing actions of the form $\overline{\langle A \rangle_v}$ are proved for use in reasoning about liveness when a weaker assertion containing $\overline{A}$ suffices to prove (7.12). Two of the assertions require an invariant $Inv2^s$ of $ICen2^s$. That invariant needs to assert type correctness of $disp$ (for C3) and that $s = 1$ implies $aw = \langle \rangle$ (for C2).

C1. $\models (s = 0) \land InpOrNot^s \Rightarrow \overline{Input}$
C2. $\models Inv2^s \land (s = 1) \land InpOrNot^s \Rightarrow \overline{\langle DispOrNot \rangle_v}$
C3. $\models Inv2^s \land Display^s \Rightarrow \overline{\langle DispOrNot \rangle_v}$
C4. $\models Ack^s \Rightarrow \overline{\langle Ack \rangle_v}$

Proving these assertions is a good way to start learning to write proofs.

Often, when showing that one program implements another, after adding a simple stuttering variable it's necessary to add a history variable to be able to define the refinement mapping. For example, suppose we split the input actions of the censor programs into two actions, where the first chooses the value of inp and the second sets the values of aw and $disp$ and sets inp to a special value $Busy$. The Ack action must also be modified by replacing $inp \in Art$ with $inp = Busy$. We could then not define $awBar$ to make (7.11) true because the input value would be forgotten when s equals 1. To define a state function $awBar$ to make (7.11) true, we would have to add a history variable that remembers what value was input.

We can avoid having to add a history variable by letting the stuttering variable carry additional information. This is done by generalizing the way stuttering steps are counted. In the censor example, instead of setting s to 1 when adding a stuttering step and to 0 otherwise, we can set it to $\langle inp \rangle$ when adding the step and to $\langle \rangle$ when not adding the step. The number of stuttering steps to be taken at any point in the execution is then the length $Len(s)$ of the sequence s. We would define $awBar$ to equal:

IF $s = \langle \rangle$ THEN aw ELSE s

In general, we can let s assume values in any set with a well-founded relation. We just require that every added stuttering step decreases the value of s.

One use of this generality is for adding stuttering steps after multiple actions. To do this, we let the value of s be a pair $\langle m, i \rangle$, where m is the

7.3. STUTTERING VARIABLES

number of remaining stuttering steps and i identifies the action. We define the well-founded ordering $\succ$ on this set of pairs by letting $\langle m, i \rangle \succ \langle n, j \rangle$ iff $m > n$. We can use this same trick to let the value of s be a tuple with additional components. Information in those other components can be used in defining the refinement mapping so it makes the stuttering steps implement the appropriate steps of the higher-level program. For simplicity, we state our theorem just for this particular use of a well-founded order. However, the conjunct $s(2) = i$ in the definition of A_i^s is added to ensure that only A_i^s performs stuttering steps added after A_i, although that matters only if s contains additional components that depend on i.

Theorem 7.4 (Post-Action Stuttering Variable)
Let T equal $\mathit{Init} \wedge \Box[\mathit{Next}]_v$, where Next equals $(\exists\, i \in I : A_i) \vee B$ for a constant set I, and v is a tuple of all the variables of T. If T^s equals $\mathit{Init}^s \wedge \Box[\mathit{Next}^s]_{vs}$ where

- s is not a variable of T and $vs \triangleq v \circ \langle s \rangle$.

- $\mathit{Init}^s \triangleq \mathit{Init} \wedge (s = \langle 0, i_0 \rangle)$ for some i_0 in I.

- $\mathit{Next}^s \triangleq (\exists\, i \in I : A_i^s) \vee B^s$

- $A_i^s \triangleq \vee\ (s(1) = 0) \wedge (s(2) = i) \wedge A_i \wedge (s' = \langle\mathit{exp}_i, i\rangle)$
  $ \vee\ (s(1) > 0) \wedge (v' = v) \wedge (s' = \langle s(1) - 1, s(2)\rangle)$
  where $\models T \Rightarrow \Box[\mathit{exp}_i \in \mathbb{N}]_v$ and exp_i is a step expression not containing s.

- $B^s \triangleq (s(0) = 0) \wedge B \wedge (s' = s)$

then $\exists\, s : T^s$ equals T.

The theorem does not assume that the actions A_i and B are mutually disjoint. A step could be both an A_i and an A_j step for $i \neq j$, or both an A_i and a B step. That should rarely be the case when applying the theorem, since it allows a nondeterministic choice of how many stuttering steps (if any) are added in some states. The action B will usually be the disjunction of actions B_j. In that case, B^s equals the disjunction of the actions $(s(0) = 0) \wedge B_j \wedge (s' = s)$.

7.3.3 Adding Stuttering Steps Before an Action

Suppose that instead of adding stuttering steps after *InpOrNot* steps of *ICen2*, we want to add them before *Ack* steps. That's a silly thing to do, but it's a silly example anyway. One thing that makes it silly is that when the *Ack* action is enabled, nothing in the state tells us whether a stuttering step is necessary. The value of *aw* is $\langle\rangle$ regardless of whether or not a *Display* step has occurred. So we'll have to add the stuttering step whether or not it's needed. But that's not a problem, since an unnecessary stuttering step can simply implement a stuttering step of *ICen1*.

For a simple stuttering variable that counts down to 0, we add stuttering steps before an action A the way we added them after A, except instead of A^s executing A in the first step when s equals 0, it executes A in the last step, when s equals 1 (unless it adds 0 stuttering steps). However, to ensure that an A^s step can be taken after those stuttering steps, the stuttering steps can begin only when A is enabled. (Once A is enabled, stuttering steps leave it enabled.) To add *exp* stuttering steps before an A step, we define:

$$A^s \triangleq \land \lor \mathbb{E}(A) \land (s = 0) \land (s' = exp)$$
$$ \lor (s > 0) \land (s' = s - 1)$$
$$ \land \text{IF } s' = 0 \text{ THEN } A \text{ ELSE } v' = v$$

Since A is enabled when $s' = 0$ is true, any enabling condition (conjunct with no primed variable) can be removed from A in the last line of the definition.

We could define Ack^s this way in $ICen2^s$ with $exp = 1$ to add a stuttering step before every Ack step. However, there's nothing in the state to indicate whether that stuttering step should implement a *Display* step or a stuttering step of *ICen1*. To define the refinement mapping that shows $ICen2^s$ implements $ICen1$, we would have to add a history variable that records whether or not the $InputOrNot^s$ step decided to display the input. Alternatively, we could add the history variable before adding the stuttering variable. We could then define Ack^s so it adds a stuttering step iff the *InpOrNot* step chose not to display the input.

To obtain the general result for adding stuttering steps before actions A_i, we modify Theorem 7.4 by changing the definition of A_i^s to:

$$A_i^s \triangleq \land \lor \mathbb{E}(A_i) \land (s(1) = 0) \land (s' = \langle exp_i, i \rangle)$$
$$ \lor (s > 0) \land (s(2) = i) \land (s' = \langle s(1) - 1, s(2) \rangle)$$
$$ \land \text{IF } s'(1) = 0 \text{ THEN } A_i \text{ ELSE } (v' = v)$$

7.3. STUTTERING VARIABLES

where exp_i is a state expression. (Although allowed, there is usually no point having primed variables in exp_i, because they equal the unprimed variables unless exp_i equals 0.)

We can also add stuttering steps both before and after A_i steps. We add a third component to s to indicate whether the next stuttering steps to be added for A_i are ones that precede or follow the A_i step. Writing a precise definition is left as an exercise for motivated readers.

7.3.4 Fairness and Stuttering Variables

As with other auxiliary variables, we add a stuttering variable to a safety property T of the form $Init \land \Box[Next]_v$. If a program is described by the property $T \land L$ for a liveness property L, then the program with the added stuttering variable s is $T^s \land L$.

To see how stuttering variables work with liveness conditions, we add fairness requirements $L1$ and $L2$ to our two censor programs to define:

$$IC1 \triangleq ICen1 \land L1 \qquad IC2 \triangleq ICen2 \land L2$$

We've shown that $ICen2^s$ implements $ICen1$ under a refinement mapping. We show here that $IC2^s$ implements $IC1$ under that same refinement mapping. That is, we show:

(7.13) $\models IC2^s \Rightarrow (IC1 \text{ WITH } aw \leftarrow awBar)$

The fairness requirements are:

$$L1 \triangleq \text{WF}_v(DispOrNot) \land \text{WF}_v(Ack)$$
$$L2 \triangleq \text{WF}_v(Display) \land \text{WF}_v(Ack)$$

(Theorem 4.8 implies that $L1$ and $L2$ are equivalent to weak fairness of $DispOrNot \lor Ack$ and $Display \lor Ack$ respectively, but it's more convenient to write them this way.) It's clear that $L1$ and $L2$ are the appropriate fairness requirements for $IC1$ and $IC2$, ensuring that an Ack step occurs after each input step. In particular, an input step of $IC2$ is a $DispOrNot$ step, after which eventually Ack is enabled—either immediately if the input is rejected or after a $Display$ step that $\text{WF}_v(Display)$ implies must occur. When Ack is enabled, $\text{WF}_v(Ack)$ implies that an Ack step must occur.

For $IC2^s$ to implement $IC1$ under a refinement mapping, it should ensure that an input step is eventually followed by an Ack^s step. In $IC2^s$, an input is entered by an $(s = 0) \land InpOrNot^s$ step. We must show that such a step is eventually followed by an Ack^s step. This appears problematic because if the step rejects the input, then it sets s to 1, in which case the only enabled action of $Next2^s$ is $(s = 1) \wedge InpOrNot^s$; and $L2$ asserts no fairness condition for that action. To show that the $(s = 0) \wedge InpOrNot^s$ step must be followed by an Ack^s step, we first show as follows that $\exists\, s : IC2^s$ is equivalent to $IC2$:

$$\begin{aligned}
\exists\, s : IC2^s &\equiv \exists\, s : ICen2 \wedge L2 &&\text{By definition of } IC2^s. \\
&\equiv (\exists\, s : ICen2^s) \wedge L2 &&\text{Because } s \text{ does not occur in } L2. \\
&\equiv ICen2 \wedge L2 &&\text{By Theorem 7.4.} \\
&\equiv IC2 &&\text{By definition of } IC2^s.
\end{aligned}$$

Any behavior that satisfies $IC2^s$ satisfies $\exists\, s : IC2^s$, so it satisfies $IC2$. An $(s = 0) \wedge InpOrNot^s$ step is an $InpOrNot$ step, which by $IC2$ must eventually be followed by an Ack step, which by definition of $ICen2^s$ must be an Ack^s step. Thus, $IC2^s$ implies that any input step is eventually followed by an Ack^s step.

In the case of the input being rejected, the necessary $(s = 1) \wedge InpOrNot^s$ step must occur to satisfy the fairness requirement $\mathrm{WF}_v(Ack)$ on the action Ack in $IC2$. If you think of the abstract program $IC2^s$ as instructions to a computer for generating behaviors, then this makes no sense. How can a fairness condition on Ack tell the computer to take an $InpOrNot^s$ step? But by now, you should understand that an abstract program is a predicate on behaviors, not instructions for generating them. Formula $ICen2^s \wedge \mathrm{WF}_v(Ack)$ implies that if a state with $s = 1$ has been reached, then there must be another $InpOrNot^s$ step and then an Ack^s step in the behavior.

This may seem weird. The source of the apparent weirdness is that ICS^2 contains a fairness condition on the action Ack, which is not a subaction of the next-state action $Next2^s$. Fairness conditions on actions not a subaction of the next-state action can lead to weirdness, including program descriptions that are not machine closed. However, in this case, we still get a machine-closed program description. In fact, this is true in general. If $\langle T, L \rangle$ is machine closed and T^s is obtained from T by adding a stuttering variable, then $\langle T^s, L \rangle$ is also machine closed. The proof is the same as the one for history variables sketched in Section 7.2.2, except in defining the behavior τ, we may have to add stuttering steps to σ as well as changing the values of the variable s. Stuttering insensitivity of L implies that $\rho \circ \tau$ still satisfies L.

We now explain the proof of (7.13). As before, define $\overline{F}$ to equal (F WITH $aw \leftarrow awBar$) for any formula F, so (7.13) asserts $\models IC2^s \Rightarrow \overline{IC1}$.

7.3. STUTTERING VARIABLES

The proof of $\models ICen2^s \Rightarrow \overline{ICen1}$ is discussed in Section 7.3.2, so we consider only the proof of $\models IC2^s \Rightarrow \overline{L1}$, which requires proving:

(7.14) (a) $\models IC2^s \Rightarrow \overline{\mathrm{WF}_v(DispOrNot)}$
       (b) $\models IC2^s \Rightarrow \overline{\mathrm{WF}_v(Ack)}$

We now sketch a proof of (7.14a). As usual when proving temporal properties, instead of assuming $IC2^s$, which is true only for a behavior starting in a state satisfying $Init2^s$, we assume this $\Box$ formula implied by $IC2^s$

$$IIC2^s \triangleq \Box Inv2 \wedge \Box[Next2^s]_{vs} \wedge L2$$

where $Inv2$ is an invariant of $ICen2^2$ that asserts some obvious invariants such as type correctness. Here is the proof sketch.

1. SUFFICES: ASSUME: $IIC2^s \wedge \Box \overline{\mathbb{E}\langle DispOrNot\rangle_v} \wedge \Box[\neg DispOrNot]_v$
   PROVE: $\Diamond\langle DispOrNot\rangle_v$

   PROOF: By (4.15), the definition of $\leadsto$, (3.21), and (3.22), since $IIC2^s$ is a $\Box$ formula.

2. $\Box((aw \neq \langle\rangle) \vee (s \neq 0))$

   PROOF: The definition of $DispOrNot$ implies that $\mathbb{E}\langle DispOrNot\rangle_v$ equals $aw \neq \langle\rangle$, so the step 1 assumption $\Box \overline{\mathbb{E}\langle DispOrNot\rangle_v}$ implies $\Box \overline{aw \neq \langle\rangle}$; and the definition of $awBar$ implies $\overline{aw \neq \langle\rangle}$ equals $(aw \neq \langle\rangle) \vee (s \neq 0)$.

3. $\Diamond\Box(aw \neq \langle\rangle) \vee \Box(s \neq 0)$

   3.1. $\Box((aw \neq \langle\rangle) \Rightarrow \Box(aw \neq \langle\rangle))$

   PROOF: The assumption $IIC2^s$ implies that $aw \neq \langle\rangle$ can be made false only by a $Display^s$ step, which by C3 is a $\langle DispOrNot\rangle_v$ step. The assumption $\Box[\neg DispOrNot]_v$ implies that such a step can't occur. Therefore, if $aw \neq \langle\rangle$ ever becomes true, then it must remain true forever.

   3.2. Q.E.D.

   PROOF: By steps 2 and 3.1 and the temporal logic tautology:
   $$\models \Box(F \vee G) \wedge \Box(F \Rightarrow \Box F) \Rightarrow (\Diamond\Box F \vee \Box G)$$

4. CASE: $\Diamond\Box(aw \neq \langle\rangle)$

   PROOF: Since $aw \neq \langle\rangle$ equals $\mathbb{E}\langle Display\rangle_v$, the case assumption and $\mathrm{WF}_v(Display)$ imply that, when $\Box(aw \neq \langle\rangle)$ becomes true, a $\langle Display\rangle_v$ step eventually occurs, and IIS^s implies that this step must be a $Display^s$

step. By C3, this $Display^s$ step is a $\overline{\langle DispOrNot\rangle}_v$ step, which implies the goal introduced by step 1.

5. CASE: $\Box(s\neq 0)$

   PROOF: The case assumption and the assumption $\Box Inv2$ imply $\Box(s=1)$. As shown above in the explanation of why a behavior of $IC2^s$ can't halt in a state with $s=1$, the property $\text{WF}_v(Ack)$ implies that, in such a state, an $(s=1)\wedge InpOrNot^s$ step must eventually occur. By C2, that is the $\langle DispOrNot\rangle_v$ step that proves the step 1 goal.

6. Q.E.D.

   PROOF: Step 3 implies that the step 4 and 5 cases are exhaustive.

The proof of (7.14b) is similar but simpler, since it doesn't have the complication of deducing from fairness of one action (Ack^s) that a step of another action ($DispOrNot^s$) of the same program must occur.

Theorem 7.2 shows how, after adding a history variable to a program, we can rewrite the program's fairness properties as fairness conditions of subactions of the modified program's next-state action. I don't know if there is a similar result for stuttering variables. Theorem 7.2 is relevant to methods other than TLA for describing abstract programs. Those other methods that I'm aware of do not assume stuttering insensitivity, so a similar result for stuttering variables seems to be of no interest.

7.3.5 Infinite-Stuttering Variables

Suppose a terminating program is described by a formula $\exists\, y:IS$, where IS implies that the value of y keeps changing forever. (IS implies that at some point, the values of all its other variables stop changing.) Suppose also that program $\exists\, y:IS$ is refined by a terminating program T with no internal variables, so all its variables eventually stop changing. The methods of adding stuttering steps to a program described so far add a finite number of stuttering steps to non-stuttering steps of the program. They can't define a state function that keeps changing forever, so they can't be used to define a refinement mapping to show that T implements $\exists\, y:IS$.

It's easy to construct an example of such programs IS and T, but I can't imagine one occurring in practice. We consider them only for completeness—and in particular, to prove the completeness theorem in Section 7.5 stating that if $\models T\Rightarrow\exists\mathbf{y}:IS$ is true for some tuple $\mathbf{y}$ of variables, then we can add auxiliary variables to T to obtain a program T^a that implements IS

under a refinement mapping. For that theorem to be true, we need to define an *infinite-stuttering* variable whose value keeps changing forever to handle this situation that never occurs in practice.

There are lots of ways to define an infinite-stuttering variable. Here is the definition used in the proof of Theorem 7.6. Let T equal $Init \land \Box[Next]_v$, where v is the tuple of all variables that appear in T, and let s not be one of those variables. We then define T^s to equal:

$$Init \land \Box[(Next \land (v' \neq v)) \lor ((s' \neq s) \land (v' = v))]_{vo\langle s \rangle} \land \Box\Diamond\langle s' \neq s\rangle_s$$

7.4 Prophecy Variables

Math XI

General Recursive Definitions We have recursively defined a function f with domain $\mathbb{N}$ by defining $f(0)$ and defining $f(n)$ in terms of $f(n-1)$ for $n > 0$. That is, we can define f by:

$f \triangleq n \in \mathbb{N} \mapsto$ IF $n = 0$ THEN exp_0 ELSE exp_1
  where f cannot occur in exp_0 and can occur in exp_1 only in the expression $f(n-1)$.

We can generalize this by allowing the value of exp_1 to depend on $f(i)$ for any $i \in \{j \in \mathbb{N} : j < n\}$. Moreover, the condition that exp_0 not depend on f can be expressed as the condition that it can depend only on $f(i)$ with $i \in \{j \in \mathbb{N} : j < 0\}$, since that allows exp_0 to depend on $f(i)$ only if i is in the empty set. We can therefore express this more general form of a recursive definition as:

RC1. $f \triangleq n \in \mathbb{N} \mapsto exp$
  where f can occur in exp only in expressions $f(i)$ with i in $\{j \in \mathbb{N} : n > j\}$.

RC1 ensures a meaningful definition of f because it implies that the value of $f(n)$ can be computed from the definition in a finite number of steps, for any $n \in \mathbb{N}$. The reason the computation terminates is that the relation $>$ is well-founded on the set $\mathbb{N}$ of natural numbers. We can generalize RC1 from $\mathbb{N}$ to any set S with a well-founded relation $\succ$ to obtain this most general form of a recursive function definition:

RC2. $f \triangleq n \in S \mapsto exp$
  where f occurs in exp only in expressions $f(i)$ with i in $\{j \in S : n \succ j\}$, and $\succ$ is a well-founded relation on S.

As an example, we can define the sum $SSum(\sigma)$ of the items of a finite sequence σ of real numbers to equal 0 if σ is the empty sequence $\langle\rangle$ and otherwise to equal the first element of σ plus the sum of its remaining elements. The definition is:

$$SSum \triangleq$$
$$\sigma \in Seq(\mathbb{R}) \mapsto \text{IF } \sigma = \langle\rangle \text{ THEN } 0$$
$$\text{ELSE } Head(\sigma) + SSum(Tail(\sigma))$$

This definition is justified by the well-founded ordering $\succ$ on $Seq(\mathbb{R})$ defined by $\sigma \succ \tau \triangleq Len(\sigma) > Len(\tau)$.

Two Set Operators If you've ever learned about sets, you should know that $S \cup T$ is the set of values that are in the set S or the set T (or both), and $S \cap T$ is the set of values that are in both S and T. We can define $\cap$ with the subsetting constructor, since $S \cap T$ equals $\{v \in S : (v \in T)\}$.[1] It is an axiom of ZF that $S \cup T$ is a set if S and T are sets.

7.4.1 Simple Prophecy Variables

We observed in Section 7.3.1 that the descriptions *Cen1* and *Cen2* of the censor system were equivalent. We showed that *Cen2* implies *Cen1*, which required adding a stuttering variable to *ICen2*. We now complete the demonstration of equivalence by showing that *Cen1* implies *Cen2*. This requires defining a state function *awBar* such that *ICen1* implies:

(*ICen2* WITH $aw \leftarrow awBar$)

However, this is impossible for the following reason. Because the refinement mapping substitutes the variables *inp* and *disp* of *ICen1* for the corresponding variables of *ICen2*, an *Input* step of *ICen1* must implement an *InpOrNot* step of *ICen2*. Besides choosing the input, the *InpOrNot* action of *ICen2* also decides whether or not that input is to be displayed, recording its decision in the value of *aw*. However, that decision is made by *ICen1* later, when executing the *DispOrNot* action. Immediately after the *Input* action, there's no information in the state of *ICen1* to determine what the value of variable *aw* of *ICen2* should be.

The solution to this problem is to have the *Input* action guess what *DispOrNot* will do, indicating its guess by setting a *prophecy variable* p to

---
[1] The parentheses disambiguate this expression, telling us that $v \in T$ is a formula while $v \in S$ is syntax.

7.4. PROPHECY VARIABLES

a value that predicts whether the input will be displayed or rejected by the *DispOrNot* step.

To make the generalization from this example more obvious, let's write action *DispOrNot* of *ICen1* as the disjunction of two actions: $DorN_{Yes}$ that displays the input and $DorN_{No}$ that doesn't. Remember that:

$$DispOrNot \triangleq \wedge \ldots \\ \wedge \vee disp' = \langle aw(1), 1 - disp(2)\rangle \\ \vee disp' = disp \\ \vdots$$

We can define $DorN_i$, for $i = Yes$ and $i = No$, by modifying the definition of *DispOrNot* to get:

$$DorN_i \triangleq \wedge \ldots \\ \wedge \vee (i = Yes) \wedge (disp' = \langle aw(1), 1 - disp(2)\rangle) \\ \vee (i = No) \wedge (disp' = disp) \\ \vdots$$

We then replace *DispOrNot* in *ICen1* by $\exists i \in \Pi : DorN_i$, where Π equals $\{Yes, No\}$. We can then add to *ICen2* an auxiliary variable p called a prophecy variable to obtain a formula $ICen2^p$ in which the *Input* action is replaced by

$$Input^p \triangleq Input \wedge (p' \in \Pi)$$

and the *DispOrNot* action is replaced by:

$$DispOrNot^p \triangleq DorN_p$$

Thus the $Input^p$ action predicts what the *DispOrNot* action will do, and $DispOrNot^p$ is modified to ensure that the prediction comes true. To complete the definition of $ICen1^p$, we can let $Init^p$ equal *Init* and Ack^p equal *Ack*, since the value of p matters only after an $Input^p$ step and before the following $DispOrNot^p$ step.

In *ICen2*, the value of *aw* is $\langle\rangle$ except after an *InpOrNot* step that chose to display the input. This implies

(7.15) $\models ICen1^p \Rightarrow (ICen2 \text{ WITH } aw \leftarrow awBar)$

where *awBar* is defined by:

$$awBar \triangleq \text{IF } aw \neq \langle\rangle \wedge (p = Yes) \text{ THEN } aw \text{ ELSE } \langle\rangle$$

To show that (7.15) implies $\models ICen1 \Rightarrow ICen2$, we have to show that p is an auxiliary variable—that is, we have to show that $\exists\, p : ICen1^p$ is equivalent to $ICen1$. To do that, we prove two things:

1. Every behavior satisfying $ICen1^p$ satisfies $ICen1$

    PROOF: It's clear that $Init^p$ equals $Init$, Act^p equals Act, and $Input^p$ implies $Input$. To complete the proof, we must show that every $DispOrNot^p$ step is a $DispOrNot$ step. It's easy to see that
    $$\mathbb{E}(DispOrNot^p) \;\Rightarrow\; (p \in \{\mathit{Yes},\mathit{No}\})$$
    is an invariant of $ICen1^p$, and to check that $DispOrNot^p$ implies $DispOrNot$ for each of those two values of p.

2. For any behavior σ satisfying $ICen1$ there is a behavior τ satisfying $ICen1^p$ such that $\sigma \simeq_p \tau$.

    PROOF: We let σ be a behavior satisfying $ICen1$ and construct the states of τ from the states of σ by specifying the value of p in each of those states, so obviously $\sigma \simeq_p \tau$. The behavior τ will satisfy $ICen1^p$ if the values chosen for p satisfy these three conditions:

    1. The value of p in the second state of a stuttering step of σ (one leaving the variables of $ICen1$ unchanged) is the same as its value in the first state of the step.

    2. After an $Input^p$ step, the value of p is either Yes or No.

    3. In the first state of a $DispOrNot$ step of σ, the value of p must make that step a $DispOrNot^p$ step of τ.

    We define the values of p in all states of τ as follows. We let p have any value in the initial state. In any other state of τ, we let the value of p be the same as its value in the previous state except if the state is the second state of an $Input$ step of σ. In that case, we let the value of p equal Yes if the next $DispOrNot$ step of σ changes $disp$; otherwise we let it equal No. (If there is no next $DispOrNot$ step, so there remain only stuttering steps, we can let p have either value.) It's easy to check that this way of defining p makes it satisfy the three conditions. END PROOF

Let's now generalize from this example. We want an action B to predict the result of the next execution of an action A. We do this by writing A as $\exists\, i \in \Pi : A_i$ for a constant set Π of possible predictions and having B predict for which value of i the next A step will be an A_i step. Action B makes the prediction by setting the variable p to equal its prediction, so we define B^p

7.4. PROPHECY VARIABLES

to equal $B \wedge (p' \in \Pi)$. The prediction is made to come true by defining A^p to equal A_p.

One way our example was special is that the prediction made by an $Input^p$ step is used by $DispOrNot^p$ in the first non-stuttering step after it is made. This allowed $ICen1^p$ to leave the new value of p unspecified by other actions. Usually, there can be steps of other actions between when the prediction is made and when it is fulfilled. Those other actions should leave the value of p unchanged. For any subaction B of the next-state action other than A, we let B^p equal either $B \wedge (p' = p)$ if it doesn't make a prediction or $B \wedge (p' \in \Pi)$ if it makes one. It doesn't matter if multiple predictions are made for the same A step; only the most recent one counts.

For simplicity, we let p always equal an element of Π. We therefore let $Init^p$ equal $Init \wedge (p \in \Pi)$. This can represent an initial prediction, or it can be overridden by a subsequent prediction. In either case, it means that we have the simple type invariant $\Box(p \in \Pi)$.

It doesn't matter if a prediction is never used—either because it is overridden by another prediction or an A step never occurs. What does matter is that a prediction must be used at most once. Our ability to choose the right prediction in the proof that $\exists p : ICen1^p$ is equivalent to $ICen1$ depended on this. To make sure that this is true, we require that A^p makes a prediction, so we define A^p to equal $A_p \wedge (p' \in \Pi)$. That prediction can always be overridden by a subsequent prediction made by a different action. The argument above that the variable p in our example was a prophecy variable then generalizes to prove:

Theorem 7.5 (Simple Prophecy Variable) Let $T \triangleq Init \wedge \Box[Next]_v$ where v is the tuple of variables in T, and let

$$Next \triangleq (\exists i \in \Pi : A_i) \vee (\exists j \in J : B_j)$$

where Π is a constant set. If p is not a variable of T,

$$T^p \triangleq Init^p \wedge \Box[Next^p]_{vp},$$
$$vp \triangleq v \circ \langle p \rangle,$$
$$Init^p \triangleq Init \wedge (p \in \Pi),$$
$$Next^p \triangleq (A_p \wedge (p' \in \Pi)) \vee (\exists j \in J : B_j \wedge C_j),$$

and each C_j equals $p' = p$ or $p' \in \Pi$, then $\models (\exists p : T^p) \equiv T$.

The theorem makes no disjointness assumption about the actions A_i and B_j, but in most applications of the theorem they will be mutually disjoint.

It is inelegant and possibly confusing to have a program make predictions that are never used—for example, by having the $DispOrNot^p$ action of $ICens1^p$ make a prediction that is always replaced by the prediction made by the $Input^p$ action. If the prediction will never be used, we can replace $p' \in \Pi$ by $p' = None$ (or $p \in \Pi$ by $p = None$ for an initial prediction), where $None$ is a value not in Π. The assertion that the prediction is never used means that the following state predicate is an invariant of T^p:

$$(p = None) \Rightarrow \neg \mathbb{E}(\exists\, i \in \Pi : A_i)$$

We could also modify $Next^p$ to let a special value of p indicate that no prediction is being made, but there is no reason to do that.

7.4.2 Predicting the Impossible and Liveness

What if a prophecy variable makes a prediction that can't be fulfilled? A prophecy variable predicts, for an action A equal to $\exists\, i \in \Pi : A_i$, the value of i for which the next A step is an A_i step. The prediction that the next A step will be an A_p step can't be fulfilled if action A_p can't be enabled until an A_j step occurs for some $j \neq p$.

Let's look at the worst case: a prediction that predicts that the next A step will be an A_i step, where A_i equals FALSE. We can write any next-state action $Next$ as

$$\exists\, i \in \{0,1\} : ((i = 1) \land Next) \lor ((i = 0) \land \text{FALSE})$$

(If $i = 0$, then a $[Next]_v$ step leaves the variables of v unchanged.) The observation that $\exists\, i \in \{0,1\} : F_i$ equals $F_0 \lor F_1$ and a bit of propositional logic show that

$$\models \exists\, i \in \{0,1\} : (p = i) \land (((i = 1) \land Next) \lor ((i = 0) \land \text{FALSE}))$$

equals $(p = 1) \land Next$. Theorem 7.5 therefore implies that if T equals $Init \land \Box[Next]_v$, then T equals $\exists\, p : T^p$ where

$$T^p \triangleq\; \land\; Init \land (p \in \{0,1\})$$
$$\land\; \Box[(p = 1) \land Next \land (p' \in \{0,1\})]_{vp}$$

In other words, if p ever becomes equal to 0, then the next-state relation of T^p is never again enabled, so the behavior halts with an infinite sequence of stuttering steps—ones that leave p and the variables of T unchanged.

But that's perfectly OK. T is a safety property; it allows behaviors that terminate at any point. The prophecy variable p is simply predicting whether the behavior will terminate before the next $Next$ step.

7.4. PROPHECY VARIABLES

If we are describing an abstract program in which $\langle Next \rangle_v$ is always enabled and its execution is never supposed to stop, then we must conjoin to T some fairness property, such as $\text{WF}_v(Next)$. If $\langle Next \rangle_v$ is enabled in every reachable state of T, then it is enabled in every reachable state of T^p, since the reachable states of T^p are reachable states of T because T equals $\exists\, p : T^p$. In that case, conjoining $\text{WF}_v(Next)$ to T^p adds the requirement that in every behavior, an infinite number of non-stuttering $Next$ steps must occur. In our worst-case example, $p = 0$ implies $Next^p =$ FALSE, so $T^p \wedge \text{WF}_v(Next)$ is satisfied only by behaviors in which infinitely many $\langle Next \rangle_v$ steps occur, and hence in which p never equals 0.

Conjoining $\text{WF}_v(Next)$ to T^p rules out finite behaviors allowed by T^p—ones in which p equals 0. Hence, the pair $\langle T^p, \text{WF}_v(Next) \rangle$ is not machine closed, so $\text{WF}_v(Next)$ is not a fairness property for T^p. This doesn't contradict Theorem 4.7, because $Next$, which is a trivial subaction of $Next$, is not a subaction of $Next^p$. In general, if predicting that the next A step is an A_p step is a nontrivial prediction, then every possible A step can't be a $Next^p$ step, so $\models A \Rightarrow Next^p$ can't be true—which by definition means A is not a subaction of $Next^p$.

As dramatically illustrated by this example, adding a prophecy variable that can make impossible predictions to a description of an abstract program with a fairness property produces a ⟨safety, liveness⟩ pair that is not machine closed. Although this is not a typical example, in practice prophecy variables often do make impossible predictions. This is usually because it's easier not to eliminate them. That's the case for the example in Section 7.6.

Programs that are not machine closed are weird, and unintentional weirdness usually indicates an error. An abstract program that describes how a concrete program works should be machine closed, because coding languages have no way of expressing liveness properties that are not fairness properties. Abstract programs that are not machine closed should almost always be avoided because they're hard to understand. However, there are exceptions [26, Section 3.2]. On the other hand, prophecy variables are added to a program only for verifying that it implements another program. There is no reason adding a prophecy variable should produce a machine-closed program.

7.4.3 General Prophecy Variables

A simple prophecy variable makes a single prediction. General prophecy variables can make multiple predictions. Those multiple predictions can be successive predictions about a single action or separate predictions about different actions. These two possibilities are illustrated with variants of the censor system. There can also be multiple predictions about multiple actions, but we won't try to be that general. The two examples illustrate the concepts. A very general definition has been described elsewhere for expert TLA$^+$ users [39].

7.4.3.1 A Sequence of Prophecies

Let's now modify the censor programs to allow the artist to submit a new picture before the censor has either displayed or rejected the previous submission. At any time, there may be a queue of submissions being processed by the censor. In the modified version of *ICen1*, called *ICenSeq1*, the censor has not yet decided whether to display or reject any of the submissions in that queue. In *ICenSeq2*, the modified version of *ICen2*, the censor decides immediately whether to accept or reject a submission and maintains only a queue of submissions to be displayed.

Formula *CenSeq1* is defined in Figure 7.6, where everything is in gray except for parts that differ from the corresponding parts of the definition of *Cen1* in Figure 7.4 other than by adding "*Seq*" to names. Because of the way we defined *Cen1*, with *aw* equal to a sequence of 0 or 1 pictures, the changes are minimal. (Recall the definitions of *Tail* and *Append* from Section 2.8.3.)

Similarly, Figure 7.7 shows the definition of *CenSeq2*, using formulas defined in Figure 7.6. Shown in black are the parts that differ from the corresponding parts in the definition of *Cen2* in Figure 7.5 by more than a name change.

In both *ICenSeq1* and *ICenSeq2*, the value of the variable *aw* is the queue being maintained by the censor. As with *ICen1* and *ICen2*, when *aw* is hidden by ∃, the two formulas are equivalent. As in the previous example, *ICenSeq2* decides whether to display or reject an input before *ICenSeq1* does. To define a refinement mapping to show *ICenSeq1* implements *ICenSeq2*, we need to add a prophecy variable *p* to *ICenSeq1* that is set by the *Input* action and predicts the decisions that will be made by the *DispOrNotSeq* action. However, this time there are multiple predictions to be remembered—one for every picture in *aw*.

You have probably figured out that this will be done by letting the value of *p* be a sequence of *Yes* or *No* values, each element of *p* predicting whether the corresponding input in the sequence *aw* will be displayed or rejected by the *DispOrNot* action. Here's how we define *ICenSeq1^p*, the formula obtained by adding the prophecy sequence variable *p* to *ICenSeq1*.

7.4. PROPHECY VARIABLES

$CenSeq1 \triangleq \exists\, aw : ICenSeq1$

$ICenSeq1 \triangleq Init \wedge \Box[NextSeq1]_v$

$v \triangleq \langle inp,\, disp,\, aw \rangle$

$InitSeq \triangleq\; \wedge\; inp = NotArt$
$\; \wedge\; aw = \langle\rangle$
$\; \wedge\; disp \in Art \times \{0, 1\}$

$NextSeq1 \triangleq InputSeq \vee DispOrNotSeq \vee AckSeq$

$InputSeq \triangleq\; \wedge\; inp = NotArt$
$\; \wedge\; inp' \in Art$
$\; \wedge\; aw' = Append(aw, inp')$
$\; \wedge\; disp' = disp$

$DispOrNotSeq \triangleq\; \wedge\; aw \neq \langle\rangle$
$\; \wedge\; \vee\; disp' = \langle aw[1],\, 1 - disp(2) \rangle$
$\; \vee\; disp' = disp$
$\; \wedge\; aw' = Tail(aw)$
$\; \wedge\; inp' = inp$

$AckSeq \triangleq\; \wedge\; inp \in Art$
$\; \wedge\; inp' = NotArt$
$\; \wedge\; (aw' = aw) \wedge (disp' = disp)$

Figure 7.6: The program *CenSeq1*.

$CenSeq2 \triangleq \exists\, aw : ICenSeq2$

$ICenSeq2 \triangleq InitSeq \wedge \Box[NextSeq2]_v$

$NextSeq2 \triangleq InpOrNotSeq \vee DisplaySeq \vee AckSeq$

$InpOrNotSeq \triangleq\; \wedge\; inp = NotArt$
$\; \wedge\; inp' \in Art$
$\; \wedge\; \vee\; aw' = Append(aw, inp')$
$\; \vee\; aw' = aw$
$\; \wedge\; disp' = disp$

$DisplaySeq \triangleq\; \wedge\; aw \neq \langle\rangle$
$\; \wedge\; disp' = \langle aw[1],\, 1 - disp(2) \rangle$
$\; \wedge\; aw' = Tail(aw)$
$\; \wedge\; inp' = inp$

Figure 7.7: The program *CenSeq2*.

Let Π be the set $\{Yes, No\}$ of predictions. The value of p should always be a sequence of elements of Π having the same length as the value of the variable aw of $ICenSeq1$. The initial predicate of $ICenSeq1^p$ is:

$$InitSeq^p \triangleq InitSeq \wedge (p = \langle \rangle)$$

In addition to appending the input to aw, the action $InputSeq^p$ must append to p the prediction of whether or not that input will be displayed:

$$InputSeq^p \triangleq InputSeq \wedge (\exists i \in \Pi : p' = Append(p, i))$$

As in $ICen1^p$, to make $DispOrNotSeq^p$ display the input iff p predicts that it will, we define $DorNSeq_i$ so that

$$DispOrNotSeq \triangleq \exists i \in \Pi : DorNSeq_i$$

where $DorNSeq_{Yes}$ displays the input and $DorNSeq_{No}$ rejects it. The definition of $DorNSeq_i$ is obtained by modifying $DispOrNotSeq$ the same way we modified $DispOrNot$ to obtain $DorN_i$ for $ICen1$. We can then define:

$$DispOrNotSeq^p \triangleq DorNSeq_{p(1)} \wedge (p' = Tail(p))$$

Note that having $DispOrNotSeq^p$ set p' to $Tail(p)$ ensures that every prediction is used only once. Since $AckSeq^p$ neither makes nor satisfies a prediction, we define:

$$AckSeq^p \triangleq AckSeq \wedge (p' = p)$$

Putting this all together we get:

$$ICenSeq1^p \triangleq InitSeq^p \wedge \Box[NextSeq1^p]_{vp}$$

where

$$NextSeq1^p \triangleq InputSeq^p \vee DispOrNotSeq^p \vee AckSeq^p$$

and vp equals $\langle inp, disp, aw, p \rangle$.

We can now show that $CenSeq1$ implements $CenSeq2$ by showing

(7.16) $\models ICenSeq1^p \Rightarrow (ICenSeq2 \text{ WITH } aw \leftarrow awBar)$

where $awBar$ is the subsequence of aw containing only the pictures that p predicts will be displayed.

To define $awBar$, we first define $OnlyYes(wsq, ysq)$ to be the subsequence of the sequence wsq consisting of all elements for which the corresponding elements of the sequence ysq equals Yes. We define $OnlyYes$ to be a function

7.4. PROPHECY VARIABLES

of two arguments with domain the set of pairs $\langle wsq, ysq \rangle$ where wsq is a sequence of elements of Art, ysq is a sequence of Yes or No values, and $Len(wsq) = Len(ysq)$. (Remember that a function of two arguments was defined in Section 2.8.3 to be a function of one argument whose domain is a set of pairs.) The definition is a recursive one, justified by the well-founded relation $\succ$ where $\langle wsq_1, ysq_1 \rangle \succ \langle wsq_2, ysq_2 \rangle$ iff the length of sequences wsq_1 and ysq_1 is greater than the length of wsq_2 and ysq_2. Since we haven't bothered to define a convenient syntax for writing recursive definitions of functions of two arguments, the definition is written somewhat informally as:

$$
\begin{aligned}
Only\,Yes(wsq, ysq) \;\triangleq\;& \\
\text{IF}\;\; wsq = \langle\rangle \;&\text{THEN}\;\; \langle\rangle \\
\text{ELSE}\;\; (&\text{IF}\;\; Head(ysq) = Yes \;\text{THEN}\;\; \langle Head(wsq) \rangle \\
&\phantom{\text{IF}\;\;} \text{ELSE}\;\; \langle\rangle \;\;) \\
&\circ\; Only\,Yes(Tail(wsq), Tail(ysq))
\end{aligned}
$$

Defining $awBar$ to equal $Only\,Yes(aw, p)$ makes (7.16) true.

It's straightforward to modify Theorem 7.5 to describe an arbitrary prophecy variable p that makes a sequence of predictions. We replace the definition of $Next^p$ in the hypothesis of the theorem by:

$$Next^p \;\triangleq\; (A_{p(1)} \land D) \lor (\exists j \in J : B_j \land C_j), \;\text{where}$$
$$D \;\;\text{equals}\;\; p' = Tail(p) \;\;\text{or}\;\; \exists i \in \Pi : p' = Append(Tail(p), i)$$
$$C_j \;\;\text{equals}\;\; p' = p \;\;\text{or}\;\; \exists i \in \Pi : p' = Append(p, i)$$

However, there's one problem: The empty sequence $\langle\rangle$ is the value of p indicating that no prediction is being made. When $p = \langle\rangle$, the value of the subscript $p(1) = i$ in this definition is undefined. That doesn't matter in our example because p and aw are sequences of the same length, so $p = \langle\rangle$ implies $aw = \langle\rangle$, which implies that $DorNSeq_i$ equals FALSE for $i \in \Pi$. Therefore, the value of the undefined subformula makes no difference. In general, to make the modified theorem valid, we need to add to its hypothesis the requirement that the following is an invariant of T^p:

$$(p = \langle\rangle) \;\Rightarrow\; \neg\, \mathbb{E}\,(\exists i \in \Pi : A_i)$$

7.4.3.2 A Set of Prophecies

To illustrate a prophecy variable that makes a set of concurrent predictions, we now modify the censor programs $CenSeq1$ and $CenSeq2$ so that instead of displaying pictures in the order in which they were submitted, the censor can display them in any order. This is represented by letting *aw* be a set rather than a sequence of pictures. It is done in the two programs *ICenSet1* and *ICenSet2*, where the first lets *aw* be the set of all unprocessed inputs and the second lets *aw* contain just the ones that will be displayed. Letting *CenSet1* and *CenSet2* be the programs obtained from these two programs by hiding *aw*, we want to show that *CenSet1* implements *CenSet2*. As you probably realize, defining a refinement mapping to show that this is true requires adding a prophecy variable p to *ICenSet1* that predicts which of the inputs in *aw* will be displayed.

Writing these two censor programs poses a problem. What if the artist submits the same picture twice? If we want the picture to be displayed twice, we would need to have two copies of it in *aw*, which means *aw* couldn't simply be a set. In the example of Section 7.6, you'll see one way of keeping multiple copies of a value in a set. But for simplicity, we'll modify the censor programs not to allow the artist to submit the same picture twice. This will be done by adding an interface variable *old* whose value is the set of all previously submitted pictures.

The definition of *CenSet1* is in Figure 7.8, with the changes from the definition of *CenSeq1* (Figure 7.6) in black. You should be able to write the definition of *CenSeq2* yourself.

To define a refinement mapping under which *ICenSet1* implements *ICenSet2*, we need to add a prophecy variable p to *ICenSet1* that predicts, for each picture in *aw*, whether or not that picture will be displayed. The obvious way to do that is to let the value of p be a function in $aw \to \Pi$, the set of functions from *aw* to Π. As before, we let Π equal the set $\{Yes, No\}$.

Since *aw* initially equals the empty set, the initial value of p should be the function whose domain is the empty set. There is just a single such function, and the easiest way to write it is as the empty sequence $\langle\rangle$, which is a (and hence the) function whose domain is the empty set. So, we define:

$$InitSet^p \triangleq InitSet \wedge (p = \langle\rangle)$$

The *InputSet*^{p} action must add a prediction of whether or not the picture *inp'* that it adds to *aw* will be displayed. Thus, it must assert that p' is the function obtained from p by adding *inp'* to its domain and letting the value of $p'(inp')$ be either element in Π. To write that action, let's define $FcnPlus(f, w, d)$ to be the function obtained from a function f by adding an element w to its domain and letting that function map w to d. The domain

7.4. PROPHECY VARIABLES

$CenSet1 \triangleq \exists\, aw : ICenSet1$

$ICenSet1 \triangleq Init \wedge \square[NextSet1]_v$

$v \triangleq \langle inp, disp, aw, old \rangle$

$InitSet \triangleq\ \wedge\ inp = NotArt$
$\ \wedge\ aw = \{\,\}$
$\ \wedge\ disp \in Art \times \{0,1\}$
$\ \wedge\ old = \{\,\}$

$NextSet1 \triangleq InputSet \vee DispOrNotSet \vee AckSet$

$InputSet \triangleq\ \wedge\ inp = NotArt$
$\ \wedge\ inp' \in Art \setminus old$
$\ \wedge\ aw' = aw \cup \{inp'\}$
$\ \wedge\ (disp' = disp) \wedge (old' = old \cup \{inp'\})$

$DispOrNotSet \triangleq\ \exists\, w \in aw\ :$
$\ \wedge \vee\ disp' = \langle w,\ 1 - disp(2)\rangle$
$\ \vee\ disp' = disp$
$\ \wedge\ aw' = aw \setminus \{w\}$
$\ \wedge\ (inp' = inp) \wedge (old' = old)$

$AckSet \triangleq\ \wedge\ inp \in Art$
$\ \wedge\ inp' = NotArt$
$\ \wedge\ (aw' = aw) \wedge (disp' = disp) \wedge (old' = old)$

Figure 7.8: The program *CenSet1*.

of f is written DOMAIN(f), so the definition is:

$FcnPlus(f, w, d) \triangleq$
$\quad x \in \{w\} \cup \text{DOMAIN}(f) \mapsto \text{IF } x = w \text{ THEN } d \text{ ELSE } f(x)$

We can then define

$InputSet^p \triangleq InputSet \wedge (\exists\, i \in \Pi : p' = FcnPlus(p, inp', i))$

To define $DispOrNotSet^p$, we define $DorNSet_i(w)$ as follows so $DispOrNotSet$ equals $\exists\, w \in aw, i \in \Pi : DorNSet_i(w)$.

$DorNSet_i(w) \triangleq\ \wedge \vee\ (i = Yes) \wedge (disp' = \langle w, 1 - disp(2)\rangle)$
$\ \vee\ (i = No) \wedge (disp' = disp)$
$\ \wedge\ aw' = aw \setminus \{w\}$
$\ \wedge\ (inp' = inp) \wedge (old' = old)$

The *DispOrNotSet^p* action will have to erase the prediction by removing from the domain of p the picture being displayed or rejected. So let's define $FcnMinus(f, w)$ to equal the restriction of f to its domain minus the element w:

$$FcnMinus(f, w) \triangleq x \in (\text{DOMAIN}(f) \setminus \{w\}) \mapsto f(x)$$

We can now define:

$$DispOrNotSet^p \triangleq$$
$$\exists w \in aw : DorNSet_{p(w)}(w) \wedge (p' = FcnMinus(p, w))$$

Since *AckSet^p* neither makes nor satisfies a prediction, its definition is simply:

$$AckSet^p \triangleq AckSet \wedge (p' = p)$$

The rest of the definition of *ICenSet1^p* should be clear.

We can then show that *CenSet1* implements *CenSet2* by showing

$$\models ICenSet1^p \Rightarrow (ICenSet2 \text{ WITH } aw \leftarrow awBar)$$

where $awBar$ equals $\{w \in aw : p(w) = Yes\}$, the set of elements in aw that p predicts will be displayed.

We won't bother writing the generalization of Theorem 7.5 for a prophecy variable p that makes a set of predictions.

7.4.3.3 Further Generalizations

We now extract from our examples a more general formulation of prophecy variables. To construct a prophecy variable, we start with certain sets of actions we'll call *action sets*. For *CenSeq1* there is one action set consisting of two actions: *DispOrNotSeq$_{Yes}$*, a *DispOrNotSeq* action that displays the picture, and *DispOrNotSeq$_{No}$*, a *DispOrNotSeq* action that doesn't display it. For *CenSet1*, for every $w \in Art$, there is an action set consisting of two actions: *DispOrNotSet$_{w,Yes}$* and *DispOrNotSet$_{w,No}$*, which are *DispOrNotSet* actions that either display or don't display the input w. Thus, there is a set of action sets, one action set defined for each w in Art.

In general, for a program T, we have a set of action sets, each of which can be written as $\{A_i : i \in \Pi\}$. (The set Π can be different for different action sets.) That set of action sets is a constant; it doesn't change during a behavior of T.

7.4. PROPHECY VARIABLES

A prophecy is a prediction about one of the program's action sets. That is, it is an element of the set Π defining the action set $\{A_i : i \in \Pi\}$. It predicts the value of i for which the next A_i step occurs. In any state, the value of a prophecy variable describes a set of predictions, some of which are active. For *CenSeq1*, the prophecy variable p equals a sequence of predictions, all for the same action set, only the first element of the sequence being active. For *CenSet1*, the prophecy variable p equals a set of prophecies, one for each action set defined by an element of aw, all of its prophecies being active.

In general, the program T^p is defined by adding the variable p in such a way that every behavior satisfying T^p satisfies T. Moreover, it ensures that no active prediction of p is ever violated. When an action predicted by an active prediction of p occurs, we say that the prediction is *fulfilled*. The initial value of p can contain prophecies. Prophecies can be added to or removed from p and/or made active or inactive by any action of T^p, so long as the following conditions are satisfied:

- No two active prophecies can be predictions for the same action set.

- For any action of T^p that adds a prophecy to p, it must be possible for the action to add a prophecy for any element of the set Π for that action set.

- An action of T^p that fulfills a prediction must remove that prediction from p. (It may also add one or more new predictions.)

The prophecy variables of *CenSeq1* and *CenSet1* made only predictions that were likely to be fulfilled. We could instead have used prophecy variables that a mathematician might consider simpler that make a lot more predictions. For *CenSeq1*, instead of having each *InputSeq* step add a prediction to p, we could have let the initial value of p be an infinite sequence of predictions. The first element of the sequence would be the active one, and each *DispOrNotSeq* action would remove that element from p. For *CenSet1*, we could have let the initial value of p be any element of $Art \to \{Yes, No\}$, predicting for each picture w whether or not it will be displayed if it is input. Since the same picture can't be input twice, the value of $p(inp)$ could be set by a *DispOrNotSet* action to a value indicating that its prediction is inactive.

We could have used an even more extravagant prophecy variable for *CenSet1*—one that predicts not only whether each picture will be displayed or rejected, but in which order they will be input. The initial value of p would be an infinite sequence of predictions $\langle w, d \rangle$, for $w \in Art$ and

$d \in \{\mathit{Yes}, \mathit{No}\}$, predicting not just if the next *DispOrNotSet* step will display or reject the input, but that it must occur with *inp* equal to w. Almost all of those predictions will be impossible to fulfill because *inp* will not equal w. But as we've seen, impossible predictions don't matter because they just require the behavior to halt, which either is allowed or else is ruled out by a liveness hypothesis. This may seem silly, but a prophecy variable that makes predictions that are almost all impossible is used in the example of Section 7.6 because it seems to provide the simplest way to define the needed refinement mapping.

7.5 The Existence of Refinement Mappings

We now state a completeness result for the auxiliary variables that we've described. Completeness means that if $\models T \Rightarrow \exists \mathbf{y} : \mathit{IS}$ is true, where $\mathbf{y}$ is a list of variables, then we can successively add a list $\mathbf{a}$ of these auxiliary variables to T to obtain a formula $T^{\mathbf{a}}$ that implies IS under a refinement mapping that substitutes state expressions of $T^{\mathbf{a}}$ for the variables $\mathbf{y}$.

Like most such completeness results, it assumes that there is a mathematical proof of the result based on the semantics of the formulas. That is, we assume not only the truth of $\models T \Rightarrow \exists \mathbf{y} : \mathit{IS}$, but that there exists a mathematical proof of its truth. Such a proof consists of an operator Φ such that for every behavior σ satisfying T, there is a behavior $\Phi(\sigma)$ satisfying IS that shows σ satisfies $\exists \mathbf{y} : \mathit{IS}$. This means approximately that we can obtain $\Phi(\sigma)$ from σ by adding and/or removing stuttering steps and changing the values of the variables of $\mathbf{y}$. The precise statement of this condition is $\Phi(\sigma) \sim_\mathbf{y} \sigma$, where the definition of $\sim_\mathbf{y}$ is the same as that of $\sim_y$ in Section 7.1.3 with $=_y$ replaced by $=_\mathbf{y}$, and $s =_\mathbf{y} t$ defined to mean that states s and t are equal except perhaps for the values they assign to the variables of $\mathbf{y}$. The assumption that there exists a mathematical proof of $\models T \Rightarrow \exists \mathbf{y} : \mathit{IS}$ is embodied in the use of Φ to construct the refinement mapping. Here is the precise statement of the theorem. It uses the notation that if $\mathbf{y}$ is the list $y_1, \ldots, y_n$ of variables and **exp** is the list $\mathit{exp}_1, \ldots, \mathit{exp}_n$ of expressions, then $\mathbf{y} \leftarrow \mathbf{exp}$ is an abbreviation for $y_1 \leftarrow \mathit{exp}_1, \ldots, y_n \leftarrow \mathit{exp}_n$.

Theorem 7.6 Let $\mathbf{x}$, $\mathbf{y}$, and $\mathbf{z}$ be lists of variables, all distinct from one another; let the variables of T be $\mathbf{x}$ and $\mathbf{z}$ and the variables of IS be $\mathbf{x}$ and $\mathbf{y}$; and let T equal $\mathit{Init} \wedge \Box[\mathit{Next}]_{\langle \mathbf{x},\mathbf{z} \rangle} \wedge L$. Let the operator Φ map behaviors satisfying T to behaviors satisfying IS such that $\Phi(\sigma) \sim_\mathbf{y} \sigma$. By adding history, stuttering, and prophecy variables to T, we can define a formula

$T^{\mathbf{a}}$ such that $\exists\,\mathbf{a}: T^{\mathbf{a}}$ is equivalent to T and a list **exp** of expressions defined in terms of Φ and the variables of $T^{\mathbf{a}}$ such that

$$\models T^{\mathbf{a}} \Rightarrow (\textit{IS} \text{ WITH } \mathbf{y} \leftarrow \mathbf{exp})$$

The theorem makes no assumption about L other than that it contains no variables besides those of $\mathbf{x}$ and $\mathbf{z}$. It doesn't even have to be a liveness property.

Here is the idea behind the theorem's proof. We first add an infinite-stuttering variable t to avoid having to worry about terminating behaviors. We then add a history variable h that remembers the entire sequence of values of all the tuples $\langle \mathbf{x}, \mathbf{z}, t \rangle$ in all the states reached thus far, including the current one. We then add a prophecy sequence variable p that predicts the infinite sequence of all future values of $\langle \mathbf{x}, \mathbf{z}, t \rangle$. This means that in all states of the behavior, the value of $h \circ p$ is the entire sequence of values of $\langle \mathbf{x}, \mathbf{z}, t \rangle$ in the complete (infinite) behavior. Moreover, the length of h indicates the position of the current state in that behavior. The values of h and p and the mapping Φ provide all the information needed to determine the values to substitute for $\mathbf{y}$ to obtain a refinement mapping under which IS is simulated. The proof in the Appendix sketches the details.

The theorem shows that these auxiliary variables are, in principle, all we need to define a refinement mapping. It and its proof do not tell us how refinement mappings are defined in practice.

7.6 The FIFO Queue

This section presents a more realistic example of the use of auxiliary variables to show that one abstract program implements another. That makes it rather long, but it's included for two reasons. The first is that it describes linearizability, which is an important concept for designing concurrent programs. The second is that stuttering and prophecy variables are not as intuitive as history variables, and a more realistic example may provide some insight into how they can be used in practice.

7.6.1 *Fifo* – A Linearizable Specification

Popular coding languages provide a small number of built-in data types such as finite-precision integers. Other data types must be implemented as objects. An object has a state and methods with which the program can read and modify parts of the state. We will ignore how objects are created and destroyed.

A simple example of such an object is a first in, first out queue, called a FIFO. We can think of the state of a FIFO as an ordinal sequence *queue* of elements from some set *Data*. A FIFO provides two methods, usually described as follows.

enqueue Takes an element of *Data* as an argument, and appends it to the end of *queue*. It returns no value.[2]

dequeue If *queue* is nonempty, it removes the first element of *queue* and returns it as the result. If *queue* is the empty sequence, it returns some special value.

An object is accessed only by executing its methods. For the purpose of correctness, the programmer needs to know nothing about how these two methods are implemented.

This kind of description is adequate for a method in a traditional program. It is inadequate for concurrent programs because it says nothing about what happens if two processes concurrently access the object. The call of a method and the return are usually described as single steps, but execution of the operation may consist of steps that occur between those two steps.

Often, it is considered an error if two processes concurrently access the same object. The object must either be accessed by only one process, or else accesses by different processes must be inside the critical section of a mutual exclusion algorithm. We're interested in objects that are meant to be accessed concurrently by multiple processes—for example, a critical section object for implementing mutual exclusion with *enter* and *exit* methods.

Maurice Herlihy and Jeannette Wing defined an object to be *linearizable* iff it acts as if the execution of a method consists of three steps: the call, the return, and between them a single step that performs the actual reading and/or modifying of the object's state [19]. The state of a linearizable object is described by internal variables. Only the call and return steps change interface variables. Linearizability has become a standard requirement for shared objects in concurrent systems.

We describe a linearizable FIFO as an abstract program. We require that execution of a *dequeue* operation when *queue* is empty waits for an element to be enqueued rather than returning a special value. This makes the FIFO more interesting because it involves process synchronization—making one process wait for another process to do something. Since the purpose of the

---

[2]Sometimes the queue can hold only some maximum number of elements, but for simplicity we assume that there is no such limit.

7.6. THE FIFO QUEUE

example is to illustrate the use of auxiliary variables, which are added only to the safety property of a program, we consider only the safety property of a FIFO.

We assume there is a set *EnQers* of processes that perform *enqueue* operations. Execution of an *enqueue* operation by process e consists of three steps: a *BeginEnq(e)* step that describes the call of the method, a *DoEnq(e)* step that modifies the variable *queue*, and an *EndEnq(e)* step that describes the return. The enqueuers communicate with the object through the interface variable *enq*, whose value is a function with domain *EnQers*. The value of *enq(e)* equals *Done* when enqueuer e is not performing an *enqueue* operation, and it equals the data value it is appending to *queue* when e is performing the operation, where *Done* is some constant not in *Data*. There is also an internal variable *enqInner*, where *enqInner(e)* is set to *Busy* by the *BeginEnq(e)* action and is set to *Done* by the *DoEnq(e)* action.

Similarly, there is a set *DeQers* of dequeuer processes, each $d \in DeQers$ performing *BeginDeq(d)*, *DoDeq(d)*, and *EndDeq(d)* steps. Dequeuers communicate with the object through the interface variable *deq*, where *deq(d)* is set to *Busy* by the *BeginDeq(d)* action and to the value that was dequeued by the *EndDeq(d)* action. There is an internal variable *deqInner*, where *deqInner(d)* is set to *Busy* by the *BeginDeq(d)* action and set by *DoDeq(d)* to the value dequeued by the *dequeue* operation. The complete definition of the abstract program is formula *Fifo* in Figure 7.9. It uses the UNCHANGED operator, where UNCHANGED exp equals $exp' = exp$. Thus, if v is a tuple $\langle v_1, \ldots, v_n \rangle$ of variables, then UNCHANGED v asserts that $v'_i = v_i$ for all i in $1..n$.

7.6.2 *POFifo* – A More General Specification

7.6.2.1 The Background

Many people, myself included, used to believe that any implementation of a FIFO had to be a more concrete version of program *IFifo*, with the value of the variable *queue* encoded in the program's state. This implied that any implementation of a FIFO should implement *IFifo* under a refinement mapping, without having to add auxiliary variables.

We were wrong. Suppose two processes concurrently execute *enqueue* operations. When the two operations' *EndEnq* steps have occurred, program *IFifo* has appended both values to *queue* in some order, determining the order in which they will be dequeued. However, in a behavior of program

$Fifo \triangleq \exists\, queue, enqInner, deqInner : IFifo$

$IFifo \triangleq Init \wedge \Box[Next]_v$

$v \triangleq \langle enq, deq, queue, enqInner, deqInner \rangle$

$Init \triangleq\ \wedge enq = (e \in EnQers \mapsto Done)$
$\qquad\qquad \wedge deq \in (DeQers \to Data)$
$\qquad\qquad \wedge queue = \langle\rangle$
$\qquad\qquad \wedge enqInner = (e \in EnQers \mapsto Done)$
$\qquad\qquad \wedge deqInner = deq$

$Next \triangleq\ \vee \exists\, e \in EnQers : BeginEnq(e) \vee DoEnq(e) \vee EndEnq(e)$
$\qquad\qquad \vee \exists\, d \in DeQers : BeginDeq(d) \vee DoDeq(d) \vee EndDeq(d)$

$BeginEnq(e) \triangleq\ \wedge enq(e) = Done$
$\qquad\qquad\qquad \wedge \exists\, D \in Data : enq' = (enq \text{ EXCEPT } e \mapsto D)$
$\qquad\qquad\qquad \wedge enqInner' = (enqInner \text{ EXCEPT } e \mapsto Busy)$
$\qquad\qquad\qquad \wedge \text{UNCHANGED } \langle deq, queue, deqInner \rangle$

$DoEnq(e) \triangleq\ \wedge enqInner(e) = Busy$
$\qquad\qquad\quad \wedge queue' = Append(queue, enq(e))$
$\qquad\qquad\quad \wedge enqInner' = (enqInner \text{ EXCEPT } e \mapsto Done)$
$\qquad\qquad\quad \wedge \text{UNCHANGED } \langle deq, enq, deqInner \rangle$

$EndEnq(e) \triangleq\ \wedge enq(e) \neq Done$
$\qquad\qquad\quad \wedge enqInner(e) = Done$
$\qquad\qquad\quad \wedge enq' = (enq \text{ EXCEPT } e \mapsto Done)$
$\qquad\qquad\quad \wedge \text{UNCHANGED } \langle deq, queue, enqInner, deqInner \rangle$

$BeginDeq(d) \triangleq\ \wedge deq(d) \neq Busy$
$\qquad\qquad\qquad \wedge deq' = (deq \text{ EXCEPT } d \mapsto Busy)$
$\qquad\qquad\qquad \wedge deqInner' = (deqInner \text{ EXCEPT } d \mapsto NoData)$
$\qquad\qquad\qquad \wedge \text{UNCHANGED } \langle enq, queue, enqInner \rangle$

$DoDeq(d) \triangleq\ \wedge deq(d) = Busy$
$\qquad\qquad\quad \wedge deqInner(d) = NoData$
$\qquad\qquad\quad \wedge queue \neq \langle\rangle$
$\qquad\qquad\quad \wedge deqInner' = (deqInner \text{ EXCEPT } d \mapsto Head(queue))$
$\qquad\qquad\quad \wedge queue' = Tail(queue)$
$\qquad\qquad\quad \wedge \text{UNCHANGED } \langle enq, deq, enqInner \rangle$

$EndDeq(d) \triangleq\ \wedge deq(d) = Busy$
$\qquad\qquad\quad \wedge deqInner(d) \neq NoData$
$\qquad\qquad\quad \wedge deq' = (deq \text{ EXCEPT } d \mapsto deqInner(d))$
$\qquad\qquad\quad \wedge \text{UNCHANGED } \langle enq, queue, enqInner, deqInner \rangle$

Figure 7.9: The program *Fifo*.

7.6. THE FIFO QUEUE

Fifo, where *queue* is hidden, there is no way to know in which order the two values appear in *queue* until that order is revealed by *dequeue* operations. In their paper defining linearizability, Herlihy and Wing gave an algorithm that implements a FIFO in which, from a state immediately after both *enqueue* operations have completed, it is possible for the two values to be dequeued in either order by two successive non-concurrent *dequeue* operations. There is no queue encoded in the algorithm. While their algorithm implements *Fifo*, there is no refinement mapping under which it implements *IFifo* without the addition of auxiliary variables. In particular, showing that their algorithm implements *Fifo* requires adding a prophecy variable that predicts the order in which data items enqueued by concurrent *enqueue* operations will be dequeued.

What is encoded in the state of their algorithm is not a linearly ordered queue of enqueued data values, but rather a partial order on the set of enqueued values that indicates the possible orders in which the values can be returned by *dequeue* operations. A partial order on a set S is a relation $\prec$ on S that is transitive and has no cycles (which implies $a \not\prec a$ for any $a \in S$). For the partial ordering $\prec$ on the set of enqueued values, the relation $u \prec w$ means that value u must be dequeued before value w. Program *IFifo* is the special case in which that partial order is a total order, meaning that either $u \prec w$ or $w \prec u$ for any two distinct enqueued values u and w.

Presented here is a program *POFifo* that is equivalent to *Fifo*, but which is obtained by hiding internal variables in a program *IPOFifo* that maintains a partially ordered set of enqueued values rather than a queue. The Herlihy–Wing algorithm can be shown to implement *IPOFifo* under a refinement mapping defined in terms of its variables, without adding a prophecy variable.

7.6.2.2 Program *POFifo*

Execution of an operation is described by a sequence of steps. In a linearizable description, there are three steps: a step of the *Begin* action, a step of the *Do* action, and a step of the *End* action. One operation execution is defined to *precede* another if its *End* step precedes the other execution's *Begin* step. If neither of two operation executions precedes the other, then the executions are said to be *concurrent*.

Since *Begin* and *End* steps change interface variables, they appear in a behavior of *Fifo*. However, a *Do* step changes only internal variables, so it is not visible in a behavior of *Fifo*. If the executions of two *enqueues* are concurrent, then a behavior of *Fifo* does not show in which order their

Do steps occurred in *IFifo*. Only if one *enqueue* execution precedes the other do we know from a behavior of *Fifo* the order in which the enqueued values appear in *queue*. Therefore, a behavior satisfies *Fifo* iff it satisfies the following two safety properties. They are stated informally, where a *value* is taken to mean a particular enqueueing of a data value.

F1. Each dequeued value has been enqueued, and an enqueued value is dequeued at most once.

F2. If an *enqueue* of a value v precedes an *enqueue* of a value w, then the *dequeue* of value w cannot precede the *dequeue* of value v.

The values enqueued by two concurrent *enqueue* executions may be dequeued in either order.

Program *IPOFifo* must maintain a set of enqueued items and some ordering relation among them. The first thing to observe is that the same data item might be enqueued twice before any item is dequeued. Since this is not a silly example, that possibility should be handled. An easy way to do that is to maintain a set of pairs $\langle d, i \rangle$ where d is the enqueued data value and i is an element of a set *Ids* of identifiers that serve to distinguish between different "copies" of an enqueued value. Let's call such a ⟨data value, identifier pair⟩ a *datum*. (We will use *datums* as the plural of *datum* because *data* suggests elements of *Data* rather than of $Data \times Id$. We will continue to call an element of *Data* a *data value*.)

IPOFifo will use an internal variable *elts* whose value is the set of currently enqueued datums. It will also have an internal variable whose value is an ordering relation $\prec$ on the set *elts*, where $u \prec w$ means that datum u must be dequeued before datum w is. For *IPOFifo* to describe a linearizable object, execution of an *enqueue* operation must consist of a *BeginPOEnq* step, followed by a *DoPOEnq* step that puts the datum in *elts*, followed by an *EndPOEnq* step. Condition F2 is satisfied if the *DoPOEnq* step that puts a datum w in *elts* adds a relation $u \prec w$ for every datum u put in *elts* by an *enqueue* operation that has completed. Of course, F1 is satisfied if every *DoPODeq* step obtains its data item from a datum that it removes from *elts*.

Given any behavior σ satisfying *IPOFifo*, we can obtain a behavior τ satisfying *IPOFifo* by moving every *DoPOEnq* step earlier in the behavior so it occurs immediately after its operation's *BeginPOEnq* step, and moving every *DoPODeq* step later in the behavior so it occurs immediately before its operation's *EndPODeq* step. Moreover, since the *Do*... steps change only internal variables, the values of the interface variables are the same in each

7.6. THE FIFO QUEUE

state of τ as in σ. Therefore, without eliminating any possible behaviors of *POFifo* (which are obtained by hiding the internal variables of *IPOFifo*), we can require that a *BeginPOEnq* step be immediately followed by the operation's *DoPOEnq* step, and that an *EndPODeq* step be immediately preceded by the operation's *DoPODeq* step. This means that there's no need for the *Do*... actions; the *BeginPOEnq* and *DoPOEnq* actions can be combined into a single action, as can the *DoPODeq* and *EndPODeq* actions. We will therefore simplify *IPOFifo* by eliminating the *Do*... actions and having only *Begin*... and *End*... actions.

We can now write the program *IPOFifo*. It will have the same constants as *IFifo* plus the set *Ids* of identifiers; and it will have the same interface variables *enq* and *deq*. It will have the internal variable *elts* whose value is the set of currently enqueued datums.

IPOFifo will need an internal variable to describe the partial order $\prec$ on the set *elts*. Mathematicians describe a relation $\prec$ on a set S as a subset of $S \times S$, where $u \prec v$ is an abbreviation for $\langle u, v \rangle \in \prec$. We'll do the same thing, except it would be confusing to use the symbol $\prec$ as a variable. We will therefore let *before* be the variable whose value is a subset of $elts \times elts$ such that $u \prec v$ means $\langle u, v \rangle \in before$.

Finally, when enqueueing a datum w, the *BeginPOEnq* step must add to $\prec$ the relation $u \prec w$ for a datum u in *elts* iff the *enqueue* operation that added u has completed. That information is not contained in the interface variable *enq* because $enq(e)$ contains only the data value that an uncompleted *enqueue* operation is enqueueing, not which datum the operation put in *elts*. Therefore, we add to *IPOFifo* an internal variable *adding* such that $adding(e)$ equals the datum in *elts* that enqueuer e put in *elts*, and equals a value *NonElt* that is not a datum if e is not currently performing an *enqueue* operation.

We use *adding* to define the following state expression, whose value is the set of datums enqueued by operations whose executions have not yet completed:

$$beingAdded \triangleq \{adding(e) : e \in EnQers\} \setminus \{NonElt\}$$

The set *beingAdded* need not be a subset of *elts* because it can contain datums that were removed from *elts* by *dequeue* operations before the operations that enqueued them have completed.

The program *POFifo* is defined in Figure 7.10. Here are explanations of the four disjuncts of the next-state action *PONext*.

BeginPOEnq(e) Enabled when $enq(e) = Done$, it:

$POFifo \triangleq \exists\, elts, before, adding : IPOFifo$

$IPOFifo \triangleq POInit \wedge \Box[PONext]_{POv}$

$POv \triangleq \langle enq, deq, elts, before, adding \rangle$

$POInit \triangleq\ \wedge\ enq = (e \in EnQers \mapsto Done)$
$\qquad\qquad\ \ \wedge\ deq \in (DeQers \to Data)$
$\qquad\qquad\ \ \wedge\ elts = \{\}$
$\qquad\qquad\ \ \wedge\ before = \{\}$
$\qquad\qquad\ \ \wedge\ adding = (e \in EnQers \mapsto NonElt)$

$PONext \triangleq\ \vee\ \exists\, e \in EnQers : BeginPOEnq(e) \vee EndPOEnq(e)$
$\qquad\qquad\quad \vee\ \exists\, d \in DeQers : BeginPODeq(d) \vee EndPODeq(d)$

$BeginPOEnq(e) \triangleq$
$\quad \wedge\ enq(e) = Done$
$\quad \wedge\ \exists\, D \in Data : \exists\, id \in \{i \in Ids : \langle D, i \rangle \notin (elts \cup beingAdded)\} :$
$\qquad \wedge\ enq' = (enq\ \text{EXCEPT}\ e \mapsto D)$
$\qquad \wedge\ elts' = elts \cup \{\langle D, id \rangle\}$
$\qquad \wedge\ before' = before \cup \{\langle el, \langle D, id \rangle \rangle : el \in (elts \setminus beingAdded)\}$
$\qquad \wedge\ adding' = (adding\ \text{EXCEPT}\ e \mapsto \langle D, id \rangle)$
$\quad \wedge\ deq' = deq$

$EndPOEnq(e) \triangleq\ \wedge\ enq(e) \neq Done$
$\qquad\qquad\qquad\ \ \wedge\ enq' = (enq\ \text{EXCEPT}\ e \mapsto Done)$
$\qquad\qquad\qquad\ \ \wedge\ adding' = (adding\ \text{EXCEPT}\ e \mapsto NonElt)$
$\qquad\qquad\qquad\ \ \wedge\ \text{UNCHANGED}\ \langle deq, elts, before \rangle$

$BeginPODeq(d) \triangleq\ \wedge\ deq(d) \neq Busy$
$\qquad\qquad\qquad\ \ \wedge\ deq' = (deq\ \text{EXCEPT}\ d \mapsto Busy)$
$\qquad\qquad\qquad\ \ \wedge\ \text{UNCHANGED}\ \langle enq, elts, before, adding \rangle$

$EndPODeq(d) \triangleq\ \wedge\ deq(d) = Busy$
$\qquad\qquad\qquad\ \wedge\ \exists\, el \in elts :$
$\qquad\qquad\qquad\quad \wedge\ \forall\, el2 \in elts : \neg(el2 \prec el)$
$\qquad\qquad\qquad\quad \wedge\ elts' = elts \setminus \{el\}$
$\qquad\qquad\qquad\quad \wedge\ deq' = (deq\ \text{EXCEPT}\ d \mapsto el(1))$
$\qquad\qquad\qquad\quad \wedge\ before' = before \cap (elts' \times elts')$
$\qquad\qquad\qquad\quad \wedge\ \text{UNCHANGED}\ \langle enq, adding \rangle$

Figure 7.10: The program *POFifo*.

7.6. THE FIFO QUEUE

- Sets $enq(e)$ to the data value D that e is enqueuing.
- Adds a datum $\langle D, id \rangle$ to $elts$ for some $id \in Ids$ for which $\langle D, id \rangle$ is not already in $elts$ or $beingAdded$.
- Modifies $before$ to add the relations $el \prec \langle D, id \rangle$ for every el in $elts$ that is not in $beingAdded$.
- Sets $adding(e)$ to $\langle D, id \rangle$, thereby adding $\langle D, id \rangle$ to $beingAdded$.

$EndPOEnq(e)$ Enabled when $enq(e)$ is a data value, it sets $enq(e)$ to $Done$ and sets $adding(e)$ to $NonElt$, thereby removing from $beingAdded$ the datum that e had enqueued.

$BeginPODeq(d)$ Enabled when $deq(d)$ is a data value, it sets $deq(d)$ to $Busy$.

$EndPODeq(d)$ Enabled when $deq(d)$ equals $Busy$ and $elts$ is not empty, which implies that $elts$ contains at least one minimal datum (a datum not preceded in the $\prec$ relation by any other datum in $elts$), since the datum in $elts$ that was added first to $elts$ must be a minimal datum. The action chooses an arbitrary minimal datum el of $elts$, removes it from $elts$, sets $deq(d)$ to its data value component, and modifies $before$ to remove all relations $el \prec el2$ for elements $el2$ of $elts$.

7.6.3 Showing *IPOFifo* Implements *Fifo*

Formulas *POFifo* and *Fifo* are equivalent. However, more important and more interesting than showing that *Fifo* refines *POFifo* is showing that *POFifo* refines *Fifo*. It's more important because *Fifo* is the generally accepted description of a FIFO. By showing that *POFifo* implements *Fifo*, we can show that an algorithm that doesn't maintain a totally ordered queue implements *Fifo* by showing that it implements *POFifo*. It's more interesting because showing that *POFifo* implements *Fifo* requires all three kinds of auxiliary variables. So, we won't discuss the problem of showing that *Fifo* refines *POFifo*.

To show that *POFifo* refines *Fifo*, we have to define a refinement mapping under which *IPOFifo* implements *IFifo*. This requires adding to *IPOFifo* first a prophecy variable, then a history variable, then a stuttering variable. They are added in the three following subsections. Adding the prophecy variable is straightforward and the necessary details are presented. How to add the other two variables and define the refinement mapping are then sketched. Rigorously defining those two programs and the refinement mapping would be a marvelous learning experience. However, the chance of doing it without making any error is small unless you use a tool to check what you have done. I used a model checker for TLA$^+$ to check that the program obtained by adding the auxiliary variables to *POFifo* implements *Fifo* under the refinement mapping described below.

7.6.3.1 The Prophecy Variable

The most significant problem in showing that *POFifo* implements *Fifo* is that *IFifo* decides the order in which concurrently enqueued values will be dequeued before *IPOFifo* does. This tells us that to define a refinement mapping under which *IFifo* is implemented by *POFifo*, we need to add a prophecy variable p to *IPOFifo*.

The simplest way I know of making the necessary predictions is with a prophecy sequence variable p that predicts the sequence of datums that will be dequeued next. The first item in the sequence predicts the datum that the next *EndPODeq* step removes from *elts*, and that step of course removes the prediction from p. The natural step to append a prediction to the sequence p is the *BeginPOEnq* step that adds a datum to *elts*. The length of p therefore always equals the number of datums in *elts*. The predictions are completely arbitrary datums, so in almost all behaviors they will be impossible to fulfill, at some point not allowing any more datums to be dequeued. But as we've seen, unfulfillable predictions are no problem. Since no predictions are made about *enqueue* operations, they can keep being performed even if the datums they enqueue can never be dequeued.

The set Π of possible predictions equals the set $Data \times Ids$ of all possible datums. The *BeginPOEnq(e)* action should append a prediction to p, and the *EndPOEnq(e)* and *BeginPODeq(d)* actions should leave p unchanged. We can therefore define three of the four subactions of the next-state action *PONext^p* of *IPOFifo^p* by:

$$BeginPOEnq^p(e) \triangleq \;\land\; BeginPOEnq(e)$$
$$ \land\; \exists\, el \in Data \times Ids : p' = Append(p, el)$$
$$EndPOEnq^p(e) \triangleq EndPOEnq(e) \land (p' = p)$$
$$BeginPODeq^p(d) \triangleq BeginPODeq(d) \land (p' = p)$$

The prediction made by the first item $p(1)$ of the sequence p is the datum that the next *EndPODeq(d)* step will remove from *elts*. The datum $p(1)$ is removed by this step iff $elts' = elts \setminus \{p(1)\}$ is true of the step. Since the

7.6. THE FIFO QUEUE

step must remove the prediction, we can define:

$EndPODeq^p(d) \triangleq$
$\quad EndPODeq(d) \wedge (elts' = elts \setminus \{p(1)\}) \wedge (p' = Tail(p))$

These four action definitions, and the observation that $Init^p$ should equal $Init \wedge (p = \langle \rangle)$ give us all the pieces of the definition of $IPOFifo^p$. I won't bother to put them together.

7.6.3.2 The History Variable qBar

We now must decide how to define *queueBar*, the state expression that is substituted for *queue* in the refinement mapping. It's easiest to think of defining *queueBar* as the sequence not of the data values to be substituted for the variable *queue* of *IFifo*, but of the sequence of datums being dequeued from *elts* by *POFifo*. We can then define the refinement mapping so it substitutes for the variable *queue* of *IFifo* the sequence of data values in the datums of *queueBar*.

Since there are no $Do\ldots$ steps in *IPOFifo*, we will have to add stuttering steps to append datums to *queueBar*. To do that, we will first add to $IPOFifo^p$ a history variable *qBar* to produce a program we'll call $IPOFifo^{pq}$. The value of *qBar* will be the sequence of datums that will appear in *queueBar*. However, datums will be appended to *qBar* by $Begin\ldots$ and $End\ldots$ steps, so stuttering steps will then have to be added to $IPOFifo^{pq}$ that append the datums in *qBar* one at a time to *queueBar*, since *IFifo* appends data values to *queue* one at a time. How those stuttering steps are added is explained in Section 7.6.3.3.

We will see that a single $BeginPOEnq^{pq}$ step may append multiple datums to *qBar*, so letting *IPOFifo* have $Do\ldots$ steps wouldn't have eliminated the need to add stuttering steps. The following definition of the history variable *qBar* is subtle. To help you understand it, I suggest you check how the definition works on the first few steps of several different behaviors of $IPOFifo^p$.

Suppose that program $IPOFifo^p$ is in a state in which it's possible for a *dequeue* operation to remove a datum from *elts*. For *qBar* to describe the datums that are in *queueBar*, the datum removed by that *dequeue* operation must be in *qBar*. An $EndPODeq^p$ step can remove only the datum $p(1)$ from *elts*, and it can remove $p(1)$ iff $p(1)$ is a minimal element for the relation $\prec$ of *elts*. Therefore, $p(1)$ must be the first element of *qBar* iff $p(1)$ is a minimal element of *elts*. If $p(1)$ can be *dequeued*, then $p(2)$ can be dequeued after it iff $p(2)$ is a minimal element of $elts \setminus \{p(1)\}$. And so on.

Define the state predicate pg to be the longest prefix of p all of whose datums can be dequeued from $elts$ if no further datums are enqueued in $elts$. It follows from the definition of $IPOFifo^p$ that pg equals the longest prefix of p satisfying the following conditions:

Q1. Every datum in pg is in $elts$.

Q2. No datum appears twice in pg.

Q3. For each $i \in 1\mathinner{.\,.} Len(pg)$ and each datum $u \in elts$, if $u \prec pg(i)$ then $u = pg(j)$ for some $j \in 1\mathinner{.\,.}(i-1)$.

We have shown that pg must be a prefix of $qBar$. Our strategy for defining $IPOFifo^{pq}$ by adding the history variable $qBar$ to $IPOFifo^p$ is to keep $qBar$ equal to pg for as long as possible. To see how to do that, let's see how pg can change.

The sequence pg can become shorter only when an $EndPODeq^p$ step occurs, in which case p is not the empty sequence and pg is a nonempty prefix of p. The step removes the first element of p and pg, so $p' = Tail(p)$, $pg' = Tail(pg)$, and $qBar' = Tail(qBar)$.

The sequence pg can be made longer by a $BeginPOEnq^p$ step as follows. Suppose the step appends the prediction u to p and adds the datum w to $elts$. The value of pg at the beginning of the step is a proper prefix of $p \circ \langle u \rangle$. If w equals the prediction in $p \circ \langle u \rangle$ immediately after pg, then w will be appended to pg iff doing so would not violate Q3. (We'll see in a moment when it would violate Q3.) If w can be appended to pg and the prediction following w in p is already in $elts$, then it might be possible to append that datum to pg as well. And so on. Thus, it's possible for the $BeginPOEnq^p$ step to append several datums to pg. If our strategy has been successful thus far and $qBar = pg$ at the beginning of the step, then a $BeginPOEnq^{pq}$ step implies $qBar' = pg'$. This makes $qBar$ a prefix of $qBar'$, as it should be because stuttering steps to be added after a $BeginPOEnq^p$ step should change $queueBar$ only by appending datums to it.

There is one situation in which it is impossible for any further datum to be appended to pg. One or more datums can be appended to pg only by a $BeginPOEnq^p$ that adds a datum w to $elts$ that can be appended to pg. However, if there is a datum u in $elts$ that is neither in the sequence pg nor in the set $beingAdded$, then adding w to $elts$ also adds the relation $u \prec w$. This relation means that w can't be appended to pg because that would violate condition Q3. Thus, if there is a datum u in $elts$ that is in neither pg nor $beingAdded$, then no datums can be added to pg. Moreover, the datum u

7.6. THE FIFO QUEUE

can never be removed from *elts* because it is not in *pg* and can never be in *pg* because no more datums can be added to *pg*. (The datum u can't be added to *beingAdded* because a *BeginPOEnq* step can't add a datum to *elts* that is already in *elts*.) Let's call a state in which there is a datum in *elts* that is not in *beingAdded* or *pg* a *blocked* state. In a blocked state, datums can be removed from the head of *pg* by $EndPODeq^p$ steps, but no new datums can be appended to *pg*. So, if and when enough $EndPODeq^p$ steps have occurred to remove all the datums from *pg*, then no more $EndPODeq^p$ steps can occur. That means that any further *dequeue* operations that are begun with a $BeginPODeq^p$ step must block, never able to complete.

Let's consider the first step that caused a blocked state—that is, causing there to be an element u in *elts* that is in neither *pg* nor *beingAdded*. Since u was added to *elts* by a $BeginPOEnq^p$ step that put u in *beingAdded*, it must be the $EndPOEnq^p$ step of the *enqueue* operation that added u to *elts* that caused the blocked state by removing u from *beingAdded*. Until that blocked state was reached, *qBar* equaled *pg*. However, since u has not been dequeued, it must be in *queueBar* after that $EndPOEnq^p$ step because that step must implement the *EndEnq* step of *IFifo*. Thus that $EndPOEnq^p$ step must append u to *qBar*. Therefore, the first blocked state is the first state in which $qBar \neq pg$. In that state, *qBar* equals $pg \circ \langle u \rangle$.

From that first blocked state on, no new datums can be added to *pg*, so the datum u can never be dequeued. Therefore, whenever an $EndPOEnq^p$ step occurs for an operation that enqueued a datum w, if w is in *elts* (so it hasn't been dequeued) and is not in *pg*, then that $EndPOEnq^p$ step must append w to *qBar*.

To recapitulate, here is how we add the history variable *qBar* to $IPOFifo^p$ to obtain the program $IPOFifo^{pq}$. These rules imply that, at any point in the behavior, *qBar* will equal $pg \circ eb$ where *pg* is the state function of $IPOFifo^p$ defined above and *eb* is a sequence of datums in *elts* that are not in *pg*. Initially, *pg* and *eb* equal $\langle \rangle$.

- An $EndPODeq^p$ step can occur only if $pg \neq \langle \rangle$. Such a step satisfies $pg' = Tail(pg)$ and $qBar' = Tail(qBar)$.

- An $EndPOEnq^p$ step that removes from *beingAdded* a datum w that is in *elts* but not in *pg* appends w to *eb* and hence to *qBar*.

- A $BeginPOEnq^p$ step that occurs when $eb = \langle \rangle$ (so $qBar = pg$) sets $qBar'$ equal to pg'.

These rules imply that a datum can never be removed from *eb*, so once *eb* is nonempty no new datums can be added to *pg* and only datums currently in *pg* can ever be dequeued.

Observe that the sequence *pg* and the set of datums in *eb* can be defined in terms of the variables of *IPOFifo^p*. A history variable is needed only to remember the order in which datums have been appended to *eb*. This suggests that it's a little simpler to make *eb* the history variable and define *qbar* to be the state expression *pg* ∘ *eb*. However, I could not have discovered this without first understanding how *qBar* should be defined.

Writing a complete definition of *IPOFifo^{pq}* is straightforward, once we have solved the problem of writing a precise mathematical definition of the state function *qBar* in terms of the variables of *IPOFifo^p*. (It took me a few tries to get the definition right, using a model checker to find my mistakes.) That definition is omitted.

7.6.3.3 Stuttering and the Refinement Mapping

Having defined *qBar* for *IPOFifo^{pq}*, adding a stuttering variable *s* and defining the refinement mapping under which the resulting program *IPOFifo^{pqs}* implements *IFifo* are comparatively straightforward. First, *s* has to add stuttering steps that allow us to define *queueBar*. Recall that *qBar* is defined so it is changed by interface actions (the only ones that *IPOFifo^{pq}* has) the way internal *Do*... actions of *IFifo* change the value of the internal variable *queue* of *IFifo*. Since *queueBar* should implement *queue* under the refinement mapping (except that *queueBar* contains datums not just the data values), it needs to be changed by stuttering steps added to *IPOFifo^{pq}*. We define the program *IPOFifo^{pqs}* by adding a stuttering variable *s* that adds steps in the following three cases. We define *queueBar* to be the state expression that equals *qBar* except as noted below.

1. *s* adds a single stuttering step before each *EndPODeq^{pq}* step. The value of *queueBar* equals *Tail(qBar)* immediately after that stuttering step.

2. *s* adds a stuttering step before each *EndPOEnq^{pq}* step that appends an element *w* to *eb* (and hence to *qBar*). Immediately after that stuttering step, *queueBar* equals *qBar* ∘ ⟨*w*⟩.

3. Following each *BeginPOEnq^{pq}* step such that *Len(pg′)* > *Len(pg)* (which implies *eb* = ⟨⟩), *s* adds *Len(pg′)* − *Len(pg)* stuttering steps. While there are *k* more of those stuttering steps left to be executed, *queueBar* equals the sequence obtained from *qBar* by removing its last *k* elements.

7.7. PROPHECY CONSTANTS

Encoding in the value of the stuttering variable s for which of the three cases the variable is being added, and in case 2 for which enqueuer e the step is an $EndPOEnq^{pq}(e)$ step, allows the value of $queueBar$ to be defined in terms of the values of s, $qBar$, and (for case 2) $adding$.

We still have to define the state functions $enqInnerBar$ and $deqInnerBar$ that are substituted for $enqInner$ and $deqInner$ in the refinement mapping under which $IPOFifo^{pqs}$ implements $IFifo$. The value of $enqInnerBar(e)$ for an enqueuer e should equal $Done$ except when $adding(e)$ equals the datum that e is enqueueing, and that datum is not yet in $queueBar$. This means that $enqInnerBar$ can be defined in terms of $adding$, $queueBar$, and s.

The value of $deqInnerBar(d)$ for a dequeuer d should equal the value of $deq(d)$ except between when d has removed the first element of $queueBar$ (by executing the stuttering step added in case 1) and before the subsequent $EndPODeq^{pqs}(d)$ step has occurred. In that case, $deq(d)$ should equal $qBar(1)$. It's therefore easy to define $deqInnerBar$ as a state function of $IPOFifo^{pqs}$ if the value of the stuttering variable s added in case 1 contains the value of d for which the following $EndPODeq^{pqs}(d)$ step is to be performed.

This completes the sketch of how auxiliary variables are added to $IPOFifo$ to define a refinement mapping under which it implies $IFifo$, showing that $POFifo$ refines $Fifo$. The intellectually challenging part was discovering how to define $qBar$. It took me quite a bit of thinking to find the definition. This was not surprising. The example of the FIFO had been studied for at least 15 years before Herlihy and Wing discovered that it could be implemented without maintaining a totally ordered queue. Given the definition of $qBar$, constructing the refinement mapping required the ability to write abstract programs mathematically—an ability that comes with practice.

7.7 Prophecy Constants

We have seen examples of showing $\models T \Rightarrow S$, where S equals $\exists \ldots : IS$, by adding an auxiliary variable a to T and showing T^a implies IS under a refinement mapping. In these examples, IS and S were safety properties. Liveness was shown by showing that T^a conjoined with the lower-level program's liveness property implies the higher-level program's liveness property.

Let's return to an example we considered in Section 7.1.3. Define IS and

T to be the two formulas defined in (7.7) and (7.8):

$$IS \triangleq \land (x = 0) \land (y \in \mathbb{N})$$
$$\land \Box[(y > 0) \land (x' = x + 1) \land (y' = y - 1)]_{\langle x,y \rangle}$$
$$T \triangleq (x = 0) \land \Box[x' = x + 1]_x \land \Diamond\Box[x' = x]_x$$

and let S equal $\exists y : IS$. We observed that formulas S and T are equivalent, so $\models T \Rightarrow S$ is true. To define a refinement mapping under which T implies IS, we have to add one or more auxiliary variables to T to obtain an expression to substitute for y.

The liveness property $\Diamond\Box[x' = x]_x$ implies that a behavior of T eventually stops incrementing x and terminates. To define the refinement mapping, we need a variable that can predict the value of x when the behavior terminates. So, we need a prophecy variable.

Because we have to predict something that is implied by a liveness property, it appears that the only kind of prophecy variable that will work is one that predicts the entire future—namely an infinite prophecy variable that predicts all the future values of x. This means adding auxiliary variables, including a prophecy variable, the way it is done in the completeness proof of Section 7.5. This is disturbingly complicated for such a simple example.

Fortunately, there is a simple way to construct the refinement mapping under which T implies IS without using a prophecy variable. We first observe that T implies that eventually x is forever equal to some natural number—more precisely:

(7.17) $\models T \Rightarrow \exists n \in \mathbb{N} : \Diamond\Box(x = n)$

This implies:

$$\models T \equiv \exists n \in \mathbb{N} : \Diamond\Box(x = n) \land T$$

By the $\exists$ Elimination Rule of Math IX, to show $(\exists n \in \mathbb{N} : \ldots) \Rightarrow S$ it suffices to prove $(n \in Nat) \land \ldots \Rightarrow S$. Therefore, to prove $T \Rightarrow \exists y : IS$, it suffices to prove:

(7.18) $\models (n \in \mathbb{N}) \land \Diamond\Box(x = n) \land T \Rightarrow \exists y : IS$

We can do this with the refinement mapping $y \leftarrow n - x$, showing:

$$\models (n \in \mathbb{N}) \land \Diamond\Box(x = n) \land T \Rightarrow (IS \text{ WITH } y \leftarrow n - x)$$

7.7. PROPHECY CONSTANTS

The generalization of this example is showing $T \Rightarrow \exists \ldots : IS$ by finding a formula L containing a constant c that does not occur in IS such that $\models T \Rightarrow \exists c : L$, and then showing:

$$\models (c \in C) \wedge L \wedge T \Rightarrow \exists \ldots : IS$$

A bound constant c used in this way is called a *prophecy constant*. It can be shown that prophecy constants are, in principle, as powerful as prophecy variables. In particular, Theorem 7.6 of Section 7.5 is true with the prophecy variable replaced by a prophecy constant. This is proved by modifying the proof of Theorem 7.6 as described in Appendix Section B.11, after the proof of that theorem.

Although in theory equivalent, prophecy variables and prophecy constants are quite different in practice. It appears that a prophecy variable is best for predicting what a safety property implies may happen, while a prophecy constant is best for predicting what a liveness property L implies must eventually happen.

Prophecy constants were introduced by Wim Hesselink, who called them "eternity variables" [20]. He did not represent programs mathematically, so he had to invent a rule for adding them to programs.

Chapter 8

Loose Ends

This chapter covers two topics that, to my knowledge, have not yet seen any industrial application. However, they might in the future become useful. The first topic is reduction, which is about verifying that a program satisfies a property by verifying that a coarser-grained version of the program satisfies it. Even if you never use it, understanding the principles behind reduction can help you choose the appropriate grain of atomicity for abstract programs. For that purpose, skimming through Sections 8.1.1–8.1.3 should suffice.

The second topic is about representing a program as the composition of component programs. We have been representing the components that make up a program, such as the individual processes in a multiprocess program, as disjuncts of the next-state action. Section 8.2 explains how the components that form a program can be described as programs. How this is done depends on why it is done. Two reasons for doing it and the methods they lead to are presented.

8.1 Reduction

8.1.1 Introduction

8.1.1.1 What Reduction Is

When writing an abstract program to describe some aspect of a concrete one, we must decide what constitutes a single step of a behavior. Stated another way, we must describe what the grain of atomicity of the next-state action should be. The only advice provided thus far is that we should use the coarsest grain of atomicity (the fewest steps) that is a sufficiently accurate representation of that aspect of the concrete program. "Sufficiently

8.1. REDUCTION

accurate" means that either we believe it is easy to make the concrete program implement that grain of atomicity, or we are deferring the problem of how those atomic actions are implemented.

Some work has addressed the problem of formalizing what makes an abstract program "sufficiently accurate", starting with a 1975 paper by Richard Lipton [41]. This work used the approach called *reduction*, which replaces a program S with an "equivalent" coarser-grained program S^R called the *reduced version* of S. Certain properties of S are verified by showing that S^R satisfies them. The program S^R is obtained from S by replacing certain nonatomic operations with atomic actions, each atomic action producing the same effect as executing all the steps of the nonatomic operation it replaces one after another, with no intervening steps of other operations. The reduced program S^R is therefore simpler and easier to reason about than program S.

It was never clear in exactly what sense S^R was equivalent to S, and the results were restricted to particular classes of programs and of the properties that could be verified. TLA enabled a new way of viewing reduction. In that view, the variables of S are replaced in S^R by "virtual" variables, and S implements S^R under a refinement mapping. The refinement mapping is not made explicit, but the relation between the values of the actual and the virtual variables is described by an invariant. This mathematical view encompasses much of the previous work on reduction for concurrent programs.

Our basic approach to writing a correct concrete program is showing that it refines an abstract program. There are two aspects to refining one program with another: data refinement and step refinement. Modern coding languages have made data refinement easier by providing higher-level, more abstract data structures. It is now almost as easy to write a program that manipulates integers as one that manipulates bit strings representing a finite set of integers. There has been much less progress in making step refinement easier. As explained in Section 7.6.1, a linearizable object allows a coarse grain of atomicity in descriptions of the code that executes operations on the object. However, the only general method of implementing a linearizable object still seems to be the one invented by Dijkstra in the 1960s: putting the code that reads and/or modifies the state of the object in a critical section.

I believe that better ways of describing the grain of atomicity will be needed if rigorous verification that concrete concurrent programs implement abstract ones is to become common practice. Reduction may provide the key to doing this. Section 8.1 provides a mathematical foundation for understanding reduction. The theorems presented here are not the most general ones possible; some generalizations can be found elsewhere [8]. Also omitted are rigorous proofs. I know of no industrial use of reduction or of tools to support it; and I have no experience using the results described here in practice. The problem it addresses is real, but I don't know if reduction is the solution.

8.1.1.2 The TLA Approach

Here is how reduction can be described in TLA. Let **x** be the variables x_1, ..., x_n of S. Reduction is usually described by letting **x** also be the variables of S^R. However, I find that reduction is easier to understand by letting the variables of S^R be different from those of S. We will let those variables be the list **X** of variables $X_1, \ldots, X_n$. The goal is then to verify that S satisfies a property P by verifying that S^R satisfies the property P WITH $\mathbf{x} \leftarrow \mathbf{X}$.

To deduce $\models S \Rightarrow P$, where S and P contain the variables **x**, from $\models S^R \Rightarrow (P$ WITH $\mathbf{x} \leftarrow \mathbf{X})$, we need a relation between the variables **x** and the variables **X**. That relation is expressed by a state predicate I^R containing the variables **x** and **X**. We then deduce that S satisfies P from the following three conditions. The formula T will be explained later; ignore it for the moment.

R1. $\models S \wedge T \Rightarrow \exists \mathbf{X} : S^R \wedge \Box I^R$

R2. $\models S^R \Rightarrow (P$ WITH $\mathbf{x} \leftarrow \mathbf{X})$

R3. $\models (P$ WITH $\mathbf{x} \leftarrow \mathbf{X}) \wedge \Box I^R \Rightarrow P$

Condition R1 is implied by theorems whose hypotheses are the conditions necessary for reduction to be possible. Condition R2 asserts that P with its variables **x** replaced by **X** is satisfied by the reduced program S^R, which should be easier to verify than that P is satisfied by the finer-grained program S. Condition R3 completes the chain of reasoning to show that S (and T, which we're ignoring) satisfies P.

Throughout this section on reduction, we abbreviate F WITH $\mathbf{x} \leftarrow \mathbf{X}$ as $\overline{F}$, for any formula F. Thus R2 and R3 can be written as

$\models S^R \Rightarrow \overline{P}$ and $\models \overline{P} \wedge \Box I^R \Rightarrow P$

We first consider the case in which S is the usual TLA safety property $\textit{Init} \wedge \Box[\textit{Next}]_{\langle \mathbf{x} \rangle}$ for an abstract program. We then consider the program described by $S \wedge F$, where F is the conjunction of fairness properties for S. Conditions R1–R3 will then have S replaced by $S \wedge F$, the reduced program

8.1. REDUCTION

$(S \wedge F)^R$ being defined to equal $S^R \wedge F^R$ where F^R is obtained by replacing each fairness condition for an action A of S with fairness of a corresponding action A^R of S^R.

The formula T in the hypothesis of R1 is a liveness assumption that will be defined below. It turns out that even when S is a safety property, so S^R is also a safety property, R1 requires a liveness assumption about S. For a program with a fairness property F, we expect $S \wedge F$ to imply T. If the program describes only safety, then it can satisfy only safety properties, so it would be strange if we required S to satisfy a liveness property to use reduction. We will see that, to show S satisfies a safety property P, showing that S satisfies a possibility condition allows us to assume that T is satisfied.

To prove the theorem that asserts R1, we construct an abstract program $S \otimes S^R$, with variables $\mathbf{x}$ and $\mathbf{X}$, that describes the programs S and S^R running simultaneously in parallel. (The symbol $S \otimes S^R$ is just an identifier that names a formula, not an expression with formulas S and S^R and an operator $\otimes$. This unusual identifier is meant to remind us what the formula means.) We then show:

R1a. $\models S \Rightarrow \exists \mathbf{X} : S \otimes S^R$

R1b. $\models S \otimes S^R \wedge T \Rightarrow S^R \wedge \Box I^R$

R1b implies $\models (\exists \mathbf{X} : S \otimes S^R \wedge T) \Rightarrow (\exists \mathbf{X} : S^R \wedge \Box I^R)$; and the variables $\mathbf{X}$ don't appear in T, so $\exists \mathbf{X} : S \otimes S^R \wedge T$ equals $(\exists \mathbf{X} : S \otimes S^R) \wedge T$. Therefore, R1a and R1b imply R1.

One property asserted by I^R is that, if the values of $\mathbf{x}$ describe a state in which none of the nonatomic operations of S being reduced is currently being executed, then $\mathbf{x} = \mathbf{X}$. The values of $\mathbf{x}$ and $\mathbf{X}$ are synchronized like this, despite the reduced program taking fewer steps than the original program, by having $S \otimes S^R$ take $\mathbf{X}$-stuttering steps—steps that leave the values of the variables $\mathbf{X}$ unchanged. R1b is satisfied because these $\mathbf{X}$-stuttering steps implement stuttering steps of S^R. R3 was satisfied in Lipton's original paper because he considered terminating programs and properties P that depend only on the initial and final states of the program. In those states, none of the nonatomic operations of S being reduced are being executed, so $\mathbf{x} = \mathbf{X}$. In what may have been the second paper published on reduction, Doeppner [10] satisfied R3 by proving only that an invariant is true when none of the reduced operations are being executed.

8.1.2 An Example

To explain reduction, we start by examining this commonly assumed rule: When reasoning about a multiprocess program in which interprocess communication is performed by atomic operations to shared data objects, the program can be represented with any grain of atomicity in which each atomic action accesses at most one shared data object.[1] The following is a statement of the rule in our science and the argument generally used to justify it.

Suppose S is a multiprocess program with a process that executes a nonatomic operation, which we call RCL, described by the statements shown in Figure 8.1. We assume this is "straight line" code, so an execution of RCL consists of $k+1+m$ steps. For now, we let S be the safety property described by the code; liveness is discussed later. We assume statements R$_i$ and L$_j$ can access only data local to the process, while statement C can also access shared data. The rule asserts that we can replace S with its reduced version S^R obtained by removing all the labels between (but not including) r_1 and o, so those $k+1+m$ statements are executed as a single step, and replacing the variables **x** with the variables **X**. It is usually claimed that we can do this because other processes can't observe when the statements R$_i$ and L$_j$ are executed, so we can pretend that they are executed in the same step as statement C.

We can reduce other operations of the same form to atomic actions as well, reducing the operations one at a time. So, it suffices to see how it's done for just this single operation RCL, which may be executed multiple times.

8.1.2.1 The Reduced Behaviors

Let R_i, C, and L_j be the TLA actions described by statements R$_i$, C, and L$_j$. An execution of RCL consists of a sequence of R_i steps, for $i \in 1..k$, followed by a C step, followed by a sequence of L_j steps, for $j \in 1..m$. In an execution of the operation during a behavior of the program, interleaved between those steps may be steps performed by other processes. (There can also be stuttering steps that leave the values of variables **x** unchanged, but they are irrelevant and we can ignore them.) A *reduced* execution of the operation execution is one in which all the steps of RCL occur one after the other, with no interleaved steps executed by other processes.

---

[1]The rule was stated in print independently by Owicki and Gries [44] and by me [29], but I think it was well known at the time.

8.1. REDUCTION

$$
\begin{array}{ll}
& \vdots \\
r_1: & \text{R}_1 \text{ ;} \\
& \vdots \\
r_k: & \text{R}_k \text{ ;} \\
c: & \text{C ;} \\
l_1: & \text{L}_1 \text{ ;} \\
& \vdots \\
l_m & \text{L}_m \text{ ;} \\
o: & \ldots \\
& \vdots
\end{array}
$$

Figure 8.1: The nonatomic operation RCL.

We transform a behavior to a *reduced* behavior, in which only reduced executions of RCL occur, by a procedure illustrated with the following portion of a behavior containing an execution of RCL, where RCL has one R_i statement ($k = 1$) and two L_j statements ($m = 2$). We show the name of the action that each step satisfies, where E_1, E_2, and E_3 are actions of other processes.

$$(8.1) \quad \cdots \; s_{41} \xrightarrow{R_1} s_{42} \xrightarrow{E_1} s_{43} \xrightarrow{C} s_{44} \xrightarrow{E_2} s_{45} \xrightarrow{E_3} s_{46} \xrightarrow{L_1} s_{47} \xrightarrow{L_2} s_{48} \; \cdots$$

Define $\mathcal{R}$ to be the state predicate that is true of a state iff that state occurs during an execution of RCL before the C action. In the part of a behavior shown in (8.1), $\mathcal{R}$ is true only in states s_{42} and s_{43}. Define $\mathcal{L}$ to be the state predicate asserting that the process is currently executing operation RCL after the C action, so in (8.1) it is true in states s_{44}–s_{47}. In general, if p is the process executing RCL of Figure 8.1, then $\mathcal{R}$ equals $pc(p) \in \{r_2, \ldots, r_k, c\}$ and $\mathcal{L}$ equals $pc(p) \in \{l_1, \ldots, l_m\}$. The behavior is currently executing RCL iff the state predicate $\mathcal{R} \vee \mathcal{L}$ is true. Thus, the operation is not being executed iff $\neg(\mathcal{R} \vee \mathcal{L})$ is true.

Because R_i and L_j actions access only process-local state, they *commute* with actions from other processes, where two actions commute iff executing them in either order has the same effect. Recall that $A \cdot B$ is defined in Section 3.4.1.4 to be the action that is satisfied by a step $s \to t$ iff there is a state u such that $s \to u$ is an A step and $u \to t$ is a B step. Actions A and B commute iff $A \cdot B$ equals $B \cdot A$. If A and B commute, then for any states s, t, and u such that $s \xrightarrow{A} u \xrightarrow{B} t$, there exists a state v such that $s \xrightarrow{B} v \xrightarrow{A} t$. By commuting R_i and L_j actions with actions of other processes, moving R_i actions to the right and L_j actions to the left, we obtain a behavior in which every execution of RCL is reduced, with no steps of other processes interleaved. For example, commuting actions in this way converts the original behavior into the reduced behavior in which the portion of the original behavior shown in (8.1) is converted to:

$$(8.2) \quad \cdots \; s_{41} \xrightarrow{E_1} u_{42} \xrightarrow{R_1} s_{43} \xrightarrow{C} s_{44} \xrightarrow{L_1} u_{45} \xrightarrow{L_2} u_{46} \xrightarrow{E_2} u_{47} \xrightarrow{E_3} s_{48} \; \cdots$$

A state s_i is changed to a possibly different state u_i if commutativity was used to commute actions A and B in $\cdots \xrightarrow{A} s_i \xrightarrow{B} \cdots$. For example, state s_{46} had to be (possibly) changed twice to arrive at u_{46} because both the E_2 and E_3 actions had to be "moved across" state number 46 of the behavior to get from (8.1) to (8.2). If σ is the original behavior (8.1), we define $\Phi(\sigma)$ to be its reduced version (8.2), obtained by transforming all executions of RCL in this way.

Note that the states s_{41} and s_{48} are the same in σ and $\Phi(\sigma)$ because RCL is not being executed in those states. States s_{43} and s_{44}, which form the C step, are also the same in the original and reduced behaviors because the C action is not commuted with any action. The reduced behavior (8.2) is also a behavior of program S because it has the same initial state as (8.1), which satisfies *Init*, and every step satisfies a subaction of the next-state action *Next*.

8.1.2.2 The Program $S \otimes S^R$

We define $S \otimes S^R$ in terms of a mapping ϕ from states in the original behavior σ to states in the reduced behavior $\Phi(\sigma)$—in our example, from states of (8.1) to states of (8.2). First, we define $\phi(s)$ for all states except the ones in a C step, which in (8.1) are all states except for s_{43} and s_{44}. We call those two states "C states" and the other states "non-C states".

We transform a behavior containing executions of RCL to a reduced behavior by a sequence of action interchanges based on commutativity. There are two kinds of interchange, both involving an E_h action of a different process: one that moves an R_i step to the right of an E_h step, and one that moves an L_j step to the left of an E_h step. To go from behavior (8.1) to behavior (8.2) requires five interchanges. Figure 8.2 shows the sequence of behaviors created by performing these interchanges, where each behavior is obtained from the preceding one by interchanging the left-most R_i or L_j action that can be moved closer to the C action. The top behavior is the original behavior (8.1) and the bottom one is the reduced behavior (8.2). Observe that every state in one behavior equals the corresponding state

8.1. REDUCTION

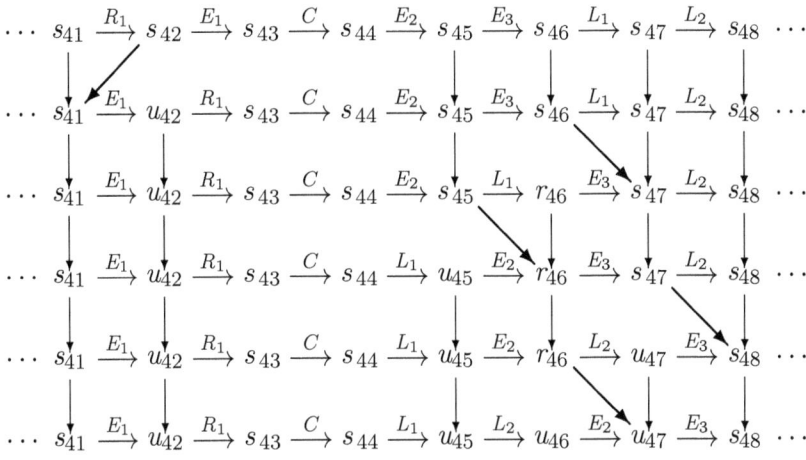

Figure 8.2: Constructing (8.2) from (8.1).

in the next behavior except for the one state across which the actions are interchanged.

The arrows in the picture are drawn according to the following rules. There is a (thin) downward pointing arrow from each non-C state that is unchanged by the interchange that yields the next behavior. From the one state in each behavior that is changed by the interchange, there is a (thick) diagonal arrow. If that state satisfies $\mathcal{R}$ (is before the C action), then the arrow points one state to the left of the changed state. If the state satisfies $\mathcal{L}$, then the arrow points one state to the right.

These arrows define a unique path from every non-C state s_i of the original behavior to a state in the reduced behavior. Define $\phi(s_i)$ to be that state in the reduced behavior. For the example in Figure 8.2, $\phi(s_{45}) = u_{47}$ because the sequence of states in the path from s_{45} in the top behavior to the bottom behavior is:

(8.3) $s_{45} \to s_{45} \to s_{45} \to r_{46} \to r_{46} \to u_{47}$

Figure 8.3 contains an arrow pointing from each non-C state s_i in the original behavior to the state $\phi(s_i)$ in the reduced behavior. Observe that for every non-C state s_i, the state $\phi(s_i)$ is a state in which operation RCL is not being executed—that is, a state satisfying $\neg(\mathcal{R} \vee \mathcal{L})$.

We define $\phi(s)$ for the C states so that if the C step is $s_i \xrightarrow{C} s_{i+1}$, then $\phi(s_i)$ is the first state to the left of s_i for which $\neg(\mathcal{R} \vee \mathcal{L})$ is true, and $\phi(s_{i+1})$ is the first state to the right of s_{i+1} for which $\neg(\mathcal{R} \vee \mathcal{L})$ is true. In other words, $\phi(s_i)$ and $\phi(s_{i+1})$ are the states of the reduced behavior in which the

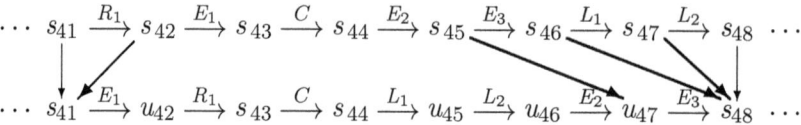

Figure 8.3: The mapping $s_i \to \phi(s_i)$ for non-C states.

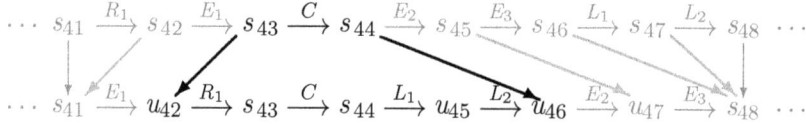

Figure 8.4: The complete mapping $s_i \to \phi(s_i)$.

execution of RCL begins and ends, respectively. The complete mapping ϕ for our example is shown in Figure 8.4, where the mapping for non-C states is in gray.

Formula $S \otimes S^R$ is defined so that it is satisfied by a behavior σ iff σ satisfies S (which describes the values of variables $\mathbf{x}$) and the values of the variables $\mathbf{X}$ in any state s_k of σ equal the values of the variables $\mathbf{x}$ in the state $\phi(s_k)$ of the reduced behavior $\Phi(\sigma)$. Since this assigns values of variables $\mathbf{X}$ to every state of every behavior σ so that the behavior satisfies $S \otimes S^R$, we see that $\models S \Rightarrow \exists \mathbf{X} : S \otimes S^R$ is true, so R1a is satisfied.

From Figure 8.4, we see that for any k:

ϕ1. If $s_k \to s_{k+1}$ is an E_h step (so E_h is an action of another process) then $\phi(s_k) \to \phi(s_{k+1})$ is also an E_h step.

ϕ2. If $s_k \to s_{k+1}$ is an R_i or L_j step, then $\phi(s_k) = \phi(s_{k+1})$.

ϕ3. If $s_k \to s_{k+1}$ is a C step, then $\phi(s_k)$ and $\phi(s_{k+1})$ are the first and last states of an execution of operation RCL in the reduced behavior $\Phi(\sigma)$, which is an execution with no interleaved steps of other process actions.

Recall that $\overline{G}$ equals G WITH $\mathbf{x} \leftarrow \mathbf{X}$ for any formula G. A step of S^R is either an $\overline{E_h}$ step, a $\overline{D}$ step, where D is an action that performs an execution of operation RCL as a single step, or a stuttering step that leaves the variables $\mathbf{X}$ unchanged. From ϕ1–ϕ3, we see that if behavior (8.1) satisfies $S \otimes S^R$ (as well as S), then each step of that behavior is either an $\overline{E_h}$ step (by ϕ1), a $\overline{D}$ step (by ϕ3) or leaves the variables $\mathbf{X}$ unchanged (by ϕ2). Hence each step of $S \otimes S^R$ satisfies the next-state action of S^R.

8.1. REDUCTION

The initial-state predicate of S^R is $\overline{Init}$ (remember that $Init$ is the initial-state predicate of S). Since operation RCL is not being executed in the initial state s_0 of (8.1), $\phi(s_0)$ equals s_0, which implies that s_0 satisfies $\overline{Init}$. Thus, if (8.1) satisfies $S \otimes S^R$, then it satisfies S^R. Therefore, $S \otimes S^R \Rightarrow S^R$ is satisfied—or so it seems.

The reasoning works in this example because the behavior (8.1) contains a complete execution of operation RCL. However, S is a safety property, which means that the process can stop executing actions at any point during the execution of the operation. The general definition of the reduced version of a behavior, which includes a possibly incomplete execution of RCL, is that actions performing steps of an RCL execution are made to occur together by commuting R_i actions to the right, L_j actions to the left, and leaving a C action unmoved. (If there is no C step, then the last R_i action can be left unmoved.) If s is the last state of a C step, $\phi(s)$ is defined to be the state after the last step of the RCL operation being executed. That state will satisfy $\neg(\mathcal{R} \vee \mathcal{L})$ iff the behavior contains a complete execution of the operation.

The one part of what we've done that's not correct in the presence of a partial execution is $\phi 3$. Statement $\phi 3$ is vacuously true if the partial execution doesn't contain a C step. In that case there are only R_i steps which correspond to stuttering steps of S^R, so the behavior of $S \otimes S^R$ is a behavior of S^R in which that RCL action doesn't occur. The problem in $\phi 3$ arises in our example if the execution contains a C step but doesn't contain both the L_1 and L_2 steps.

The solution is to rule out such behaviors. That's what the hypothesis T in R1 and R1b does. Formula T must assert that any execution of RCL that includes the C step must complete. The operation has performed the C step but has not completed iff $\mathcal{L}$ is true. So we want to allow only behaviors in which it is not the case that $\mathcal{L}$ eventually becomes true and remains true forever. Such behaviors are ones satisfying $\neg \Diamond \Box \mathcal{L}$, which is equivalent to $\Box \Diamond \neg \mathcal{L}$. So, we can restate R1b as this assumption:

$$\models S \otimes S^R \wedge (\Box \Diamond \neg \mathcal{L}) \Rightarrow S^R \wedge \Box I^R$$

The argument showing $S \otimes S^R$ implies S^R for the behavior (8.1) applies to all behaviors of the program of Figure 8.1 satisfying $\Box \Diamond \neg \mathcal{L}$. That is, we have shown:

$$\models S \otimes S^R \wedge (\Box \Diamond \neg \mathcal{L}) \Rightarrow S^R$$

is satisfied by this program S. To complete the proof of R1b, we must define I^R and show that it is an invariant of $S \otimes S^R$. Since we have seen that S

satisfies R1a, this will show that it satisfies R1 with T equal to $\Box\Diamond\neg\mathcal{L}$. The assumption $\Box\Diamond\neg\mathcal{L}$ is discussed in Section 8.1.4.

8.1.2.3 The Invariant I^R

The invariant I^R of $S\otimes S^R$ that relates the values of the variables $\mathbf{x}$ to those of the variables $\mathbf{X}$ follows from three additional properties of the mapping ϕ. We can see why those properties hold from Figures 8.2–8.4.

The most obvious of these properties follows from the observation that if $\neg(\mathcal{R}\vee\mathcal{L})$ is true in a state s, then only downward pointing arrows are drawn from it in the figures. This shows:

$\phi4$. For any state s in which $\neg(\mathcal{R}\vee\mathcal{L})$ is true, $\phi(s) = s$.

For the next property, look at the path (8.3) from the state s_{45} to the state $\phi(s_{45})$, which equals u_{47}. Follow that path in Figure 8.2. Observe that each step in the path either leaves the state unchanged (is a stuttering step) or else is an L_1 or L_2 step. (To see this, look at the horizontal arrows just above the diagonal arrows.) We can see from the figure that this is true of the path from state s to state $\phi(s)$ for the states s_{46} and s_{47} as well. The rule for drawing the arrows implies that this is true in general, for all executions of the program of Figure 8.1. The path from every non-C state s for which $\mathcal{L}$ is true to $\phi(s)$ consists of a sequence of steps each of which is either a stuttering step or an L_j step for some j. From Figure 8.4, it's clear that this is also true for the C state for which $\mathcal{L}$ is true.

Let's define L to equal $L_1 \vee \ldots \vee L_m$, so any L_j step is an L step. We have seen that we can get from a state s in which $\mathcal{L}$ is true to the state $\phi(s)$ by a sequence of stuttering steps and/or L steps. Recall that in Section 5.1.2, for any action A we defined A^+ to equal $A \vee (A \cdot A) \vee (A \cdot A \cdot A) \vee \ldots$. Therefore, a step $s \to t$ satisfies $([L]_{\langle\mathbf{x}\rangle})^+$, which we abbreviate $[L]^+_{\langle\mathbf{x}\rangle}$, iff we can get from state s to state t by a sequence of L steps or steps that leave the variables $\mathbf{x}$ unchanged. Let's write the subscript $\langle\mathbf{x}\rangle$ as simply $\mathbf{x}$, so $[A]_{\mathbf{x}}$ and $\langle A\rangle_{\mathbf{x}}$ mean $[A]_{\langle\mathbf{x}\rangle}$ and $\langle A\rangle_{\langle\mathbf{x}\rangle}$ for any action A.

We have thus seen:

$\phi5$. For any state s in which $\mathcal{L}$ is true, $s \to \phi(s)$ is an $[L]^+_{\mathbf{x}}$ step.

Following the path from s to $\phi(s)$ backwards for states s in which $\mathcal{R}$ is true similarly leads to the following statement, where R equals $R_1 \vee \ldots \vee R_k$.[2]

---

[2] The action R bears no relation to the superscript R in S^R. It is traditional to name the action R for Right-mover because of the way the reduced behavior is constructed; and there seems to be no better superscript than R to signify *reduced*.

8.1. REDUCTION

$\phi 6$. For any state s in which $\mathcal{R}$ is true, $\phi(s) \to s$ is an $[R]_{\mathbf{x}}^+$ step.

Finally, Figure 8.4 shows that for any state s of the original behavior, $\phi(s)$ is always a state in the reduced behavior in which the RCL operation is not being executed, so $\neg(\mathcal{R} \vee \mathcal{L})$ is true for $\phi(s)$. Because the rule for drawing the arrows in Figure 8.2 creates a leftward pointing arrow whenever an R step is moved to the right and a rightward pointing arrow whenever an L step is moved to the left, this is true in general. Therefore, we have:

$\phi 7$. For any state s, the state predicate $\neg(\mathcal{R} \vee \mathcal{L})$ is true in state $\phi(s)$.

Statements $\phi 4$–$\phi 7$ give us relations between s and $\phi(s)$ for all states s of a behavior of our example program. We now have to turn them into relations between the values of the variables $\mathbf{x}$ and the variables $\mathbf{X}$ in any state s in a behavior of $S \otimes S^R$.

It's easy to do this for $\phi 4$. The values of the variables $\mathbf{X}$ in state s are the values of $\mathbf{x}$ in $\phi(s)$. Since $\phi(s) = s$ if s satisfies $\neg(\mathcal{R} \vee \mathcal{L})$, this means that $\mathbf{x} = \mathbf{X}$ is true for any reachable state of $S \otimes S^R$ satisfying $\neg(\mathcal{R} \vee \mathcal{L})$. In other words:

(8.4) $\quad \neg(\mathcal{R} \vee \mathcal{L}) \Rightarrow (\mathbf{X} = \mathbf{x}) \quad$ is an invariant of $S \otimes S^R$

To express the relations between $\mathbf{x}$ and $\mathbf{X}$ implied by $\phi 5$ and $\phi 6$, we need a bit of notation. For any action A containing only the variables $\mathbf{x}$, a step $s \to t$ satisfies A iff formula A is true when we substitute for the variables $\mathbf{x}$ their values in state s and for $\mathbf{x}'$ their values in state t. Therefore, $\phi(s) \to s$ is an $[R]_{\mathbf{x}}^+$ step iff $[R]_{\mathbf{x}}^+$ is true when we substitute the values of $\mathbf{x}$ in $\phi(s)$ for the variables $\mathbf{x}$ and the values of $\mathbf{x}$ in s for the primed variables $\mathbf{x}'$. But the values of $\mathbf{x}$ in $\phi(s)$ are by definition the values of $\mathbf{X}$ in state s. So $\phi(s) \to s$ is an $[R]_{\mathbf{x}}^+$ step iff s satisfies the formula we get by substituting $\mathbf{X}$ for $\mathbf{x}$ and $\mathbf{x}$ for $\mathbf{x}'$ in $[R]_{\mathbf{x}}^+$. Using the construct AWITH defined in Section 6.4.4.1, we write the formula produced by these substitutions as:

$[R]_{\mathbf{x}}^+$ AWITH $\mathbf{x} \leftarrow \mathbf{X}, \mathbf{x}' \leftarrow \mathbf{x}$

so formula $\phi 6$ implies:

(8.5) $\quad \mathcal{R} \Rightarrow ([R]_{\mathbf{x}}^+$ AWITH $\mathbf{x} \leftarrow \mathbf{X}, \mathbf{x}' \leftarrow \mathbf{x}) \quad$ is an invariant of $S \otimes S^R$

Remember that in this formula, the definition of $[R]_{\mathbf{x}}^+$ must be fully expanded before the AWITH substitution is performed.

We can obtain a similar relation between $\mathbf{x}$ and $\mathbf{X}$ from $\phi 5$. The statement that $s \to \phi(s)$ is an $[L]_{\mathbf{x}}^+$ step is equivalent to the statement that state

s is satisfied by the formula obtained from $[L]_{\mathbf{x}}^+$ by substituting for variables $\mathbf{x}$ their values in state s and substituting for $\mathbf{x}'$ the values of $\mathbf{x}$ in state $\phi(s)$, the latter being the values of $\mathbf{X}$ in state s. Therefore, $\phi 5$ implies the following, where $\mathbf{x} \leftarrow \mathbf{x}$ has been eliminated from the AWITH formula, since it just states that $\mathbf{x}$ is substituted for itself:

(8.6) $\mathcal{L} \Rightarrow ([L]_{\mathbf{x}}^+ \text{ AWITH } \mathbf{x}' \leftarrow \mathbf{X})$ is an invariant of $S \otimes S^R$

Finally, since the values of $\mathbf{X}$ in state s equal the values of $\mathbf{x}$ in state $\phi(s)$, from $\phi 7$ we obtain:

(8.7) $\neg(\mathcal{R} \vee \mathcal{L})$ WITH $\mathbf{x} \leftarrow \mathbf{X}$ is an invariant of $S \otimes S^R$

The invariant I^R of $S \otimes S^R$ relating the values of $\mathbf{x}$ and $\mathbf{X}$ is the conjunction of the invariants (8.4)–(8.7):

$$\begin{aligned} I^R \triangleq\ & \wedge\ \neg(\mathcal{R} \vee \mathcal{L}) \Rightarrow (\mathbf{X} = \mathbf{x}) \\ & \wedge\ \mathcal{R} \Rightarrow ([R]_{\mathbf{x}}^+ \text{ AWITH } \mathbf{x} \leftarrow \mathbf{X}, \mathbf{x}' \leftarrow \mathbf{x}) \\ & \wedge\ \mathcal{L} \Rightarrow ([L]_{\mathbf{x}}^+ \text{ AWITH } \mathbf{x}' \leftarrow \mathbf{X}) \\ & \wedge\ \neg(\mathcal{R} \vee \mathcal{L}) \text{ WITH } \mathbf{x} \leftarrow \mathbf{X} \end{aligned}$$

8.1.3 Reduction In General

So far, we have been considering reduction of an operation RCL of one process of a multiprocess program having the form shown in Figure 8.1. We now extend this to a more general situation. First, some observations about reducing RCL.

The invariant I^R is described in terms of the actions R and L, which are the disjunction of the actions R_i and L_j, respectively. The fact that R and L were defined in this particular way was irrelevant. All we required was that an execution of the operation RCL consists of a sequence of R steps followed by a C step followed by a sequence of L steps. We didn't need actions E_h of other processes to commute with each of the actions R_i and L_j. In drawing the diagrams illustrated by Figures 8.2 and 8.4, we didn't have to identify the subactions of R and L that are involved. We could have replaced each R_i by R and each L_i by L. We only needed to assume that each action of another process commutes with R and L, not with each R_i and L_j individually. (For example, an $E_h \cdot L_1$ step could be an $L_2 \cdot E_h$ step.) Similarly, we didn't have to require that R and L commute with particular actions of other processes. We just required R and L to commute with the disjunction of the next-state relations of all the other processes—an action we will call E.

8.1. REDUCTION

Furthermore, we didn't need to require that R and L commute with E. To move R steps to the right, we just required that for any pair of steps $s \xrightarrow{R} u \xrightarrow{E} t$ there is a pair of steps $s \xrightarrow{E} v \xrightarrow{R} t$ for some state v. This condition can be stated as the requirement $R \cdot E \Rightarrow E \cdot R$. When this formula holds, we say that R *right-commutes* with E, and that E *left-commutes* with R. Similarly, to move L steps to the left, we don't need $E \cdot L$ to equal $L \cdot E$; we need only require $E \cdot L \Rightarrow L \cdot E$, which asserts that L left-commutes with E (and E right-commutes with L).

Finally, suppose that A is another action of the same process containing the RCL operation, so A does not allow steps that implement the RCL operation. Since the next step of the process after an R step can only be an R step or a C step, an A step cannot follow an R step. This implies that $R \cdot A$ must equal FALSE, which means that $R \cdot A \Rightarrow A \cdot R$ is trivially true. Similarly, the only step of the process that can immediately precede an L step is an L step or a C step. Therefore, $A \cdot L$ must equal FALSE, so $A \cdot L \Rightarrow L \cdot A$ must be true. Therefore, other actions of the process containing RCL satisfy the same commutativity requirements as actions of other processes. This implies that we can completely forget about processes. We just assume that the program's next-state action equals $E \lor R \lor C \lor L$, where R right-commutes with E and L left-commutes with E. If we represent the program as a collection of processes, there is no need for R, C, and L steps to all be steps of the same process.

What we need to require is that execution of an RCL operation consists of a sequence of R steps followed by a C step followed by a sequence of L steps. To express this requirement, we generalize $\mathcal{R}$ and $\mathcal{L}$ from assertions about a process's control state to arbitrary state predicates satisfying certain conditions. We take as primitives the state predicates $\mathcal{R}$ and $\mathcal{L}$ and the actions E and M such that the program's next state relation equals $E \lor M$, where M describes the operation to be reduced. The actions R, C, and L will be defined in terms of $\mathcal{R}$, $\mathcal{L}$, and M. We therefore assume the original program S is defined by:

$$S \triangleq \mathit{Init} \land \Box[E \lor M]_{\mathbf{x}}$$

As in our example, we assume that $\mathcal{R}$ is true when execution of the operation described by M is in its first phase, where execution has begun but the C action has not yet been executed; and $\mathcal{L}$ is true when execution is in its second phase, where the C action has been executed but the operation execution has not yet terminated. This is implied by the following assumptions on executions of an operation described by the action M:

M1. In the initial state, M is not in the middle of an execution, expressed by $\mathit{Init} \Rightarrow \neg(\mathcal{R} \vee \mathcal{L})$.

M2. An E step can't change the current phase of an execution of M, expressed by $E \Rightarrow (\mathcal{R}' \equiv \mathcal{R}) \wedge (\mathcal{L}' \equiv \mathcal{L})$.

M3. An M step can't go from the second phase to the first phase, expressed by $\neg(\mathcal{L} \wedge M \wedge \mathcal{R}')$.

M4. The two phases are disjoint, expressed by $\neg(\mathcal{R} \wedge \mathcal{L})$.

We can define the actions R, L, and C in terms of M, $\mathcal{R}$, and $\mathcal{L}$ by:

$$R \triangleq M \wedge \mathcal{R}' \qquad L \triangleq \mathcal{L} \wedge M \qquad C \triangleq (\neg \mathcal{L}) \wedge M \wedge (\neg \mathcal{R}')$$

A complete execution of the operation described by M consists of a sequence of M steps beginning and ending in a state in which the M operation is not being executed—in other words, in a state satisfying $\neg(\mathcal{R} \vee \mathcal{L})$. Therefore, the action M^R that executes the complete operation as a single step for the variables $\mathbf{X}$ is:

$$M^R \triangleq (\neg(\mathcal{R} \vee \mathcal{L}) \wedge M^+ \wedge \neg(\mathcal{R} \vee \mathcal{L})') \text{ with } \mathbf{x} \leftarrow \mathbf{X}$$

We can therefore define S^R as follows, where Init^R and E^R are Init and E with the variables $\mathbf{x}$ replaced by the variables $\mathbf{X}$:

$$S^R \triangleq \mathit{Init}^R \wedge \Box[E^R \vee M^R]_{\mathbf{X}}$$

If $\mathcal{R}$ always equals FALSE, then R equals FALSE so there is no R action. Similarly, there is no L action if $\mathcal{L}$ always equals FALSE. If there is neither an R nor an L action, then M equals C and S^R equals (S with $\mathbf{x} \leftarrow \mathbf{X}$), so reduction accomplishes nothing.

Ignoring liveness, reduction is described in TLA by a theorem asserting that R1 (with T equal to $\Box\Diamond\neg\mathcal{L}$) is implied by the definitions of S, R, L, M, and S^R above, assumptions M1–M4, and the commutativity relations assumed of R, L, and E.

M1–M4 and the commutativity relations are action formulas. (Remember that a state predicate is an action whose value depends only on the first state of a step.) Those action formulas don't have to be true of all possible steps, just on steps in behaviors satisfying S. (The action formulas are usually meaningless for states not satisfying some type-correctness predicate.) If $\mathbf{x}$ is the list of all variables that can appear in S and A, then the assertion that an action formula A is true for all steps of behaviors satisfying S can be written as $\models S \Rightarrow \Box[A]_{\mathbf{x}}$. Here is reduction, without liveness, expressed as a theorem.

8.1. REDUCTION

Theorem 8.1 Assume *Init*, $\mathcal{L}$, and $\mathcal{R}$ are state predicates, M and E are actions, **x** is a list of all variables appearing in these formulas, and **X** is a list of the same number of variables different from the variables **x**. Define

$$S \triangleq \mathit{Init} \wedge \Box[E \vee M]_{\mathbf{x}} \qquad R \triangleq M \wedge \mathcal{R}' \qquad L \triangleq \mathcal{L} \wedge M$$
$$\mathit{Init}^R \triangleq \mathit{Init} \text{ WITH } \mathbf{x} \leftarrow \mathbf{X} \qquad E^R \triangleq E \text{ WITH } \mathbf{x} \leftarrow \mathbf{X}$$
$$M^R \triangleq (\neg(\mathcal{R} \vee \mathcal{L}) \wedge M^+ \wedge \neg(\mathcal{R} \vee \mathcal{L})') \text{ WITH } \mathbf{x} \leftarrow \mathbf{X}$$
$$S^R \triangleq \mathit{Init}^R \wedge \Box[E^R \vee M^R]_{\mathbf{X}}$$
$$I^R \triangleq \wedge \neg(\mathcal{R} \vee \mathcal{L}) \Rightarrow (\mathbf{X} = \mathbf{x})$$
$$\wedge \mathcal{R} \Rightarrow ([R]_{\mathbf{x}}^+ \text{ AWITH } \mathbf{x} \leftarrow \mathbf{X}, \mathbf{x}' \leftarrow \mathbf{x})$$
$$\wedge \mathcal{L} \Rightarrow ([L]_{\mathbf{x}}^+ \text{ AWITH } \mathbf{x}' \leftarrow \mathbf{X})$$
$$\wedge \neg(\mathcal{R} \vee \mathcal{L}) \text{ WITH } \mathbf{x} \leftarrow \mathbf{X}$$

and assume:

(1) $\models \mathit{Init} \Rightarrow \neg(\mathcal{R} \vee \mathcal{L})$

(2) $\models S \Rightarrow \Box [\wedge E \Rightarrow (\mathcal{R}' \equiv \mathcal{R}) \wedge (\mathcal{L}' \equiv \mathcal{L})$
$\wedge \neg(\mathcal{L} \wedge M \wedge \mathcal{R}')$
$\wedge \neg(\mathcal{R} \wedge \mathcal{L})$
$\wedge R \cdot E \Rightarrow E \cdot R$
$\wedge E \cdot L \Rightarrow L \cdot E \,]_{\mathbf{x}}$

Then $\models S \wedge \Box \Diamond \neg \mathcal{L} \Rightarrow \exists \mathbf{X} : S^R \wedge \Box I^R$.

Assumption (1) and the first three conjuncts in the action of assumption (2) are the conditions M1–M4, which assert that an execution of the operation described by the action M consists of a sequence of L steps followed by a C step followed by a sequence of R steps. The final two conjuncts in the action of assumption (2) are the assumptions that R right-commutes with E and L left-commutes with E.

In practice, R, L, and E will be defined to be the disjunction of subactions. This allows us to decompose the proofs of those commutativity conditions by using the following theorem that is proved in the Appendix.

Theorem 8.2 If $A \equiv \exists i \in I : A_i$ and $B \equiv \exists j \in J : B_j$ for actions A_i and B_j, then:

$$\models (\forall i \in I, j \in J : A_i \cdot B_j \Rightarrow B_j \cdot A_i) \Rightarrow (A \cdot B \Rightarrow B \cdot A)$$

By this theorem, to show that R right-commutes with E, it suffices to show that each subaction in the definition of R right-commutes with each subaction in the definition of E. Similarly, L left-commutes with E if each subaction of L left-commutes with each subaction of E.

8.1.4 The Hypothesis $\Box\Diamond\neg\mathcal{L}$

Formula $\Box\Diamond\neg\mathcal{L}$ is a liveness property. When we add liveness conditions to S and hope to use reduction to prove that it satisfies a liveness property P, we would expect S to imply $\Box\Diamond\neg\mathcal{L}$. But we wouldn't expect to have to add a liveness property to S in order to verify that it satisfies a safety property. In fact, to verify a safety property, we don't have to prove that $\neg\mathcal{L}$ is always eventually true. The following theorem implies that, to verify S satisfies a safety property, we can simply assume that $\Box\Diamond\neg\mathcal{L}$ is true if it is always *possible* for $\neg\mathcal{L}$ to eventually become true. To understand the theorem, recall that Section 5.1.2 defines what it means for it to be always possible for a state predicate Q to eventually become true—namely, that the program $\mathit{Init} \wedge \Box[\mathit{Next}]_\mathbf{x}$ implies $\Box\mathbb{E}([\mathit{Next}]_\mathbf{x}^+ \wedge Q')$. (See (5.1).) This theorem is proved in the Appendix:

Theorem 8.3 If S equals $\mathit{Init} \wedge \Box[\mathit{Next}]_\mathbf{x}$, P is a safety property, and Q is a state predicate such that $\models S \Rightarrow \Box\mathbb{E}([\mathit{Next}]_\mathbf{x}^+ \wedge Q')$, then $\models S \wedge \Box\Diamond Q \Rightarrow P$ implies $\models S \Rightarrow P$.

The theorem allows us to replace the formula T in R1b (which we later defined to equal $\Box\Diamond\neg\mathcal{L}$) with $\Box\,\mathbb{E}([\mathit{Next}]_\mathbf{x}^+ \wedge \neg\mathcal{L}')$. Section 5.1.2 explains that we can verify this possibility condition by finding a fairness condition F for S and verifying $\models S \wedge F \Rightarrow \Box\Diamond\neg\mathcal{L}$. This is the only case I know of in which a possibility condition is used to verify a correctness property.

8.1.5 Adding Liveness

Theorem 8.1 allows us to deduce safety properties of the program S from safety properties of the coarser-grain program S^R. We also want to deduce liveness properties of S from liveness properties of S^R. We deduce liveness properties of a program from fairness properties of program actions. To deduce liveness properties of S by proving liveness properties of S^R, we extend Theorem 8.1 so its conclusion is

(8.8) $\models S \wedge F \wedge \Box\Diamond\neg\mathcal{L} \;\Rightarrow\; \exists \mathbf{X} : S^R \wedge \Box I^R \wedge F^R$

where F is the conjunction of fairness properties of subactions of the next-state action $E \vee M$ of S and F^R is the conjunction of fairness properties of subactions of the next-state action $E^R \vee M^R$ of S^R.

To understand how this is done, it helps to think in terms of the program $S \otimes S^R$, a behavior of which is a behavior both of S (described by the values of variables $\mathbf{x}$) and of S^R (described by the values of variables $\mathbf{X}$) whose

8.1. REDUCTION

existence is asserted by (8.8). We expect S to satisfy (8.8) because $S \otimes S^R$ satisfies:

$$(8.9) \quad \models S \otimes S^R \wedge F \wedge \Box\Diamond\neg\mathcal{L} \;\Rightarrow\; S^R \wedge \Box I^R \wedge F^R$$

Formula F^R should assert fairness of subactions A^R of $E^R \vee M^R$. For simplicity, we consider only actions A^R that are subactions of either E^R or M^R, which I expect will usually be the case. When it is not the case, the requirements for deducing fairness of A^R include requirements for deducing fairness of both $A^R \wedge E^R$ and $A^R \wedge M^R$ [8].

8.1.5.1 Fairness of Subactions of E^R

We defined S^R so that E^R equals $\overline{E}$. (Recall that we defined $\overline{G}$ to equal G WITH $\mathbf{x} \leftarrow \mathbf{X}$ for any formula G.) Property $\phi 1$ of Section 8.1.2.2 for our example generalizes to show that, in any behavior of $S \otimes S^R$, an E step is also an $\overline{E}$ step.

Because each E^R step corresponds to a single E step in a behavior of $S \otimes S^R$, we expect fairness of a subaction A^R of E^R to be implied by fairness of a single subaction A of E. In other words, we expect this to be true:

$$(8.10) \quad \models S \otimes S^R \wedge \mathrm{XF}_\mathbf{x}(A) \;\Rightarrow\; \mathrm{XF}_\mathbf{x}(A^R)$$

where XF is either WF or SF. By (4.14) and (4.23) we have

$$\begin{aligned}
\mathrm{XF}_\mathbf{x}(A) &\equiv (\boxtimes\!\boxtimes \mathbb{E}\langle A\rangle_\mathbf{x} \Rightarrow \Box\Diamond\langle A\rangle_\mathbf{x}) \\
\mathrm{XF}_\mathbf{x}(A^R) &\equiv (\boxtimes\!\boxtimes \mathbb{E}\langle A^R\rangle_\mathbf{x} \Rightarrow \Box\Diamond\langle A^R\rangle_\mathbf{x})
\end{aligned}$$

where $\boxtimes\!\boxtimes$ means $\Diamond\Box$ if XF is WF and $\Box\Diamond$ if XF is SF. These formulas and a little temporal logic imply that to prove (8.10) it suffices to prove these two theorems:

$$(8.11) \quad \models S \otimes S^R \;\Rightarrow\; (\Box\Diamond\langle A\rangle_\mathbf{x} \Rightarrow \Box\Diamond\langle A^R\rangle_\mathbf{x})$$

$$(8.12) \quad \models S \otimes S^R \;\Rightarrow\; \Box(\mathbb{E}\langle A^R\rangle_\mathbf{x} \Rightarrow \mathbb{E}\langle A\rangle_\mathbf{x})$$

We make (8.11) true by requiring every $\langle A\rangle_\mathbf{x}$ step in a behavior of $S \otimes S^R$ to be an $\langle A^R\rangle_\mathbf{x}$ step. Every E step in a behavior of $S \otimes S^R$ is an E^R step because E^R equals $\overline{E}$. This suggests that we want A^R to equal $\overline{A}$. (Note that $\overline{\langle A\rangle_\mathbf{x}}$ equals $\langle \overline{A}\rangle_\mathbf{X}$ because $\overline{\mathbf{x}}$ equals $\mathbf{X}$.)

Every E step in a behavior of $S \otimes S^R$ is an E^R step because of property $\phi 1$, and that property holds because of the commutativity assumptions of action E with respect to actions R and L. Therefore, we must require that $\langle A \rangle_\mathbf{x}$ satisfies the same commutativity relation as E, namely:

$$(8.13) \quad \models S \Rightarrow \Box[(R \cdot \langle A \rangle_\mathbf{x} \Rightarrow \langle A \rangle_\mathbf{x} \cdot R) \wedge (\langle A \rangle_\mathbf{x} \cdot L \Rightarrow L \cdot \langle A \rangle_\mathbf{x})]_\mathbf{x}$$

With this assumption, defining A^R to equal $\overline{A}$ will make (8.11) true.

The commutativity relations satisfied by E were used to define the mapping ϕ, which in turn was used to define S^R. For example, in Figures 8.2–8.4, the state u_{42}, which equals $\phi(s_{43})$, was chosen when right-commuting R_1 with E_1 so that $s_{41} \to u_{42}$ is an E_1 step and $u_{42} \to s_{43}$ is an R_1 step. Suppose that A is a subaction of E_1 and $s_{41} \to s_{42}$ is an $\langle A \rangle_\mathbf{x}$ step. Nothing in the construction in those figures, which describes the choice of ϕ used to define S^R in Theorem 8.1, ensures that the E_1 step $s_{41} \to u_{42}$ is also an $\langle A \rangle_\mathbf{x}$ step. However, the assumption (8.13) ensures that we could have chosen u_{42} to make $s_{41} \to u_{43}$ an $\langle A \rangle_\mathbf{x}$ step.

In general, we can use (8.13) to ensure that every E step in the original behavior that is an $\langle A \rangle_\mathbf{x}$ step remains an $\langle A \rangle_\mathbf{x}$ step whenever that step is commuted with an R or L step, so it remains an $\langle A \rangle_\mathbf{x}$ step in the reduced behavior. We can therefore define S^R so that (8.12) is true, so this is not a problem when we want to ensure that (8.10) holds for a single action A. However, we may want (8.10) to hold for multiple subactions A of E, and a single E step can be an $\langle A \rangle_\mathbf{x}$ step for more than one of those subactions A. We will return to this problem in Section 8.1.5.3. Now, we consider making (8.12) true.

We can deduce (8.12) from these two theorems:

$$(8.14) \quad (a) \quad \models S \otimes S^R \Rightarrow \Box(\mathbb{E}\langle A^R \rangle_\mathbf{x} \Rightarrow \overline{\mathbb{E}\langle A \rangle_\mathbf{x}})$$
$$ (b) \quad \models S \otimes S^R \Rightarrow \Box(\overline{\mathbb{E}\langle A \rangle_\mathbf{x}} \Rightarrow \mathbb{E}\langle A \rangle_\mathbf{x})$$

Since $\langle A^R \rangle_\mathbf{x}$ equals $\overline{\langle A \rangle_\mathbf{x}}$ and formulas $\mathbb{E}\overline{\langle A \rangle_\mathbf{x}}$ and $\overline{\mathbb{E}\langle A \rangle_\mathbf{x}}$ contain only the variables $\mathbf{X}$, (8.14a) is equivalent to:

$$(8.15) \quad \models S^R \Rightarrow \Box(\mathbb{E}\overline{\langle A \rangle_\mathbf{x}} \Rightarrow \overline{\mathbb{E}\langle A \rangle_\mathbf{x}})$$

If $\mathbb{E}$ were not a weird operator (see Section 6.4.4.3), $\mathbb{E}\overline{\langle A \rangle_\mathbf{x}}$ would be equivalent to $\overline{\mathbb{E}\langle A \rangle_\mathbf{x}}$; and we expect that equivalence to be true for most actions $\langle A \rangle_\mathbf{x}$. However, because it is not always true, we have to add (8.15) as an assumption.

To see what is required to make (8.14b) true, we consider what assumption is required to ensure that $\overline{P} \Rightarrow P$ is true for an arbitrary state predicate P with free variables $\mathbf{x}$. The free variables of $\overline{P}$ are $\mathbf{X}$, and the relation between the values of $\mathbf{x}$ and $\mathbf{X}$ is described by the invariant I^R of $S \otimes S^R$.

8.1. REDUCTION

There are three cases, depending on whether $\mathcal{R}$ is true, $\mathcal{L}$ is true, or neither is true:

$\mathcal{R}$ true: The conjunct
$$\mathcal{R} \;\Rightarrow\; ([R]_{\mathbf{x}}^{+} \text{ AWITH } \mathbf{x} \leftarrow \mathbf{X},\; \mathbf{x}' \leftarrow \mathbf{x})$$
of I^R asserts that, in this case, we can arrive at the values of $\mathbf{x}$ in the current state by starting in a state in which the values of $\mathbf{x}$ equal the current values of $\mathbf{X}$ and executing a sequence of R steps. This means that $\overline{P} \Rightarrow P$ is true if, starting in a state satisfying P and executing a sequence of R steps, we reach a state in which P is true. This is true iff, starting in a state satisfying P and repeatedly executing single R steps, we keep reaching states satisfying P. In other words, if $P \wedge R \Rightarrow P'$ is true in any state satisfying $\mathcal{R}$ of a behavior of $S \otimes S^R$, then $\overline{P} \Rightarrow P$ is true.

$\mathcal{L}$ true: A similar argument based on the conjunct
$$\mathcal{L} \;\Rightarrow\; ([L]_{\mathbf{x}}^{+} \text{ AWITH } \mathbf{x}' \leftarrow \mathbf{X})$$
of I^R shows that if $L \wedge P' \Rightarrow P$ is true in any state satisfying $\mathcal{L}$ in a behavior of $S \otimes S^R$, then $\overline{P} \Rightarrow P$ is true.

Neither $\mathcal{R}$ nor $\mathcal{L}$ true: The conjunct $\neg(\mathcal{R} \vee \mathcal{L}) \Rightarrow (\mathbf{X} = \mathbf{x})$ of I^R shows that $\overline{P} \equiv P$ is true for any state satisfying $\neg(\mathcal{R} \vee \mathcal{L})$ in a behavior of $S \otimes S^R$.

Let's review what we have shown. We can deduce (8.10) from (8.11) and (8.12). If (8.13) is true, then we can choose S^R of Theorem 8.1 to make (8.11) true for a single subaction A of E. We can deduce (8.12) from (8.14a) and (8.14b). We can deduce (8.14a) from (8.15). And finally, we can deduce (8.14b) from the conditions obtained above for proving $\overline{P} \Rightarrow P$, substituting $\mathbb{E}\langle A \rangle_{\mathbf{x}}$ for P. Putting all this together, we have shown that the program S^R of Theorem 8.1 can be chosen to make (8.10) true, for a single subaction A of E, if the following two conditions are satisfied:

$$(8.16) \quad \models S \;\Rightarrow\; \Box [\wedge \; (R \cdot \langle A \rangle_{\mathbf{x}} \Rightarrow \langle A \rangle_{\mathbf{x}} \cdot R) \wedge (\langle A \rangle_{\mathbf{x}} \cdot L \Rightarrow L \cdot \langle A \rangle_{\mathbf{x}})$$
$$\wedge \; \mathbb{E}\langle A \rangle_{\mathbf{x}} \wedge R \;\Rightarrow\; (\mathbb{E}\langle A \rangle_{\mathbf{x}})'$$
$$\wedge \; L \wedge (\mathbb{E}\langle A \rangle_{\mathbf{x}})' \;\Rightarrow\; \mathbb{E}\langle A \rangle_{\mathbf{x}} \;]_{\mathbf{x}}$$
$$\models S^R \;\Rightarrow\; \Box \,(\overline{\mathbb{E}\langle A \rangle_{\mathbf{x}}} \;\Rightarrow\; \overline{\mathbb{E}\langle A \rangle_{\mathbf{x}}})$$

8.1.5.2 Fairness of Subactions of M^R

Deducing fairness properties of subactions of M^R from fairness properties of actions of S is more complicated than for subactions of E^R because an M^R step is the result of executing multiple actions of S as a single step. The simplest and probably most common case is when we want the reduced program to satisfy fairness of the M^R action itself. So, we begin by examining this case.

Action M^R is the action obtained by executing the entire operation consisting of a sequence of R steps, followed by a C step, followed by a complete sequence of L steps, with the variables $\mathbf{X}$ substituted for the variables $\mathbf{x}$. For our example program of Figure 8.1, where the values of variables $\mathbf{X}$ in state s were defined to be the values of $\mathbf{x}$ in state $\phi(s)$, condition $\phi 3$ implies that M^R equals $\overline{C}$. This means that in any behavior of $S \otimes S^R$, a C step is an M^R step. It suggests that we should be able to deduce fairness of the M^R action of S^R from fairness of the C action of S.

Now suppose A is a subaction of C and A^R is the action obtained by executing the entire operation consisting of a sequence of R steps, followed by an A step, followed by a complete sequence of L steps, with the variables $\mathbf{X}$ substituted for the variables $\mathbf{x}$. The same argument shows that A^R equals $\overline{A}$, and that in any behavior of $S \otimes S^R$, an A step is an A^R step. Moreover, any A^R step is also an M^R step, so A^R is a subaction of M^R. So, it is reasonable to consider deriving fairness of a subaction A^R of M^R when A^R is obtained in this way from a subaction A of C. Since our goal is not to obtain the most general results, we consider only this case.

First, we must define A^R precisely for a subaction A of C. An A^R step is obtained by combining a sequence of R steps followed by an A step followed by a sequence of L steps into a single step, and then substituting $\mathbf{X}$ for $\mathbf{x}$. The definitions of R, C, and L in terms of $\mathcal{R}$ and $\mathcal{L}$ and assumptions M1–M4 imply that A^R equals $\overline{A^\rho}$ where A^ρ is defined by

(8.17) $\quad A^\rho \triangleq \neg(\mathcal{R} \vee \mathcal{L}) \wedge ([R]_{\mathbf{x}}^+ \cdot A \cdot [L]_{\mathbf{x}}^+) \wedge \neg(\mathcal{R} \vee \mathcal{L})'$

We want condition (8.10) to be true for this choice of A and A^R. As before, we do this by making (8.11) and (8.12) true, starting with (8.11). In a behavior satisfying $S \otimes S^R$, every A step is an A^R step. However, (8.11) requires every $\langle A \rangle_{\mathbf{x}}$ step to be an $\langle A^R \rangle_{\mathbf{x}}$ step. This is not true for A an arbitrary subaction of C. It's not even necessarily true for $A = C$, for the following reason.

Recall that Figure 8.4 shows two behaviors that satisfy S, the bottom one being the reduced version of the top one. The action labels describe the

8.1. REDUCTION

changes of the values of the variables $\mathbf{x}$. The top behavior satisfies $S \otimes S^R$, where the values of variables $\mathbf{X}$ in a state s_i of that behavior are the values of $\mathbf{x}$ in the corresponding state $\phi(s_i)$ of the bottom sequence. The step $s_{43} \to s_{44}$ of the top behavior is a $\overline{C}$ step iff $u_{42} \to u_{46}$ is a C step. If one of the variables $\mathbf{x}$ has different values in states s_{43} and s_{44}, there is no reason why its value should differ in states u_{42} and u_{46}. Step $s_{43} \to s_{44}$ would be a $\langle C \rangle_\mathbf{x}$ step but not a $\langle \overline{C} \rangle_\mathbf{x}$ step if the values of all the variables $\mathbf{x}$ are the same in states u_{42} and u_{46}. To be able to deduce (8.11) when A is C and A^R is M^R, we need the assumption that if $s_{43} \to s_{44}$ is a $\langle C \rangle_\mathbf{x}$ step, then $\mathbf{x}' \neq \mathbf{x}$ is true of step $u_{42} \to u_{46}$.

Since every A step in a behavior of $S \otimes S^R$ is an A^R step, we can deduce that every $\langle A \rangle_\mathbf{x}$ step is an $\langle A^R \rangle_\mathbf{X}$ step from this assumption:

$$\models S \Rightarrow \Box[(\langle A \rangle_\mathbf{x})^\rho \Rightarrow (\mathbf{x}' \neq \mathbf{x})]_\mathbf{x}$$

There is seldom any reason for a program's next-state action to allow stuttering steps, and modifying it to disallow stuttering steps does not change the program. An A step of the program will usually be an $\langle A \rangle_\mathbf{x}$ step; and if it isn't, A can be replaced by $\langle A \rangle_\mathbf{x}$. So for simplicity, we strengthen this assumption to:

(8.18) $\quad \models S \Rightarrow \Box[A^\rho \Rightarrow (\mathbf{x}' \neq \mathbf{x})]_\mathbf{x}$

We have shown that (8.18) implies that in a behavior of $S \otimes S^R$, every $\langle A \rangle_\mathbf{x}$ step is an $\langle A^R \rangle_\mathbf{X}$ step. In other words, we have shown that it implies:

(8.19) $\quad \models S \otimes S^R \Rightarrow \Box[\langle A \rangle_\mathbf{x} \Rightarrow \langle A^R \rangle_\mathbf{X}]_{\mathbf{x},\mathbf{X}}$

This assertion implies (8.11).

The assumption (8.18) makes (8.11) true, so we now have to make (8.12) true. But we can't expect (8.12) to hold in general for the following reason. Since A^R equals $\overline{A^\rho}$, we expect $\mathbb{E}\langle A^R \rangle_\mathbf{X}$ to imply $\mathbb{E}\langle A^\rho \rangle_\mathbf{x}$. By (8.17), $\mathbb{E}\langle A^\rho \rangle_\mathbf{x}$ equals $\mathbb{E}\langle \neg(\mathcal{R} \vee \mathcal{L}) \wedge [R]_\mathbf{x}^+ \cdot A \cdot \ldots \rangle_\mathbf{x}$, which implies $\mathbb{E}(\neg(\mathcal{R} \vee \mathcal{L}) \wedge (R \vee A))$ (since $\mathbb{E}(U \cdot V)$ implies $\mathbb{E}(U)$ for any actions U and V). We can therefore expect $\mathbb{E}\langle A^R \rangle_\mathbf{X}$ to imply $\mathbb{E}\langle A \rangle_\mathbf{x}$, as required by (8.12), only when there is no R action.

A sequence of R steps may have to occur between when A^ρ becomes enabled and when A becomes enabled, so fairness assumptions for R as well as a fairness assumption for A may be required to imply fairness of A^ρ. Instead of assuming a fairness condition on L actions to ensure that operation M completes after a C step occurs, we simply assumed that the operation completes by adding the assumption $\Box\Diamond\neg\mathcal{L}$. Similarly, instead of assuming a fairness condition on R actions to ensure that the necessary enabling condition of C occurs, we simply assume that the enabling condition eventually occurs.

As an example, suppose we want to deduce weak fairness of A^R from strong fairness of A. (Because fairness of A^R requires fairness of more than just A, there's no reason not to have different kinds of fairness for the two actions.) By (8.19) and the definition (4.12) of WF, to prove $\text{WF}_\mathbf{x}(A^R)$ it suffices to prove $\Diamond\Box\mathbb{E}\langle A^R\rangle_\mathbf{x} \leadsto \langle A\rangle_\mathbf{x}$. Just as we split the proof of (8.12) into the two conditions of (8.14), we split the proof of $\Diamond\Box\mathbb{E}\langle A^R\rangle_\mathbf{x} \leadsto \langle A\rangle_\mathbf{x}$ into proving:

(8.20) (a) $\Box(\mathbb{E}\langle A^R\rangle_\mathbf{x} \Rightarrow \overline{\mathbb{E}\langle A^\rho\rangle_\mathbf{x}})$
 (b) $\Diamond\Box\mathbb{E}\langle A^\rho\rangle_\mathbf{x} \leadsto \langle A\rangle_\mathbf{x}$

This may seem wrong because we have $\overline{\mathbb{E}\langle A^\rho\rangle_\mathbf{x}}$ in (8.20a) and $\mathbb{E}\langle A^\rho\rangle_\mathbf{x}$ in (8.20b) when the two formulas should be equal. However, the following reasoning shows that they are equal. The definition of A^ρ and conditions E3 and E4 of Section 6.4.4.2 imply that $\mathbb{E}\langle A^\rho\rangle_\mathbf{x}$ equals $\neg(\mathcal{R}\vee\mathcal{L})\wedge\mathbb{E}\langle A^\rho\rangle_\mathbf{x}$. The invariant I^R implies that $\neg(\mathcal{R}\vee\mathcal{L}) \Rightarrow (\mathbf{x} = \mathbf{X})$ and $\overline{\neg(\mathcal{R}\vee\mathcal{L})}$ are true, so $S\otimes S^R$ implies that $\mathbb{E}\langle A^\rho\rangle_\mathbf{x}$ always equals $\overline{\mathbb{E}\langle A^\rho\rangle_\mathbf{x}}$. We make S^R implying (8.20a) one of our requirements for deducing that $\text{WF}_\mathbf{x}(A^R)$ is satisfied. We now consider (8.20b).

By (3.33b) of Section 3.4.2.8 and the tautology $\models \neg\langle A\rangle_\mathbf{x} \equiv [\neg A]_\mathbf{x}$, to prove (8.20b) it suffices to prove:

(8.21) $\Diamond\Box\mathbb{E}\langle A^\rho\rangle_\mathbf{x} \wedge \Box[\neg A]_\mathbf{x} \leadsto \langle A\rangle_\mathbf{x}$

By the definition (4.22) of SF and transitivity of $\leadsto$, to deduce (8.21) from $\text{SF}_\mathbf{x}(A)$, it suffices to prove that S implies:

(8.22) $\Diamond\Box\mathbb{E}\langle A^\rho\rangle_\mathbf{x} \wedge \Box[\neg A]_\mathbf{x} \leadsto \Box\Diamond\mathbb{E}\langle A\rangle_\mathbf{x}$

We have seen that to deduce $\text{WF}_\mathbf{x}(A^R)$ from $\text{SF}_\mathbf{x}(A)$, it suffices to show (8.18) and:

(8.23) (a) $\models S^R \Rightarrow \Box(\mathbb{E}\langle A^R\rangle_\mathbf{x} \Rightarrow \overline{\mathbb{E}\langle A^\rho\rangle_\mathbf{x}})$
 (b) $\models S \Rightarrow (\Diamond\Box\mathbb{E}\langle A^\rho\rangle_\mathbf{x} \wedge \Box[\neg A]_\mathbf{x} \leadsto \Box\Diamond\mathbb{E}\langle A\rangle_\mathbf{x})$

For the other three possible pairs of fairness conditions on A^R and A, the same argument shows that we can deduce $\text{SF}_\mathbf{x}(A^R)$ instead of $\text{WF}_\mathbf{x}(A^R)$ by replacing $\Diamond\Box$ with $\Box\Diamond$ in (8.23b); and we can assume $\text{WF}_\mathbf{x}(A)$ instead of $\text{SF}_\mathbf{x}(A)$ by replacing $\Box\Diamond$ with $\Diamond\Box$ in (8.23b).

8.1. REDUCTION

8.1.5.3 The Reduction Theorem with Fairness

We have described the assumption needed to infer that the reduced program satisfies a fairness condition on a single action A^R if the original program satisfies a fairness condition on a single action A. We now combine this into a theorem for inferring that the reduced program satisfies the conjunction of countably many fairness conditions A_i^R. This is simple, except for one problem mentioned above for the case in which A^R is a subaction of E^R.

Recall that to satisfy (8.11), we constrained the construction of the function ϕ illustrated in Figures 8.2–8.4 so that if an E step is an A step in the original behavior, then the corresponding E step in the reduced behavior is also an A step. With multiple actions A_i, if the E step in the original behavior is both an A_i and an A_j step for $j \neq i$, it might be impossible to make the E step in the transformed behavior both an A_i and an A_j step.

However, to satisfy (8.11), it's not necessary for every E step that's an A step in the original behavior to remain an A step in the reduced behavior. It's only necessary to ensure that if there are infinitely many A steps in the original behavior, then infinitely many of them are A steps in the reduced behavior. With countably many such actions A_i, it's possible to construct the reduced behavior so that for every i for which there are infinitely many A_i steps in the original behavior, there are infinitely many A_i steps in the reduced behavior. This is done using Theorem 4.1 of Math V the same way it is used in the proof of Theorem 4.7 in the Appendix.

We can now put together the assumptions we derived above for deducing fairness of an action A^R from fairness of an action A for individual actions A into a theorem for deducing fairness of a countable number of actions A_i^R from fairness of actions A_i. The requirements for A_i a subaction of E (and A_i^R a subaction of E^R) come from (8.16). The requirements for A_i a subaction of C (and A_i^R a subaction of M^R) come from (8.18) and (8.23) plus the modification of (8.23) for additional fairness conditions of A and A^R.

Theorem 8.4 With the definitions and assumptions (1) and (2) of Theorem 8.1, let $C \triangleq (\neg \mathcal{L}) \wedge M \wedge (\neg \mathcal{R}')$ and let

$$\models F \Rightarrow \forall i \in I : \mathrm{YF}_\mathbf{x}^i(A_i) \qquad F^R \triangleq \forall i \in I : \mathrm{ZF}_\mathbf{x}^i(A_i^R)$$

where I is a countable set and YF^i and ZF^i are WF or SF for each $i \in I$; and assume either:

- A_i is a subaction of E, $A_i^R \triangleq \overline{A_i}$, YF^i equals ZF^i,

$$\models S \;\Rightarrow\; \Box[\wedge\; (R \cdot \langle A_i \rangle_{\mathbf{x}} \Rightarrow \langle A_i \rangle_{\mathbf{x}} \cdot R) \wedge (\langle A_i \rangle_{\mathbf{x}} \cdot L \Rightarrow L \cdot \langle A_i \rangle_{\mathbf{x}})$$
$$\wedge\; \mathbb{E}\langle A_i \rangle_{\mathbf{x}} \wedge R \;\Rightarrow\; (\mathbb{E}\langle A_i \rangle_{\mathbf{x}})'$$
$$\wedge\; L \wedge (\mathbb{E}\langle A_i \rangle_{\mathbf{x}})' \;\Rightarrow\; \mathbb{E}\langle A_i \rangle_{\mathbf{x}}]_{\mathbf{x}}, \quad \text{and}$$
$$\models S^R \;\Rightarrow\; \Box(\overline{\mathbb{E}\langle A_i \rangle_{\mathbf{x}}} \;\Rightarrow\; \overline{\mathbb{E}\langle A_i \rangle_{\mathbf{x}}})$$

or

- A_i is a subaction of C,

$$A_i^\rho \;\triangleq\; \neg(\mathcal{R} \vee \mathcal{L}) \wedge ([R]_{\mathbf{x}}^+ \cdot A_i \cdot [L]_{\mathbf{x}}^+) \wedge \neg(\mathcal{R} \vee \mathcal{L})',$$
$$A_i^R \;\triangleq\; \overline{A_i^\rho},$$
$$\models S \;\Rightarrow\; \Box[A_i^\rho \Rightarrow (\mathbf{x}' \neq \mathbf{x})]_{\mathbf{x}},$$
$$\models S^R \;\Rightarrow\; \Box(\mathbb{E}\langle A_i^R \rangle_{\mathbf{x}} \Rightarrow \overline{\mathbb{E}\langle A_i^\rho \rangle_{\mathbf{x}}}), \quad \text{and}$$
$$\models S \wedge F \;\Rightarrow\; (\boxtimes\boxtimes^Z \mathbb{E}\langle A_i^\rho \rangle_{\mathbf{x}} \wedge \Box[\neg A_i]_{\mathbf{x}} \;\leadsto\; \boxtimes\boxtimes^Y \mathbb{E}\langle A_i \rangle_{\mathbf{x}})$$

where for Q either Y or Z, $\boxtimes\boxtimes^Q$ is $\Diamond\Box$ if QF is WF, and it is $\Box\Diamond$ if QF is SF.[3]

Then $\models S \wedge F \wedge \Box\Diamond\neg\mathcal{L} \;\Rightarrow\; \exists\mathbf{X} : S^R \wedge \Box I^R \wedge F^R$.

8.1.6 An Example: Making Critical Sections Atomic

A standard concurrent coding practice is to "protect" accesses to shared data by putting them in critical sections. Recall that Section 4.2.2.1 defined a critical section to be a piece of code in a process such that no two processes can be executing their critical sections at the same time. We can consider this coding practice to be an application of reduction in which the reduced program executes the entire critical section, including its waiting and exiting code, as a single action.

We assume that critical sections are implemented with the trivial mutual exclusion algorithm *LM* described in Figure 4.6 of Section 4.2.6.1 that uses Dijkstra's *P* and *V* semaphore operations. (Correctness of a mutual exclusion algorithm can be expressed as the requirement that it implements *LM* under a suitable refinement mapping.) We assume the program is described with pseudocode, using a semaphore variable *sem* and a variable *pc* to describe the control state. The variable *sem* initially equals 0 and is accessed by a process p only by P_p and V_p actions that execute the $P(sem)$ and $V(sem)$ operations. These actions are written in TLA as follows, where the

---

[3] For example, if $\text{YF}_{\mathbf{x}}^i(A_i)$ is $\text{SF}_{\mathbf{x}}^i(A_i)$ and $\text{ZF}_{\mathbf{x}}^i(A_i^R)$ is $\text{WF}_{\mathbf{x}}^i(A_i^R)$, this condition is:
$$\models S \wedge F \;\Rightarrow\; (\Diamond\Box\mathbb{E}\langle A_i^\rho \rangle_{\mathbf{x}} \wedge \Box[\neg A_i]_{\mathbf{x}} \;\leadsto\; \Box\Diamond\mathbb{E}\langle A_i \rangle_{\mathbf{x}})$$

8.1. REDUCTION

UNCHANGED formulas assert that all program variables other than sem and pc are left unchanged:

$$P_p \triangleq \land\ pc(p) = \ldots$$
$$\land\ (sem = 1) \land (sem' = 0)$$
$$\land\ pc' = (pc\ \text{EXCEPT}\ p \mapsto \ldots)$$
$$\land\ \text{UNCHANGED}\ \ldots$$

$$V_p \triangleq \land\ pc(p) = \ldots$$
$$\land\ sem' = 1$$
$$\land\ pc' = (pc\ \text{EXCEPT}\ p \mapsto \ldots)$$
$$\land\ \text{UNCHANGED}\ \ldots$$

The value of sem is therefore always either 0 or 1. An execution of a critical section by process p consists of a P_p step, followed by steps satisfying actions $CS_{p,1}, \ldots, CS_{p,k_p}$ that represent executions of statements in the critical section, followed by a V_p step. The assumption that shared data is accessed only within a critical section means that if an action E_q describes a statement of process q outside a critical section (meaning not a P_q, $CS_{q,j}$, or V_q action), then each action $CS_{p,i}$ commutes with E_q if $p \neq q$.

We can reduce a program using critical sections in this way by making execution of each critical section a single step. This is done by a sequence of applications of our reduction theorems, each one reducing one critical section of a single process. When doing multiple reductions, it would get confusing if we introduced new variables for each reduction. We therefore consider the reduced version S^R of a program S to be the program S^R described in our theorems, except with $\mathbf{x}$ substituted for $\mathbf{X}$. In our theorems, the M^R that executes the operation described by action M as a single step is defined to equal M^ρ WITH $\mathbf{x} \leftarrow \mathbf{X}$. When we use the variables $\mathbf{x}$ instead of $\mathbf{X}$ for the reduced program, M^R becomes M^ρ.

To apply the theorems to a critical section of a process p, we let M_p equal $P_p \lor CS_{p,1} \lor \ldots \lor CS_{p,k_p} \lor V_p$, so M^p is replaced in the reduced program by M_p^ρ. We could let any of those actions be the action C, but it is most convenient to let C be the P_p action, so there is no action R and action L is $CS_{p,1} \lor \ldots \lor CS_{p,k_p} \lor V_p$. By Theorem 8.2, it suffices to show that V_p and each $CS_{p,i}$ left-commutes with every action of every process $q \neq p$. (Action L trivially left-commutes with any action of process p not a subaction of M_p.) The possible actions of process q are P_q, V_q, $CS_{q,j}$ for some j, an action E_q not in a critical section, and M_q^ρ if the operation described by M_q has already been reduced. Here is why V_p and $CS_{p,i}$ commute with each of those actions of process $q \neq p$:

P_q: V_p left-commutes with P_q because the mutual exclusion algorithm implies that V_p is not enabled when a process $q \neq p$ is in its critical section, so $P_q \cdot V_p$ equals FALSE; $CS_{p,i}$ commutes with P_q because it does not access sem or $pc(q)$ (meaning that it does not depend on or modify sem or $pc(q)$).

V_q: V_p commutes with V_q because any two $V(sem)$ operations commute; $CS_{p,i}$ commutes with V_p because it does not access sem or $pc(q)$.

$CS_{q,j}$: $CS_{q,j} \cdot V_p$ and $CS_{q,j} \cdot CS_{p,i}$ both equal FALSE because a $CS_{q,j}$ step leaves process q inside its critical section, which by the mutual exclusion algorithm implies process q is outside its critical section so neither $CS_{p,i}$ nor V_p is enabled.

E_q: V_p commutes with E_q because E_q does not access sem or $pc(p)$; and $CS_{p,i}$ commutes with E_q because of the assumption that actions describing a statement inside a critical section commute with all actions describing statements not in another process's critical section.

M_q^ρ: Both $M_q^\rho \cdot V_p$ and $M_q^\rho \cdot CS_{p,i}$ equal FALSE because an M_q^ρ step leaves $sem = 1$, while the mutual exclusion algorithm implies that V_p and $CS_{p,i}$ are enabled only when $sem = 0$.

This shows that S implies $E \cdot L \Rightarrow L \cdot E$, so since there is no R action, we can apply Theorem 8.1. There is still the formula $\Box \Diamond \neg \mathcal{L}$ to deal with. If the program has fairness assumptions, then we expect $\Box \Diamond \neg \mathcal{L}$ to be implied by fairness assumptions of the L actions. If not, then by Theorem 8.3 we can verify safety properties by showing that, after executing process p's P_p statement, it is always possible for execution of the critical section to complete. It's hard to imagine an application of mutual exclusion that would allow a behavior in which it is impossible for some process ever to exit its critical section.

We now consider deducing fairness properties of the reduced program. First, let action A describe a statement outside any critical section. If the statement is in process p, then A^ρ equals A so fairness of A^ρ is equivalent to fairness of A. If A is an action of a process other than p, the argument above shows that L commutes with $\langle A \rangle_\mathbf{x}$. If $\langle A \rangle_\mathbf{x}$ is a subaction of the next-state action of S, then an $L \wedge (\mathbb{E}\langle A \rangle_\mathbf{x})'$ step ends in a state in which an $\langle A \rangle_\mathbf{x}$ step can occur, which by commutativity of L and $\langle A \rangle_\mathbf{x}$ implies it begins in a state in which an $\langle A \rangle_\mathbf{x}$ step can occur, so S implies $\Box (L \wedge (\mathbb{E}\langle A \rangle_\mathbf{x})' \Rightarrow \mathbb{E}\langle A \rangle_\mathbf{x})$. We expect $\Box (\mathbb{E}\langle A_i \rangle_\mathbf{x} \Rightarrow \overline{\mathbb{E}\langle A_i \rangle_\mathbf{x}})$ to be true, since substitution has been found to distribute over $\mathbb{E}$ for most actions. (However, there is

8.1. REDUCTION

little experience with the substitution $\mathbf{x} \leftarrow \mathbf{X}$ that occurs in reduction.) If this formula is true, then by Theorem 8.4 we can deduce fairness of A^ρ from fairness of A.

We expect the most common fairness property for a subaction of M_p^ρ to be fairness of M_p^ρ itself. In this case C is P_p, and we expect to deduce a fairness condition of M_p^ρ from the same fairness condition of the P_p action. There is no R action, so the definitions of P_p and M_p^ρ imply $M_p^\rho \Rightarrow (\mathbf{x}' \neq \mathbf{x})$ and $\mathbb{E}\langle M_p^\rho \rangle_\mathbf{x} \Rightarrow \mathbb{E}\langle P_p \rangle_\mathbf{x}$. (In the unlikely case that process p does nothing but repeatedly execute the critical section, so M_p^ρ leaves $pc(p)$ unchanged, we need to add the assumption that M_p^ρ changes some other variable.) The only remaining requirement to deduce from Theorem 8.4 that fairness of P_p implies fairness of M_p^ρ is:

$$\models S^R \Rightarrow \Box(\mathbb{E}\langle M^R \rangle_\mathbf{x} \Rightarrow \overline{\mathbb{E}\langle M^\rho \rangle_\mathbf{x}})$$

Since $\langle M^R \rangle_\mathbf{x}$ equals $\overline{\langle M^\rho \rangle_\mathbf{x}}$, this is true if substitution distributes over $\mathbb{E}$ for the action $\langle M^\rho \rangle_\mathbf{x}$.

We have described the mathematics underlying the use of mutual exclusion to implement atomic operations. We have ignored the question of what that achieves. We use mutual exclusion to view execution of the critical section as a single step, but is that a correct view? The answer lies in condition R3 of Section 8.1.1.2, which tells us when we can deduce that the original program satisfies a property that the reduced program satisfies. The only part of the invariant I^R that seems useful in condition R3 is the conjunct $\neg(\mathcal{R} \vee \mathcal{L}) \Rightarrow (\mathbf{X} = \mathbf{x})$, which asserts that the variables of the original program and the reduced one have equal values when no process is executing its critical section.

8.1.7 Another Example: Pipelining

Here is a sketch of a simple example of reduction that is interesting in part because each operation being reduced contains actions performed by two different processes. The example is a very abstract view of one stage in a pipelined computation—a view that tells us nothing about what is being computed.

The program S performs a sequence of computations. Each computation presumably obtains some input, does some computation, and then produces some output—but that is irrelevant. What concerns us is that the computations are pipelined as follows so they can be performed concurrently by two processes. Process 1 performs the first part of the computation to obtain a partial result that it appends to the end of a FIFO queue. Process 2 removes the partial result from the head of the queue and completes the computation. Process 1 can therefore get ahead of process 2, performing its part of the ith computation while process 2 is still performing its part of the jth computation, for $i > j$. The reduced program S^R replaces these two processes with a single process that performs each computation as a single atomic action. The property we want to prove by reduction presumably involves how the computed values are used after they are computed, when they have the same values in the original and reduced programs, so condition R3 is satisfied.

We describe steps of process 1 by an action $Cmp1 \vee Send$, where that process's part of a computation consists of a finite sequence of $Cmp1$ steps followed by a single $Send$ step that appends the partial result to the tail of the queue. Steps of process 2 are described by an action $Rcv \vee Cmp2$, where that process's part of the computation consists of a single Rcv step that removes the partial result from the head of the queue followed by a finite sequence of $Cmp2$ steps. The contents of the queue are described by the variable $qBar$, which is accessed only by the $Send$ and Rcv actions. We assume that the two processes communicate only through the FIFO $qBar$, an assumption expressed by these conditions: $Cmp1$ commutes with the process 2 actions Rcv and $Cmp2$, and $Cmp2$ commutes with the process 1 actions $Cmp1$ and $Send$. Since $qBar$ is the only shared variable accessed by Rcv and $Send$, it doesn't matter in which order these two actions are executed in a state where the queue is nonempty. Thus, we have:

(8.24) $\models (qBar \neq \langle \rangle) \Rightarrow (Send \cdot Rcv \equiv Rcv \cdot Send)$

The program may contain other processes that can interact in some way with processes 1 and 2. For example, process 1 may obtain its input from a third process and process 2 may send its output to a fourth process.

The program's next-state action is $M \vee O$, where M describes processes 1 and 2 and O describes any other processes. We rewrite M in the form $\exists n \in \mathbb{N}^+ : M_n$, where $\mathbb{N}^+$ is the set of positive integers and M_n is an action whose steps describe a complete execution of the nth computation. To do this, we assume state functions $snum$ and $rnum$ whose values are the numbers of $Send$ and Rcv actions, respectively, that have been executed. Initially, $snum = rnum = 0$. The $Send$ action increments $snum$ by 1 and the Rcv action increments $rnum$ by 1. We can then define:

(8.25) $M_n \triangleq \vee (snum = n - 1) \wedge (Cmp1 \vee Send)$
$ \vee ((rnum = n - 1) \wedge Rcv) \vee ((rnum = n) \wedge Cmp2)$

8.1. REDUCTION

We recursively define the nth reduction of the program to be the one obtained by reducing the operations M_1, ..., M_n in that order. To define the nth reduction, define:

$$Cmp1_n \triangleq (snum = n - 1) \wedge Cmp1$$
$$Send_n \triangleq (snum = n - 1) \wedge Send$$
$$Rcv_n \triangleq (rnum = n - 1) \wedge Rcv$$
$$Cmp2_n \triangleq (rnum = n) \wedge Cmp2$$

so M_n equals $Cmp1_n \vee Send_n \vee Rcv_n \vee Cmp2_n$. The actions R, C, and L for the nth reduction are:

$$R_n \triangleq Cmp1_n \qquad C_n \triangleq Send_n \qquad L_n \triangleq Rcv_n \vee Cmp2_n$$

Again, with multiple reductions we let the reduced program have the same variables as the original program, so the nth reduction replaces the action M_n with M_n^ρ.

The remaining action E for this reduction is the disjunction of these actions: the action O describing the other processes, the already reduced actions M_k^ρ for $k < n$, and the subactions of M_k for $k > n$. To apply Theorem 8.1, we must show that R_n right-commutes with these actions and L_n left-commutes with them.

That R_n right-commutes and L_n left-commutes with O must be assumed. The commutativity relations hold for M_k^ρ with $k < n$ because an R_n step is enabled only after an M_k^ρ step, which implies $R_n \cdot M_k^\rho$ equals FALSE (so R_n right commutes with M_k^ρ), and which also implies that L_n cannot be enabled immediately after an M_k^ρ step, so $M_k^\rho \cdot L_n$ also equals FALSE.

What remains to be shown is that $Cmp1_n$ (the action R_n) right commutes with M_k, and that Rcv_n and $Cmp2_n$ (whose disjunction equals L_n) left commutes with M_k, for $k > n$. For that, we have to show that each of the four actions whose disjunction equals M_k satisfy those commutativity conditions. We will use the commutativity relations we assumed above: that $Cmp1$ commutes with $Cmp2$ and Rcv, and that $Cmp2$ commutes with $Send$. The assumption that $Cmp2$ commutes with $Send$ implies that $Cmp2_i$ commutes with $Send_j$ for all i and j. This follows from the definitions of $Cmp2_i$ and $Send_j$, because $Cmp2$ does not depend on or modify $snum$ and $Send_j$ does not depend on or modify $rnum$. Similarly, $Cmp1_i$ commutes with Rcv_j and $Cmp2_j$ for all i and j. These assumptions are called the *commutativity assumptions* in the following proof sketches of the required commutativity relations. Recall that we are assuming $k > n$.

$Cmp1_n$ **right-commutes with** $Cmp1_k$ **and** $Send_k$
  $Cmp1_n \cdot Cmp1_k$ and $Cmp1_n \cdot Send_k$ equal FALSE because $snum = n-1$ after a $Cmp1_n$ step; $Cmp1_k$ and $Send_k$ are enabled iff $snum = k-1$; and $k > n$.

$Cmp1_n$ **right-commutes with** Rcv_k **and** $Cmp2_k$
  By the commutativity assumptions.

Rcv_n **left-commutes with** $Cmp1_k$
  By the commutativity assumptions.

Rcv_n **left-commutes with** $Send_k$
  A $Send_k$ step is enabled only if $snum = k-1$; the step leaves $rnum$ unchanged; and Rcv_n is enabled only if $rnum = n-1$. Therefore, $Send_k \cdot Rcv_n$ enabled implies $snum = k-1$ and $rnum = n-1$, so $k > n$ implies $snum > rnum$ which implies $qBar \neq \langle\rangle$. By (8.24), this implies $Send_k \cdot Rcv_n \equiv Rcv_n \cdot Send_k$.

Rcv_n **left-commutes with** Rcv_k **and** $Cmp2_k$
  $Rcv_k \cdot Rcv_n$ and $Cmp2_k \cdot Rcv_n$ equal FALSE because a Rcv_k or $Cmp2_k$ step ends in a state with $rnum = k$ which by $k > n$ implies $rnum \neq n-1$, so Rcv_n is not enabled in that state.

$Cmp2_n$ **left-commutes with** $Cmp1_k$ **and** $Send_k$
  By the commutativity assumptions.

$Cmp2_n$ **left-commutes with** Rcv_k **and** $Cmp2_k$
  A Rcv_k or $Cmp2_k$ step ends with $rnum = k$, and $Cmp2_n$ is enabled only if $rnum = n$, which is false because $k > n$. Therefore a $Cmp2_n$ step cannot follow a Rcv_k or $Cmp2_k$ step, so $Rcv_k \cdot Cmp2_n$ and $Cmp2_k \cdot Cmp2_n$ equal FALSE.

This handles the commutativity assumptions of Theorem 8.1. We still have the hypothesis $\Box\Diamond\neg\mathcal{L}$ in the theorem's conclusion to deal with. By Theorem 8.3, to use reduction for verifying safety properties, we don't need that hypothesis. We only have to show that any finite behavior satisfying the safety property S can be extended to a behavior that completes each M_n operation in which the C_n action has occurred. This means showing that Process 2 cannot deadlock. This should be easy to show unless process 2 may have to wait for another process to do something—for example, until another process is ready to receive process 2's output.

For reasoning about liveness, we would expect the hypothesis $\Box\Diamond\neg\mathcal{L}$ to be satisfied by adding fairness conditions to process 2 actions, and perhaps to other processes, to ensure that the operation will complete once process 1's *Send* action occurs. The obvious fairness condition we want the reduced program to satisfy is fairness of M^ρ. If an M_n^ρ action is enabled, then no M_i^ρ action with $i \neq n$ can be enabled until an M_n^ρ step occurs. This implies that (weak or strong) fairness of M^ρ is equivalent to fairness of M_n^ρ for all n. For each n, ensuring fairness of M_n^ρ is the second case in Theorem 8.4, with A_i equal to C_n, which equals $Send_n$. The assumption $\models S \wedge F \Rightarrow \ldots$ in that case of the theorem will have to be implied by fairness conditions on subactions of $Cmp1$.

8.2 Decomposing and Composing Programs

We think of a program as consisting of multiple components. Most often those components are processes. However, a process of an abstract program need not correspond to a process (or thread) in a coding language. As we saw in Section 1.5, Euclid's algorithm can be viewed as a multiprocess program. In general, any disjunct of a program's next-state action can be thought of as a process, and we may be able to write the next-state action in more than one way as the disjunction of subactions. We now use the term *component* instead of *process* for what is described by a disjunct of the program's next-state action.

In this section, we describe a program as the conjunction of separate programs, each describing one of the program's components. There are two reasons for doing this. The first is that we have the program and want to decompose the problem of verifying its correctness into the simpler tasks of verifying correctness of each of its components. We call this procedure *decomposing programs* and consider it in Section 8.2.1. The second reason is because the program is implemented using existing components whose correctness has been verified. We want to deduce correctness of the program from correctness of the components, without knowing how the components are implemented. This procedure is called *composition* and is considered in Section 8.2.2.

There is little reason to decompose a program if we are proving its correctness. Decomposition structures the proof in three parts: (1) showing that the program is equivalent to the conjunction of programs describing the components, (2) showing that each of those programs satisfies a property, and (3) showing that the conjunction of those properties implies correctness of the original program. Such a proof can be rewritten as an ordinary correctness proof of the original algorithm by a simple rearrangement of the steps of those three parts. But math provides many ways to structure a proof, and deciding in advance to structure it by decomposition might rule out better proofs.

The one good reason to decompose the verification of a program in this way is that it may make it easier to use a tool to verify correctness. For example, a model checker might be able to verify correctness of individual components but not correctness of the complete program. Decomposition would allow using model checking to perform part of the verification, and then using the results presented here to prove that correctness of the components implies correctness of the entire program. This approach has been applied to a nontrivial example [25], but I don't know of any case in which it has been used in industry.

Composition is useful if an engineer wants to verify correctness of a program that describes a system built using an existing component whose behavior is specified by an abstract program. Up until now, we have described a program by a formula that is satisfied by behaviors in which the program to be implemented, which I will here call the actual program, and its environment are both acting correctly. There was no need for the mathematical description to separate the actual program and its environment, since it makes no difference if an execution is incorrect because the programmer didn't understand what the code would do or what the environment would do. However, if a program is implemented using a component purchased elsewhere, it is important to know if an incorrect behavior is due to an incorrect implementation of the actual program or of the component, which is part of the environment.

For composition, we therefore describe a program with two formulas, formula M describing the correct behavior of the actual program and a formula E describing correct behavior of its environment. These formulas are combined into a single formula, written $E \mathrel{+\!\!\!\!\Rightarrow} M$, that can be thought of as being true of a behavior iff M is true as long as E is (so M is always true if E is always true). Formula $E \mathrel{+\!\!\!\!\Rightarrow} M$ is what is called a rely/guarantee description of the program [23].

Currently, implementing actual programs with precisely specified existing components seems likely to arise in practice only for components that are traditional programs that perform a computation and stop; and where execution of the component can be considered to be a single step of the complete program. In that case, there is no need for TLA. As explained in Appendix Section A.5, the safety property of the component can be specified by a Hoare triple; and termination is the only required liveness property. Composition in TLA is needed only if the existing component interacts with

8.2. DECOMPOSING AND COMPOSING PROGRAMS

its environment in a more complex way that must be described with a more general abstract program. Such reusable, precisely specified components do not seem to exist now. Perhaps someday they will.

The results presented here come from a single paper [2]. The reader is referred to that paper for the proofs. To make reading it easier, much of the notation used here—including the identifiers in formulas—is taken from that paper.

8.2.1 Decomposing Programs

8.2.1.1 Writing a Program as a Conjunction

As an example, we take Euclid's algorithm, described in Section 1.5. Instead of x and y, let's name the variables a and b. Also, instead of having the algorithm compute the GCD of two particular numbers, we'll let it nondeterministically choose the initial values of a and b and compute their GCD.

To write the algorithm in TLA, let's first define formulas that describe the initial values of each of the variables, how they are changed in the next-state action, and fairness of the actions that change them, where $\mathbb{N}^+$ is the set of positive integers. Here are those formulas for the variable a:

$$Init_a \triangleq a \in \mathbb{N}^+$$
$$Next_a \triangleq (a > b) \land (a' = a - b) \land (b' = b)$$
$$L_a \triangleq \text{WF}_{\langle a \rangle}(Next_a)$$

The formulas $Init_b$, $Next_b$, and L_b are obtained from these formulas by interchanging a and b. Note that L_a is equivalent to $\text{WF}_{\langle a,b \rangle}(Next_a)$ because $Next_a$ implies $b' = b$, and similarly, L_b is equivalent to $\text{WF}_{\langle a,b \rangle}(Next_b)$.

We can describe Euclid's algorithm with the following TLA formula M:

$$M \triangleq Init_M \land \Box[Next_M]_{\langle a,b \rangle}$$
$$Init_M \triangleq Init_a \land Init_b$$
$$Next_M \triangleq Next_a \lor Next_b$$
$$L_M \triangleq L_a \land L_b$$

Formula M is equivalent to the conjunction of M_a and M_b, defined by:

$$M_a \triangleq Init_a \land \Box[Next_a]_a \land L_a$$
$$M_b \triangleq Init_b \land \Box[Next_b]_b \land L_b$$

The equivalence of M and $M_a \land M_b$ follows by simple logic from:

$$\models \Box[Next_a]_a \land \Box[Next_b]_b \equiv \Box[Next_a \lor Next_b]_{\langle a,b \rangle}$$

This result follows from the equivalence of $\Box(F \wedge G)$ and $\Box F \wedge \Box G$, for any formulas F and G, and from

$$[Next_a]_a \wedge [Next_b]_b \equiv [Next_a \vee Next_b]_{\langle a, b \rangle}$$

which follows from the definition of $[\ldots]_{\ldots}$, the equivalence of $(a' = a) \wedge (b' = b)$ and $\langle a, b \rangle' = \langle a, b \rangle$, and:

(8.26) $\models Next_a \Rightarrow (b' = b) \qquad \models Next_b \Rightarrow (a' = a)$

That M is equivalent to $M_a \wedge M_b$ depends only on (8.26), not on any other properties of $Next_a$ and $Next_b$, and not on the definitions of $Init_a$, $Init_b$, L_a, or L_b. Moreover, it remains true if each variable a and b is replaced by a tuple of variables, as long as those two tuples have no variable in common and (8.26) is satisfied. In other words, if a program consists of two components, each modifying different variables than the other, then the program can be decomposed as the conjunction of two programs, each describing one of the components.

The following theorem generalizes this example from two to n components. It replaces M_a and M_b by processes M_i for $i \in 1..n$, replaces a and b by the lists m_i of variables modified by each component i, and replaces (8.26) by the requirement that for each i, the next-state action $Next_i$ of M_i implies $\langle m_j \rangle' = \langle m_j \rangle$ for $j \neq i$.[4]

Theorem 8.5 If $m_1, \ldots, m_n$ are each lists of variables, with all the variables in all the lists distinct, $N \triangleq 1..n$, and

$$m \triangleq m_1, \ldots, m_n$$
$$M_i \triangleq Init_i \wedge \Box[Next_i]_{\langle m_i \rangle} \wedge L_i$$
$$M \triangleq \forall i \in N : M_i$$
$$\models M \Rightarrow \Box[\forall i, j \in N : Next_i \wedge (i \neq j) \Rightarrow (\langle m_j \rangle' = \langle m_j \rangle)]_m$$

then

$$\models M \equiv (\forall i \in N : Init_i) \wedge \Box[\exists i \in N : Next_i]_{\langle m \rangle} \wedge (\forall i \in N : L_i)$$

We can further generalize this theorem to allow hiding of variables local to components. Suppose that for each component i, we might want to hide

---

[4]We are abandoning our convention of naming a list of variables with a boldface letter and adopting the notation of [2], where each m_i is a list of variables that we could write $m_{i,1}, \ldots, m_{i,n_i}$ but won't.

8.2. DECOMPOSING AND COMPOSING PROGRAMS

a sublist y_i of the variable list m_i, where the variables y_i do not appear in any M_j with $j \neq i$. We can then define M by

$$M \triangleq \forall i \in N : (\exists y_i : M_i)$$

where if y_i is the empty tuple, then $\exists y_i : M_i$ equals M_i. We must modify the hypothesis $\models M \Rightarrow \Box[\ldots]_m$ by replacing m_j with the variables of m_j not in y_j, and make this the conclusion:

$$\models M \equiv \exists y_1, \ldots, y_n :$$
$$(\forall i \in N : \mathit{Init}_i) \wedge \Box[\exists i \in N : \widehat{\mathit{Next}_i}]_{\langle m \rangle} \wedge (\forall i \in N : L_i)$$

where $\widehat{\mathit{Next}_i} \triangleq \mathit{Next}_i \wedge \forall j \in N \setminus \{i\} : y'_j = y_j$.

Another generalization is to require only that different components modify different parts of the state, not necessarily different variables. For example, suppose the components are processes and process i modifies $pc(i)$, where the value of the variable pc is always a function whose domain is the set N. In the hypothesis $\models M \Rightarrow \Box[\ldots]_m$, we can replace the expression $\langle m_j \rangle' = \langle m_j \rangle$ by a state predicate ν_j, where the predicates ν_i must satisfy only the additional hypothesis:

$$\models M \Rightarrow \Box[(\forall i \in N : \nu_i) \Rightarrow (m' = m)]_{\langle m \rangle}$$

For the example in which process i modifies $pc(i)$, we can define ν_i so it implies $(\exists S : pc \in (N \to S)) \wedge (pc'(i) = pc(i))$.

For simplicity, we consider only decomposing programs as described by Theorem 8.5. The rest of what we say about program decomposition can be generalized to these more general ways to decompose programs.

8.2.1.2 Decomposing Proofs

We now consider decomposing the verification that a program is correct into the verification that its components are correct. Let's start with a program with two variables c and d and two components, each component modifying one of the variables. Let's suppose we have decomposed the program into the conjunction $M_c^l \wedge M_d^l$, and we have decomposed its correctness property into $M_c \wedge M_d$, where M_c and M_d are correctness conditions for the two components. We have to verify:

(8.27) $\models M_c^l \wedge M_d^l \Rightarrow M_c \wedge M_d$

and we'd like to do this by verifying that M_c^l satisfies M_c and that M_d^l satisfies M_d. We can obviously do that if we can verify

$$\models M_c^l \Rightarrow M_c \quad \text{and} \quad \models M_d^l \Rightarrow M_d$$

However, those conditions are unlikely to be true. The component program M_c^l is unlikely to satisfy M_c when used as a component of an arbitrary program. Its correctness will depend upon some property of its environment M_d^l. Similarly, correctness of M_d^l will depend upon some property of M_c^l.

We can obviously reduce verification of (8.27) to verifying

$$\models M_c^l \wedge M_d^l \Rightarrow M_c \quad \text{and} \quad \models M_c^l \wedge M_d^l \Rightarrow M_d$$

but that doesn't reduce the amount of work involved. However, suppose that correctness of M_c^l doesn't depend on its environment being the component M_d^l, but just requires its environment to satisfy the correctness condition M_d of that component, and similarly correctness of M_d^l just requires that the other component satisfies M_c. We would then like to reduce verification of (8.27) to verifying:

$$(8.28) \quad \models M_d \wedge M_c^l \Rightarrow M_c \quad \text{and} \quad \models M_c \wedge M_d^l \Rightarrow M_d$$

This would reduce the amount of work because M_c and M_d are probably significantly simpler than M_c^l and M_d^l. Can we do that?

Let's consider the following trivial example, where each component initializes its variable to 0 and keeps setting its variable's value to the value of the other component's variable.

$$(8.29) \quad M_c^l \triangleq (c = 0) \wedge \Box[(c' = d) \wedge (d' = d)]_c$$
$$\wedge \text{WF}_c((c' = d) \wedge (d' = d))$$
$$M_d^l \triangleq (d = 0) \wedge \Box[(d' = c) \wedge (c' = c)]_d$$
$$\wedge \text{WF}_d((d' = c) \wedge (c' = c))$$

We take as the correctness condition of each component that its variable always equals 0:

$$M_c \triangleq \Box(c = 0) \quad \text{and} \quad M_d \triangleq \Box(d = 0)$$

Condition (8.28) is satisfied because each component's variable keeps setting its variable to 0 (that is, it can take nothing but stuttering steps) if the other component's variable always equals 0. As we would hope, the correctness condition (8.27) is also satisfied because the program consisting of those two components keeps both c and d always equal to 0.

Now let's replace M_c and M_d by the properties asserting that c and d eventually equal 1:

$$M_c \triangleq \Diamond(c = 1) \quad M_d \triangleq \Diamond(d = 1)$$

8.2. DECOMPOSING AND COMPOSING PROGRAMS

while keeping M_c^l and M_d^l the same. Condition (8.28) is still satisfied because each component eventually sets its variable to 1 if the other component sets its variable to 1. However, (8.27) is not satisfied. Changing the correctness conditions doesn't change the behavior of the program, which is to take nothing but stuttering steps.

We might ask why we can't deduce (8.27) from (8.28) in this example. However, the real question is why we *can* deduce it in the first example. Deducing (8.27) from (8.28) is deducing, from the assumption that correctness of each component implies correctness of the other, that both components are correct. This is circular reasoning, and letting $M_c = M_d =$ FALSE shows that it allows us to deduce that any program implies FALSE, from which we can deduce that the program satisfies any property.

So, why does (8.28) imply (8.27) in the first case? Why can we deduce that both components leave their variables equal to 0 from the assumption that each component leaves its variable equal to 0 if the other process leaves its variable equal to 0? The reason is that neither process can set its variable to a value other than 0 until the other one does. Stated more generally, we can deduce that both components in a two-component program satisfy their correctness properties if neither component can violate its correctness property until after the other does. So we want to replace (8.28) by:

(8.30) $\models \forall k \in \mathbb{N}$:
$\quad$ (M_d true through state $k-1$)
$\quad \wedge$ (M_c^l true through state k) $\Rightarrow$ (M_c true through state k)

plus the same condition with c and d interchanged, where F true through state -1 is taken to be true for any property F.

To express (8.30) precisely, we have to say what it means for a property F to be true through state k. If F is a safety property, it means that F is true of the finite behavior $\sigma(0) \to \ldots \to \sigma(k)$, which means it's true of the (infinite) behavior obtained by repeating the state $\sigma(k)$ forever. It follows from Theorems 4.4 and 4.5 that any property F equals $\mathcal{C}(F) \wedge L$ where L is a liveness property such that $\langle \mathcal{C}(F), L \rangle$ is machine closed. By the definition of machine closure (in Section 4.2.2.2), any finite behavior that satisfies $\mathcal{C}(F)$ can be completed to a behavior satisfying $\mathcal{C}(F) \wedge L$, which equals F. Therefore, the only way a behavior can fail to satisfy F through state k is for it not to satisfy $\mathcal{C}(F)$ through state k, so F is true through state k means that $\mathcal{C}(F)$ is true through state k. We should therefore replace M_d, M_c^l, and M_c by $\mathcal{C}(M_d)$, $\mathcal{C}(M_c^l)$, and $\mathcal{C}(M_c)$ in (8.30). For a safety property, true through state k means true if all states i with $i > k$ equal state k, so we can rewrite the resulting condition as:

(8.31) $\models \forall k \in \mathbb{N}$:
$\qquad$ (every state after state k equals state k) $\Rightarrow$
$\qquad\qquad ((\mathcal{C}(M_d)$ true through state $k-1) \wedge \mathcal{C}(M_c^l) \Rightarrow \mathcal{C}(M_c))$

Next, let v be the tuple of all variables in these formulas. We can then replace the assertion "every state ... state k" in (8.31) with "$v' = v$ from state k on". By predicate logic, if k does not appear in R or S, then

$$(\forall k : P \Rightarrow (Q \wedge R \Rightarrow S)) \equiv ((\exists k : P \wedge Q) \wedge R \Rightarrow S)$$

We can therefore rewrite (8.31) as follows, abbreviating "true through state" as "tts":

(8.32) $(\exists k \in \mathbb{N} : (v' = v$ from state k on$) \wedge (\mathcal{C}(M_d)$ tts $k-1))$
$\qquad \wedge\, \mathcal{C}(M_c^l) \Rightarrow \mathcal{C}(M_c)$

If we define F_{+v} to equal

$$\exists k \in \mathbb{N} : (v' = v \text{ from state } k \text{ on}) \wedge (\mathcal{C}(F) \text{ tts } k-1)$$

we can then write (8.32) and the condition obtained from it by interchanging c and d as:

(8.33) $\models \mathcal{C}(M_d)_{+v} \wedge \mathcal{C}(M_c^l) \Rightarrow \mathcal{C}(M_c)$
$\qquad \models \mathcal{C}(M_c)_{+v} \wedge \mathcal{C}(M_d^l) \Rightarrow \mathcal{C}(M_d)$

From (8.33), we can infer:

(8.34) $\models \mathcal{C}(M_c^l) \wedge \mathcal{C}(M_d^l) \Rightarrow \mathcal{C}(M_c) \wedge \mathcal{C}(M_d)$

The theorems to be stated require a slightly weaker definition of F_{+v}, which makes the conditions (8.33) stronger (so they still imply (8.34)). Let F_{+v}^{old} be the formula that we have been calling F_{+v}. We now define F_{+v} to equal $F_{+v}^{old} \vee F$. With this definition, (8.33) implies its two conditions also hold with the "$+v$" removed. If F is a safety property, then F_{+v} is a safety property but F_{+v}^{old} usually isn't. In fact, if F is a safety property then F_{+v} equals $\mathcal{C}(F_{+v}^{old})$. In practice, the change should seldom make a difference in (8.34) because we don't expect liveness properties to be useful for proving safety properties, so we wouldn't expect $F \wedge G \Rightarrow H$ to be true for safety properties G and H without $\mathcal{C}(F) \wedge G \Rightarrow H$ also being true.

The formula F_{+v} has been defined semantically. However, to verify (8.33) directly, we have to write $\mathcal{C}(F)_{+v}$ as a formula for a given formula F. It's

8.2. DECOMPOSING AND COMPOSING PROGRAMS

easy to write $\mathcal{C}(F)$ if F has the usual form $Init \wedge \Box[Next]_w \wedge L$, where w is the tuple of variables in the formulas and L is the conjunction of fairness properties of subactions of $Next$. In that case, the definition of machine closure (Section 4.2.2.2) and Theorem 4.7 (Section 4.2.7) imply $\mathcal{C}(F)$ equals $Init \wedge \Box[Next]_w$. We can then write F_{+v} as follows:

$$F_{+v} \triangleq \exists h : \widehat{Init} \wedge [\widehat{Next}]_{w \circ v \circ \langle h \rangle}$$
$$\text{where } \widehat{Init} \triangleq (Init \wedge (h = 0)) \vee (h = 1)$$
$$\widehat{Next} \triangleq \vee (h = 0) \wedge \vee (h' = 0) \wedge [Next]_w$$
$$\vee h' = 1$$
$$\vee (h = 1) \wedge (h' = h) \wedge (v' = v)$$

While writing F_{+v} is easy enough, we usually don't have to for the same reason that we didn't have to use the $+v$ subscripts in (8.27). Our example has one feature that we didn't use in our generalization—namely, that no single program step can make both M_c and M_d false. Here's how to use that feature in general. For safety properties F and G, define $F \perp G$ to be true of a behavior σ iff for every $k \in \mathbb{N}$, if $F \wedge G$ is true of $\sigma(0) \to \ldots \to \sigma(k)$ then $F \vee G$ is true of $\sigma(0) \to \ldots \to \sigma(k+1)$. Understanding why the following theorem is true is a good test that you understand the definition of F_{+v}.

Theorem 8.6 If F, G, and H are safety properties, v is a tuple of variables containing all variables of F, and $\models H \Rightarrow (F \perp G)$, then $\models F \wedge H \Rightarrow G$ implies $\models F_{+v} \wedge H \Rightarrow G$.

For our example, in which M_c and M_d are safety properties, $\models \mathcal{C}(M_c^l) \Rightarrow (M_c \perp M_d)$ and $\models \mathcal{C}(M_d^l) \Rightarrow (M_c \perp M_d)$ are true and allow us to remove $+v$ from the conditions (8.33). These properties are true because the example satisfies these two conditions:

- We can express correctness of the program as $M_c \wedge M_d$, where only a step of component c can violate M_c and only a step of component d can violate M_d. This seems to be a requirement for decomposing verification of the program into verification of its components to make sense. For example, mutual exclusion can't be expressed as the conjunction of invariance properties that can each be violated by only one process. I therefore expect that attempting to decompose verification of a mutual exclusion algorithm in this way would complicate the task.

- No step is both a c step and a d step. This condition means that a step in a behavior of the program consists of a step of a single component.

It is the case if the components are processes in a program written in the kind of pseudocode we have been using, which is modeled after the most popular coding languages. I believe that all the engineers I have worked with find this to be the most natural way to describe concurrent programs.

We have obtained the assumptions we need to deduce (8.34). But we want to verify (8.27), which is (8.34) with the $\mathcal{C}$ operators removed. Since F implies $\mathcal{C}(F)$ for any property F, we can remove the $\mathcal{C}$s from the left-hand side of the implication (8.34). But we need additional assumptions to be able to infer that $M_c^l \wedge M_d^l$ implies the liveness parts of M_c and M_d. Since we know that $M_c^l \wedge M_d^l$ implies $\mathcal{C}(M_c) \wedge \mathcal{C}(M_d)$, we can use the following assumptions to deduce (8.27).

(8.35) $\models \mathcal{C}(M_d) \wedge M_c^l \Rightarrow M_c$ and $\models \mathcal{C}(M_c) \wedge M_d^l \Rightarrow M_d$

Condition (8.33) allows us to assume that other components satisfy their safety conditions when showing that a component satisfies its safety condition. However, (8.35) allows us to use the liveness property of only that component when showing that the component satisfies its liveness requirement. It would be circular reasoning to assume M_d when verifying M_c and assume M_c when verifying M_d. However, we can do it for one of the components. For example, if we show that $\mathcal{C}(M_c) \wedge M_d^l$ implies M_d, we can then assume M_d when showing that M_c^l implies M_c. We can therefore replace $\mathcal{C}(M_d)$ by M_d in (8.35), since $\mathcal{C}(M_d) \wedge M_d$ equals M_d. (But we then can't also replace $\mathcal{C}(M_c)$ by M_c.)

For any decomposition of a program into two components M_c^l and M_d^l with correctness properties M_c and M_d, we have deduced (8.27) from (8.33) and (8.35). The following theorem, which follows easily from Theorem 1 of [2], generalizes this to a program with n components M_i^l, each with correctness property M_i. The theorem is first stated, then explained.

Theorem 8.7 (Decomposition Theorem) If for all $i \in 1..n$:

1. $\models \forall j \in 1..n : \mathcal{C}(M_j) \Rightarrow E_i$

2. (a) $\models \mathcal{C}(E_i)_{+v} \wedge \mathcal{C}(M_i^l) \Rightarrow \mathcal{C}(M_i)$
   (b) $\models E_i \wedge M_i^l \wedge (\forall j \in 1..(i-1) : M_j) \Rightarrow M_i$

then $\models (\forall i \in 1..n : M_i^l) \Rightarrow (\forall i \in 1..n : M_i)$

The theorem's conclusion is the obvious generalization of (8.27). There are two hypotheses for each component i. Let's first ignore hypothesis 1 and take E_i to be the conjunction of all the $\mathcal{C}(M_j)$ for $j \neq i$. Hypothesis 2(a) for component M_i^l then generalizes the first condition of (8.33) for component M_c^l, replacing the correctness condition $\mathcal{C}(M_d)$ of the other component with the conjunction $\mathcal{C}(M_j)$ of all the other components. Hypothesis 2(b) makes the similar generalization of (8.35), where allowing the use of all M_j with $j < i$ in the proof of M_i generalizes the observation we made about being able to weaken one of the conditions of (8.35). Hypothesis 1 generalizes what we did for two components in two ways:

- It allows E_i to be the conjunction of all formulas $\mathcal{C}(M_j)$, including $j = i$. This can obviously be done for hypothesis 2(b). It might seem to turn hypothesis 2(a) into a tautology by conjoining the right-hand side $\mathcal{C}(M_i)$ of the implication to the left-hand side, resulting in circular reasoning. However, the subscript $+v$ turns it from circular reasoning into induction on the number of steps in a finite behavior.

- Instead of using the conjunction of $\mathcal{C}(M_j)$ for all the components' correctness properties M_j in hypothesis 2, it allows E_i to be any property implied by that conjunction that is strong enough to satisfy hypothesis 2. I expect E_i will always be a safety property, but it's conceivable that it might not be.

The theorem does not make any assumption about v. That's because if w is the tuple of all variables appearing in the formulas (including in v), then F_{+w} implies F_{+v}. Thus, if hypothesis 2(a) is satisfied for any state function v, then it's satisfied with v equal to the tuple of all variables in the formulas. Letting v equal that tuple produces the weakest (hence easiest to satisfy) hypothesis.

8.2.2 Composing Components

In Section 8.2.1, we decomposed a given program as the conjunction of components. We now assume we are given a collection of components and define the program to be the conjunction of those components. As a tiny example, assume we want to write a program that satisfies the property $\Box(c = 0) \land \Box(d = 0)$, and we want to do it by conjoining a c component that implements $\Box(c = 0)$ and a d component that implements $\Box(d = 0)$. We find that someone has written a program M_x^l that satisfies $\Box(x = 0)$

when run in an environment that satisfies $\Box(y = 0)$. So, we decide to write our program as $M_c^l \wedge M_d^l$ where:

$$M_c^l \triangleq (M_x^l \text{ WITH } x \leftarrow c, \, y \leftarrow d)$$
$$M_d^l \triangleq (M_x^l \text{ WITH } x \leftarrow d, \, y \leftarrow c)$$

This silly example captures the most important aspect of specifying components: No real device will satisfy a specification such as $\Box(c = 0)$ when executed in an arbitrary environment. For example, a process will not be able to compute the GCD of two numbers if other processes can at any time arbitrarily change the values of its variables.

We want to deduce that $M_c^l \wedge M_d^l$ implies $\Box(c = 0) \wedge \Box(d = 0)$ from the properties that components c and d satisfy, without knowing what M_c^l and M_d^l are. The property that the c component satisfies is that if its environment satisfies $\Box(d = 0)$ then the component satisfies $\Box(c = 0)$; and d satisfies the same condition with d and c interchanged. The obvious way to express these two properties is $\Box(d = 0) \Rightarrow \Box(c = 0)$ and $\Box(c = 0) \Rightarrow \Box(d = 0)$, but those two properties obviously don't imply $\Box(c = 0) \wedge \Box(d = 0)$. We need to find the right way to express mathematically the condition that a component satisfies the property M if its environment satisfies the property E. We do this by assuming that the condition is expressed by a formula $E \overset{+}{\Rightarrow} M$ and figuring out what the definition of $\overset{+}{\Rightarrow}$ should be, given the assumption that the definition should make this true:

(8.36) $\models \Box(d = 0) \overset{+}{\Rightarrow} \Box(c = 0)$ and $\models \Box(c = 0) \overset{+}{\Rightarrow} \Box(d = 0)$
   implies $\models \Box(c = 0) \wedge \Box(d = 0)$

We first ask when we can deduce this:

(8.37) $\models E_1 \overset{+}{\Rightarrow} M_1$ and $\models E_2 \overset{+}{\Rightarrow} M_2$ implies $\models M_1 \wedge M_2$

The answer lies in Theorem 8.7. Since (8.37) doesn't mention the programs M_1^l and M_2^l, it should be true if we let those programs equal TRUE. Substituting TRUE for them, the conclusion of Theorem 8.7 for $n = 2$ is $M_1 \wedge M_2$. We define $\overset{+}{\Rightarrow}$ so that hypotheses 2(a) and 2(b) are equivalent to $E_i \overset{+}{\Rightarrow} M_i$. The definition is:

$$E \overset{+}{\Rightarrow} M \triangleq (\mathcal{C}(E)_{+v} \Rightarrow \mathcal{C}(M)) \wedge (E \Rightarrow M)$$

where v is the tuple of all variables in E and M. The theorem then implies that (8.37) is true if hypothesis 1 is satisfied, that hypothesis asserting:

(8.38) $\models \mathcal{C}(M_1) \wedge \mathcal{C}(M_2) \Rightarrow E_1$ and $\models \mathcal{C}(M_1) \wedge \mathcal{C}(M_2) \Rightarrow E_2$

8.2. DECOMPOSING AND COMPOSING PROGRAMS

These conditions are true for our example, so (8.36) is true.

The conclusion of Theorem 8.7 is $\models M_1 \wedge M_2$, which asserts that the composition of the components satisfies M_1 and M_2 assuming nothing about its environment. We need a more general theorem whose conclusion is $\models E \xrightarrow{+} M_1 \wedge M_2$, asserting that the composition satisfies $M_1 \wedge M_2$ if its environment satisfies E. There is actually a stronger result, asserting that the composition satisfies $\models E \xrightarrow{+} M$ for any property M implied by $E \wedge M_1 \wedge M_2$. Here is the theorem, generalized from two to n components. It is Theorem 3 of [2].

Theorem 8.8 (Composition Theorem) If

1. $\models \forall i \in 1..n : \mathcal{C}(E) \wedge (\forall j \in 1..n : \mathcal{C}(M_j)) \Rightarrow E_i$
2. (a) $\models \mathcal{C}(E)_{+v} \wedge (\forall j \in 1..n : \mathcal{C}(M_j)) \Rightarrow \mathcal{C}(M)$
   (b) $\models E \wedge (\forall j \in 1..n : M_j) \Rightarrow M$

then $\models (\forall j \in 1..n : E_j \xrightarrow{+} M_j) \Rightarrow (E \xrightarrow{+} M)$

It's instructive to compare Theorems 8.7 and 8.8. They both make no assumption about v, since letting it equal the tuple of all variables in the formulas yields the weakest hypothesis 2(a). Hypothesis 1 differs only in Theorem 8.8 having the additional conjunct $\mathcal{C}(E)$. This conjunct (which weakens the hypothesis) is expected because, if M is the conjunction of the M_i, then the M in the conclusion of Theorem 8.7 is replaced in Theorem 8.8 by $E \xrightarrow{+} M$.

As we observed for Theorem 8.7, hypothesis 1 of Theorem 8.8 pretty much requires the E_i to be safety properties. However, when applying Theorem 8.8, we can choose to make them safety properties by moving the liveness property of E_i into the liveness property of M_i. More precisely, suppose we write E_i as $E_i^S \wedge E_i^L$, where E_i^S is a safety property and E_i^L a liveness property such that $\langle E_i^S, E_i^L \rangle$ is machine closed; and we similarly write M_i as $M_i^S \wedge M_i^L$. We can then replace E_i by E_i^S and M_i by $M_i^S \wedge (E_i^L \Rightarrow M_i^L)$.[5] This replaces the property $E_i \xrightarrow{+} M_i$ by the stronger property:

(8.39) $E_i^S \xrightarrow{+} (M_i^S \wedge (E_i^L \Rightarrow M_i^L))$

It is stronger because if the environment doesn't satisfy its liveness property E_i^L, then $E_i \xrightarrow{+} M_i$ is satisfied no matter what the component does; but in

---

[5]By definition of machine closure, $\langle M_i^S, M_i^L \rangle$ machine closed implies $\langle M_i^S, E_i^L \Rightarrow M_i^L \rangle$ is also machine closed, because M_i^L implies $E_i^L \Rightarrow M_i^L$.

that case, (8.39) still requires the component to satisfy its safety property M_i^S if the environment satisfies its safety property E_i^S. The two formulas should be equivalent in practice because machine closure of $\langle E_i^S, E_i^L \rangle$ implies that, as long as the environment satisfies its safety property, the component can't know that the environment's entire infinite behavior will violate its liveness property.

Theorem 8.8 has been explained in terms of M_i being the property satisfied by a component whose description M_i^l we don't know, with M a property we want the composition of the components to satisfy. It can also be applied by letting M_i be the actual component M_i^l and letting M be the composition $\forall\, i \in 1\mathinner{.\,.}n : M_i^l$ of those components. The theorem then tells us under what environment assumption E the composition will behave properly if each M_i^l behaves properly under the environment assumption E_i. However, there is a problem when using it in this way. To explain the problem, we return to our two components c and d whose composition satisfies $\Box(c = 0) \land \Box(d = 0)$.

The definitions M_c^l and M_d^l in (8.29) were written for components c and d intended to be composed with one another. They were not written to describe a component that satisfies its desired property only if the environment satisfies its property. We now want to define them and their environment assumptions E_c and E_d so that:

$$\models (E_c \overset{+}{\Rightarrow} M_c^l) \Rightarrow \Box(c = 0)$$
$$\models (E_d \overset{+}{\Rightarrow} M_d^l) \Rightarrow \Box(d = 0)$$

The definition of M_c^l asserts that the value of d cannot change when the value of c changes (because of the conjunct $d' = d$ in the next-state relation) and d cannot change when c doesn't change (because of the subscript $\langle c, d \rangle$). That's a property of its environment. If we want d to satisfy that property, we should state it in E_c, not inside the definition of M_c^l. So, the definition of M_c^l should be

$$M_c^l \triangleq (c = 0) \land \Box[c' = d]_c \land \mathrm{WF}_c(c' = d)$$

and the definition of M_d^l should be similarly changed.

If you recall how we decomposed programs in Section 8.2.1.1, expressed in Theorem 8.5, you will realize that the conjuncts $d' = d$ and $c' = c$ in the original definitions of M_c^l and M_d^l were there so that the next-state action of the conjunction of M_c^l and M_d^l would be the disjunction of their next-state

8.2. DECOMPOSING AND COMPOSING PROGRAMS

actions. With these new definitions, the next-state action of $M_c^l \wedge M_d^l$ equals

$$[\vee (c' = d) \wedge (d' = d)$$
$$\vee (d' = c) \wedge (c' = c)$$
$$\vee (c' = d) \wedge (d' = c)]_{\langle c, d \rangle}$$

The additional disjunct $(c' = d) \wedge (d' = c)$ describes a step that is performed jointly by the two components. If we want the composition of the two components to allow such steps, then there is no problem. However, components are often processes, and in all the examples we've considered, each step is a step of exactly one process. Program descriptions in which each step is performed by a single component are called *interleaving* descriptions.[6]

Suppose we want to consider only interleaving program descriptions. We would take the approach used in Theorem 8.5 that for each i, there is a list m_i of variables that can be modified only by component M_i^l. It would be nice to let E_i assert that any step that changes a variable other than one of the variables of m_i must leave all the variables of m_i unchanged. However, this is impossible because there are infinitely many variables other than the ones in m_i, and a formula E_i can mention only finitely many of them.

Instead, we modify Theorem 8.8 so its conclusion is:

$$(8.40) \quad \models G \wedge (\forall j \in 1\mathinner{\ldotp\ldotp} n : E_j \overset{\pm}{\Rightarrow} M_j) \Rightarrow (E \overset{\pm}{\Rightarrow} G \wedge M)$$

for a property G. We can then apply the theorem with M_i equal to M_i^l, M equal to $\forall i \in 1\mathinner{\ldotp\ldotp} n : M_i^l$, and G the property asserting that if $i \neq j$, then a step can't change both $\langle m_i \rangle$ and $\langle m_j \rangle$. Formula $G \wedge M$ is the interleaving description that is presumably what we intended the composition of the components M_i^l to mean.

In the same way as we could generalize Theorem 8.5, we can replace $\langle m_j \rangle' = \langle m_j \rangle$ in the definition of G by a step predicate ν_j and have G assert that every step must satisfy $\nu_i \vee \nu_j$ for $i \neq j$.

You can write the theorem whose conclusion is (8.40) by yourself. All you have to do is apply Theorem 8.8 substituting $n+1$ for n, letting E_{n+1} equal TRUE, letting M_{n+1} equal G, and replacing M with $G \wedge M$. The hypotheses of Theorem 8.8 after making these substitutions are the hypotheses of the theorem.

---

[6] An interleaving description is often taken to mean any description of a program's executions as sequences of states and/or events, so by that meaning all TLA program descriptions are interleaving descriptions.

Appendix A

Miscellany

A.1 Ordinary Math Summary

This is a summary of all the ordinary math introduced in the main text of the book. Each subsection indicates in [square brackets] the sections where the operators it describes were introduced. Section A.1.5 introduces an operator not described earlier that is used in the appendix. In this summary, *variable* means a variable of ordinary math, which is a constant in temporal logic.

A.1.1 Arithmetic [Section 2.1, Math I]

Ordinary Operators $+$, $-$, $*$ (multiplication), $/$ (real-number division), $>$, $\geq$, $<$, $\leq$.

The Operator % For integers m and n, if $n > 0$ then $m \% n$ is the unique integer r satisfying $0 \leq r < n$ and $m = d * n + r$, for some integer d.

A.1.2 Propositional Logic [Sections 2.4 and 2.9.2]

Booleans TRUE and FALSE

Operators For any Boolean values A and B:

$\neg A$ Equals TRUE iff A equals FALSE.
$A \wedge B$ Equals TRUE iff both A and B equal TRUE.
$A \vee B$ Equals TRUE iff A or B or both equal TRUE.
$A \Rightarrow B$ Equals FALSE iff A equals TRUE and B equals FALSE.
$A \equiv B$ Equals TRUE iff A equals B.

A.1. ORDINARY MATH SUMMARY

Conjunction/Disjunction Lists An aligned list of formulas $A_1, \ldots, A_n$ "bulleted" by $\wedge$ like this:

$$\wedge\ A_1$$
$$\vdots$$
$$\wedge\ A_n$$

equals $(A_1) \wedge \ldots \wedge (A_n)$. The analogous notation is also used for $\vee$.

A.1.3 Predicate Logic [Section 2.7, Math IX]

$\forall v : F$ Equals TRUE iff F equals TRUE for all values of the variable v.

$\exists v : F$ Equals TRUE iff F equals TRUE for some value of the variable v.

$\forall v \in S : F$ Equals $\forall v : (v \in S) \Rightarrow F$.

$\exists v \in S : F$ Equals $\exists v : (v \in S) \wedge F$.

$\models F$ A meta-formula that is true iff formula F is true for any assignment of values to its variables.

$\exists$ **Introduction Rule** $\models (F \text{ WITH } v \leftarrow exp) \Rightarrow (\exists v : F)$

$\exists$ **Elimination Rule** $\models F \Rightarrow G$ implies $\models (\exists v : F) \Rightarrow (\exists v : G)$

A.1.4 Sets [Section 2.5, Math II, Math V, Math VI, Math XI]

$v \in S$ Equals TRUE iff v is an element of the set S.

$\{exp_1, \ldots, exp_n\}$ The set for which $v \in S$ equals TRUE iff v equals one (or more) of the expressions exp_i.

Sets of Numbers

     $\mathbb{R}$ The set of all real numbers.

     $\mathbb{I}$ The set of all integers.

     $\mathbb{N}$ The set of all non-negative integers (natural numbers).

     $m \mathbin{..} n$ The set of all integers i satisfying $m \leq i \leq n$.

$\#(S)$ The number of elements in S, if S is a finite set.

$S \subseteq T$ Equals TRUE iff every element of set S is an element of set T.

$S \cap T$ The set of all elements in both S and T.

$S \cup T$ The set of all elements in S or T or both.

$S \setminus T$ The set of all elements in S that are not elements of T.

$\{v \in S : F\}$ The set of all values of the variable v for which $(v \in S) \wedge F$ equals TRUE.

$\{exp : v \in S\}$ The set of all values of exp obtained by substituting an element of S for v.

Countable Set A set S is countable iff there is a mapping M such that this formula equals TRUE: $\forall s \in S : \exists n \in \mathbb{N} : M(n) = s$.

A.1.5 The CHOOSE Operator

Mathematicians often define something in terms of its properties. For example, they might define $\sqrt{r}$ for a real number r to be the non-negative real number such that $(\sqrt{r})^2 = r$. We can express such a definition using an operator invented by the mathematician David Hilbert in the 1920s. I didn't learn about this operator until some 25 years after I completed my studies; I suspect it's still unknown to most mathematicians. Hilbert called it ε, but I think it's better to call it CHOOSE. We can use this operator to define the square root as follows:

$$\sqrt{r} \triangleq \text{CHOOSE } s \in \mathbb{R} : (s \geq 0) \wedge (s^2 = r)$$

The CHOOSE operator is much like $\exists$ in that CHOOSE $v \in S : F$ is defined to equal CHOOSE $v : (v \in S) \wedge F$, where the scope of the bound variable v does not include S. The expression CHOOSE $v : F$ is defined to equal a value e that makes F true when e is substituted for v. If there is no such e, then the value of the expression is unspecified. If there is more than one such value e, then the expression can equal any one of those values. For example, define the mapping $ASqrt$ by:

$$ASqrt(r) \triangleq \text{CHOOSE } s \in \mathbb{R} : s^2 = r$$

Then $ASqrt(4)$ might equal 2 and $ASqrt(9)$ might equal -3. Since this is math, $\models ASqrt(4) = ASqrt(4)$ is true. The value of $ASqrt(4)$ may be 2 or -2. But whichever value it equals, like every mathematical expression with no free variable, it always equals the same value.

Formally, CHOOSE is defined by the following rules:

(A.1) (a) $\models (\exists v : F) \Rightarrow (F \text{ WITH } v \leftarrow (\text{CHOOSE } v : F))$
(b) $\models (\forall v : F \equiv G) \Rightarrow ((\text{CHOOSE } v : F) = (\text{CHOOSE } v : G))$

A.1. ORDINARY MATH SUMMARY

If there is more than one value of x for which F equals TRUE, then CHOOSE $x : F$ can equal any of those values. But it always equals the same value.

No matter how often I repeat that the CHOOSE operator always chooses the same value, there are engineers who think that CHOOSE is nondeterministic, possibly choosing a different value each time it's evaluated; and they try to use it to describe nondeterminism in a program. I've also heard computer scientists talk about "nondeterministic functions".[1] There's no such thing. There's no nondeterminism in mathematics. Nondeterminism is important in concurrent programs, and Section 3.3 shows that it's easy to describe mathematically. Adding nondeterminism to math for describing nondeterminism in a program makes as much sense as adding water to math for describing fluid dynamics.

An expression CHOOSE $v : F$ is most often used when there is only a single choice of v that makes F true, as in the definition of $\sqrt{r}$ above. Sometimes, it appears within an expression whose value doesn't depend on which value of v satisfying F is chosen.

A.1.6 Functions [Section 2.8.2, Math II]

A function f is a mapping that is a value such that $f(e)$ is defined only on its domain, which is a set.

DOMAIN(f) The domain of f, if f is a function.

$v \in S \mapsto exp$ The function f with domain S such that $f(v) = exp$ for all values of the variable v in the set S.

$D \to S$ The set of all functions f with domain D such that $\forall v \in D : f(v) \in S$ equals TRUE.

f EXCEPT $exp_1 \mapsto exp_2$ If f is a function, then this equals the function:
$$v \in \text{DOMAIN}(f) \mapsto \text{IF } v = exp_1 \text{ THEN } exp_2 \text{ ELSE } f(v)$$

A function of n arguments, for $n > 1$, is one whose domain is a set of n-tuples, where $f(v_1, \ldots, v_n)$ is an abbreviation of $f(\langle v_1, \ldots, v_n \rangle)$.

A.1.7 Sequences [Section 2.8.3, Math VII]

A finite *ordinal sequence* σ of length n, also called an n-tuple, is a function σ with domain $1 \ldots n$. We can write such a function σ as $\langle \sigma(1), \ldots, \sigma(n) \rangle$.

---

[1] I must confess that, many years ago, I used that term in a paper [29].

An infinite ordinal sequence is a function with domain the set of all positive integers.

A finite *cardinal sequence* σ of length n is a function σ with domain $0..(n-1)$. We can write such a function σ as $\sigma(0) \to \ldots \to \sigma(n-1)$, if $n > 0$. An infinite cardinal sequence is a function with domain the set $\mathbb{N}$ of all natural numbers.

Except for *Append*, all the following operators that take sequences as arguments are defined for both ordinal and cardinal sequences.

$Len(\sigma)$ The length of the sequence σ.

$\sigma \circ \tau$ The concatenation of the finite sequence σ and the finite or infinite sequence τ, where the sequences are both ordinal or both cardinal.

$Head(\sigma)$ The first element ($\sigma(1)$ or $\sigma(0)$) of the nonempty (positive-length) sequence σ.

$Tail(\sigma)$ The sequence obtained by removing the first element of the nonempty sequence σ.

$Append(\sigma, exp)$ The sequence $\sigma \circ \langle exp \rangle$ for an ordinal sequence σ.

$Seq(S)$ The set of all ordinal sequences σ such that $\sigma(i) \in S$ for all $i \in \text{DOMAIN}(\sigma)$.

$S_1 \times \ldots \times S_n$ The set of all n-tuples σ such that $\sigma(i) \in S_i$ for all i in $1..n$, for any integer $n > 1$.

A.1.8 Notation [Section 2.9.1, Chapter 6 introduction]

IF P THEN exp_1 ELSE exp_2
: Equals exp_1 if P equals TRUE and exp_2 if P equals FALSE.

E WITH $v_1 \leftarrow exp_1, \ldots, v_m \leftarrow exp_m$
: The expression obtained by simultaneously substituting every expression exp_i for the variable v_i in expression E.

A.1.9 Recursive Definitions [Math IV, Math XI]

Recursive function definitions are defined using the CHOOSE operator introduced in Section A.1.5 above. For example, the recursive definition of the factorial function ! in Math IV is an abbreviation for

$$! \triangleq \text{CHOOSE } f :$$
$$f = (n \in \mathbb{N} \mapsto \text{IF } n = 0 \text{ THEN } 1 \text{ ELSE } n * f(n-1))$$

In general, any recursive definition with no definition parameters can be expressed this way in terms of CHOOSE. Such a definition has the form $g \triangleq M(g)$ for some mapping M. This definition is an abbreviation for

$$g \triangleq \text{CHOOSE } f : f = M(f)$$

The rule (A.1a) implies $\models (\exists f : M(f)) \Rightarrow (g = M(g))$.

Sometimes we want to write a recursive definition of a mapping that takes an argument and isn't a function. For example here is a definition of the operator $\#$, where $\#(S)$ is defined in Math II to equal the number of elements in S, for any finite set S. This operator can't be a function because its domain would have to be the collection of all finite sets, which is too big to be a set. (The one-to-one correspondence $S \leftrightarrow \{S\}$ implies that the collection of finite sets is at least as big as the collection of all sets.) However, it's intuitively clear that the following recursive definition of $\#$ defines $\#(S)$ for any finite set S:

$$\#(S) \triangleq \text{IF } S = \{\} \text{ THEN } 0$$
$$\text{ELSE } 1 + \#(S \setminus \{\text{CHOOSE } e : e \in S\})$$

In general, a recursive definition of a mapping M has the form:

(A.2) $M(v) \triangleq Def(v, M)$

where Def is called a *higher-order mapping* because it takes a mapping as its second argument. Allowing recursive definitions of mappings in ZF without introducing logical inconsistency is tricky. A method of doing this by translating a recursive definition to a non-recursive one was apparently first given in this century [17]. That work essentially showed that for any value v such that the recursive computation of $M(v)$ defined by (A.2) terminates, $M(v)$ equals $Def(v, M)$.

A.2 Structured Proofs

To understand structured proofs, we need to understand what a completely rigorous proof would be. We therefore pretend that our proofs appear in a completely rigorous book of ordinary math, written for a reader who knows ZF. The book consists of a sequence of global definitions, theorems, and the proofs of some of the theorems. (Theorems without proofs are axioms.) A proof is either a *terminal* proof (corresponding to a paragraph proof in an informal proof) or a sequence of proof steps, each with a proof. Mathglish can appear only in comments, which would not be needed by sufficiently brilliant mathematicians (or computers).

A *context* consists of a collection of definitions, formulas that can be assumed to be true, and constant and variable declarations. Every definition, theorem, proof, and proof step occurs in a context. The *context* of a global definition or a theorem consists of all previous global definitions and theorems. Every proof step and proof also has associated with it a formula called its *current goal*. The contexts and current goals of proofs and proof steps are described below. We state here only that the context and current goal of the first step of a proof are the same as for the proof.

The statement of a theorem or proof step asserts a formula. That formula should be provable using the formulas and definitions of the context of the theorem or step. The statement of a theorem and of most proof steps has the form

(A.3) ASSUME: $F_1, \ldots, F_n$
       PROVE: G

where G is a formula called the statement's *goal* and each F_i is an *assumption* that is either a formula or a NEW declaration. (When $n = 0$, so there is no assumption, the statement is written simply as G.) If there is no NEW declaration, statement (A.3) asserts the formula

(A.4) $F_1 \wedge \ldots \wedge F_n \Rightarrow G.$

By propositional logic, $(P \wedge Q) \Rightarrow R$ is equivalent to $P \Rightarrow (Q \Rightarrow R)$, so (A.4) is equivalent to:

(A.5) $F_1 \Rightarrow (F_2 \Rightarrow (\ldots \Rightarrow (F_n \Rightarrow G)\ldots))$

A NEW declaration has the form NEW $v \in S$ for a constant[2] v and an expression S. For every such NEW assumption F_i in (A.3), the "$F_i \Rightarrow$" in (A.5) is replaced by "$\forall v \in S :$". For example, the statement

ASSUME: P, NEW $v \in S$, Q
PROVE: G

asserts the formula $P \Rightarrow (\forall v \in S : (Q \Rightarrow G))$. The scope of the bound variable v is the assumption Q and the goal G; it does not include P or S. The Safe Scoping Rule implies that no constant (or variable) named v is declared in the context of the theorem or step.

---

[2] Formal reasoning about $\exists$ might require NEW v declarations for variables v, but we will not do such reasoning.

A.2. STRUCTURED PROOFS

The context of the proof of (A.3) contains everything in the context of that statement, plus the additional formulas assumed to be true consisting of all the assumptions F_i that are formulas and all the assumptions $v \in S$ from assumptions NEW $v \in S$, plus declarations of all the constants introduced by NEW assumptions. The scope of such a declaration consists of all subsequent assumptions in the ASSUME clause, the goal G, and the proof of the statement. The current goal of the proof of (A.3) is G.

If (A.3) is a proof step, then the context of the next proof step (if there is one) contains everything in that step plus the formula (A.5) asserted by (A.3).

There are two abbreviations for a step of the form (A.3). The statement CASE P is an abbreviation for ASSUME: P PROVE: G, where G is the step's current goal. The other abbreviation is Q.E.D., which must be the statement of the last step of a proof. It is an abbreviation for the formula that is the step's current goal.

A definition step makes one or more definitions that are local to the current proof. It consists of DEFINE followed by one or more definitions. Such a step has no proof. The context of the next step is the same as the definition step's context with those definitions added to it. The goal of the next step is the same as that of the definition step.

The only other kind of step is a *suffices* step whose statement is:

(A.6)   SUFFICES: ASSUME: $F_1, \ldots, F_n$
                PROVE: G

(If there are no assumptions F_i, then the "ASSUME:" and "PROVE:" are omitted.) Suppose that the current goal of this statement is H. Statement (A.6) asserts that to prove H, it suffices to prove G under the additional assumptions $F_1, \ldots F_n$. In other words, the statement asserts the formula $A \Rightarrow H$ where A is the assertion made by the ASSUME/PROVE. The context of the proof of (A.6) is the same as for the statement:

     ASSUME: A   PROVE: H

The context of the following step consists of the context of the SUFFICES step with the added assumptions F_i. This means that F_i is assumed true if it is a formula, and if it is NEW $v \in S$ then the context contains the declaration of v and the assumption that $v \in S$ is true. The current goal of the following step is G.

Finally, there is a terminal proof. It specifies which formulas and definitions in the proof's context are used to prove its current goal. A formula in the context that comes from a previous theorem or step is identified by its name. Steps are numbered like sections in the main body of this book, so the 4th step of the proof of the 5th step of the proof of the 2nd step of a theorem is step 2.5.4. (It can be abbreviated as $\langle 3 \rangle 4$, meaning it is step 4 of a depth-3 proof.) The other formulas in a context come from ASSUME clause assumptions, and for our purpose there is no need to consider how they are identified. Definitions are identified by the name of the defined symbol, so definition steps need no number.

Of course, this is not a completely formal book. Our proofs contain many formulas written in Mathglish, and the terminal proofs attempt to explain why the current goal follows from the assertions and definitions in the current context. But you should now understand what that context is and what the proof has to prove.

A.3 Why Not All Mappings Are Sets

Section 2.8.2 states that a function is a special kind of mapping that is assumed to be a value—meaning that it's a set, although we don't know what its elements are. This raises the question of why we can't simply assume that all mappings are sets. The answer is provided by the following theorem, whose proof is due to Stephan Merz. It asserts that there has to be a mapping that is not a set. Although we could assume that some mappings other than functions are sets, the theorem means that we can't assume all mappings are sets. For simplicity, we let functions be the only mappings that we assume to be sets.

Theorem There exists a mapping that is not a set.

1. SUFFICES: ASSUME: Every mapping is a set.
           PROVE: FALSE

   PROOF: Obvious.

   DEFINE M to be the mapping such that $M(S) = S$ if S is a set that is a mapping.

2. $M(S)(U) = S(U)$ for every mapping S and every set U.

   PROOF: Since we are assuming that every mapping S is a set, M is a mapping on the collection of all mappings, and by definition $M(S) = S$ for every mapping S, so $M(S)(U) = S(U)$ for every set U.

DEFINE *Russell* to be the mapping on the collection of all sets that are mappings such that $Russell(S) \triangleq \text{CHOOSE } U : U \neq M(S)(S)$.

3. *Russell* is a mapping such that $Russell(S) \neq M(S)(S)$ for all sets S that are mappings.

   PROOF: The value of any syntactically correct formula is a set, even if its elements are unspecified. Therefore, $M(S)(S)$ is a set, and for any set T there exists a set U such that $U \neq T$. Thus, *Russell* is a mapping such that $Russell(S) \neq M(S)(S)$ for every mapping S.

4. $Russell(S) \neq S(S)$ for all sets S that are mappings.

   PROOF: Substituting S for U in step 2 shows $S(S)$ equals $M(S)(S)$, which by step 3 is unequal to $Russell(S)$.

5. Q.E.D.

   PROOF: Since *Russell* is a mapping, and all mappings are assumed to be sets, substituting *Russell* for S in step 4 proves $Russell(Russell) \neq Russell(Russell)$, which equals FALSE.

A.4 How Not to Write x'''

Here is an amusing paradox. It's illegal to prime a primed expression, so it's illegal to write x'' or x''' if x is a variable. However, consider this definition:

(A.7) $F(n) \triangleq \text{IF } n = 0 \text{ THEN } x \text{ ELSE } F(n-1)'$

It apparently defines $F(3)$ to equal x'''. It doesn't. To see why not, let's simplify things by defining F to be a function with domain $\mathbb{N}$:

$$F \triangleq \text{CHOOSE } f : f = (n \in \mathbb{N} \mapsto \text{IF } n = 0 \text{ THEN } x \text{ ELSE } f(n-1)')$$

In this definition, f and n are bound constants, so $f(n-1)$ is a constant expression; and $exp' = exp$ for any constant expression exp. Therefore, this definition of F is equivalent to

$$F \triangleq \text{CHOOSE } f : f = (n \in \mathbb{N} \mapsto \text{IF } n = 0 \text{ THEN } x \text{ ELSE } f(n-1))$$

which defines $f(n)$ to equal x for all $n \in \mathbb{N}$.

If we defined F as a mapping by (A.7), using the meaning of that definition described in [17], we would see that $F(n)$ equals an expression (CHOOSE $f : \ldots$)(n) where the primed expression in "$\ldots$" is a constant. Again, we would obtain $F(n) = x$ for all $n \in \mathbb{N}$.

This example illustrates why we should not write a recursive definition that contains an expression that isn't a constant or a state expression. There's no problem applying a recursively defined mapping to a step expression. It should also be all right to apply one to a temporal logic formula, though I can't imagine why we would want to do that. Recursively defined mappings are used to define the meaning of temporal logic operators, but those are mappings of ordinary math whose definitions contain no primes or temporal operators.

A.5 Hoare Logic

Hoare logic is a science of traditional programs developed by C. A. R. (Tony) Hoare [22]. Programs are described in a coding language, and the logic's goal is to prove properties of concrete programs. However, Hoare intended it also to be applied to abstract programs written in code as well as to concrete programs.

In Hoare logic, a program is viewed as a relation between the initial and the final states of its execution. A formula of the logic has the form $\{P\}S\{Q\}$, where S is a program (written in code) and P and Q are state predicates. This formula asserts that if program S is executed starting in a state in which P is true and the execution terminates, then Q is true in the final state of the execution. The formula $\{P\}S\{Q\}$ is called a Hoare triple, P is called its precondition, and Q is called its postcondition. Hoare logic provides a way of showing that a program S satisfies a Hoare triple.

The following is the Hoare logic rule for a program consisting of the single assignment statement $x := exp$, where x is a variable and exp is an expression:

(A.8) $\models (P \text{ WITH } x \leftarrow exp) \Rightarrow Q$ implies $\{P\} \, x := exp \, \{Q\}$

There are also rules for deriving a Hoare triple for a program from Hoare triples of its components. Here are three such rules:

(A.9) $\{P\}S\{R\}$ and $\{R\}T\{Q\}$ imply $\{P\} \, S;T \, \{Q\}$

(A.10) $\{P \wedge R\}S\{Q\}$ and $\{P \wedge \neg R\}T\{Q\}$ imply
$\quad \{P\}$ if R then S else T end if $\{Q\}$

(A.11) $\models P \Rightarrow I$ and $\{I \wedge R\}S\{I\}$ and $\models I \wedge \neg R \Rightarrow Q$ imply
$\quad \{P\}$ while R do S end while $\{Q\}$

A.5. HOARE LOGIC

Such rules decompose the proof of a Hoare triple for any program to proofs of Hoare triples for elementary statements of the language, such as assignment statements.

It was quickly realized that pre- and postconditions are not adequate to describe what a program should do. For example, suppose S is a program to sort an array x of numbers. The obvious Hoare triple for it to satisfy has a precondition asserting that x is an array of numbers and a postcondition asserting that x is sorted. But this Hoare triple is true of a program that simply sets all the elements of the array x to 0. A postcondition needs to be able to state a relation between the final values of the variables and their initial values. Various ways were proposed for doing this, one of them being to allow formulas P and Q to contain constants whose values are the same in the initial and final states. For example, the precondition for a sorting program could assert that the constant $x0$ equals x, and the postcondition could assert that the elements of the array x are a sorted permutation of the elements of $x0$.

Viewing a program as a relation between initial and final states means that it can be described mathematically as a formula of the Logic of Actions. If we represent the program S as an LA formula, then $\{P\}S\{Q\}$ is the assertion $\models P \wedge S \Rightarrow Q'$; and the Hoare logic rules follow from rules of LA. For example, the program $S; T$ is represented in LA as $S \cdot T$, where "·" is the action composition operator defined in Section 3.4.1.4. The Hoare Logic rule (A.9) is equivalent to this LA rule:

$$\models P \wedge S \Rightarrow R' \text{ and } \models R \wedge T \Rightarrow Q' \text{ imply } \models P \wedge (S \cdot T) \Rightarrow Q'$$

The program **if** R **then** S **else** T **end if** is represented by the LA formula $(R \wedge S) \vee (\neg R \wedge T)$, and rule (A.10) becomes the propositional-logic tautology:

$$\models (P \wedge R \wedge S \Rightarrow Q') \wedge (P \wedge \neg R \wedge T \Rightarrow Q') \Rightarrow$$
$$(P \wedge ((R \wedge S) \vee (\neg R \wedge T)) \Rightarrow Q')$$

Hoare's rule (A.8) for assignment statements is obtained from LA by representing the statement $x := exp$ as $(x' = exp) \wedge ((v_{\tilde{x}})' = v_{\tilde{x}})$, where $v_{\tilde{x}}$ is the tuple of all program variables other than x. It is valid because $\models P \wedge (x' = exp) \wedge ((v_{\tilde{x}})' = v_{\tilde{x}}) \Rightarrow Q'$ equals $\models (P \text{ WITH } x \leftarrow exp) \Rightarrow Q$ if $v_{\tilde{x}}$ is a tuple containing all variables other than x that appear in P or exp.

Rule (A.11) is a bit tricky because, when executed in a state in which R equals FALSE, the **while** statement leaves all variables unchanged. We can represent that **while** statement by

$$((R \wedge S)^+ \wedge \neg R') \vee (\neg R \wedge (v' = v))$$

where v is the tuple of all program variables and $(\ldots)^+$ is defined in Section 3.4.1.4. With this representation of the **while** statement, (A.11) can be derived from the following rule of LA, where I is any state predicate and A any action:

(A.12) $\quad \models I \wedge A \Rightarrow I'$ implies $\models I \wedge A^+ \Rightarrow I'$

The LA definition of a Hoare triple implies that the validity of rule (A.11) is proved by the following theorem:

Theorem A.1 Assume:
1. $\models P \Rightarrow I$
2. $\models I \wedge R \wedge S \Rightarrow I'$
3. $\models I \wedge \neg R \Rightarrow Q$
4. v is the tuple of all variables occurring in Q.

Prove: $\models P \wedge ((R \wedge S)^+ \wedge \neg R') \vee (\neg R \wedge (v' = v)) \Rightarrow Q'$

1. Suffices: Assume: $P \wedge ((R \wedge S)^+ \wedge \neg R') \vee (\neg R \wedge (v' = v))$
   Prove: Q'

   Proof: Because assumptions 1–3 have the form $\models \ldots$, proving that they imply a formula $F \Rightarrow G$ proves that they imply $\models (F \Rightarrow G)$, and $F \Rightarrow G$ is proved by assuming F and proving G.

2. Case: $P \wedge (R \wedge S)^+ \wedge \neg R'$

   2.1. $I \wedge (R \wedge S)^+ \Rightarrow I'$
      Proof: By assumption 2 and (A.12), with $R \wedge S$ substituted for A.

   2.2. $P \wedge (R \wedge S)^+ \Rightarrow I'$
      Proof: By 2.1 and assumption 1.

   2.3. I'
      Proof: By 2.2 and the step 2 case assumption

   2.4. $\neg R'$
      Proof: By the step 2 case assumption

   2.5. Q.E.D.
      Proof: By 2.3, 2.4, and assumption 3 (since $\models F$ implies $\models F'$ for any state predicate F).

3. Case: $P \wedge \neg R \wedge (v' = v)$

   Proof: By assumptions 1 and 3, $P \wedge \neg R$ implies Q, which by $v' = v$ and assumption 4 implies Q'.

A.6. ANOTHER WAY TO LOOK AT SAFETY AND LIVENESS

4. Q.E.D.

PROOF: By the step 1 assumption, steps 2 and 3 cover all possibilities.

A.6 Another Way to Look at Safety and Liveness

This section provides a different view of safety and liveness based on viewing behavior predicates as sets of behaviors. This view was first recognized by Gordon Plotkin. I find that it helps me understand safety and liveness. To understand it, we first need some more math.

A.6.1 Metric Spaces

A metric space M is a set with a distance function δ that assigns a non-negative real number $\delta(p, q)$, called the distance between p and q, to all elements p and q of M. The function δ must satisfy these conditions for all elements p, q, and r of M:

M1. $\delta(p, q) = 0$ iff $p = q$.

M2. $\delta(p, q) = \delta(q, p)$

M3. $\delta(p, q) \leq \delta(p, r) + \delta(r, q)$.

Do you see why these conditions imply $\delta(p, q) \geq 0$ for all p and q in M?

The set $\mathbb{R}$ of real numbers is a metric space with $\delta(p, q)$ equal to $|p - q|$, where $|r|$ is the absolute value of the number r, defined by

$$|r| \triangleq \text{IF } r \geq 0 \text{ THEN } r \text{ ELSE } -r$$

An infinite plane, represented as in analytic geometry by the set $\mathbb{R} \times \mathbb{R}$ of pairs of real numbers, is a metric space with $\delta(\langle x_1, y_1 \rangle, \langle x_2, y_2 \rangle)$ defined to equal $\sqrt{(x_1 - x_2)^2 + (y_1 - y_2)^2}$. I find that thinking of a metric space M as the set of points in a plane is a good way to visualize the concepts presented here.

For a metric space M, the distance $\widehat{\delta}(p, S)$ from $p \in M$ to a nonempty subset S of M is defined to be the largest number r such that $r \leq \delta(p, q)$ for all $q \in S$.[3] For example, if S is the set of all points $\langle x, y \rangle$ in the plane such that $x < 3$, then $\widehat{\delta}(\langle 4, 7 \rangle, S)$ equals 1 because $\widehat{\delta}(\langle 4, 7 \rangle, S) > 1$ for all q

---

[3] To handle the uninteresting case of S equal to the empty set, we can define $\widehat{\delta}(p, \{\})$ to equal ∞, which is a value satisfying $r < \infty$ for all $r \in \mathbb{R}$.

in S and there are elements q of S such that $\delta(\langle 4,7 \rangle, q)$ is arbitrarily close to 1.

For any metric space M and subset S of M, if $p \in S$ then $\widehat{\delta}(p, S) = 0$ because condition M1 implies $\delta(p, p) = 0$. In general, $\widehat{\delta}(p, S) = 0$ for $p \in M$ iff for every $e > 0$ there exists $q \in S$ such that $\delta(p, q) < e$.

The closure operation $\mathcal{C}$ on subsets of a metric space M is defined by letting $\mathcal{C}(S)$ be the set $\{p \in M : \widehat{\delta}(p, S) = 0\}$ of all elements M that are a distance 0 from S. For example, if M is the plane, let OD and CD be the open and closed disks of radius 1 centered at the origin, defined by:

$$OD \triangleq \{p \in M : \delta(p, \langle 0,0 \rangle) < 1\}$$
$$CD \triangleq \{p \in M : \delta(p, \langle 0,0 \rangle) \leq 1\}$$

Both $\mathcal{C}(OD)$ and $\mathcal{C}(CD)$ equal CD.

Theorem A.2 For any subset S of a metric space, $S \subseteq \mathcal{C}(S)$ and $\mathcal{C}(S) = \mathcal{C}(\mathcal{C}(S))$.

PROOF: The definition of $\mathcal{C}$ and property M1 imply $S \subseteq \mathcal{C}(S)$ for any set S, which implies $\mathcal{C}(S) \subseteq \mathcal{C}(\mathcal{C}(S))$ for any S. Therefore, to show $\mathcal{C}(S) = \mathcal{C}(\mathcal{C}(S))$, it suffices to assume $p \in \mathcal{C}(\mathcal{C}(S))$ and show $p \in \mathcal{C}(S)$. By definition of $\mathcal{C}$ and $\widehat{\delta}$, we do this by assuming $e > 0$ and showing there exists $q \in S$ with $\delta(q, p) < e$. Because $p \in \mathcal{C}(\mathcal{C}(S))$, there exists $u \in \mathcal{C}(S)$ with $\delta(p, u) < e/2$; and $u \in \mathcal{C}(S)$ implies there exists $q \in S$ with $\delta(q, u) < e/2$. By M2 and M3, this implies $\delta(p, q) < e$. END PROOF

As you will have guessed by its name, the operator $\mathcal{C}$ on behavior predicates is a special case of the closure operator $\mathcal{C}$ on metric spaces. But for now, forget about behavior predicates and just think about metric spaces.

A set S that, like CD, equals its closure is said to be *closed*. The following result shows that for any set S, its closure $\mathcal{C}(S)$ is the smallest closed set that contains S.

Theorem A.3 For any subsets S and T of a metric space, if T is a closed set and $S \subseteq T$ then $\mathcal{C}(S) \subseteq T$.

PROOF: It follows from the definition of $\mathcal{C}$ that $S \subseteq T$ implies $\mathcal{C}(S) \subseteq \mathcal{C}(T)$, and the definition of a closed set implies $T = \mathcal{C}(T)$. END PROOF

For any subset S of a metric space M, the *boundary* of S is defined to be the set of all $p \in M$ with $\widehat{\delta}(p, S) = 0$ and $\widehat{\delta}(p, M \setminus S) = 0$. The boundary of both disks OD and CD is $\{p \in M : \delta(p, \langle 0,0 \rangle) = 1\}$, the circle of radius

A.6. ANOTHER WAY TO LOOK AT SAFETY AND LIVENESS

1 centered at the origin. For any metric space M and $S \subseteq M$, any element p of M with $\hat{\delta}(p, S) = 0$ that is not in S must be in $M \setminus S$ and therefore must satisfy $\hat{\delta}(p, M \setminus S) = 0$. This shows that the closure of any set S is the union of S and the boundary of S.

A subset S of a metric space M is said to be *dense* iff $\mathcal{C}(S) = M$. A dense set is one that, for any element p of M, contains p or elements of M arbitrarily close to p. As an example, let's call a finite-digit real number one that can be written in decimal notation with a finite number of digits—for example, 123.5432. The set of all pairs of finite-digit numbers is dense in the plane because any real number can be approximated arbitrarily closely with a finite-digit number. Thus, for any pair of real numbers $\langle x, y \rangle$ and any $e > 0$, we can find a pair of finite-digit numbers $\langle p, q \rangle$ within a distance e of $\langle x, y \rangle$ by choosing p and q such that $|x - p|$ and $|y - q|$ are both less than $e/\sqrt{2}$.

Theorem A.4 Any subset S of a metric space equals $\mathcal{C}(S) \cap D$ for a dense set D.

PROOF: Let M be the metric space and let D equal $S \cup (M \setminus \mathcal{C}(S))$. The set D consists of all elements of M except those elements in the boundary of S that are not in S. It follows from this that $\mathcal{C}(S) \cap D = S$. Since elements in the boundary of S are a distance 0 from S, which is a subset of D, they are a distance 0 from D. Therefore all elements in M are a distance 0 from D, so D is dense. END PROOF

What we're interested in is not the distance function δ, but the closure operator $\mathcal{C}$. Imagine that the plane was an infinite sheet of rubber that was then stretched and shrunk unevenly in some way. Define the distance between two points on the original plane to be the distance between them after the plane was deformed. For example, if the plane was stretched to make everything twice as far apart in the y direction but the same distance apart in the x direction, then $\delta(\langle x_1, y_1 \rangle, \langle x_2, y_2 \rangle)$ would equal $\sqrt{(x_1 - x_2)^2 + (2 * (y_1 - y_2))^2}$. As long as the stretching and shrinking is continuous, meaning that the rubber sheet is not torn, the boundary of a set S in the plane after it is deformed is the set obtained by deforming the boundary of S. This implies that the new distance function produces the same closure operator as the ordinary distance function on the plane.

Topology is the study of properties of objects that depend only on a closure operation, which need not be generated by a metric space. But we are interested in a closure operator that is generated by a particular kind of metric space, and it helps me to think in terms of its distance function.

A.6.2 The Metric Space of Behaviors

Safety and liveness will be explained by viewing behaviors as elements of a metric space. In particular, we will see that:

- The operator $\mathcal{C}$ on behavior predicates corresponds to the operator C on sets of behaviors.

- Safety predicates correspond to closed sets of behaviors.

- Liveness predicates correspond to dense sets of behaviors.

Doing this poses two problems. The first is that mathematicians describe metric spaces as sets, and the collection of all behaviors isn't a set. I believe that all the results about metric spaces that we need would remain true if metric spaces were arbitrary collections rather than sets, but I haven't checked this. So for the rest of this section, we assume that the collection of all behaviors is a set, which we call $\mathbb{B}$. For example, we can let a *behavior* here mean an infinite sequence of states in which each variable satisfies some type invariant. Since our purpose is an intuitive understanding of safety and liveness, there's no need to be very rigorous.

The second problem is that we are relating properties, which are temporal-logic formulas, to sets of behaviors. Recall that the meaning $[\![F]\!]$ of a property F is a Boolean-valued mapping on behaviors. There's a standard way of identifying predicates on a set with subsets of that set: we identify the predicate P with the subset consisting of all elements e such that $P(e)$ equals TRUE. (This is the basis of Venn diagrams, which you have probably seen.) We can therefore identify the property F with the subset $\overline{\overline{F}}$ of $\mathbb{B}$ defined by:

$$\overline{\overline{F}} \triangleq \{b \in \mathbb{B} : [\![F]\!](b)\}$$

Under this identification, the propositional logic operators $\wedge$, $\vee$, $\Rightarrow$, and $\equiv$ correspond to the set-theoretic operators $\cap$, $\cup$, $\subseteq$, and $=$. That is, for any properties F and G:

$$\models \overline{\overline{F \vee G}} = (\overline{\overline{F}} \cup \overline{\overline{G}}) \qquad \models \overline{\overline{F \Rightarrow G}} = (\overline{\overline{F}} \subseteq \overline{\overline{G}})$$
$$\models \overline{\overline{F \wedge G}} = (\overline{\overline{F}} \cap \overline{\overline{G}}) \qquad \models \overline{\overline{F \equiv G}} = (\overline{\overline{F}} = \overline{\overline{G}})$$

We're interested in the closure operator on sets of behaviors, which can be the same for many different distance functions. The property of the distance

A.6. ANOTHER WAY TO LOOK AT SAFETY AND LIVENESS

function that provides the closure operator we want is that behaviors with a long prefix in common are close together. More precisely, for two different behaviors σ and τ, define $o(\sigma, \tau)$ to be the largest n such that σ and τ have the same prefix of length $n - 1$—that is, the largest value n such that $\forall i \in 0 \mathinner{..} (n-1) : \sigma(i) = \tau(i)$. Thus, $o(\sigma, \tau)$ equals 1 iff $\sigma(0) = \tau(0)$ and $\sigma(1) \neq \tau(1)$. (There is no such n iff $\sigma = \tau$, in which case we let $o(\sigma, \tau) = \infty$, where $\infty > i$ for all $i \in \mathbb{N}$.) We get the right closure operator on sets of behaviors if δ satisfies this property:

> For any $e > 0$, there is an $n \in \mathbb{N}$ such that $o(\sigma, \tau) > n$ implies $\delta(\sigma, \tau) < e$, for any behaviors σ and τ.

The simplest choice of δ satisfying this and the properties of a distance function for a metric space is $\delta(\sigma, \tau) \triangleq 1/(1 + o(\sigma, \tau))$ for $\sigma \neq \tau$. (Of course, $\delta(\sigma, \tau) = 0$ if $\sigma = \tau$.)

With the correspondence between the operator $\mathcal{C}$ on behavior predicates and the closure operator on this metric space, Theorems 4.3 and 4.4 of Section 4.1.3 are immediate consequences of Theorems A.2–A.4 of Section A.6.1. I find it more elegant to deduce the results about behavior predicates from the corresponding results about metric spaces than to prove them directly. But that might be because I was educated as a mathematician. Whichever you prefer, I hope that having an alternative way of thinking about safety and liveness helps you understand those concepts.

Appendix B

Proofs

Most of the proofs here are structured proofs. To understand them, you should first read Appendix Section A.2.

B.1 Invariance Proof of *Increment*

Figure 3.5 in Section 3.4.1.1 defines the initial predicate *Init* and next-state action *Next* for the RTLA formula describing a program having the inductive invariant *Inv*. As described in Section 3.4.1.3, to prove the invariance of *Inv* we had to prove the two conditions of (3.10). As with most programs, the proof of the first condition is simple. Here, we describe the proof of the second condition, which is:

Theorem $Next \wedge Inv \Rightarrow Inv'$

If the program were described in TLA instead of RTLA, the disjunct *Stutter* would be removed from the definition of *Next*; and *Next* in the theorem would be replaced by $[Next]_v$, where v is the tuple $\langle x, t, pc \rangle$ of variables. The proof of the theorem would be essentially the same, the only difference being that the action *Stutter* would be replaced everywhere by its second conjunct, which is $v' = v$.

The proof of the theorem is decomposed hierarchically. The first two levels are determined by the logical structure of the theorem. There are two standard ways to decompose the proof of a formula of the form $F \Rightarrow G$:

- Write F in the form $F_1 \vee \ldots \vee F_m$ and prove $F_i \Rightarrow G$ for all i.

- Write G in the form $G_1 \wedge \ldots \wedge G_n$ and prove $F \Rightarrow G_j$ for all j.

B.1. INVARIANCE PROOF OF INCREMENT

In this case, we can do both, proving $F \Rightarrow G$ by proving $F_i \Rightarrow G_j$ for all i and j, performing the two decompositions in either order. We can do the first decomposition by writing *Next* as a disjunction (since $(P \vee Q \vee \ldots) \wedge \mathit{Inv}$ equals $(P \wedge \mathit{Inv}) \vee (Q \wedge \mathit{Inv}) \vee \ldots$), and we can do the second decomposition because *Inv* is defined to be the conjunction of three formulas. We do the first decomposition first.

Expanding the definitions of *Next* and *PgmStep* and using some propositional and predicate logic, including this rule:

$$\models (\exists v \in S : F \vee G) \equiv (\exists v \in S : F) \vee (\exists v \in S : G)$$

we see that *Next* $\wedge$ *Inv* is equivalent to:

$$(\forall p \in \mathit{Procs} : \mathit{aStep}(p) \wedge \mathit{Inv}) \vee (\forall p \in \mathit{Procs} : \mathit{bStep}(p) \wedge \mathit{Inv})$$
$$\vee (\mathit{Stutter} \wedge \mathit{Inv})$$

Writing each $\forall$ assertion as an ASSUME/PROVE, the top level of the proof is:

1. ASSUME: NEW $p \in \mathit{Procs}$, $\mathit{aStep}(p)$, Inv
   PROVE: Inv'

2. ASSUME: NEW $p \in \mathit{Procs}$, $\mathit{bStep}(p)$, Inv
   PROVE: Inv'

3. ASSUME: *Stutter*, *Inv*
   PROVE: Inv'

   PROOF: By the definitions of *Stutter*, *Inv*, *TypeOK*, and *NumberDone*, since a *Stutter* step leaves the three variables unchanged, which by definition of *Inv* implies that the value of *Inv* is unchanged.

4. Q.E.D.

   PROOF: By steps 1–3 and the definition of *Next*.

Steps 3 and 4 are simple enough that there is no need to decompose their proofs. You should try to understand why these steps, and the others whose proofs are given here, follow from the facts and definitions mentioned in their proofs. To help you, a little bit of explanation has been added to some of the proofs.

We now have to prove steps 1 and 2. They can both be decomposed using the definition of *Inv* as a conjunction. We consider the proof of step 1. Here is the first level of its decomposition.

    1.1. *TypeOK*$'$

1.2. $\forall i \in Procs : (pc'(i) = b) \Rightarrow (t'(i) \leq NumberDone')$

1.3. $x' \leq NumberDone'$

1.4. Q.E.D.
  PROOF: By steps 1.1–1.3 and the definition of Inv.

Step 1.2 is the most difficult one to prove, so we examine its proof. The standard way to prove a formula of this form is to assume $i \in Procs$ and $pc'(i) = b$ and prove $t'(i) \leq NumberDone'$. So, the first step of the proof should be a SUFFICES step asserting that it suffices to make those assumptions and prove $t'(i) \leq NumberDone'$. Thus far, we have used only the logical structure of the formulas, without thinking about what the formulas mean. We can go no further that way. To write the rest of the proof of step 1.2, we have to ask ourselves why an $aStep(p)$ step starting in a state with Inv true produces a state with $t'(i) \leq NumberDone'$ true.

When I asked myself that question, I realized that the answer depends on whether or not i is the process p executing the step. That suggested proving the two cases $i \neq p$ and $i = p$ separately, asserting them as CASE statements. In figuring out how to write those two proofs, I found that both of them required proving $NumberDone' = NumberDone$. Moreover, this was true for the same reason in both cases—namely, that an $aStep$ step of any process leaves $NumberDone$ unchanged. Therefore, I could prove it once in a single step that precedes the two CASE statements. This produced the following level-3 proof:

  1.2.1. SUFFICES: ASSUME: NEW $i \in Procs$, $pc'(i) = b$
              PROVE: $t'(i) \leq NumberDone'$
    PROOF: Obvious.
  1.2.2. $NumberDone' = NumberDone$

  1.2.3. CASE: $i = p$

  1.2.4. CASE: $i \neq p$

  1.2.5. Q.E.D.
    PROOF: By steps 1.2.3 and 1.2.4.

This leaves three steps to prove. Here is the proof of step 1.2.4, which I think is the most interesting one.

1.2.4.1. $(t'(i) = t(i)) \wedge (pc'(i) = pc(i))$

PROOF: By step 1 (which implies $aStep(p)$ and Inv), the step 1.2.4 case assumption, and the definitions of $aStep$, Inv, and $TypeOK$, which together imply that the values of $t(i)$ and $pc(i)$ are unchanged. (The definition of $TypeOK$ is needed because type correctness is required to deduce this.)

1.2.4.2. $pc(i) = b$

PROOF: By step 1.2.4.1 and the step 1.2.1 assumption $pc'(i) = b$.

1.2.4.3. $t(i) \leq NumberDone$

PROOF: By step 1.2.4.2, the step 1 assumption (which implies Inv), and the second conjunct in the definition of Inv.

1.2.4.4. Q.E.D.

PROOF: Steps 1.2.4.1, 1.2.4.3, and 1.2.2 imply $t'(i) \leq NumberDone'$, which is the current goal (introduced in step 1.2.1).

The purpose of this example is to illustrate the science of proving correctness of concurrent programs. The program and its proof are very simple.[1] The example shows how proving that a program satisfies a property can be hierarchically decomposed into proving simple mathematical assertions whose proofs require no understanding of why the program works or what it's supposed to do. How this can be done for real abstract programs is an engineering problem that is outside the scope of this book.

B.2 Proof of Theorem 4.3

Theorem 4.3 If F is a property, then $\mathcal{C}(F)$ is a safety property such that $\models F \Rightarrow \mathcal{C}(F)$ and, for any safety property G, if $\models F \Rightarrow G$ then $\models \mathcal{C}(F) \Rightarrow G$.

PROOF: Let F be a property. Extend the definition of $\natural$ in Section 3.5.3 in the obvious way to finite behaviors ρ so that $\natural\rho$ equals ρ with stuttering steps removed.

1. ASSUME: F is a property.
   PROVE: $\mathcal{C}(F)$ is a property.

   1.1. SUFFICES: ASSUME: σ is a behavior.

---

[1] To check the level-1 proof, the TLA$^+$ proof checker requires only that step 2 be decomposed to a two-step proof, and that it be told to use two simple facts about the cardinality of finite sets that it easily deduces from a standard library of such facts.

PROVE: σ satisfies $\mathcal{C}(F)$ iff $\natural\sigma$ does.

PROOF: By definition of a property, it suffices to show that $\mathcal{C}(F)$ is SI. By definition of SI, it suffices to assume σ is a behavior and show σ satisfies $\mathcal{C}(F)$ iff $\natural\sigma$ does.

1.2. ASSUME: σ satisfies $\mathcal{C}(F)$.
PROVE: $\natural\sigma$ satisfies $\mathcal{C}(F)$.

PROOF: By definition of $\mathcal{C}$ (Section 4.1.3), it suffices to assume ρ is a nonempty finite prefix of $\natural\sigma$ and show it is a prefix of a behavior satisfying F. Since ρ is a prefix of $\natural\sigma$, it equals $\natural\tau$ for some prefix τ of σ, so σ satisfies $\mathcal{C}(F)$ implies $\tau \circ \nu$ satisfies F for some behavior ν. Since F is SI and ρ is obtained from τ by removing stuttering steps, $\rho \circ \nu$ also satisfies F, so ρ is a prefix of a behavior satisfying F.

1.3. ASSUME: $\natural\sigma$ satisfies $\mathcal{C}(F)$.
PROVE: σ satisfies $\mathcal{C}(F)$.

PROOF: By definition of $\mathcal{C}$, it suffices to show that any finite nonempty prefix ρ of σ is the prefix of a behavior satisfying F. Since $\natural\rho$ is a prefix of $\natural\sigma$, by hypothesis there is a behavior τ such that $(\natural\rho) \circ \tau$ satisfies F. Since F is SI and $\rho \circ \tau$ differs from $(\natural\rho) \circ \tau$ only by stuttering steps, $\rho \circ \tau$ too satisfies F. Thus ρ is the prefix of a behavior satisfying F.

1.4. Q.E.D.
PROOF: By steps 1.1–1.3.

2. $\mathcal{C}(F)$ is a safety predicate.

2.1. ASSUME: ρ is a prefix of a behavior that satisfies $\mathcal{C}(F)$.
PROVE: $\rho^\uparrow$ satisfies $\mathcal{C}(F)$.

2.1.1. Let σ be a behavior such that $\rho \circ \sigma$ satisfies F; let $\phi(n)$ be the sequence of states consisting of n copies of the final state of ρ, for any $n \in \mathbb{N}$; and let $\tau(n)$ equal $\rho \circ \phi(n) \circ \sigma$. Then $\tau(n)$ satisfies F for all $n \in \mathbb{N}$.

PROOF: A behavior σ such that $\rho \circ \sigma$ satisfies F exists by the step 2.1 assumption and the definition of $\mathcal{C}$. That $\tau(n)$ satisfies F follows from: (i) $\natural\tau(n)$ equals $\natural(\rho \circ \sigma)$ by definition of $\phi(n)$ and $\tau(n)$, (ii) $\rho \circ \sigma$ satisfies F, and (iii) F is SI.

2.1.2. Every finite prefix of $\rho^\uparrow$ is a finite prefix of $\tau(n)$, for some n.
PROOF: By the definitions of $\tau(n)$ and of $\rho^\uparrow$.

2.1.3. Q.E.D.
PROOF: By steps 2.1.1 and 2.1.2, every finite prefix of $\rho^\uparrow$ is a prefix

B.3. PROOF OF THEOREM 4.4

of a behavior satisfying F. By definition of $\mathcal{C}$, this implies $\rho^\uparrow$ satisfies $\mathcal{C}(F)$, which proves the step 2.1 goal.

2.2. ASSUME: σ is a behavior such that $\rho^\uparrow$ satisfies $\mathcal{C}(F)$ for every finite prefix ρ of σ.
PROVE: σ satisfies $\mathcal{C}(F)$.

    2.2.1. SUFFICES: ASSUME: ρ a prefix of σ.
                    PROVE: ρ a prefix of a behavior satisfying F.
PROOF: By definition of $\mathcal{C}(F)$.

    2.2.2. Every prefix of $\rho^\uparrow$ is a prefix of a behavior satisfying F.
PROOF: By the steps 2.2 and 2.2.1 assumptions and the definition of $\mathcal{C}(F)$.

    2.2.3. Q.E.D.
PROOF: The step 2.2.1 goal follows from 2.2.2, since ρ is a prefix of $\rho^\uparrow$.

2.3. Q.E.D.
PROOF: By steps 2.1 and 2.2 and the definition of safety.

3. ASSUME: G a safety property and $\models F \Rightarrow G$.
PROVE: $\models \mathcal{C}(F) \Rightarrow G$

PROOF: It suffices to assume σ is a behavior satisfying $\mathcal{C}(F)$ and prove it satisfies G. Since G is a safety property, it suffices to show that any finite prefix ρ of σ satisfies G. By definition of $\mathcal{C}$, ρ is a prefix of a behavior satisfying F, and therefore by hypothesis satisfying G. Since G is a safety property, this implies ρ satisfies G.

4. Q.E.D.
PROOF: Steps 1–3 are the assertions of the theorem.

B.3 Proof of Theorem 4.4

Theorem 4.4 Every property F is equivalent to $\mathcal{C}(F) \wedge L$ for a liveness property L.

DEFINE $L \triangleq F \vee \neg \mathcal{C}(F)$

1. F is equivalent to $\mathcal{C}(F) \wedge L$.

    PROOF: By $\models (F \Rightarrow \mathcal{C}(F))$ (from Theorem 4.3) and propositional logic.

2. L is a liveness property.

2.1. SUFFICES: ASSUME: ρ is a finite behavior.
   PROVE: ρ is a prefix of a behavior τ satisfying L.
   PROOF: By definition of liveness, since L is a property because the operators of propositional logic preserve stuttering insensitivity, and $\mathcal{C}(F)$ is a property by Theorem 4.3.

2.2. CASE: ρ is the prefix of a behavior τ satisfying F.
   PROOF: By definition of L, if τ satisfies F then it satisfies L.

2.3. CASE: ρ is not the prefix of any behavior satisfying F.
   PROOF: By definition of $\mathcal{C}(F)$, if ρ were the prefix of a behavior satisfying $\mathcal{C}(F)$, then it would be the prefix of a behavior satisfying F. The CASE assumption therefore implies that any behavior τ having ρ as a prefix does not satisfy $\mathcal{C}(F)$, so it satisfies $\neg \mathcal{C}(F)$ and therefore satisfies L by definition of L.

2.4. Q.E.D.
   PROOF: Steps 2.2 and 2.3 cover all possibilities.

3. Q.E.D.
   PROOF: By steps 1 and 2.

B.4 Proof of Theorem 4.5

Theorem 4.5 ASSUME: S a safety property and L a liveness property.
   PROVE: $\langle S, L \rangle$ is machine closed iff $\mathcal{C}(S \wedge L) \equiv S$.

1. ASSUME: $\langle S, L \rangle$ is machine closed.
   PROVE: $\mathcal{C}(S \wedge L) \equiv S$

   1.1. $\mathcal{C}(S \wedge L) \Rightarrow S$
      PROOF: Theorem 4.3 implies $\models S \Rightarrow \mathcal{C}(S)$, so $\models S \wedge L \Rightarrow \mathcal{C}(S)$. That theorem also implies $\mathcal{C}(S)$ is a safety property and therefore $\models \mathcal{C}(S \wedge L) \Rightarrow \mathcal{C}(S)$. Since S is a safety property, it equals $\mathcal{C}(S)$, so $\models \mathcal{C}(S \wedge L) \Rightarrow \mathcal{C}(S)$ implies $\mathcal{C}(S \wedge L) \Rightarrow S$.

   1.2. $S \Rightarrow \mathcal{C}(S \wedge L)$
      PROOF: It suffices to assume a behavior σ satisfies S and prove σ satisfies $\mathcal{C}(S \wedge L)$. By definition of machine closure, every finite prefix of σ can be completed to a behavior of $S \wedge L$. By definition of $\mathcal{C}$, this implies σ satisfies $\mathcal{C}(S \wedge L)$.

   1.3. Q.E.D.

PROOF: By steps 1.1 and 1.2.

2. ASSUME: $\mathcal{C}(S \wedge L) \equiv S$
   PROVE: $\langle S, L \rangle$ is machine closed.

   PROOF: By definition of machine closure, it suffices to assume ρ is a finite behavior satisfying S and prove ρ can be completed to a behavior satisfying $S \wedge L$. By definition of what it means for a finite behavior to satisfy a property, $\rho^\uparrow$ satisfies S. Since $S \equiv \mathcal{C}(S \wedge L)$, behavior $\rho^\uparrow$ satisfies $\mathcal{C}(S \wedge L)$. By definition of $\mathcal{C}$, this implies every prefix of $\rho^\uparrow$ can be completed to a behavior satisfying $S \wedge L$, and ρ is a prefix of $\rho^\uparrow$.

3. Q.E.D.
   PROOF: By steps 1 and 2.

B.5 Proof of Theorem 4.6

Theorem 4.6 ASSUME: $\models (E\,\mathcal{U}\,P) \equiv (\Diamond P \wedge E\,\mathcal{U}\,P) \vee (\neg \Diamond P \wedge \Box E)$
PROVE: $\models ((E\,\mathcal{U}\,P) \rightsquigarrow P) \equiv (\Box E \rightsquigarrow P)$.

1. SUFFICES: $\models ((E\,\mathcal{U}\,P) \Rightarrow \Diamond P) \equiv (\Box E \Rightarrow \Diamond P)$
   PROOF: By (3.20) and (3.19), since $F \rightsquigarrow G$ equals $\Box(F \Rightarrow \Diamond G)$.

2. $\models ((E\,\mathcal{U}\,P) \Rightarrow \Diamond P) \equiv\ \wedge (\Diamond P \wedge E\,\mathcal{U}\,P) \Rightarrow \Diamond P$
   $\wedge (\neg \Diamond P \wedge \Box E) \Rightarrow \Diamond P$
   PROOF: By the theorem's assumption and the propositional logic tautology $\models ((F \vee G) \Rightarrow H) \equiv (F \Rightarrow H) \wedge (G \Rightarrow H)$.

3. Q.E.D.
   PROOF: $\models \Diamond P \wedge E\,\mathcal{U}\,P \Rightarrow \Diamond P$ is a propositional logic tautology, which by step 2 implies $\models ((E\,\mathcal{U}\,P) \Rightarrow \Diamond P) \equiv (\neg \Diamond P \wedge \Box E \Rightarrow \Diamond P)$, which with the propositional logic tautology $\models (\neg \Diamond P \wedge \Box E \Rightarrow \Diamond P) \equiv (\Box E \Rightarrow \Diamond P)$ proves the step 1 goal.

B.6 Proof of Theorem 4.7

Theorem 4.7 Let *Init* be a state predicate, *Next* an action, and v a tuple of all variables occurring in *Init* and *Next*. If A_i is a subaction of *Next* for all i in a countable set I, then the pair

$$\langle\ \textit{Init} \wedge \Box[\textit{Next}]_v,\ \forall i \in I\ :\ \text{XF}^i_v(A_i)\ \rangle$$

is machine closed, where each XF_v^i may be either WF_v or SF_v.

DEFINE $S \triangleq Init \wedge \Box[Next]_v$

1. SUFFICES: ASSUME: ρ is a finite behavior satisfying S.
   PROVE: There exists a behavior σ having ρ as a prefix that satisfies S and $SF_v(A_i)$, for all $i \in I$.

   PROOF: By definition of machine closure, it suffices to show that any finite behavior ρ satisfying S is the prefix of a behavior σ satisfying $S \wedge \forall i \in I : XF_v^i(A_i)$. Since $SF_v(A_i)$ implies $WF_v(A_i)$, it suffices to show that σ satisfies $SF_v(A_i)$ for all $i \in I$.

2. Choose $f \in (\mathbb{N} \to I)$ such that each $i \in I$ equals $f(n)$ for infinitely many $n \in \mathbb{N}$. Define τ_j for each $j \in \mathbb{N}$ as follows. Let $\tau_0 = \rho$, and for $j > 0$, define τ_j such that:

   if τ_{j-1} is a prefix of a finite behavior μ satisfying S and ending in a state in which $\langle A_{f(j-1)} \rangle_v$ is enabled.

   then τ_j equals the finite behavior obtained by appending to μ a state that makes the last step of τ_j an $\langle A_{f(j-1)} \rangle_v$ step.

   else τ_j is obtained from τ_{j-1} by adding a stuttering step.

   For all $j \in \mathbb{N}$, τ_j is a prefix of and shorter than τ_{j+1}, and τ_j satisfies S.

   PROOF: Theorem 4.1 of Math V shows the existence of f. By construction, each τ_j is a prefix of and shorter than τ_{j+1}. We must just show that τ_j satisfies S. The proof is by induction. It is true for $j = 0$ since τ_0 equals ρ, which satisfies S by the step 1 assumption. So we complete the proof by assuming $j > 0$ and τ_{j-1} satisfies S and proving as follows that τ_j satisfies S.

   If the **if** condition in the definition of τ_j is true, then τ_j satisfies S because τ_{j-1} does and τ_j is obtained by appending to τ_{j-1} an $\langle A_{f(j-1)} \rangle_v$ step, which is a *Next* step by the hypothesis that $\models A_i \Rightarrow Next$ for all $i \in I$. If the **if** condition is false, then τ_j satisfies S because S is stuttering insensitive, τ_{j-1} satisfies S, and τ_j is obtained by adding a stuttering step to τ_{j-1}.

3. Let σ be the behavior having every τ_j as a prefix. Then σ is a behavior satisfying S having the prefix ρ.

   PROOF: The behavior σ exists (and is unique) because each τ_j is a prefix of and shorter than τ_{j+1}. Since ρ equals τ_0, it is a prefix of σ. Step 2 asserts that every prefix τ_j of σ satisfies S. By definition of S, this implies σ satisfies S.

B.7. PROOF OF THEOREM 4.8

4. σ satisfies $\mathrm{SF}_i(A)$ for all $i \in I$.

   PROOF: Step 2 asserts that for any $i \in I$, there are infinitely many $j \in \mathbb{N}$ such that $i = f(j-1)$. If the **if** condition in the definition of τ_j is true for all of those values of j, then σ contains an $\langle A_i \rangle_v$ step for each of those values of j, so σ satisfies $\Box \Diamond \langle A_i \rangle_v$. If the **if** condition is false for any such j, then τ_{j-1} cannot be extended to any finite behavior containing an $\langle A_i \rangle_v$ step. Hence, $\Box \neg \mathbb{E} \langle A_i \rangle_v$ is true for the suffix of σ obtained by removing the prefix τ_{j-1}. Therefore, σ satisfies $\Diamond \Box \neg \mathbb{E} \langle A_i \rangle_v$, which equals $\neg \Box \Diamond \mathbb{E} \langle A_i \rangle_v$. By (4.23), in either case σ satisfies $\mathrm{SF}_v(A_i)$.

5. Q.E.D.

   PROOF: The theorem follows from steps 1, 3, and 4.

B.7 Proof of Theorem 4.8

Theorem 4.8 Let A_i be an action for each $i \in I$, let $Q \triangleq \exists i \in I : A_i$, and let XF be either WF or SF. Then

$$\models (\forall i \in I : \Box(\mathbb{E}\langle A_i \rangle_v \wedge \Box[\neg A_i]_v \Rightarrow$$
$$\Box[\neg Q]_v \wedge \Box(\mathbb{E}\langle Q \rangle_v \Rightarrow \mathbb{E}\langle A_i \rangle_v))$$
$$\Rightarrow (\mathrm{XF}_v(Q) \equiv \forall i \in I : \mathrm{XF}_v(A_i))$$

1. SUFFICES: ASSUME: $\forall i \in I : \Box(\mathbb{E}\langle A_i \rangle_v \wedge \Box[\neg A_i]_v \Rightarrow$
   $$\Box[\neg Q]_v \wedge \Box(\mathbb{E}\langle Q \rangle_v \Rightarrow \mathbb{E}\langle A_i \rangle_v))$$
   PROVE: $\mathrm{XF}_v(Q) \equiv \forall i \in I : \mathrm{XF}_v(A_i)$

   PROOF: Obvious.

   DEFINE $\boxtimes\boxtimes$ to equal $\Diamond\Box$ if XF is WF, and $\Box\Diamond$ if XF is SF.

2. $\mathrm{XF}_v(Q) \Rightarrow \forall i \in I : \mathrm{XF}_v(A_i)$

   2.1. SUFFICES: ASSUME: $\mathrm{XF}_v(Q)$, NEW $i \in I$, $\boxtimes\boxtimes \mathbb{E}\langle A_i \rangle_v \wedge \Diamond\Box[\neg A_i]_v$
        PROVE: FALSE
        PROOF: By (4.14) and (4.23), since $F \Rightarrow G$ is equivalent to $F \wedge \neg G \Rightarrow$ FALSE and $\neg\Box\Diamond\langle A_i \rangle_v$ equals $\Diamond\Box[\neg A_i]_v$.

   2.2. $\Diamond(\Box[\neg Q]_v \wedge \Box(\mathbb{E}\langle Q \rangle_v \Rightarrow \mathbb{E}\langle A_i \rangle_v))$
        PROOF: $\boxtimes\boxtimes \mathbb{E}\langle A_i \rangle_v$ implies $\Box\Diamond \mathbb{E}\langle A_i \rangle_v$, and $\Box\Diamond \mathbb{E}\langle A_i \rangle_v \wedge \Diamond\Box[\neg A_i]_v$ implies $\Diamond(\mathbb{E}\langle A_i \rangle_v \wedge \Box[\neg A_i]_v)$ by temporal reasoning. Therefore, the step 2.1 assumption implies $\Diamond(\mathbb{E}\langle A_i \rangle_v \wedge \Box[\neg A_i]_v)$, which by the step 1 assumption implies 2.2.

2.3. $\Diamond\Box[\neg Q]_v \land \Diamond\Box(\mathbb{E}\langle Q\rangle_v \equiv \mathbb{E}\langle A_i\rangle_v)$

PROOF: By step 2.2, because $\Diamond(\Box F \land \Box G)$ equals $\Diamond\Box F \land \Diamond\Box G$ for any F and G, and $\Box(\mathbb{E}\langle Q\rangle_v \Rightarrow \mathbb{E}\langle A_i\rangle_v)$ implies $\Box(\mathbb{E}\langle Q\rangle_v \equiv \mathbb{E}\langle A_i\rangle_v)$ because the definition of Q implies $\models A_i \Rightarrow Q$, which by the definition of $\mathbb{E}$ in Section 4.2.1 implies $\models \mathbb{E}\langle A_i\rangle_v \Rightarrow \mathbb{E}\langle Q\rangle_v$.

2.4. $\Box\Diamond\langle Q\rangle_v$

PROOF: $\boxtimes\boxtimes F$ and $\Diamond\Box(F \equiv G)$ imply $\boxtimes\boxtimes G$, for any F and G. Therefore step 2.3 and the step 2.1 assumption $\boxtimes\boxtimes \mathbb{E}\langle A_i\rangle_v$ imply $\boxtimes\boxtimes \mathbb{E}\langle Q\rangle_v$. By definition of XF, the step 2.1 assumption $\mathrm{XF}_v(Q)$ and $\boxtimes\boxtimes \mathbb{E}\langle Q\rangle_v$ imply $\Box\Diamond\langle Q\rangle_v$.

2.5. Q.E.D.

PROOF: Since $\Diamond\Box[\neg Q]_v$ is equivalent to $\neg\Box\Diamond\langle Q\rangle_v$, steps 2.3 and 2.4 imply FALSE, the goal introduced in step 2.1.

3. $(\forall i \in I : \mathrm{XF}_v(A_i)) \Rightarrow \mathrm{XF}_v(Q)$

3.1. SUFFICES: ASSUME: $(\forall i \in I : \mathrm{XF}_v(A_i)) \land \boxtimes\boxtimes \mathbb{E}\langle Q\rangle_v$
PROVE: $\Box\Diamond\langle Q\rangle_v$

PROOF: By (4.14) and (4.23).

3.2. $\mathbb{E}\langle Q\rangle_v \Rightarrow \Diamond\langle Q\rangle_v$

3.2.1. SUFFICES: ASSUME: $(i \in I) \land \mathbb{E}\langle A_i\rangle_v$
PROVE: $\Diamond\langle Q\rangle_v$

PROOF: By predicate logic (the $\exists$ Elimination rule), since Q equals $\exists i \in I : A_i$, so $\mathbb{E}\langle Q\rangle_v$ equals $\exists i \in I : \mathbb{E}\langle A_i\rangle_v$ by rule $\mathbb{E}2$ of Section 6.4.4.2.

3.2.2. CASE: $\Diamond\langle A_i\rangle_v$

PROOF: $\Diamond\langle Q\rangle_v$ follows from the case assumption and $\models A_i \Rightarrow Q$.

3.2.3. CASE: $\Box[\neg A_i]_v$

PROOF: Assumption $\mathbb{E}\langle A_i\rangle_v$ from step 3.2.1, the case assumption, and the step 1 assumption imply $\Box(\mathbb{E}\langle Q\rangle_v \Rightarrow \mathbb{E}\langle A_i\rangle_v)$. This, the temporal logic tautology $\models \Box(F \Rightarrow G) \Rightarrow (\boxtimes\boxtimes F \Rightarrow \boxtimes\boxtimes G)$, and the step 3.1 assumption $\boxtimes\boxtimes \mathbb{E}\langle Q\rangle_v$ imply $\boxtimes\boxtimes \mathbb{E}\langle A_i\rangle_v$. Since $i \in I$ by the step 3.2.1 assumption, the step 3.1 assumption implies $\mathrm{XF}_v(A_i)$, which by $\boxtimes\boxtimes \mathbb{E}\langle A_i\rangle_v$ and the definition of XF implies $\Diamond\langle A_i\rangle_v$, which by $\models A_i \Rightarrow Q$ implies $\Diamond\langle Q\rangle_v$.

3.3. Q.E.D.

PROOF: All assumptions in effect at step 3.2 are $\Box$ formulas so, as explained in Section 4.2.4, we can deduce $\Box(\mathbb{E}\langle Q\rangle_v \Rightarrow \Diamond\langle Q\rangle_v)$ from 3.2.

This and the temporal logic tautology
$$\models \Box(F \Rightarrow \Diamond G) \Rightarrow (\boxtimes\boxtimes F \Rightarrow \Box\Diamond G)$$
imply $\boxtimes\boxtimes \mathbb{E}\langle Q\rangle_v \Rightarrow \Box\Diamond Q$, which by the step 3.1 assumption $\boxtimes\boxtimes \mathbb{E}\langle Q\rangle_v$ implies the step 3.1 goal $\Box\Diamond Q$.

4. Q.E.D.

PROOF: By steps 1–3.

B.8 Proof Sketch of Theorem 4.9

Theorem 4.9 Let $\mathbf{x}$ be the list $x_1, \ldots, x_n$ of variables and let F be a property such that $F(\sigma)$ depends only on the values of the variables $\mathbf{x}$ in σ, for any behavior σ. There exists a formula S equal to $\mathit{Init} \wedge \Box[\mathit{Next}]_{\langle\mathbf{x},y\rangle} \wedge \mathrm{WF}_{\langle\mathbf{x},y\rangle}(\mathit{Next})$, where Init and Next are defined in terms of F, y is a variable not among the variables $\mathbf{x}$, and the variables of S are $\mathbf{x}$ and y, such that $\models F \Rightarrow [\![G]\!]$ iff $\models S \Rightarrow G$, for any property G. If F is a safety property, then the conjunct $\mathrm{WF}_{\langle\mathbf{x},y\rangle}(\mathit{Next})$ is not needed.

PROOF SKETCH: For any behavior σ, let $\sigma|_\mathbf{x}$ be the infinite sequence of n-tuples of values such that $\sigma|_\mathbf{x}(i)$ equals the value of $\langle\mathbf{x}\rangle$ in state $\sigma(i)$. The basic idea is to define S so that the value of y in any state i of a behavior of S always equals $(\sigma|_\mathbf{x})^{+i}$ for some behavior σ satisfying F, and $\mathbf{x}$ always equals $y(0)$. (Remember that τ is the infinite sequence $\tau(0) \to \tau(1) \to \cdots$, and τ^{+i} equals $\tau(i) \to \tau(i+1) \to \cdots$.)

To do this, for any infinite sequence τ of n-tuples of values, we define $\widetilde{F}(\tau)$ to equal $F(\sigma)$ for any behavior σ such that $\sigma|_\mathbf{x}$ equals τ. This uniquely defines $\widetilde{F}$ because, by hypothesis, the value of $F(\sigma)$ depends only on the values of the variables $\mathbf{x}$ in the behavior σ. Define $\mathit{IsTupleSeq}$ to be the mapping such that $\mathit{IsTupleSeq}(\tau)$ is true iff τ is an infinite cardinal sequence of n-tuples of arbitrary values. We then define S by letting:

$$\mathit{Init} \triangleq \exists \tau : \wedge \mathit{IsTupleSeq}(\tau) \wedge \widetilde{F}(\tau)$$
$$\wedge\, (y = \tau) \wedge (\langle\mathbf{x}\rangle = \tau(0))$$
$$\mathit{Next} \triangleq (y' = \mathit{Tail}(y)) \wedge (\langle\mathbf{x}\rangle' = y'(0))$$

With this definition, $F(\sigma)$ equals TRUE for a behavior σ iff there is a behavior satisfying S in which the initial value of y is $\sigma|_\mathbf{x}$. Notice that σ is a halting behavior iff τ ends with an infinite sequence of identical n-tuples. When y equals that value $\mathit{Tail}(y) = y$, so $\langle\mathit{Next}\rangle_{\langle\mathbf{x},y\rangle}$ equals FALSE and S allows only stuttering steps from that point on.

Eliminating the conjunct $\text{WF}_{\langle \mathbf{x},y \rangle}(\textit{Next})$ allows S to halt even if the behavior y initially equals $\sigma|_\mathbf{x}$ for a non-halting behavior σ that satisfies F. That makes no difference if F is a safety property, since in that case every finite prefix of σ also satisfies F. END PROOF SKETCH

B.9 Proof of Theorem 7.2

Theorem 7.2 With the assumptions of Theorem 7.1, for all $i \in I$ let B_i be a subaction of A_i such that

$$(*) \quad T \wedge (i \neq j) \;\Rightarrow\; \Box[\neg(B_i \wedge A_j)]_v$$

for all j in I; and let $B_i^h \triangleq \langle B_i \rangle_v \wedge (h' = exp_i)$. Then

$$T \wedge (\forall i \in I : \text{XF}^i_v(B_i)) \;\equiv\; \exists h : T^h \wedge (\forall i \in I : \text{XF}^i_{vh}(B_i^h))$$

where each XF^i is either WF or SF.

1. ASSUME: $i \in I$
   PROVE: $\langle B_i^h \rangle_{vh} \equiv \langle B_i \wedge (h' = exp_i) \rangle_v$
   1.1. $\langle B_i^h \rangle_{vh} \equiv B_i \wedge (v' \neq v) \wedge (h' = exp_i) \wedge (vh' \neq vh)$
       PROOF: By the definitions of B_i^h, $\textit{Next}^i$, and $\langle \ldots \rangle_{\ldots}$.
   1.2. $\langle B_i^h \rangle_{vh} \equiv B_i \wedge (v' \neq v) \wedge (h' = exp_i)$
       PROOF: By step 1.1, since $vh = v \circ \langle h \rangle$ implies $(v' \neq v) \wedge (vh' \neq vh) \equiv (v' \neq v)$.
   1.3. Q.E.D.
       PROOF: By step 1.2 and the definition of $\langle \ldots \rangle_v$.

2. ASSUME: $i \in I$
   PROVE: $\mathbb{E}\langle B_i^h \rangle_{vh} \equiv \mathbb{E}\langle B_i \rangle_v$
   PROOF: By step 1 because exp is assumed not to contain h', so rules E3 and E5 of Section 6.4.4.2 imply $\mathbb{E}\langle B_i \wedge (h' = exp_i) \rangle_v$ equals $\mathbb{E}\langle B_i \rangle_v$.

DEFINE $\boxtimes\boxtimes^i$ to equal $\Diamond\Box$ if XF^i is WF and to equal $\Box\Diamond$ if XF^i is SF.

3. ASSUME: $T^h \wedge \forall i \in I : \text{XF}^i_{vh}(B_i^h)$
   PROVE: $T \wedge \forall i \in I : \text{XF}^i_v(B_i)$
   3.1. SUFFICES: ASSUME: $(i \in I)$
               PROVE: $\text{XF}^i_v(B_i)$
       PROOF: By Theorem 7.1, T^h implies T. Therefore, if suffices to prove $\forall i \in I : \text{XF}^i_v(B_i)$ to prove step 3.

B.9. PROOF OF THEOREM 7.2

3.2. SUFFICES: ASSUME: $\Box\boxdot^i \mathbb{E}\langle B_i\rangle_v$
     PROVE: $\Box\Diamond\langle B_i\rangle_v$
   PROOF: By (4.14) and (4.23).

3.3. $\Box\boxdot^i \mathbb{E}\langle B_i^h\rangle_{vh}$
   PROOF: By the step 3.2 assumption and step 2. (Since step 2 is not in the scope of any assumptions, it implies $\Box(\mathbb{E}\langle B_i^h\rangle_{vh} \equiv \mathbb{E}\langle B_i\rangle_v)$.)

3.4. $\Box\Diamond\langle B_i^h\rangle_{vh}$
   PROOF: The step 3 assumption implies $\text{XF}_{vh}^i(B_i^h)$, which by step 3.3, (4.14), and (4.23) implies $\Box\Diamond\langle B_i^h\rangle_{vh}$.

3.5. Q.E.D.
   PROOF: Step 3.4 and step 1 imply $\Box\Diamond\langle B_i \wedge (h' = exp_i)\rangle_v$, which implies the goal introduced in step 3.2.

4. ASSUME: $T \wedge \forall i \in I : \text{XF}_v^i(B_i)$
   PROVE: $\exists h : T^h \wedge \forall i \in I : \text{XF}_{vh}^i(B_i^h)$

   4.1. SUFFICES: ASSUME: $T^h \wedge (i \in I)$
        PROVE: $\text{XF}_{vh}^i(B_i^h)$
      PROOF: Theorem 7.1 shows that T implies $\exists h : T^h$. This implies that to prove $T \wedge F$ implies $\exists h : (T^h \wedge G)$ for any F and G, it suffices to prove that $T \wedge F \wedge T^h$ implies G.[2] Thus, the step 4 assumption shows that to prove the step 4 goal, it suffices to prove T^h implies $\forall i \in I : \text{XF}_{vh}^i(B_i^h)$, which is asserted by this step's ASSUME/PROVE.

   4.2. SUFFICES: ASSUME: $\Box\boxdot^i \mathbb{E}\langle B_i^h\rangle_{vh}$
        PROVE: $\Box\Diamond\langle B_i^h\rangle_{vh}$
      PROOF: By (4.14) and (4.23).

   4.3. $\Box\boxdot^i \mathbb{E}\langle B_i\rangle_v$
      PROOF: By the step 4.2 assumption and step 2.

   4.4. $\Box\Diamond\langle B_i\rangle_v$
      PROOF: The step 4 assumption implies $\text{XF}_v^i(B_i)$, which by step 4.3, (4.14), and (4.23) implies $\Box\Diamond\langle B_i\rangle_v$.

   4.5. Q.E.D.
      PROOF: By hypothesis, B_i is a subaction of A_i. By hypothesis (*) and the step 4 assumption (which implies T), $B_i \wedge A_j$ equals FALSE if $i \neq j$. Hence a B_i step must be an A_i^h step. By definition of A_i^h and the step

---

[2] To understand this reasoning, convince yourself that it is sound for formulas of ordinary math (not temporal logic) when $\exists$ is replaced by $\exists$.

4.1 assumption (which implies T^h), every B_i step is a $B_i \wedge (h' = exp_i)$ step. Therefore, step 4.4 and step 1 imply $\Box\Diamond\langle B_i^h\rangle_{vh}$, which is the goal introduced by step 4.2.

5. Q.E.D.

PROOF: Steps 3 and 4 imply that $T \wedge (\forall i \in I : \mathrm{XF}^i_v(B_i))$ is equivalent to $\exists h : T^h \wedge (\forall i \in I : \mathrm{XF}^i_{vh}(B_i^h))$.

B.10 Proof Sketch of Theorem 7.3

Theorem 7.3 Let T equal $Init \wedge \Box[Next]_{\langle \mathbf{x}\rangle}$ where $\mathbf{x}$ is the list of all variables of S; let F be a safety property such that $F(\sigma)$ depends only on the values of the variables $\mathbf{x}$ in σ, for any behavior σ; and let h be a variable not one of the variables $\mathbf{x}$. We can add h as a history variable to T to obtain T^h and define a state predicate I_F in terms of F such that $\models [\![T]\!] \Rightarrow F$ is true iff I_F is an invariant of T^h.

PROOF SKETCH: Define T^h as follows:

$T^h \triangleq Init^h \wedge \Box[Next^h]_{\langle \mathbf{x},h\rangle}$
$Init^h \triangleq Init \wedge (h = \langle \mathbf{x}\rangle)$
$Next^h \triangleq Next \wedge (h' = Append(h, \langle \mathbf{x}\rangle'))$

Since h is a history variable, so $\exists h : T^h$ is equivalent to T, to every behavior σ satisfying T there is a corresponding behavior satisfying T^h that has the same values of the variables of $\mathbf{x}$ as σ. Since F does not depend on h, this means that $\models [\![T]\!] \Rightarrow F$ iff $\models [\![T^h]\!] \Rightarrow F$.

We now define $\rho|_x$ and $\widetilde{F}$ to be the same as in the proof of Theorem 4.9, except for finite behaviors ρ. We define $\rho|_\mathbf{x}$ to be the finite cardinal sequence of n-tuples of the same length as ρ such that $\rho|_\mathbf{x}(i)$ equals the value of $\langle \mathbf{x}\rangle$ in state $\rho(i)$; and we define $\widetilde{F}$ to be the predicate on finite sequences of n-tuples of values such that $\widetilde{F}(\rho|_x)$ equals $F(\rho)$ (which by definition equals $F(\rho^\uparrow)$). We then define I_F to equal $\widetilde{F}(h)$.

Much as in the proof of Theorem 4.9, for any behavior τ, a finite prefix ρ of τ satisfies F iff $\widetilde{F}(\rho|_\mathbf{x})$ is true, which is true iff $\widetilde{F}(h)$ is true of the last state of ρ. Every state of τ is the last state of some finite prefix of τ, and the safety property F is true of τ iff it is true of every finite prefix of τ, so F is true of τ iff I_F is true of every state of τ. This proves that I_F is an invariant of T^h iff T^h satisfies F; and T satisfies F iff T^h does, because F depends only on the variables $\mathbf{x}$. END PROOF SKETCH

B.11 Proof Sketch of Theorem 7.6

Theorem 7.6 Let **x**, **y**, and **z** be lists of variables, all distinct from one another; let the variables of T be **x** and **z** and the variables of IS be **x** and **y**; and let T equal $\mathit{Init} \wedge \Box[\mathit{Next}]_{\langle \mathbf{x},\mathbf{z} \rangle} \wedge L$. Let the operator Φ map behaviors satisfying T to behaviors satisfying IS such that $\Phi(\sigma) \sim_\mathbf{y} \sigma$. By adding history, stuttering, and prophecy variables to T, we can define a formula $T^\mathbf{a}$ such that $\exists \mathbf{a} : T^\mathbf{a}$ is equivalent to T and a tuple **exp** of expressions defined in terms of Φ and the variables of $T^\mathbf{a}$ such that

$$\models T^\mathbf{a} \Rightarrow (IS \text{ WITH } \mathbf{y} \leftarrow \mathbf{exp})$$

PROOF SKETCH: We first add an infinite stuttering variable t to T, defining T^t to equal

$$\wedge \; \mathit{Init} \wedge \Box[(\mathit{Next} \wedge (v' \neq v)) \vee ((t' \neq t) \wedge (\langle \mathbf{x}, \mathbf{z} \rangle' = \langle \mathbf{x}, \mathbf{z} \rangle))]_{\langle \mathbf{x},\mathbf{z},t \rangle}$$
$$\wedge \; L \wedge \Box\Diamond\langle t' \neq t \rangle_t$$

In addition to handling the weird case described in Section 7.3.5, this simplifies the proof by not having to consider terminating behaviors, since T^t doesn't allow them.

Let m be the number of variables in **x**, **z**, and t. We next define T^{th} by adding to T^t a history variable h whose value in any state is a cardinal sequence of m-tuples. The initial value of h is the one-element sequence whose single element is the value of $\langle \mathbf{x}, \mathbf{z}, t \rangle$ in the initial state. Each step that does not leave $\langle \mathbf{x}, \mathbf{z}, t \rangle$ unchanged appends to h the new value of $\langle \mathbf{x}, \mathbf{z}, t \rangle$. For a behavior σ satisfying T^{th} that has no stuttering steps (steps leaving **x**, **z**, and t unchanged), the value of variable h always equals the sequence $h(0), \ldots, h(\mathit{Len}(h) - 1)$ of m-tuples such that each $h(i)$ equals the value of $\langle \mathbf{x}, \mathbf{z}, t \rangle$ in state $\sigma(i)$ for all $i < \mathit{Len}(h)$.

We now add to T^{th} a prophecy variable p that always makes an infinite sequence of prophecies. The value of p in state $\sigma(i)$ of a behavior σ satisfying T^{thp} is the infinite sequence of m-tuples such that in state $\sigma(i)$, the value of $p(0)$, the next prediction made by p, is the m-tuple that equals the next value of $\langle \mathbf{x}, \mathbf{z}, t \rangle$ different from its current value. This is a generalized prophecy variable with predictions in the collection (not a set) of m-tuple of values. It is defined by writing the next-state action Next^{th} as $\exists i : A_i$, where

$$A_i \triangleq (i = \langle \mathbf{x}, \mathbf{z}, t \rangle') \wedge \mathit{Next}^{th}$$

and defining the next-state action Next^{thp} of T^{thp} by

$$\mathit{Next}^{thp} \triangleq A_{p(0)} \wedge \mathit{Next}^{th} \wedge (p' = \mathit{Tail}(p))$$

A $Next^{thp}$ step removes the first element from p and appends that element to the end of h. Therefore, the value of $h \circ p$ remains unchanged throughout any behavior that satisfies T^{thp}. The value of $h \circ p$ during a behavior σ satisfying T^{thp} equals the sequence of values of $\langle \mathbf{x}, \mathbf{z}, t \rangle$ in the entire behavior σ, except that σ may have additional (stuttering) steps that leave $\langle \mathbf{x}, \mathbf{z}, t \rangle$ unchanged.

In any state of a behavior satisfying T^{thp}, the value of $(h \circ p)(Len(h)-1)$ (the last element in the sequence h of m-tuples of values) is the current value of $\langle \mathbf{x}, \mathbf{z}, t \rangle$. The variables h and p, together with the mapping Φ contain all the information needed to define a refinement mapping under which T^{thp} implements IS. To see how this is done, we need some notation.

For any behavior σ and state expression exp, define $\sigma|_{exp}$ to be the infinite sequence of values such that $(\sigma|_{exp})(i)$ equals the value of exp in state $\sigma(i)$, for all $i \in \mathbb{N}$. Thus $\sigma|_{\langle \mathbf{x}, \mathbf{z}, t \rangle}$ is the sequence of m-tuples of values of $\langle \mathbf{x}, \mathbf{z}, t \rangle$ in the states of σ. Define the mapping $\widetilde{\Phi}$ from sequences of m-tuples of values to behaviors so that $\widetilde{\Phi}(\rho)$ equals $\Phi(\sigma)$ for some behavior σ such that $\sigma|_{\langle \mathbf{x}, \mathbf{z}, t \rangle} = \rho$. (It doesn't matter what values the states of σ assign to variables other than those in $\mathbf{x}$, $\mathbf{z}$, and t since they don't affect whether or not σ satisfies T.) We are assuming that $\Phi(\sigma)$ satisfies IS and $\Phi(\sigma) \sim_{\mathbf{y}} \sigma$. Therefore, for any behavior satisfying T^{thp}, for the value of $h \circ p$ in any state of that behavior, $\widetilde{\Phi}(h \circ p)$ satisfies IS and $\widetilde{\Phi}(h \circ p) \sim_{\mathbf{y}} \sigma$ for some behavior σ such that $\sigma|_{\langle \mathbf{x}, \mathbf{z}, t \rangle} = h \circ p$.

To understand how to construct the needed refinement mapping, we consider a simpler version of the theorem that would be true if we were using RTLA rather than TLA, so we didn't have the complication introduced by stuttering insensitivity. In that case, $\widetilde{\Phi}(h \circ p)$ would satisfy $\widetilde{\Phi}(h \circ p) \simeq_{\mathbf{y}} \sigma$ instead of $\widetilde{\Phi}(h \circ p) \sim_{\mathbf{y}} \sigma$. This means that the behavior $\Phi(\sigma)$ satisfying IS is constructed from a behavior σ with $\sigma|_{\langle \mathbf{x}, \mathbf{z}, t \rangle}$ equal to $h \circ p$ by just changing the value of the variables $\mathbf{y}$ in each state of σ (without adding or removing stuttering steps). For any state s, let $s_{\mathbf{y}}$ be the list of values of the variables $\mathbf{y}$ in that state. For σ to satisfy IS, the values of $\mathbf{y}$ in any state $\sigma(i)$ of the behavior σ should equal the values of $\Phi(\sigma)(i)_{\mathbf{y}}$, the values of $\mathbf{y}$ in the corresponding state of $\Phi(\sigma)$.[3] Remember that state number i of σ corresponds to the m-tuple $(h \circ p)(i)$ with $i = Len(h) - 1$. Therefore, the values assigned to $\mathbf{y}$ by the refinement mapping under which T^{thp} implements IS should in each state equal the values of $\mathbf{y}$ in state number $Len(h) - 1$ of $\widetilde{\Phi}(h \circ p)$. In

---

[3]This means that for each variable y_j of $\mathbf{y}$, the value of y_j in any state $\sigma(i)$ should equal the value of y_j in $\Phi(\sigma)(i)$.

B.11. PROOF SKETCH OF THEOREM 7.6

other words, we have:

(B.1) $\quad \models T^{thp} \Rightarrow (\text{IS WITH } \mathbf{y} \leftarrow (\widetilde{\Phi}(h \circ p)(Len(h) - 1))_{\mathbf{y}})$

Let's now return to the actual situation in which $\widetilde{\Phi}(h \circ p) \sim_{\mathbf{y}} \sigma$ (rather than $\widetilde{\Phi}(h \circ p) \simeq_{\mathbf{y}} \sigma$). The behavior $\widetilde{\Phi}(h \circ p)$ is constructed from the behavior σ, where $\sigma|_{\langle \mathbf{x}, \mathbf{z}, t \rangle}$ equals the value of $h \circ p$ in every state of σ, by possibly adding stuttering steps to σ and then modifying the values of $\mathbf{y}$ in its states. (There are no stuttering steps to remove from σ because we defined T^t and the history variable h so that h is a sequence of m-tuples no two successive elements of which are equal.)

To fix (B.1) to handle these stuttering steps, we have to add a stuttering variable s to T^{thp} to obtain the program T^{thps} that adds to the behavior σ satisfying T^{thp} the stuttering steps needed to produce a behavior τ such that the state $\tau(i)$ corresponds to the state $\widetilde{\Phi}(h \circ p)(i)$ for every $i \in \mathbb{N}$. The behavior $\widetilde{\Phi}(h \circ p)$ tells us where those stuttering steps must be added: each step $\widetilde{\Phi}(h \circ p)(i) \to \widetilde{\Phi}(h \circ p)(i+1)$ that leaves the value of $\langle \mathbf{x}, \mathbf{z}, t \rangle$ unchanged corresponds to a stuttering step added to the behavior σ satisfying T^{thp} to form τ.

Define the function f in $(\mathbb{N} \to \mathbb{N})$ in terms of $h \circ p$ as follows. Let $f(0) = 0$, and for all $i \in \mathbb{N}$, let $f(i+1)$ be the smallest number greater than $f(i)$ such that the value of $\langle \mathbf{x}, \mathbf{z}, t \rangle$ in state $\widetilde{\Phi}(h \circ p)(f(i+1))$ is different from its value in state $\widetilde{\Phi}(h \circ p)(f(i))$. (Such a number $f(i+1)$ exists for the value of $h \circ p$ in any reachable state of T^{thp} because adding the infinite-stuttering variable t ensured that $\Box \Diamond (t' \neq t)$ is true for every behavior of T^{thp}.)

To construct $\widetilde{\Phi}(h \circ p)$ from a behavior σ with $\sigma|_{\langle \mathbf{x}, \mathbf{z}, t \rangle} = h \circ p$, we have to add stuttering steps to make each state number i of σ correspond to state number $f(i)$ of $\widetilde{\Phi}(h \circ p)$. The stuttering variable s added to T^{thp} to define T^{thps} has to add $f(i+1) - f(i) - 1$ stuttering steps between states number i and $i+1$ of a behavior of T^{thp}. That means adding $f(Len(h)) - f(Len(h) - 1) - 1$ stuttering steps after every step of the next-state action of T^{thp}. (Of course no stuttering step is added if $f(Len(h)) - f(Len(h) - 1) = 1$.) We then define k to be a state expression whose value in any behavior satisfying T^{thps} is the number of steps of the next-state action of T^{thps} that have occurred so far. We can define k in terms of the values of f and s, or we can simply add k as a history variable to T^{thps}. However we define it, we can express the corrected version of (B.1) that handles stuttering insensitivity by:

$\models T^{thps} \Rightarrow (\text{IS WITH } \mathbf{y} \leftarrow (\widetilde{\Phi}(h \circ p)(k))_{\mathbf{y}})$

which completes the proof. END PROOF SKETCH

Replacing the Prophecy Variable with a Prophecy Constant

Theorem 7.6 is true if we use a prophecy constant, as defined in Section 7.7, instead of a prophecy variable. This is proved by modifying the proof sketch of Theorem 7.6 as follows. After adding the auxiliary variables t and h, we add to T^{th} a prophecy constant c whose value is the infinite sequence of m-tuples that are the values of $\langle \mathbf{x}, \mathbf{z}, t \rangle$ in the entire behavior. In other words,

$$T^{thc} \triangleq \exists c : P(h, c) \wedge T^{th}$$

where $P(h, c)$ asserts that c is an infinite sequence of m-tuples such that, in every state, h equals the sequence of the first $Len(h)$ elements of c. We then define p to be the state function such that, in any state, $h \circ p$ equals c. The proof is then the same as the rest of the proof of Theorem 7.6, using this as the definition of p.

B.12 Proof of Theorem 8.2

The proof uses the following assertion, which the definition of the action composition operator "·" implies is true for all actions A_i and B_j:

(B.2) $\models (\exists i \in I : A_i) \cdot (\exists j \in J : B_j) \equiv (\exists i \in I, j \in J : A_i \cdot B_j)$

Theorem 8.2 If $A \equiv \exists i \in I : A_i$ and $B \equiv \exists j \in J : B_j$ for actions A_i and B_j, then:

$$\models (\forall i \in I, j \in J : A_i \cdot B_j \Rightarrow B_j \cdot A_i) \Rightarrow (A \cdot B \Rightarrow B \cdot A)$$

PROOF: It suffices to assume $A_i \cdot B_j \Rightarrow B_j \cdot A_i$ for all $i \in I$ and $j \in J$ and prove $A \cdot B \Rightarrow B \cdot A$. Here is the proof:

$A \cdot B \equiv (\exists i \in I, j \in J : A_i \cdot B_j)$ by (B.2)
$\quad \Rightarrow (\exists i \in I, j \in J : B_j \cdot A_i)$ we assume $A_i \cdot B_j \Rightarrow B_j \cdot A_i$ for all i and j
$\quad \equiv B \cdot A$ by (B.2), substituting $I \leftarrow J$, $J \leftarrow I$, $A_i \leftarrow B_j$, and $B_j \leftarrow A_i$.

END PROOF

B.13 Proof of Theorem 8.3

Theorem 8.3 If S equals $Init \wedge \Box[Next]_\mathbf{x}$, P is a safety property, and Q is a state predicate such that $\models S \Rightarrow \Box\mathbb{E}([Next]_\mathbf{x}^+ \wedge Q')$, then $\models S \wedge \Box\Diamond Q \Rightarrow P$ implies $\models S \Rightarrow P$.

B.13. PROOF OF THEOREM 8.3

1. $\langle S, \Box\Diamond Q\rangle$ is machine closed.

    1.1. SUFFICES: ASSUME: ρ is a finite behavior satisfying S
    PROVE: ρ is a prefix of a behavior satisfying $S \wedge L$
    PROOF: By definition of machine closure.

    1.2. There is a mapping Φ such that if μ is any finite behavior satisfying S, then $\Phi(\mu)$ is a finite behavior ending in a state satisfying Q such that $\mu \circ \Phi(\mu)$ satisfies S.
    PROOF: The hypothesis $\models S \Rightarrow \Box\mathbb{E}([Next]_{\mathbf{x}}^+ \wedge Q')$ implies that the action $[Next]_{\mathbf{x}}^+ \wedge Q'$ is enabled in the last state of μ. Therefore, there is a finite behavior ψ beginning with the last state of μ and containing at least two states such that the last state of ψ satisfies Q and every step of ψ satisfies $[Next]_{\mathbf{x}}^+$. Let $\Phi(\mu)$ equal $Tail(\psi)$. Then $\mu \circ \Phi(\mu)$ satisfies S by definition of S, because μ satisfies $Init$ and $\Box[Next]_{\mathbf{x}}$ and every step of ψ is a $[Next]_{\mathbf{x}}^+$ step; and the last state of $\mu \circ \Phi(\mu)$ satisfies Q.

    DEFINE τ_i for $i \in \mathbb{N}$ by: $\tau_0 \triangleq \rho$
    $$\tau_{i+1} \triangleq \tau_i \circ \Phi(\tau_i) \text{ for all } i \in \mathbb{N}$$

    1.3. Q.E.D.
    PROOF: Let σ be the (unique) behavior such that each τ_i is a prefix of σ, so ρ (which equals τ_0) is a prefix of σ. Each finite prefix of σ is a prefix of some τ_i and therefore satisfies S. Since S is a safety property, this implies σ satisfies S. For all $i \in \mathbb{N}$, τ_{i+1} has at least one more state satisfying Q than τ_i does, so σ satisfies $\Box\Diamond Q$.

2. $S = \mathcal{C}(S \wedge \Box\Diamond Q)$

    PROOF: By step 1 and Theorem 4.5.

3. Q.E.D.

    PROOF: By step 2, the assumption that P is a safety property, and Theorem 4.3.

Bibliography

[1] Martín Abadi and Leslie Lamport. An old-fashioned recipe for real time. *ACM Transactions on Programming Languages and Systems*, 16(5):1543–1571, September 1994. This paper has an appendix published by ACM only online that contains proofs. Other online versions of the paper might not contain the appendix.

[2] Martín Abadi and Leslie Lamport. Conjoining specifications. *ACM Transactions on Programming Languages and Systems*, 17(3):507–534, May 1995. This paper has an appendix published by ACM only online that contains proofs. Online versions of the paper might not contain the appendix.

[3] Bowen Alpern and Fred B. Schneider. Defining liveness. *Information Processing Letters*, 21(4):181–185, October 1985.

[4] E. A. Ashcroft. Proving assertions about parallel programs. *Journal of Computer and System Sciences*, 10:110–135, February 1975.

[5] Selma Azaiez, Damien Doligez, Matthieu Lemerre, Tomer Libal, and Stephan Merz. Proving determinacy of the PharOS real-time operating system. In Michael Butler, Klaus-Dieter Schewe, Atif Mashkoor, and Miklós Biró, editors, *5th Intl. Conf. Abstract State Machines, Alloy, B, TLA, VDM, and Z (ABZ 2016)*, volume 9675 of Lecture Notes in Computer Science, pages 70–85. Springer, 2016.

[6] Arthur Bernstein and Paul K. Harter, Jr. Proving real time properties of programs with temporal logic. In *Proceedings of the Eighth Symposium on Operating Systems Principles*, pages 1–11, New York, 1981. ACM. Operating Systems Review 15(5).

[7] James E. Burns and Nancy A. Lynch. Bounds on shared memory for mutual exclusion. *Inf. Comput.*, 107(2):171–184, 1993.

[8] Ernie Cohen and Leslie Lamport. Reduction in TLA. In David Sangiorgi and Robert de Simone, editors, *CONCUR'98 Concurrency Theory*, volume 1466 of Lecture Notes in Computer Science, pages 317–331. Springer-Verlag, 1998.

[9] E. W. Dijkstra. Solution of a problem in concurrent programming control. *Communications of the ACM*, 8(9):569, September 1965.

[10] Thomas W. Doeppner, Jr. Parallel program correctness through refinement. In *Fourth Annual ACM Symposium on Principles of Programming Languages*, pages 155–169. ACM, January 1977.

[11] Laurent Doyen, Goran Frehse, George J. Pappas, and André Platzer. Verification of hybrid systems. In Edmund M. Clarke, Thomas A. Henzinger, Helmut Veith, and Roderick Bloem, editors, *Handbook of Model Checking*, pages 1047–1110. Springer, 2018.

[12] Cynthia Dwork, Nancy Lynch, and Larry Stockmeyer. Consensus in the presence of partial synchrony. *Journal of the ACM*, 35(2):288–323, April 1988.

[13] Michael Fischer. Re: Where are you? Email message to Leslie Lamport. Arpanet message sent on June 25, 1985 18:56:29 EDT, number 8506252257.AA07636@YALE-BULLDOG.YALE.ARPA (47 lines), 1985.

[14] Michael J. Fischer, Nancy Lynch, and Michael S. Paterson. Impossibility of distributed consensus with one faulty process. *Journal of the ACM*, 32(2):374–382, April 1985.

[15] R. W. Floyd. Assigning meanings to programs. In *Proceedings of the Symposium on Applied Math., Vol. 19*, pages 19–32. American Mathematical Society, 1967.

[16] Aman Goel, Stephan Merz, and Karem A. Sakallah. Towards an automatic proof of the bakery algorithm. In Marieke Huisman and António Ravara, editors, *Formal Techniques for Distributed Objects, Components, and Systems*, volume 13910 of Lecture Notes in Computer Science, pages 21–28. Springer, 2023.

[17] Georges Gonthier and Leslie Lamport. Recursive operator definitions. Research Report RR-9341, INRIA Saclay Île de France, 2020. https://inria.hal.science/hal-02598330/file/RR-9341.pdf.

[18] Thomas A. Henzinger, Zohar Manna, and Amir Pnueli. What good are digital clocks? In Werner Kuich, editor, *Automata, Languages and Programming, 19th International Colloquium, ICALP92, Vienna, Austria, July 13–17, 1992, Proceedings*, volume 623 of Lecture Notes in Computer Science, pages 545–558. Springer, 1992.

[19] Maurice P. Herlihy and Jeannette M. Wing. Linearizability: A correctness condition for concurrent objects. *ACM Transactions on Programming Languages and Systems*, 12(3):463–492, January 1990.

[20] Wim H. Hesselink. Eternity variables to prove simulation of specifications. *ACM Trans. Comput. Log.*, 6(1):175–201, 2005.

[21] C. A. R. Hoare. Proof of correctness of data representations. *Acta Informatica*, 1:271–281, 1972.

[22] C. A. R. Hoare. An axiomatic basis for computer programming. *Communications of the ACM*, 12(10):576–583, October 1969.

[23] Cliff B. Jones. Specification and design of (parallel) programs. In R. E. A. Mason, editor, *Information Processing 83: Proceedings of the IFIP 9th World Congress*, pages 321–332, Amsterdam, September 1983. IFIP, North-Holland.

[24] R. M. Keller. Formal verification of parallel programs. *Communications of the ACM*, 19(7):371–384, July 1976.

[25] R. P. Kurshan and Leslie Lamport. Verification of a multiplier: 64 bits and beyond. In Costas Courcoubetis, editor, *Computer-Aided Verification: Proceedings of the Fifth International Conference, CAV'93*, volume 697 of Lecture Notes in Computer Science, pages 166–179, Berlin, June 1993. Springer-Verlag.

[26] Peter Ladkin, Leslie Lamport, Bryan Olivier, and Denis Roegel. Lazy caching in TLA. *Distributed Computing*, 12(2/3):151–174, 1999.

[27] Leslie Lamport. The Paxos algorithm or how to win a Turing award. Web page. https://lamport.azurewebsites.net/tla/paxos-algorithm.html.

[28] Leslie Lamport. TLA—temporal logic of actions. A web page at https://lamport.azurewebsites.net/tla/tla.html.

[29] Leslie Lamport. Proving the correctness of multiprocess programs. *IEEE Transactions on Software Engineering*, SE-3(2):125–143, March 1977.

[30] Leslie Lamport. The mutual exclusion problem—part II: Statement and solutions. *Journal of the ACM*, 32(1):327–348, January 1986.

[31] Leslie Lamport. Hybrid systems in TLA+. In Robert L. Grossman, Anil Nerode, Anders P. Ravn, and Hans Rischel, editors, *Hybrid Systems*, volume 736 of Lecture Notes in Computer Science, pages 77–102, Berlin, Heidelberg, 1993. Springer-Verlag.

[32] Leslie Lamport. The temporal logic of actions. *ACM Transactions on Programming Languages and Systems*, 16(3):872–923, May 1994.

[33] Leslie Lamport. Proving possibility properties. *Theoretical Computer Science*, 206(1–2):341–352, October 1998.

[34] Leslie Lamport. Fairness and hyperfairness. *Distributed Computing*, 13(4):239–245, November 2000.

[35] Leslie Lamport. *Specifying Systems*. Addison-Wesley, Boston, 2003.

[36] Leslie Lamport. Real-time model checking is really simple. In Dominique Borrione and Wolfgang Paul, editors, *Correct Hardware Design and Verification Methods, 13th IFIP WG 10.5 Advanced Research Working Conference, CHARME 2005, Saarbrücken, Germany, October 3–6, 2005, Proceedings*, volume 3725 of Lecture Notes in Computer Science, pages 162–175. Springer, 2005.

[37] Leslie Lamport. The PlusCal algorithm language. In Martin Leucker and Carroll Morgan, editors, *Theoretical Aspects of Computing, ICTAC 2009*, volume 5684 of Lecture Notes in Computer Science, pages 36–60. Springer-Verlag, 2009.

[38] Leslie Lamport. How to write a 21st century proof. *Journal of Fixed Point Theory and Applications*, March 2012. `DOI:10.1007/s11784-012-0071-6`.

[39] Leslie Lamport and Stephan Merz. Auxiliary variables in TLA+. arXiv:1703.05121 (`https://arxiv.org/abs/1703.05121`) Also available, together with TLA+ specifications, at `http://lamport.azurewebsites.net/tla/auxiliary/auxiliary.html`.

[40] Mark H. Liffiton and Karem A. Sakallah. Algorithms for computing minimal unsatisfiable subsets of constraints. *J. Autom. Reason.*, 40(1):1–33, 2008.

[41] Richard J. Lipton. Reduction: A method of proving properties of parallel programs. *Communications of the ACM*, 18(12):717–721, December 1975.

[42] Chris Newcombe, Tim Rath, Fan Zhang, Bogdan Munteanu, Marc Brooker, and Michael Deardeuff. How Amazon Web Services uses formal methods. *Communications of the ACM*, 58(4):66–73, April 2015.

[43] Brian M. Oki and Barbara H. Liskov. Viewstamped replication: A new primary copy method to support highly-available distributed systems. In *Proceedings of the Seventh Annual ACM Symposium on Principles of Distributed Computing*, pages 8–17. ACM Press, August 1988.

[44] S. Owicki and D. Gries. An axiomatic proof technique for parallel programs I. *Acta Informatica*, 6(4):319–340, 1976.

[45] Susan Owicki and David Gries. Verifying properties of parallel programs: An axiomatic approach. *Communications of the ACM*, 19(5):279–284, May 1976.

[46] Susan Owicki and Leslie Lamport. Proving liveness properties of concurrent programs. *ACM Transactions on Programming Languages and Systems*, 4(3):455–495, July 1982.

[47] Marshall Pease, Robert Shostak, and Leslie Lamport. Reaching agreement in the presence of faults. *Journal of the ACM*, 27(2):228–234, April 1980.

[48] Amir Pnueli. The temporal logic of programs. In *Proceedings of the 18th Annual Symposium on the Foundations of Computer Science*, pages 46–57. IEEE, November 1977.

[49] Eric Verhulst, Raymond T. Boute, José Miguel Sampaio Faria, Bernard H. C. Sputh, and Vitaliy Mezhuyev. *Formal Development of a Network-Centric RTOS*. Springer, New York, 2011.

[50] Hagen Völzer and Daniele Varacca. Defining fairness in reactive and concurrent systems. *Journal of the ACM*, 59(3):13:1–13:37, 2012.

[51] J. Wensley et al. SIFT: Design and analysis of a fault-tolerant computer for aircraft control. *Proceedings of the IEEE*, 66(10):1240–1254, October 1978.

Index

$'$ (prime), 53, 56–58
$\mapsto$ (function constructor), 30, 269
$\models$, 16, 55, 267
$\setminus$ (set difference), 129, 268
$\neg$ (negation), 18, 266
$\rightarrow$ (in cardinal sequence), 32, 59, 270
$\rightarrow$ (set of functions), 46, 269
$\rightarrow$ (step), 56
$\twoheadrightarrow$ (temporal operator), 262
$\rightsquigarrow$, see leads to
$\ldots^+$ (action operator), 59, 113
$\ldots^+$ (suffix operator), 62
$\ldots^\uparrow$ (finite-behavior completion), 81
$\ldots^R$ (reduced version of program), 221
$[\ldots]^+_{\langle\ldots\rangle}$, 113, 230
$\bot$, 259
F_{+v}, 258–259
$\times$ (Cartesian product), 31, 270
$=_y$, 167
$\simeq_y$, 167
$\sim_y$, 168
$\sim_{\mathbf{y}}$, 202
$\#$ (cardinality), 46, 267, 271
$\Rightarrow$ (implication), 18, 266
$\equiv$ (equivalence), 18, 266
$\triangleq$ (equals by definition), 19
$\mathinner{\ldotp\ldotp}$ (integer interval), 22, 267
$\cdot$, see action composition
$*$ (multiplication), 14
$\circ$ (sequence concatenation), 128, 270
$\oplus$, 129

$\Box$ (always), 59, 62–64
  formula, 96
$\Box\Diamond$ (infinitely often), 66–67
$\Diamond$ (eventually), 64–66
$\Diamond\Box$ (eventually always), 66
$\subseteq$ (is a subset of), 22, 267
$[\ ]_v$ (action operator), 73
$[\![\ ]\!]$ (meaning), 14, 15, 22, 55, 60
$\langle\ \rangle_v$ (action operator), 77
$\langle\ \rangle$ (tuple notation), 31, 269
$\lfloor\ \rfloor$, 132
$\wedge$, see conjunction
$\cap$ (set intersection), 188, 267
$\vee$, see disjunction
$\cup$ (set union), 188, 267
$!$ (factorial), 70, 270
$\%$ (mod), 37, 266
$\natural$, 75
$\natural_y$, 168
$\forall$ (universal quantification), 25, 267
$\exists$, see existential quantification
$\exists\!\!\!\exists$ (temporal existential quantification), 83, 165–169
  definition, 167
$\exists\!\!\!\exists$ (temporal existential quantification)
  reasoning about, 166–167
$\exists\!\!\!\exists_{\text{RTLA}}$, 167
$\in$ (is an element of), 21, 267
$\notin$ (is not an element of), 99
$:\in$, 118

Abadi, Martín, xiv, 115

abstract program, 3
abstraction, 136
accuracy, 112, 161
action, 55, 56
   commuting, 225
action composition, 58, 277
   weirdness, 160
Add program, 128
AddS program, 129
AddSeq program, 132
algebra, 14
algorithm
   concurrent, 1
   distributed, 1, 136
   Euclid's, *see* Euclid's algorithm
   Fischer's, 117–121
   Paxos, 138–144
   Paxos voting, 139–142
   random, 47
Alpern, Bowen, 81
always, 59
   possible, 112
always eventually, 66
   possible, 113
and, 18
Append, 129, 270
Apt, Krzysztof, xiv
arguments of mapping, 32
arithmetic, 13–14, 266
   Boolean, 18–21
array, 46
array variable, 90
associative, 20
ASSUME/PROVE, 79–80, 272
   with SUFFICES, 147
assumption (of proof), 272
atomic operation, 45
atomicity, grain of, 45, 58
await statement, 90
AWITH, 155

axiom, 16

Batson, Brannon, xiv
beauty, 131
behavior, 59, 60
   halting, 39
   predicate, 76
   reduced, 224–226
   Zeno, 121–123
behavioral property, 5
Bhagavad Gita, 89
Boolean, 14
Boolean arithmetic, 18–21
bound constant, 57, 60
bound variable, 22, 26–28
bounded quantifier, 25
Broy, Manfred, xiv
Burns, James E., 98

$\mathcal{C}$, 84–85
   operator on metric space, 280
cardinal sequence, 31, 270
CASE proof step, 175, 273
Chandy, K. Mani, xiv
CHOOSE, 268–269
circular definition, 29
clock, hour-minute, 71
closed set, 280
coding language, 4
Cohen, Ernie, xiv
commutative, 20
commuting actions, 225
   left-, 233
   right-, 233
completion of a finite behavior, 81
component, 251
   composing, 261–265
composition, 251, 261–265
   action, *see* action composition
   theorem, 263

concatenation of sequences, 128, 270
concrete program, 5
concurrent algorithm, 1
conjunction, 18, 266
   list, 32–33, 267
consensus, 136–138
constant, 55
   bound, 57, 60
   prophecy, 217–219
constant expression, 57
context, 17, 272
   of an expression, 27
correctness, 5
countable set, 80, 268
critical section, 88
   making atomic, 244–247
current goal (of proof), 147

data refinement, 126
datum, 208
deadlock, 91
   freedom, 97
decomposing program, 251, 253–261
decomposing proof, 255–261
decomposition theorem, 260
DEFINE, 273
define statement, 132
definition, 28
   circular, 29
   in an expression, 116
   in proof, 273
   of TLA, 76–77
   recursive, 70–71, 187–188, 270–271
dense set, 281
Dijkstra, Edsger, xiv, 2, 88
discrete time, 123–125
disjunction, 18, 266
   list, 32–33, 267
distance function, 279
distributed algorithm, 1, 136

distributes over, 20
Doligez, Damien, xiv
DOMAIN, 30, 269
domain of a function, 30, 269
Dwork, Cynthia, 136

$\mathbb{E}$, 87, 155–161
   computing it, 156–158
   weirdness, 160
element, 21
empty set, 22
enabled, 87
enabling condition, 50
Engberg, Urban, xiv
engineer, 2
equivalence, 18
Euclid's algorithm, 6–9
   decomposed, 253
   termination, 69
   two-process version, 9
   type correctness, 23
eventually, 64–66
eventually always, 66
EXCEPT, 47, 91, 269
execution as a state sequence, 7
existential quantification, 25, 267
   ∃ Elimination, 164, 267
   ∃ Introduction, 163, 267
   reasoning about, 163
expression, 14
   constant, 57
   context of, 27
   definition in, 116
   meaningless, 23–24
   state, 56
   step, 55, 56

F_{12}, 82
factorial, 70, 270
failure, 47, 136

INDEX

fairness, 87
   for history variable, 173
   semantic definition, 109–110
   strong, 106
   weak, 94
FALSE, 14, 266
FGSqrs program, 44–46
FIFO queue, 203–217
Fischer's algorithm, 117–121
Fischer, Michael, 115, 138
Floyd, Robert, 42
FLP theorem, 138
for all, 25
formula, 14
   □, 96
   state, 56
   temporal, 60
Fraenkel, Abraham, 21
free variable, 27
function, 30–31, 269
   of multiple arguments, 32, 269

GCD, 7
Gilkerson, Ellen, ii
goal (of proof), 272
   current, 147
Gonthier, Georges, xiv
grain of atomicity, 45, 58
Gray, Jim, xiv
greatest common divisor (GCD), 7
Greek letters, 15
Grønning, Peter, xiv

halting behavior, 39
Head, 128, 270
Herlihy, Maurice, 204
Hesselink, Wim, 219
hidden variable, 165
hierarchically structured proofs, 146–147

higher-order mapping, 271
Hilbert, David, 268
history independence, 35
history variable, 169–175
Hoare logic, 58, 161, 276–279
Hoare, Tony, 276
Hochstein, Lorin, xiv
hybrid system, 125

$\mathbb{I}$ (set of integers), 21, 267
   is countable, 80
I1 and I2, 43, 57, 61
if and only if, 18
IF/THEN/ELSE, 32, 270
iff (if and only if), 19
implementation
   is implication, 73
   see also refinement
implication, 18
implies, 18, 19
Increment program, 48–51, 53, 61
   invariance proof, 284–287
inductive invariant, 43
infinite-stuttering variable, 186
infinitely often, 66–67
Init, 53
initial predicate, 41
input, user, 47
interface variable, 164
interleaving description, 265
internal variable, 164
interpretation, 15, 55
invariance property, 8
invariant, 8, 43
   inductive, 43
   type, 43

Kuppe, Markus, xiv
Kurshan, Robert, xiv

LA (Logic of Actions), 55

labels in pseudocode, 41
Ladkin, Peter, xiv
language, coding, 4
Langworthy, David, xiv
leads to, 68–69
    proving, 100–104
leads-to lattice, 100
left-commute, 233
Len, 129, 270
LET/IN, 116
linear-time temporal logic, 59
linearizable, 204
Lipton, Richard, 221
Liskov, Barbara, 136
livelock, 97
liveness property, 8
    another view of, 279–283
    as dense set, 282
    definition, 81–82
    refinement proof, 152
    traditional program, 86
LM algorithm, 105
lock, 104
logic
    Hoare, 58, 161, 276–279
    predicate, 26, 267
    propositional, 18–21, 266
    temporal, 3, 59
logic of actions, 53–59
Lynch, Nancy, xiv, 136, 138

machine closed, 93, 193
mapping, 14, 28–29
    arguments of, 32
    higher-order, 271
    not a set/value, 29, 274–275
    refinement, *see* refinement mapping
    set constructor, 116, 268
    time-translation, 123
math, ordinary, 2, 12, 266–271

mathematical induction
    simple, 37
    strong, 37
Mathglish, 17
meaningless expression, 23–24
Melliar-Smith, Michael, xiv
Merz, Stephan, xiv
message passing in Paxos, 142
meta-formula, 16
metric space, 279–282
    of behaviors, 282–283
model checking, 5
    catches type errors, 24
    real-time program, 123
mutual exclusion, 88

$\mathbb{N}$ (set of natural numbers), 22, 267
    > well-founded on, 176
negation, 18
NEW declaration, 272
Next, 53
nondeterminism, 6, 47
    none in math, 269
not, 18
number, real, 13

OB algorithm, 98–104, 145–155
Oki, Brian, 136
One-Bit algorithm, 98–104, 145–155
or, 18
ordinal sequence, 31, 269
ordinary math, 2, 12, 266–271
Owicki, Susan, xiv

Palais, Richard, xiv
paradox, amusing, 275
parameter, 29
partial order, 207
Paterson, Michael, 138
Paxos algorithm, 138–144
    implementation, 144–145

INDEX

Paxos voting algorithm, 139–142
pc, 44
pipelining, 247–251
plane, infinite, 279
planetary motion, 34–35, 71
Plotkin, Gordon, 279
PlusCal, 45
   label convention, 41
Pnueli, Amir, 59
possibility, 111–114
postcondition, 276
precedence, 20
precondition, 276
predicate, 14
   behavior, 76
   initial, 41
   state, 76
   step, 41
predicate logic, 26, 267
   in TLA, 76
process, 1
   starved, 87, 97
process statement, 48
program
   abstract, 3
   concrete, 5
   decomposing, 251, 253–261
   real-time, 115–125
   reduced version, 221
   traditional, 1
   written as conjunction, 253–255
program state, 131
program variable, 13, 53
proof
   assumption, 272
   by contradiction, 52
   CASE step, 175, 273
   correctness, 3
   decomposing, 255–261
   goal, 272

   machine-checked, 5
   of leads to, 100–104
   of liveness properties, 66
   paragraph, 13, 52, 80, 146
   Q.E.D. step, 53, 273
   step numbering, 146, 274
   structured, 3, 52, 146–147, 271–274
   SUFFICES step, 147
   terminal, 271
property, 76
   behavioral, 5
   invariance, 8
prophecy constant, 217–219
prophecy variable, 187–202
propositional logic, 18–21, 266
   in TLA, 76

Q.E.D. (proof step), 53, 273
quantification, 25–26
   existential, 25, 267
   universal, 25, 267
quantifier, 25
   bounded, 25
   scope of, 26
   unbounded, 25
queue, FIFO, 203–217

$\mathbb{R}$ (set of real numbers), 21, 267
   as metric space, 279
real number, 13
real-time program, 115–125
recursive definition, 70–71, 187–188, 270–271
reduced behavior, 224–226
reduced version of program, 221
reduction, 220–251
reduction theorem, 235, 243
redundancy, 44
redundancy, 44

refinement, 126
  data, 126
  invariance under, 135
  proof of liveness, 152
  proof of safety, 149
  step, 126
refinement mapping, 130
  existence of, 202–203
  two views of, 131
right-commute, 233
Rosetta spacecraft, 10
RTLA, 59–70
Russell's paradox, 23, 52
Russell, Bertrand, 23

safe scoping rule, 28, 272
safety property, 8
  another view of, 279–283
  as closed set, 282
  definition, 81–82
  refinement proof, 149
satisfies, 56
Schneider, Fred, xiv, 81
Scholten, Carel, xiv
scientist, 2
scope
  of a quantifier, 26
  of variable declaration, 27
scoping, safe, 28, 272
semantics, 12, 14
  of ZF, 22
semaphore, binary, 104
Seq, 129, 270
sequence
  cardinal, 31, 270
  concatenation, 128, 270
  operators on, 128, 269
  ordinal, 31, 269
set, 21, 22
  closed, 280
  dense, 281
  difference, 129, 268
  enumerated, 22, 267
  mapping constructor, 116, 268
  subset constructor, 22, 117, 268
SF, 106
Shostak, Robert, xiv
SI, 75
skip statement, 88
Sqrs program, 40–43
starvation of process, 87, 97
state, 62
  of Euclid's algorithm, 7
  program, 131
  reachable, 112–113
state expression, 56
state formula, 56
state number, 39
state predicate is TLA formula, 76
step, 39, 56
  refinement, 126
  stuttering, 39
step expression, 55, 56
step predicate, 41
Stockmeyer, Larry, 136
strong fairness, 106
stuttering insensitive, 74–75
stuttering step, 39, 72–74
  adding after action, 178–181
  adding before action, 182–183
  of a program, 75
stuttering variable, 175–186
  fairness, 183–186
  infinite, 186
subaction, 107
subset, 22
subset constructor, 22, 117, 268
substitution, notation for, 127
substitutive, 69
SUFFICES proof step, 147

symmetry under time translation, 123

Tail, 128, 270
tautology, 26, 63
temporal logic, 3, 59
termination, 5, 8, 39
  of Euclid's algorithm, 69
testing, 6
theorem, 16
  composition, 263
  decomposition, 260
  FLP, 138
there exists, 25
TLA, 3
  definition, 76–77
TLA$^+$, 2, 10, 45
TLC, 115
topology, 281
traditional program, 1
  liveness property, 86
transitive, 20
TRUE, 14, 266
tuple, 31, 269
Tuttle, Mark, xiv
type, 23–24
type invariant, 43

$\mathcal{U}$ (until operator), 93–94, 108
unbounded quantifier, 25
UNCHANGED, 205
universal quantification, 25, 267

valid, 16
value, 21
Varacca, Daniele, 110
variable, 55
  array, 90
  auxiliary, 163–219
  bound, 22, 26–28
  free, 27
  hidden, 165

hiding, 163–169
history, 169–175
infinite-stuttering, 186
infinitely many, 17
interface, 164
internal, 164
mathematical, 13, 53
program, 13, 53
prophecy, 187–202
stuttering, 175–186
variable capture, 28
variables statement, 40
Venn diagram, 282
Verhulst, Eric, 10
Virtuoso, 10
Vogt, Friedrich H., xiv
Völzer, Hagen, 110

weak fairness, 94
well-founded relation, 176, 187
WF, 94
while statement, 40
Wing, Jeannette, 204
WITH (substitution), 127, 270

x (list notation), 84

y (list notation), 202
Yu, Yuan, xiv

Zeno behavior, 121–123
Zermelo, Ernst, 21
ZF set theory, 21–23

For EU product safety concerns, contact us at Calle de José Abascal, 56–1°, 28003 Madrid, Spain or eugpsr@cambridge.org.

www.ingramcontent.com/pod-product-compliance
Ingram Content Group UK Ltd.
Pitfield, Milton Keynes, MK11 3LW, UK
UKHW050709260326
469255UK00025B/106